PENGUIN BOOKS

Towards a Just Society

Thomas S. Axworthy is Executive Director of the CRB Foundation and an Adjunct Lecturer at the John F. Kennedy School of Government, Harvard University. He was Principal Secretary to Prime Minister Trudeau from 1981 to 1984. Among his previously published works are *Marching to a Different Drummer: An Essay on the Liberals and Conservatives in Convention* (co-authored with Martin Goldfarb) (Toronto, 1988) and *Our American Cousins* (edited) (Toronto, 1987).

Pierre Elliott Trudeau joined the staff of the office of the Privy Council in Ottawa in 1949. In 1952 he returned to Montreal, where he practised law, specializing in labour law and civil liberties, and from 1961, he taught constitutional law at the University of Montreal. Elected to the Parliament of Canada for the riding of Mount Royal in 1965, he became prime minister in 1968. On his retirement from politics in 1984, he joined the firm of Heenan Blaikie in Montreal as counsel. His previously published works include *Federalism and the French Canadians* (Toronto, 1968), *Approaches to Politics* (Toronto, 1970) and *Lifting the Shadow of War* (Edmonton, 1987).

Patricia Claxton was founding president of the Literary Translators' Association and has taught translation at the University of Montreal. She has translated books by Gabrielle Roy, Nicole Brossard, Fernand Ouellet and Marcel Trudel, and stories, poems and articles by Naïm Kattan, André Roy, France Théoret and Pierre Elliott Trudeau. She has won and been shortlisted for the Governor General's Award and has received three Canada Council honourable mentions for her translations.

TOWARDS A JUST SOCIETY

The Trudeau Years

Edited by

Thomas S. Axworthy
Pierre Elliott Trudeau

Translations into English by Patricia Claxton

Penguin Books

PENGUIN BOOKS
Published by the Penguin Group
Penguin Books Canada Ltd, 10 Alcorn Avenue, Toronto, Ontario, Canada M4V 3B2
Penguin Books Ltd, 27 Wrights Lane, London W8 5TZ, England
Penguin Putnam Inc., 375 Hudson Street, New York, New York 10014, U.S.A.
Penguin Books Australia Ltd, Ringwood, Victoria, Australia
Penguin Books (NZ) Ltd, cnr Rosedale and Airborne Roads, Albany, Auckland 1310,
New Zealand

Penguin Books Ltd, Registered Offices: Harmondsworth, Middlesex, England

First published in Viking by Penguin Books Canada Limited, 1990

Published in Penguin Books, 1992
Published in this edition, 2000

10 9 8 7 6 5 4 3 2

Original publisher, Penguin Books Canada Limited.
French edition published by Le Jour, éditeur.

Manufactured in Canada.

Canadian Cataloguing in Publication Data

Main entry under title:

Towards a just society

Issued also in French under title: Les années Trudeau.
Includes bibliographical references.

ISBN 0-14-029867-3

1. Canada - Politics and government - 1968–1979.*
2. Canada - Politics and government - 1980–1984.*
3. Trudeau, Pierre Elliott, 1919– .
4. Liberal Party of Canada.
I. Axworthy, Tom, 1947–   II. Trudeau, Pierre Elliott, 1919–.

FC625.T68 2000   971.064′4   C90-095722-0
F1034.2.T68 2000

Visit Penguin Canada's web site at www.penguin.ca

One name is missing from the list of authors of this book: the name of a man who believed deeply in Canada and passionately in the importance of working for justice in his country. He died before being able to contribute to the present volume; but the history written here would not have happened, had it not been for the extraordinary man of action that was

JEAN MARCHAND

Acknowledgments

The idea for this book originated with a group of friends and colleagues who meet regularly with us over lunch. Some became contributors and others did not, but we would like to thank Michael Pitfield, Marc Lalonde, Gérard Pelletier, James Coutts and Theodore Johnson for spending so much time in thinking through the thrust of the book.

Anne Marriott has done a superb job in co-ordinating and organizing the efforts of fifteen authors, and our research assistant, Denis Stevens, spent many long hours in the library locating documents and checking on our facts. We want to thank them for their enthusiasm and good spirits in what has turned out to be quite an arduous process.

Kathryn Dean and Cynthia Good of Penguin Books have provided expert editorial assistance, and Patricia Claxton and Normand Paiement have made a major contribution through their sensitive translations.

The generous efforts of Hélène Tanghe and the editorial staff of Le Jour, éditeur, have made possible the simultaneous publication of the book in both official languages.

We want to thank, too, all our former colleagues who worked so hard in the many policy areas not covered in the book because of problems of space. Hundreds, and perhaps even thousands, of individuals made a contribution to the policies of the four Liberal governments from 1968 to 1984 and we and, as we believe, the country as a whole, are in their debt.

Thomas S. Axworthy
Pierre Elliott Trudeau
Montreal, Quebec
January, 1990

Contents

TOWARDS A JUST SOCIETY

Introduction to the Hardcover Edition

Thomas S. Axworthy
Pierre Elliott Trudeau

History is never neutral. Values are the prisms through which we refract events, personalities and causes. "Historical facts," Carl Becker writes, "are not out there in the world of the past, but in here, in the mind of the historian."[1]

What is true for the historian is doubly so for the engaged participant. Writing memoirs, as Gérard Pelletier has noted in his excellent volumes *Years of Impatience* and *Years of Choice,*[2] is a tricky business. Recollections become disjointed, imagination coats events with a rosy hue and fiction begins to edge out fact. To prevent this process of romanticism from running too deep, we have decided to publish a book of essays now while our memories are still clear and our pens still have some bite.

This book is about change. More precisely, it is about how one group of decision makers anticipated, interpreted and reacted to the multiple changes which transformed the world and Canadian society between 1968 and 1984.

The overwhelming impact of change on our lives is perhaps a cliché, but no less true for all that. Arthur Schlesinger, Jr., has calculated that the last two lifetimes have seen more change than the planet's 798 put together.[3] In the latter part of the twentieth century, technology has leapt ahead. The number of states has shot upward. Interdependence has increased.

1

Communication networks have girded the globe. "A law of acceleration," Henry Adams warned, "definite and constant as any law of mechanics, cannot be supposed to relax its energy to suit the convenience of man."[4]

Canada has hardly been immune to Adams' law of acceleration. During the sixteen years described in our essays, Canadians witnessed a changing world balance of power, a transformation of the economic paradigm, an information explosion of global proportions, the emergence of a new definition of the role of women, the birth of environmentalism, the rise of multiculturalism, the sustained impact of the baby boom on education, jobs and housing, an intense outburst of nationalism in Quebec, a shift of power towards the provinces and a quantum leap in the desire and expectations of Canadians that government could simultaneously deliver more wealth and more equity. To say the least, it was a turbulent era in which to govern: more than once we ruefully agreed with Ralph Waldo Emerson that "things are in the saddle and ride mankind."

Every politician in every society has to adjust to change. Otto von Bismarck, no shrinking violet when it came to self-confidence, wrote that the leaders of states travel on a stream of time which they can neither create nor direct, but upon which they can steer with more or less skill and experience.[5] How societies emerge from that voyage depends upon the wisdom of their leadership.

The essays in this book describe the voyage we took together as Canadians from 1968 to 1984. Our central purpose in writing the book is to describe how one group of decision makers tried to cope with the stream of change in their time. With the exception of two distinguished historians who provide a more detached view, almost all our collaborators had important roles to play, as Cabinet ministers, public officials or political advisors. To help Canadians better understand the complexity of self-government, we felt there was particular merit in asking different participants, from their different vantage points, to describe events that they had helped to shape. Each contributor, of course, bears responsibility only for his or her particular contribution. We invite the reader to join a participants' seminar.

This volume is not an apologia. Mistakes are admitted, omissions are noted. There are many things we regret about our time in office—most of all the things left undone. Poverty was reduced, but as we left office, there were still too many poor. Social security was enhanced but we failed to implement our plans to assist the working poor. Many measures were taken to assist the West but we failed to gain the support of Westerners. The Charter of Rights and Freedoms was won over provincial opposition but only at the cost of a pernicious "notwithstanding clause" that has already been used to reduce the rights of Canadians—an outcome that we foresaw, and deplored, but were forced to accept, lest the Charter be entirely lost. The Constitution was patriated from Great Britain but, again because of the intransigence of the provinces, only with an amending clause that dropped our proposal for a referendum, a device that truly would have made citizens arbiters of their own fate.

How best to assess our efforts? In his memoirs, Gérard Pelletier approvingly quotes the criterion of Jean-Paul Desbiens: "Every time an official measure results or might result in a little more security or dignity for poor people I know, it has my support."[6] This is the type of standard that we gladly endorse: not the words of speech writers or the promises of politicians, but real, actual improvements in condition. In Canada from 1968 to 1984, was poverty reduced? foreign aid increased? social security improved? Were civil liberties better protected? Did real income rise? Was Canadian ownership of the economy increased? Did the arts flourish?

In short, was Canada a better place in 1984 than in 1968? That is the test readers should apply to the pages that follow. Our goal was not to redeem the past but to be just in our own time. Judge us by that and we will accept the verdict.

Finally, there is one further reason why we believe that Canadians may be interested in an account of our government: we freely admit that we were animated by a particular set of values. Today, these values are under attack. So, beyond the management of change, which is the task of governments everywhere, or a mere accumulation of laws and decisions during our time in office, there is another dimension of the Liberal governments from 1968 to 1984 that merits attention.

We went to Ottawa not to gain power for power's sake but to transform our society according to a set of liberal values. Make no mistake, we were an ideological government—ideological in the sense that we were motivated by an overarching framework of purpose. That framework was grounded in the supreme importance we attached to the dignity and rights of individual human beings. As one of the co-editors wrote many years ago in *Vrai*: "The aim of life in society is the greatest happiness of everyone, and this happiness is attained only by being just toward each and every person."[7]

We believe that ultimately history turns on such values and ideas—not economic determinism, nor dialectical materialism, nor the great-man theory of Carlyle. Best expressed in the philosophy of Hegel, this concept of history places primacy on the principles that underlie the organizations and actions of man. "Thought is, indeed, essential to humanity," wrote Hegel. "It is this that distinguishes us from the brutes." Thus, "the idea is in truth the leader of peoples and of the world."[8] Ideas, not personalities or force, are in the words of Lord Acton "the spiritual property that gives dignity and grace and intellectual value to history."[9]

The essays in this book demonstrate that we tried to be a government of ideas. Sadly, these ideas are today being undermined on all fronts—by the business community, by the provinces and, most importantly, by the Conservative party of Brian Mulroney. This is a book of history, but the ideas that animated our efforts from 1968 to 1984 are every bit as compelling today as they were during our years of power. The differences between our recent past and our dithering present are profound:

- We fought for a Canada where individual rights, including linguistic rights, would be respected across the land. Through the Meech Lake Accord, the Mulroney government favours instead special status for one province, and that inevitably propels us towards a two nations concept of Canada, in which three provincial signatories of the Accord have already reduced the linguistic rights of their minorities.
- We fought for a strong federal government capable of initiating programs that would equalize opportunities for

Canadians wherever they happened to live. Again through the Meech Lake Accord, the Mulroney government favours a massive decentralization of power to the provinces. Already one of the most decentralized countries on earth, under Meech Lake, Canada would become a confederacy, a mere marriage of convenience between the provinces.

- We fought for an independent Canadian economy and foreign policy so that we would have the ability to create and maintain a distinctive way of life in our part of North America: the Mulroney government, through the Free Trade Agreement with the United States, the dismantling of the Foreign Investment Review Agency (FIRA) and its advocacy of a continental energy and resources policy, has accepted and accentuated north-south integration.
- We fought for a fairer, more humane Canada, in which the power of government was a necessary instrument in the quest for a more just society. The Mulroney government sees the state as part of the problem, not part of the solution, and accepts the primacy of the market as the only regulator that matters.

This book is not about the future. It is about the past. But that past contends with all that is going on at present. It is up to Canadians to decide which of these conflicting visions appeals to them most. For ourselves, the goal of a Just Society—a humane, caring, freedom-loving society of many peoples, traditions and beliefs—is still a beacon that compels us forward. Our goals were perhaps too vast. Our hopes were perhaps too high. Our abilities were perhaps too limited. But we say, along with Robert Browning, that "a man's reach should exceed his grasp, or what's a heaven for?"

PART I

The Tempest Bursting: Canada in 1992

"I muse upon my country's ills.
The tempest bursting from the waste of Time."

–Herman Melville
Misgivings

Political discourse tends towards the apocalyptic. Propelled by the twin needs of the media for drama and the politician for attention, political rhetoric invariably transforms problems into crises, slights into humiliations, wants into non-negotiable demands, and self-imposed deadlines into doomsday clocks. Meanwhile, for the average citizen, life goes on pretty much the same. As the Arab proverb says, "The dog barks but the caravan moves on."

So we are very conscious about the risks of exaggerating the threats or underestimating the capacity of Canadians to surmount difficulties or at least ignore the ravings of the political class. This essay argues, in fact, that the old image of Canadians as a divided people held together by enlightened political élites who heroically bargain to bridge yawning gaps is now totally out of date, if it ever was true. Today the opposite is more nearly the case: whatever language we speak, Canadians basically agree about most things, our system of values is nearly uniform, and on a day-to-day basis we live together quite amicably. It is the political élites who passionately fight over status and power. Canada is a success, looking for a problem. We are a united people divided by our leaders.

Yet, however strong the basic tolerance and common sense of Canadians, it is difficult to assess the state of the nation in 1992 without a sense of foreboding. There does seem to be a tempest bursting. Since the first edition of *Towards a Just Society* was published in the winter of 1990, the world outside our borders has been transformed. The Cold War has ended,

Germany has reunited and freedom has come to Russia and the former Soviet empire, but neither Canadians nor Americans seem to be taking much joy from these triumphs. Instead, the prevailing sentiment is one of apprehension: a war has been fought in the Persian Gulf; a Canadian peacekeeper has died in the former Yugoslavia; and there is special concern about the impact of the new global economy on Canada's traditional resource strengths. The world once knocked on our door; now we must work hard even to get outsiders to take a look. A prominent journalist captured this sentiment well in reporting on a conversation with a Quebec federalist about the Canada-U.S. Free Trade Agreement and English-speaking Canadians' fears about economic and cultural survival. "What you are really saying," said the Quebecker, "is that English Canadians are now living at risk in the same way Quebeckers have had to live at risk throughout their history. Welcome aboard."[1]

While buffeted by global trends, Canada in the past two years has also endured a series of self-induced woes. Three issues in particular have predominated:

- a deep recession has gripped the country since the winter of 1990, causing unemployment to soar, profits to fall, companies to fail and food banks to proliferate;
- since the failure of the Meech Lake Accord in June 1990, the country has witnessed a constitutional spectacle variously and charitably described as "the Mad Hatter's tea party" and the "Keystone Cops at work." Like Stephen Leacock's famous rider, Messrs. Mulroney and Clark leapt astride the constitutional stallion and have ridden madly off in all directions.
- for his part, in 1990 Mr. Bourassa unleashed upon an unsuspecting world the Bélanger-Campeau[2] circus, followed by the 1991 Allaire report[3] of the Quebec Liberal party. Bélanger-Campeau resulted in committing the Quebec government to holding a referendum no later than October 26, 1992, and the Allaire report recommended something even Mr. Lévesque never dared to propose: sovereignty-association with equalization payments.

As a result of all this, the mood of Canadians is grim.[4] People are discouraged about the economy and weary of constitutional squabbles. The feeling of constitutional fatigue is palpable. Confidence in the political leadership of all parties is at an all-time low. Discontent with our political system has led to the creation of two regional parties: the Bloc Québécois, and the Reform Party in the West. Quebec will likely face another referendum about its future sometime in the next twelve months and there may be a national referendum as well. Tension between the Mohawks of Oka and Kahnawake and Quebec's provincial police, La Sûreté du Québec, which erupted into an armed confrontation in the summer of 1990, remains high. As *The Economist* magazine asked recently: "What's a nice country like Canada doing in a mess like this?"[5]

Nationalism in Quebec, the ravages of recession and a confused Conservative constitutional policy are hardly new occurrences in Canada. By themselves, they would not merit any special attention, nor is their existence any cause for excessive lamentations about the future of the country. Quebec nationalism has been a force since the Conquest, there have been debates about the proper role of the state in economic development since the 1820s, and the position of the provinces vis-à-vis the national government has preoccupied us since 1867. On the face of it, nothing new here.

But the crux of the argument of this essay is that the sad events of 1990–1992 are not isolated phenomena. They result from, and in many cases are inspired by, the philosophy of the Conservative government of Brian Mulroney. In Canadian history there have been moments when federal politicians flirted with Quebec nationalists. There have certainly been times when the federal government practised laissez-faire economics. And there have been Ottawa governments that espoused the provincialist cause in federal-provincial conflicts. But prior to Brian Mulroney there has *never* been a federal government that unleashed all three decentralist forces at one and the same time.

For tactical reasons, Brian Mulroney struck an alliance with Quebec nationalism in 1984, brought separatists and nationalists into his caucus and Cabinet and has been trying to ride that tiger ever since. For ideological reasons, Conservatives and their business allies oppose the concept of an active state, favour market remedies to any problem and oppose the post-1945 social welfare – Keynesian consensus. For political and historical reasons, the Conservatives also find it convenient to promote a "community of communities" view of federalism, which necessitates giving away a goodly number of federal powers.

Antagonism to Ottawa is the single thread uniting these disparate elements. Nationalists, free-enterprise ideologists and provincialists may agree on little else, but they all want to see the federal government weakened. The particular skill of Brian Mulroney has been the creation and, even more impressively, the maintenance of this coalition of the antis. But if the unity of the Conservative party has endured, the unity of the country is much more in doubt. Any one of these decentralist forces would challenge the fabric of Canada as we have come to know it; to face all three simultaneously puts unprecedented stress on the country's foundations.

Yet Canada has proven to be a resilient country. Even if the forces of collective rights, laissez-faire economics and provincialism do their worst, the outer shell of the country may survive. What will be lost, though, is any dream of a Just Society. A just society is motivated by the supreme importance we attach to the dignity and rights of the individual human being; ethnic nationalism promotes the group. A just society promotes equal life chances for all; laissez-faire economics lets the market chips fall where they may. A just society is prepared to use the federal government to promote a minimum standard of citizenship everywhere in Canada; a confederacy of provinces reduces to insignificance the instrument of national will. To us, the primary issue is not *whether* Canada endures, but what *kind* of Canada endures. Our answer to that question informs the rest of this essay.

—— The Collectivist Folly ——————————

> *"I love my country too much to be a nationalist."*
>
> —Albert Camus
> *Letters to a German Friend*

Liberals believe that the individual is the unit of supreme value in our society. Each of us has a special dimension, a uniqueness that cries out to be realized. The purpose of life is to realize that potential, to become whatever it is we are capable of becoming. The role of the state is to provide the conditions in which individuals have the broadest possible choice in deciding upon their definition of the good life. "Let us not abandon the fundamental principle," writes Ernest Renan, "that man is a rational and moral being before he is penned up in this or that language, before he is a member of this or that race, before he adheres to this or that culture."[6]

If individualism, self-definition and choice are liberalism's defining characteristics, nationalists believe that humankind belongs to groups, that the character of the individuals who compose the group are shaped by, and cannot be understood apart from, the group, that maintenance of the group or national identity is the dominant value in politics and the supreme end of political life and that therefore the only legitimate type of government is national self-government. "Nationalism," as Ernest Gellner defines it, "is primarily a political principle which holds that the political and the national unity should be congruent."[7]

In Canada, the traditional force of Quebec nationalism has been joined by a new strain of aboriginal nationalism. Ovide Mercredi, the national chief of the status Indian organizations—the Assembly of First Nations—caused an uproar in Quebec in February 1992 by denying the right of self-determination to Quebec but advocating it for the First Nations within Quebec. He did so by employing concepts and arguments that had been the stock-in-trade of Quebec nationalists for generations. "Self-determination is not a right of a 'province,'" Mercredi told the Committee of the National Assembly examining sovereignty. "It is a right of all peoples. Are the 'people of Quebec' a 'people' in the international legal sense? The population of Quebec is made up of a wide range of racial and ethnic groups. It cannot be considered to be a single 'people' with the right of self-determination ... Are French Quebeckers and First Nations within Quebec part of a single people? If this is your view, then it is contrary to our right to self-determination and self-identification."[8] That set the cat among the pigeons!

In assessing the merits of individualism versus collectivism as the core organizing concept of society, we are perfectly aware that there is no one single standard to determine objectively what is the best choice. But ideas do have consequences, and one can examine concepts according to operational criteria, such as what concept applies best to the complex entity that is humankind. Are the goals realistic or utopian? And since no idea is perfect and all have unintended impacts, which concept has the least potential for doing harm and the most potential for doing good? By applying such criteria to the collectionist concept of ethnic nationalism or group identity, we make the following arguments:

- It conforms neither to the breadth of the human spirit nor to the reality of the world as it exists. There is more to humanity than group identity and far more groups than there ever can be states. The attempt to identify the group with the state is logically flawed;
- Nationalist analysis tends toward self-deception. Nationalists do not have a monopoly on this fault, of course, but since nationalism deals in the world of identity, symbols, myths and grievances, this accent on emotionalism is often at variance with the world of reality;
- Nationalism can be dangerous, and the world has suffered and is suffering still from its excesses. By celebrating the inclusion of some within the group, nationalists must by definition exclude others. The excluded often become real or imagined adversaries.

_____ Ethnicity and Territory _____

The need to belong to a group has been recognized, since Aristotle, as a natural requirement on the part of human beings. Families, tribes, estates, races, religions, parties or nations all have their claim on the emotions of humankind. Liberals do not deny the value of group identity or cultural diversity – we extol them. Freedom of association is a right of citizens in any liberal state. But we refuse to make this value pre-eminent, because it it only one good out of many. In different times and on different issues, citizens will identify with their local neighbourhood, their city, their trade union, their professional association, their ethnic group, their province, their country or humankind as a whole. By putting the accent on individual self-determination, liberalism responds to this multiplicity of identities. Vaclav Havel captures this idea well with his metaphor of the "open house." Establishing a state on the basis of ethnic identity, race, religion or ideology he writes: "... means making a single stratum of our house superior to the others."[9]

By making group or ethnic identity the basis of the state, we fail to take into account our diversity as human beings. By extolling one aspect of our personality, nationalism demeans others. And there is an even greater problem with the theory: there are many more groups than there can possibly be states. If the logic of nationalism is that state and ethnic groups should be congruent, as Mazzini desired with his call of "every nation a state," what do we do about the fact that there are only two hundred states but over eight thousand identifiable language or ethnic groups? Does the logic of national self-determination require an ever greater splintering? If Quebec nationalists, for example, claim the right to split Canada apart because they are a "people" and as a "people" have the right to national self-determination, they can hardly deny this right to Quebec's aboriginal community. And since the aboriginal community is composed of thirty-five to fifty distinct peoples, six hundred bands and eleven languages, will each of these "peoples" in turn demand a separate state?

Liberals, then, agree with nationalists on the virtue of identity. A person must enjoy the freedom to be different than others. To make an informed judgment about the qualities of the good life, citizens should have the opportunity to benefit from a rich cultural diversity. We disagree that society should be based on this principle alone, however, and in fact any state so constituted would be sowing the seeds of its own destruction. Once the virus of national self-determination takes hold, it infects group after group. Equal rights for all is both fairer and safer. Lord Acton got it right a long time ago: the greatest adversary of the rights of nationalities is the modern theory of nationality.[10]

_____Emotionalism over Reason_____

Liberals recognize that nationalism is rooted in grievance. Isaiah Berlin writes that the origins of "nationalism, as distinct from mere national consciousness—the sense of belonging to a nation—is in the first place a response to a patronizing or disparaging attitude towards the traditional values of a society, the result of wounded pride and a sense of humiliation in its most socially conscious members, which in due course produces anger and self-assertion."[11] To combat nationalism we must seek out the reasons for the disillusionment, understand why the alienation began and institute reforms that attack the cause of the injustice.

All minorities have fears. The status of the French language in North America, for example, has been perilous since 1760. In 1839 Lord Durham proposed the assimilation of French Canada. In 1890 the Manitoba Schools question ended Cartier's dream of a bilingual West. Regulation 17 in Ontario, the conscription debates, Ottawa's lack of sensitivity to francophones until the 1960s and periodic outbursts of anti–French Canadian emotions like the *Gens de l'air* episode in 1976 or the trampling of the Quebec flag in 1990, remind us all that tolerance cannot be taken for granted. The flawed responses of Quebec nationalists to these sad events—ultramontane Catholicism in the 1880s, Duplessis's siege mentality in the 1940s and '50s, and the nostrums of special status and separation since the 1960s—should not divert us from the very real difficulties involved in preserving and promoting the French fact in North America.

Similarly, it hardly bears repeating that whether or not one agrees with the rhetoric of Canada's native leaders, the plight of the aboriginal community is a national disgrace. Tremendous deprivation leads to harsh words. In 1984 at a federal-provincial conference called to discuss the concept of native self-government, the Government of Canada compiled a shocking set of statistics describing the condition of status Indians, and the situation has not improved since then:

- life expectancy was ten years less than for the population as a whole;
- violent deaths were three times the national rate. Suicides, particularly in the fifteen-to-twenty-four age group, were more than six times the national rate;
- between 50 and 70 percent were on social assistance;

- one in three families lived in overcrowded conditions. Less than 50 percent of Indian houses were properly serviced, compared to a national level of more than 90 percent.

Third World living conditions for aboriginal communities have finally led to a nationalism also typical of the Third World.

Yet, however real the grievances that nationalists protest, one of the first victims of their anger is reason. The rejection of reason is the prime characteristic of folly or self-deception, and self-deception, writes Barbara Tuchman, "consists in assessing a situation in terms of pre-conceived fixed notions while ignoring or rejecting any contemporary signs. It is acting according to wishes while not allowing one's self to be deflected by the facts."[12] Nationalism – the obsession with group identity as the prime characteristic of humanity – is almost by definition an enemy of reason and balance.

The Allaire and Bélanger-Campeau reports—those two recent additions to the catechism of Quebec nationalism—provide textbook primers of nationalism's capacity to delude.[13] A few examples will suffice.

First, as scholars like Daniel Bell have long noted about the phenomenon,[14] since nationalism springs from a sense of grievance, it soon attracts a professional grievance industry, writers and intellectuals who are skilled in articulating, if not sharing, the problems of the masses. Scribes, intellectuals, journalists, bureaucrats and politicians all begin to have a vested interest in victimization. If the original problems have been overcome or if basic rights in large measure have been achieved, then this progress must be ignored. Or if this is too inconvenient, a new threshold must be invented and the goal posts moved again.

An air of pessimism thus pervades the analysis of Allaire and Bélanger-Campeau about the state of Canada. Allaire declares that "from many points of view, Canadian federalism has been unable to fulfil its promises. The situation has worsened over the past few decades."[15] Bélanger-Campeau, for its part, while lauding Quebec as a modern society which has evolved only because of its own strenuous efforts and with little help from the rest of the country, condemns the 1982 Constitution because "The Constitution Act, 1982, also constitutionalized the principle of the preservation and enhancement of the multicultural heritage of Canadians, thus imposing on Quebec a constitutional viewpoint which did not necessarily coincide with its reality within Canada: the latter was defined as a multicultural society, without constitutional recognition of the principle of "Canadian duality" and of Quebec's distinctiveness. The multicultural Canadian society, being predominantly English-speaking, can easily become indifferent to Quebec's distinct identity and its unique linguistic and cultural position in Canada."[16]

The gloomy, even despairing, description of Canadian federalism found in Allaire and Bélanger-Campeau would undoubtedly amaze the authors of the 1992 United Nations report on human development which declared that Canada ranked first according to its indices of the quality of life. Canada's indifference to the French language and Quebec culture would also surprise the 295,000 anglophone children enrolled in French immersion programs, and Quebec's artists and filmmakers who know that they receive 40 percent of Ottawa's cultural grants while having only 25 percent of the population.

The fact of the matter is that the future of French in Quebec has never looked better. We should relish this success, celebrate it as a genuine Canadian achievement, and move to relax restrictions like Bill 178, which reflect the worst of nationalism's fears, rather than the reality of the progress of the French language within Quebec. Our message to the nationalists should be, "Lighten up!" Victories for French have been won. Enjoy them.

The population of francophones in Quebec has increased from 79 percent in 1931 to 83 percent in 1986. In Montreal, francophones have increased from 66 percent of the population in 1971 to 70 percent in 1986. Demographic projections made by the Conseil de la langue française show that Quebec will be 87 percent francophone in the year 2021. More importantly, because of bilingualism, 93.5 percent of Quebeckers could speak French in 1986, compared to 85 percent in 1931. Unilingual English-speaking Quebeckers have declined from 13.8 percent of the population in 1931 to 5.7 percent in 1986. If the problem in the 1960s was, in René Lévesque's phrase, the "Westmount Rhodesians," today 60 percent of those "Rhodesians" speak French. In 1971, 13.4 percent of Canadians were bilingual, but by 1986 this figure had increased to 16.2 percent. In Quebec, non-francophones are twice as likely to be bilingual (60 percent) as francophones (30 percent), and today there are more than two million students, more than half of all anglophone students, enrolled in core French and immersion projects, an increase of 35 percent since 1970. Indeed, a higher proportion of anglophone children aged five to fourteen outside Quebec can hold a conversation in French (7 percent) than francophone children of the same age in Quebec can hold a conversation in English (5 percent).[17]

If one demand of the Quiet Revolution was that the English-speaking minority in Quebec learn French (now achieved) and another that the French fact be recognized in Ottawa (now achieved), a third was that French Canadians should assume a greater control of their economic destiny (they should be *"Maîtres chez nous"*) and that the income disparities between the English and French should diminish. Here, too, the speed of the catch-up of Quebec francophones has been, according to economist John McCallum, "really quite miraculous and perhaps unprecedented in comparison with other disadvantaged groups."[18] In 1961, in Quebec, francophone businesses employed 47 percent of Quebec citizens, anglophone businesses 39 percent and foreign capital 14 percent. In 1987 francophone entrepreneurs controlled 62 percent of the employees, anglophones 31 percent and foreigners 8 percent. Income disparities have all but disappeared: in 1961 the average anglophone living in Montreal earned 51 percent more than the average francophone. By 1980 this gap had declined to 9 percent or to zero if one corrects for education. In 1970 a bilingual anglophone made on average $1,500 a year more than a bilingual francophone. In 1980, both made $19,500.[19]

All this has been achieved in a Canada which, according to Allaire and Bélanger-Campeau, is indifferent to Quebec and under a federal system that has been stifling Quebec's development. The truth is that Quebeckers have progressed so far and so fast largely because of their own efforts but also because they have had two governments—Quebec City and Ottawa—working on their behalf. If the essential goal is the preservation of French in North America, why would Quebec nationalists want to secede from the one million other francophones in the

rest of Canada and the hundreds of thousands of English speak-
ers who are becoming bilingual because of immersion, and
forego the support of 20 million English-speaking taxpayers
who help to pay not only for bilingualism but also for cultural
institutions like Radio-Canada and the National Film Board?
All Quebeckers have succeeded in preserving the vitality of
French. Now they are joined in this noble pursuit by the goodwill of millions of English-speaking Canadians, the persever-
ance of a million francophones outside Quebec, the efforts of
several hundreds of thousands of immersion students and all
the resources of the Government of Canada.

Yet at this precise moment of strength, Quebec nationalists
want to break a linguistic partnership that has finally taken hold
after two hundred years of effort. As Kant once remarked: "Out
of the crooked timber of humanity no straight thing was ever
made."[20]

If a reluctance to shed outworn images from the past is one
characteristic of nationalist self-deception, another one,
according to Isaiah Berlin, is a "pathological exaggeration of
one's real or imaginary virtues, resentment and hostility
towards the proud, the happy and the successful."[21] Here, too,
the Allaire and Bélanger-Campeau reports are rich in examples. Both reports agree that Canada is in a desperate state and
that a central cause of this malady is an arrogant federal government committed to centralization. Bélanger-Campeau, for
example, describes "the vision of an exclusive national Canadian identity which emphasizes the centralization of powers
and the existence of a strong 'national' government."[22] Allaire
chimes in with a claim that "the constitutional wishes of the
federal and Quebec governments were fundamentally different. They were not speaking the same language ... Quebec
was attempting to move federalism in the direction of a new
distribution of powers, while Canada was tending toward
greater centralization."[23]

Forget the fact that what the authors of the two reports are
complaining about in their definition of centralization is a
Charter of Rights and Freedom which, far from giving any
additional powers to the Government of Canada, gives citizens
in every part of the land the right to resist arbitrary authority.
The Charter of Rights is a profoundly decentralizing reform

which takes power away from *all* governments and gives it to the people. Forget, too, that during this supposed orgy of centralization the federal percentage of total government revenues declined from 50 percent in 1969 to 43 percent in 1983.

Even taking the Allaire and Bélanger-Campeau bogeyman of a powerful centralizing federal government at face value, what do we then make of the analysis that the progress of the Québécois is solely due to the efforts of the province? Bélanger-Campeau writes that since the 1960s, "Quebec charted the course necessary to ensure the emergence of a modern, complete society open to the world ... The Quebec government acted as a driving force and rallying point for the reconquering of political, linguistic and economic levers."[24] The federal ogre – so prominent in the pages discussing the failure of Canadian federalism – suddenly disappears when it is time to discuss *"la société moderne."* The truth is, of course, that Quebeckers, like all Canadians, have progressed since the 1960s, and that a dynamic federalism made up of strong provinces and a strong national government played an important part in this evolution.

This tendency to exaggerate strengths and minimize risk is most evident in the Bélanger-Campeau analysis of the economic impact of separation. Here the optimistic assumptions of the report border on deception. Bélanger-Campeau assumes that after separation Quebec would assume only 18.5 percent of Canada's public debt, a figure far lower than Quebec's share of Canada's population. Even Mr. Parizeau has mentioned in public that the share would be closer to 25 percent.[25] With that optimistic assumption in place, the commission minimizes the positive impact of federal transfers and glosses over possible problems in transition costs, declines in growth, out-immigration, trade relations with the rest of Canada and Quebec adherence to the Canada-U.S. Free Trade Agreement.

This exercise in fiscal utopianism, however, inspired a spate of other studies that made more realistic judgments. First, virtually all the studies made the point that Quebec could have a viable economy after separation.[26] Small economies can do as well as large ones. But every study also detailed the very large risks that Quebec would run. The question is what possible gains are worth the risks? Some of the risks include the following:

- Quebec would almost certainly have to assume its 25 percent per capita share of the federal debt of $400 billion (i.e., $100 billion). When added to the existing Quebec debt of $33 billion, Quebec would have to service a debt of approximately $133 billion. The new country of Quebec would begin as one of the most indebted nations of the world. To develop a market for Quebec securities large enough to service a debt of $133 billion would take at least five to ten years;

- Quebec's budget deficit for 1992–93 is forecast at $4.2 billion. In addition, Hydro-Québec and other institutions have considerable debits. According to the 1992–93 provincial budget, Quebec's net total long-term public-sector borrowing will be $10.2 billion. Given the likelihood of reduced growth and a high-risk premium on Quebec debt after separation and the certainty of the loss of federal transfers, a consensus in recent studies is that Quebec's deficit will increase from the $3–4 billion range to the $10–17 billion range.

- Quebec is already a relatively large borrower ($10 billion), and its deficit would likely go up by another $10 billion. In addition, it would have to finance its share of the federal debt, another $10 billion. Quebec borrowing could shoot from $10 billion, or 6 percent of GNP, to over $30 billion, or 19 percent of GNP. Such a debt ratio would call for savage tax increases or service cuts. Such a risk cannot be simply wished away;

- As part of Canada, Quebec has the best of both worlds when it comes to economic autonomy. Federal politicians from Quebec have an influence over Ottawa's monetary and fiscal policy, and like Canadians everywhere, Quebeckers benefit from Canada's membership in international organizations like the Group of Seven Economic Summits of Industrialized Nations. But because it is a province, Quebec has been largely spared international scrutiny of interventionist institutions like the Caisse de depôt et placement du Québec or Hydro-Québec. If Quebec became independent and sought to join the proposed North American Free Trade Agreement with Canada (the United States and Mexico, for instance), the United States would likely demand that Quebec stop using state instruments like the "Caisse" that form the basis of "Quebec Inc." Quebec already has real autonomy. What greater benefits could accrue from legal sovereignty?

- Future projections about debt loads, growth and risk are all in the realm of conjecture. The impact of the anglophone exodus on Montreal, however, is a proven fact. Between 1976 and 1986, 200,000 anglophones, mainly Montrealers, left Quebec, and 54,000 entered, leaving a net emigration of 150,000. One consequence of this was a permanent increase in the unemployment rate of Montreal. The difference between unemployment in Montreal and Toronto jumped from a 1966–75 average gap of 1.5 percentage points to an average of nearly 5 percentage points between 1981 and 1990. On the other hand, the Quebec-Ontario gap – excluding the two major cities – has remained stable at 3 to 4 percentage points since 1970.[27]

It stands to reason that if 200,000 relatively wealthy and educated citizens leave, an economy will be poorer. Having already inflicted this burden on Montreal, nationalist policy would go further. Public opinion polls have indicated that in the event of separation, as many as half of Quebec anglophones would leave. Montreal already has the highest urban unemployment rate and urban poverty rate in Canada. Separation would only make it worse.

If Quebec were oppressed, or like Eastern Europe or the Baltic republics held by force in an empire, then assuming such economic risks on behalf of independence would be justified. But Quebec is not in the same position as these states. It is part of one of the freest and most civilized places on earth, the country which rates highest in human development, according to the United Nations. What possible gain would be worth such stupendous risks? Even Pierre-Marc Johnson, the former Parti québécois premier, is now one of those who no longer ask such questions. "About 80 percent of Quebec's requirements have already been met within Confederation," Johnson pointed out in a recent interview with Canadian Press: "Historically, Quebec was oppressed but that hasn't been the case for some time." Economically, Quebec has made large gains in control over its economy, Johnson said, "but we still have considerable Canadian assets." There are reasons for separatism, he suggested, but few of these conditions now apply to Quebec.[28]

Faced with difficult arguments like Johnson's, nationalists respond by a tried-and-true tactic: they move the goal posts. If federalism is contributing to the traditional goal of promoting the French language and culture in North America and if francophones have advanced economically within the system – in other words, if the grievances have been answered – why not, then, change the battleground to symbolism and power? Make the powers, privileges and status of the spokespersons for the group the talisman of society's concern, not the actual change of condition of the group itself. Transform group needs into interest group needs. This is what has happened in Quebec. The test of Canada's interest in the preservation of the French fact or the success in federalism in doing so, is no longer the actual linguistic or economic progress of francophones. The acid test is now whether the politicians and the bureaucrats of the government of Quebec get more power.

Again Allaire and Bélanger-Campeau are illustrative. In answer to the question "What does Quebec want anyway?" Allaire answers, not language security or economic advance – since these have largely been achieved – but "it has demanded greater powers for its development. Quebec's prime ministers have always sought a more decentralized federal system."[29] Bélanger-Campeau was even more explicit: "Quebec wanted to preserve and restore its autonomy in its fields of exclusive jurisdiction and, in a number of sectors, enjoy broader autonomy to ensure the development of Quebec society."[30]

A lust for power among politicians and bureaucrats is hardly a new phenomenon in Canada or anywhere else, but it should not be dignified with names like "special status" or "distinct society." It is what it is – a power grab. It is not enough that Mr. Bourassa says, I want a power because I want it. The question should be, want it to do what, and why would you do it better than other levels of government?

Two examples will suffice. Mr. Bourassa, as everyone knows, wants a Quebec defined as a distinct society in the Canadian constitution. Quebec is distinct, as the Bélanger-Campeau Commission says, because it is ". . . the only political entity in North America in which a French-speaking majority enjoys autonomous democratic institutions."[31] Bourassa told the National Assembly on June 18, 1987, that: "The entire constitution, including the Charter, will be interpreted and applied in the light of the section proclaiming our distinctness as a society. As a result, in the experience of our legislative authority, we will thus be able to consolidate existing positions and make new gains."[32] Powers, then, were the real game.

Jacques Parizeau also relished the potential of the distinct society provision. He told the late Barbara Frum on the *Journal* on October 25, 1989, that: "If we come to power, there is no doubt that I'm going to use – if the Meech Lake clause of a distinct society that hasn't been watered down is still there – I'm going to use that for everything it's worth. It's remarkable how much we could get through that clause if the courts say, well, yes, in some circumstances, it can overrule certain dispositions of the Charter of Rights. If the courts ever say that, my God, what a weapon it could be for people who have the sort of, shall we say, political project that I have."[33] The enthusiasm of Quebec's provincial leaders for the distinct society clause, then, is to be able to use this weapon against the Charter of Rights (without having the opprobrium of using the notwithstanding clause, a power they already have), and perhaps to use it as a lever to gain new jurisdictions.

Ambitions to have additional powers to limit civil liberties or to gain the upper hand in federal-provincial power games are less than exalted and certainly not worth all the effort that has been devoted to them. If the real goal is to promote the distinctiveness of Quebec by ensuring that the French language thrives, then the real danger is not the Canadian Charter of Rights, but the declining quality of the French being taught in Quebec's public schools.[34] Here the province has all the power it needs and not even the president of the St. Jean Baptiste Society can blame Ottawa for the problem. At the University of Montreal 40 percent of the students entering the university fail required French tests, and at the Université du Québec, the percentage is near 50 percent. And these are students who have passed through the secondary and CEGEP system. What about the 36 percent of Quebec young people, including the astounding rate of 42 percent of males, who drop out of secondary schools entirely? Quebeckers are dropping out at the same rate

as inner-city blacks in the United States. What is their future –
in French, in North America? Jean-Paul Desbiens, who as Frère
Untel opened the eyes of Quebeckers to the quality of their educational system prior to the Quiet Revolution, declared recently
that "we are forced to admit that our public school system has
been a failure."[35]

Literacy and learning are also aided by a good library
system. Here, too, Quebec lags behind the rest of Canada. In
1990, Quebec had 161 libraries compared to 534 in Ontario;
Toronto spent over $150 million on its library system in 1990;
Montreal only $38 million.[36] Other cultural institutions are
similarly deprived.

Public education and cultural dissemination are difficult;
making speeches about humiliation and distinct societies is
easy. Educators across North America are struggling with the
problem of dropouts, and English admission offices for large
universities complain as strenuously about the quality of
English as their colleagues do about French in Quebec. The
point is, if we are worried about the substance of the
problem – how to transmit and pass on to succeeding generations the beauties and complexities of one of the world's great
languages – then public education, language training and cultural creation would be the priority, not distinct society desig-
nations or special status. By getting sidetracked by the
ambitions of politicians for more power, Quebeckers work less
on the problems that count.

So, too, with the environment. The Allaire report recom-
mends that the province be given exclusive legislative authority over environmental matters and that the federal
government's spending power be eliminated. Quebec's Young
Liberals are the strongest backers of the Allaire report – but
they would have responded better to the environmental concerns of their generation by examining how the province was
using the powers it already possesses.

The list of Quebec environmental horror stories seems
endless.[37] In August 1988, a fire at a PCB warehouse in St.
Basil le Grand forced 3,500 residents to evacuate their homes
for nineteen days. Four years after that disaster, only 14 of 68
hazardous waste sites considered top priority have been
cleaned up, and in total only 24 of 333 sites discovered have

been restored. Beluga whales are on the way to extinction in the St. Lawrence and beaches close every summer because of health hazards, but across Quebec manufacturers and companies continue to dump raw sewage into the St. Lawrence. Quebec City alone dumps 51 tonnes of raw sewage into the St. Lawrence every day–enough to fill the 15,000-seat Colisée hockey arena three times over. Only one-third of Quebec cities, towns and villages have functional sewage installations, compared with 95 percent in Ontario.

If one were really concerned with protecting the environment rather than a power base, then one would advocate that a multiplicity of actors be involved in environmental protection at many levels. If only one jurisdiction has control, it could become prey to a dominant local power–Hydro-Québec, for example, or local industrial concerns. If only one jurisdiction has power, it becomes possible to attract local industries for jobs and export the pollution and waste to your neighbours. Environmental authority has to move up, towards international agreements and global understanding, not down to become the exclusive domain of one actor.

___ Colliding Groups _____

The self-deluding fallacies to which nationalism is susceptible – outmoded images, exaggerated virtue, élitist hijacking–hurt most the prospects of the group that is supposedly being promoted. But there is a darker side to nationalism, and this, too, has to be examined if we are to make a judgment about what principles should best govern the state: maximum freedom for equal citizens or group power and identity. Nationalism often veers from pride in one's group to antagonism towards another. A nation is a group of people who share a feeling of belonging. Daniel Bell writes: "If one looks down the dark ravines of history, one sees that groups need some other group to hate. The strength of a primordial attachment is that emotional cohesion derives not only from some inner consciousness of kind, but from some external definition of an adversary as well."[38]

Sensitive nationalists are well aware of the dangers in moving from pride in the group to opposing another group simply because it is different. Leon Dion, for example, has written that "it is one thing to feel a strong emotional affinity with one's fellow compatriots: it is quite another to use this affinity as a basis for interpreting social reality or for a doctrine that turns hatred of the 'other' into a moral negative."[39]

But others are not so careful. In Canada there is a history of anglophobia in Quebec and of francophobia in the rest of the country. By concentrating on group identity rather than individuals, nationalism leads to stereotyping, and stereotyping is an essential stepping stone to racial or ethnic hostility. By defining, too, belief in the overall need to belong to a group or nation and advocating the overriding need to maintain the identity of the group, there is an additional and essential problem: What if group goals collide? Why should my group have any more legitimacy than your group? What happens if we want the same thing? This is the particular conundrum of Quebec and aboriginal nationalism: if both are peoples and if people have the right to self-determination, what do you do about the problem of both these peoples inhabiting the same territory?

Force is not the Canadian way, and we have never experienced the extremes of ethnic violence that have periodically swept Europe. But the confrontation between Quebec and aboriginal nationalism is already troubling enough. Both nationalisms use the language of grievance and humiliation, both use the concept of peoplehood to promote the right of national self-determination, and these various "peoples" inhabit the same place. We should draw back from this abyss before it engulfs us. The claptrap of national self-determination must be discarded. What counts is improving the life chances of every Canadian, not protecting the abstract rights of "peoples."

No single individual is responsible for its rise or for the periodic outbursts of nationalism that have occurred throughout the history of Quebec and Canada. Quebec nationalism was born long before Brian Mulroney and it will likely exist as a political force long after he is gone. But our current prime minister bears a heavy responsibility for its present virulent state.

In 1983, in his campaign for the Conservative leadership, he attacked Joe Clark's supporters in Quebec: "To try to curry the favour of the Parti québécois organization during a leadership campaign is dangerous to the candidate who does it, it's dangerous to the future of the party he seeks to lead, and it's dangerous to the united country he seeks to govern."[40] Unfortunately for all of us, Mr. Mulroney did not heed his own advice. In 1984 he was busy recruiting nationalist and separatist supporters as Conservative candidates. One of those he recruited to the cause was his separatist friend Lucien Bouchard, who wrote the 1984 Sept-Îles speech announcing the Conservative's constitutional policy. The leader of the Bloc Québécois has revealed in his memoirs that: "I wrote the speech as though I was to be the one to give it, giving free reign to the indignation I felt over Quebec being set aside."[41] Mulroney then re-opened the Pandora's box of the constitution, accepted the "distinct society" clause as the centrepiece of the Meech Lake proposals and defended those proposals by using the traditional Quebec nationalist language of "humiliation" and "rejection." Since the failure of Meech Lake, the creation of the Bloc Québécois and the rise of separatism in Quebec, the prime minister has turned his rhetoric against the separatists and now makes a passionate defence of Canada. But the tiger he awakened has teeth and is not easily led. As Franklin Roosevelt once advised: "No man can tame a tiger into a kitten by stroking it."[42]

Yet whatever their apparent strength, aboriginal and Quebec nationalism do not have to win the day. Native self-government, for example, can proceed without debates over peoplehood, and in principle, Canadians have nothing to fear from this development. Indeed, the possibility that the aboriginal community may win constitutional entrenchment of the right to self-government is the most positive aspect of the latest round of constitutional negotiations. In 1982 the federal government fought for native rights and over the objections of the provinces succeeded in passing amendments confirming existing treaty rights and committing the First Ministers to hold a series of federal and provincial conferences on the issue of native self-government. We invited aboriginal leaders to attend these conferences so that for the first time they could approach elected politicians as equals. In 1983 a House of Commons special committee, ably chaired by Liberal MP Keith Penner, recommended aboriginal self-government, and in June 1984 our government introduced the Indian Self-Government Act.[43] Work on native self-government was well advanced when we left office in 1984.

No demons will be unleashed by natives running their reserves, by land claim settlements that give local bands wide discretion over health, education and other municipal services, or by the natural evolution of the Yukon and Northwest territories into provinces. Land claims are especially important. At present the 600 bands of status Indians comprise half a million Canadians on 2,225 reserves spread across the country. They control an area nearly half the size of Nova Scotia. To reduce their dependence on government assistance, this land base should be greatly increased so that natives can enjoy higher rents from resources like timber sales or mineral rights. But the Charter of Rights should apply to natives just as it does to every Canadian (as native women have requested) and the extravagant claims about self-determination should be dropped in favour of the tougher but much more productive task of raising living standards. Native Canadians should enjoy all the good that Canada has to offer while being able to develop their identity and culture. But self-government cannot be allowed to become a code word for isolation. It could so easily become synonymous with self-induced ghettos.

Quebec is not a monolith. Nationalism has always been a powerful force in the province, but at every stage of its development it has been opposed by Quebeckers who believed that individual choice was more important than group-sanctioned norms. In the 1840s and 1850s Étienne Parent advocated modern economic development while nationalists were clinging to the farm; Bishop Laflèche called the faithful to ultramontanism but he was opposed by Wilfrid Laurier, who, in 1877, made the best defence for individual conscience in Canadian intellectual history; Duplessis held Quebec back, but Paul-Émile Borduas in the arts, Father Lévesque in the social sciences and Jean Marchand in the union movement pointed the way to a modern Quebec, and in our day a new generation of Cité libristes are using their talents and pens to dissect the nationalist corpus.

Francophone Quebeckers want to have the good life. They want to define the qualities of that good life themselves. They also want to live that good life in French and to pass on to their children their linguistic heritage. A society based on equal rights and partnerships with other like-minded Canadians has a better chance of achieving this balanced agenda than a society that concentrates solely on ethnic group identity. Given a real choice, the men and women of Quebec will once again repudiate the nationalist élite, as they did in 1980.

This debate between individual choice and collectivism preoccupies much of the globe. Religious fundamentalism, particularly militant Islam, is on the rise in a variety of states. Ethnic nationalism has turned murderous in Europe. In Canada, democratic and free, collectivism has taken on the more benign form of ethnic nationalism parties like the Parti québécois or advocacy associations like the Assembly of First Nations. But even in this tolerant state, the excesses of collectivism are not unknown. Future generations will cringe at Premier Bourassa bragging about Bill 178 by saying that "never before in the history of Quebec has a government suspended fundamental liberties to protect the French language and culture."[44] But if one Quebecker has given voice to collectivism's premise that the rights of some are more important than equal treatment for all, another, Chief Justice Jules Deschênes, in a judgment on Bill 101, made a classic defence of individuals, equal in eloquence to Laurier's 1877 speech against ultramontanism. Deschênes pointed out the cruel dilemma presented by collectivism, whether it appears in its religious, ethnic, or ideological strain. There is, he stated, no homogeneity left in the world. Deschênes' judgment, which rejected portions of Bill 101, deserves to be quoted:

> However – Quebec argues – a collective right implies that it was established in the interest of and for the benefit of the collectivity, and not for each of its members. The limitation on this collective right may well involve the loss of the right by certain members of the collectivity, but the right is not denied to the group as a whole: it is simply limited.
>
> The court is amazed, to use a euphemism, to hear this argument from a government which prides itself in maintaining in America the flame of French civilization with its promotion of spiritual values and its traditional respect for liberty.
>
> In fact, Quebec's argument is based on a totalitarian

conception of society to which the court does not subscribe. Human beings are, to us, of paramount importance
and nothing should be allowed to diminish the respect due
to them. Other societies place the collectivity above the
individual. They use the Kilkhoze steamroller and see
merit only in the collective result even if some individuals
are left by the wayside in the process.

This concept of society has never taken root here – even
if certain political initiatives seem at times to come dan-
gerously close to it – and this court will not honour it with
its approval. Every individual in Canada should enjoy his
rights to the full when in Quebec, whether alone or as a
member of a group; and if the group numbers 100 persons,
the one hundredth has as much right to benefit ... He
cannot simply be counted as an accidental loss in a collective operation: our concept of human beings does not
accommodate such a theory.[45]

Human beings are not the means to an end. They are the end.
They should *never* be treated as the means to someone else's
end. Freedom offers human beings the choice to self-define and
self-develop. It is the individual merit and potential of the
citizen that counts, not the group that he or she is from. In our
universe, individuals are at the centre.

_____ An Equal Race _____

> *"The moral test of government is how it treats*
> *those who are in the dawn of life, the children;*
> *those who are in the twilight of life, the aged;*
> *and those who are in the shadows of life*
> *– the sick, the needy, and the handicapped."*

– Hubert H. Humphrey[46]

The Mulroney government did not champion the cause of
Quebec nationalists. It merely responded – ineptly and
naïvely – to this dynamic force. But in mounting an attack on the
post-1945 Keynesian social welfare consensus, the Conservative party itself has been the battering ram. The promotion of an
unfettered market has been as destabilizing to the personal

security of Canadians as nationalism has been to the tranquillity of the constitutional order. By weakening the power of the state, limiting social security and forcing the burden of economic adjustment on individuals rather than society, the Mulroney government has subjected Canada to a second series of shocks.

Change, innovation and enterprise enliven liberty. As Ralf Dahrendorf writes, "Rigidity, stagnation, and sclerosis are enemies of freedom."[47] Markets, which are a daily economic referendum, therefore hold no terrors for liberals. After all, Adam Smith, who theorized that the market is the most efficient means for co-ordinating the numerous private purposes of a heterogenous society, is one of the founding fathers of classical liberalism. To ensure a good quality of life, individuals must have access to an adequate stock of provisions, and free enterprise markets are the best way to provide provisions. Consumer dissatisfaction, in fact, was one of the prime forces in destroying communism in Central and Eastern Europe.

But if adequate provisions are critical to one aspect of the liberal design for expanding life's choices, equal entitlements are the other part of the equation. Modern liberalism's premise and promise consist in the idea that *every* citizen should have the opportunity to develop to the fullest. Personal emancipation for all is the just society's goal. Liberalism's failure resides in the gap between this promise and performance.

Inequality blights our society. All of us are different as individuals, but inequality is almost always the product of society itself. Those who have greater resources go to the best schools, have the best health care, acquire the most influential friends and wield the most power. The one million children who live in poverty in Canada will suffer from malnutrition, drop out of school in the greatest numbers, have the least job security and be the most at risk. As one social agency said about these children, they are *Born to Fail*.[48] For too many, the just society's promises are a hoax. It is not an equal race, R.H. Tawney taught us, if many of the contestants are lame.[49]

Equal opportunity is, therefore, critical to our definition of liberty. There must be a connection between "being free to" and "being able to." Or in the words of Anthony Crosland, "Until we are truly equal we will not be truly free."[50] Liberty and equality, rights and opportunities, provisions and entitlements – they march best when they march together.

To equalize opportunity for those left out of life's lottery, modern liberalism has used the instrument of the state both to guide markets and to redistribute the wealth that markets produce. There is, thus, a tension, although not necessarily a conflict, between the demands of the market and the requirements of equal opportunity.[51] Markets, left totally on their own, create a pattern of distribution that neglects the needs of the less wealthy in favour of the immediate financial interest of the prosperous. Therefore, modern liberalism has developed the concept of the mixed economy, where "resources are largely allocated through the market but in which public money intervenes in a significant role to supplement, contain, manipulate or direct market forces for public ends."[52] The welfare state joins the mixed economy as an essential foundation of modern liberalism: the state incurs part of the risk for individuals by assuming much of the cost of health care, unemployment insurance and pensions, and redistributes income through the progressive income tax. John Maynard Keynes and William Beveridge stand side by side with Adam Smith and John Stuart Mill in the pantheon of liberalism.

This "Keynesian–social welfare consensus" existed in Canada from 1944 to 1984, and it had many successes. Internationally, Canada was a champion of the GATT-Breton Woods system of multilateral trade, and through successive tariff-cutting rounds, the protectionist legacy of the 1930s was discarded. Despite all the heat of the 1988 election campaign, for example, Canada had already achieved the reality of free trade with the United States long before any agreement was signed: thanks to the GATT and the Autopact, 80 percent of the trade in goods between our two countries was tariff-free by the mid-1980s. Canada, in fact, gave up significant concessions over energy and investment to receive slight U.S. tariff cuts on a minority of our trade, which in time would likely have occurred within GATT anyway. In 1984, too, Canada enjoyed a surplus of over $20 billion in trade with the U.S., a figure not even remotely approached since the signing of the agreement. Canada was an open economy and a significant world trader long before the Conservatives came to power.

Domestically, the era of the Keynesian consensus saw a

tremendous investment boom in plant, equipment and public infrastructure. The public sector invested in capital projects like the Trans-Canada Highway system and natural gas pipelines, which, in turn, spurred private-sector spending. Education was massively expanded to accommodate the demands of the baby boom generation. University enrolment, for example, grew from 35,000 before World War II to over 400,000 students by the mid-1980s. As a consequence, throughout most of this period, real per-capita income grew every year, business profits were high and government resources were buoyant. Wealth creation led to wealth distribution.

In 1944 the King government introduced family allowances, thereby ushering in the modern welfare state. Every subsequent decade saw a major social advance: in the 1950s health insurance, in the 1960s medicare and the Canada Pension Plan, in the 1970s the expansion of the unemployment insurance system and the child tax credit, and in the early 1980s expansion of the Guaranteed Income Supplement to lift the aged from poverty. In 1984 the expansion stopped. A new era – self-proclaimed – was upon us. The age of neo-conservatism had arrived.

On November 8, 1984, Michael Wilson presented to Parliament *A New Direction for Canada: An Agenda for Economic Renewal*. This document somewhat sententiously proclaimed that: "On September 4, Canadians voted for change ... they voted for a change in policies and change in the approach of government to the making of those policies. That is our mandate and our challenge."[53] As a matter of fact, if Canadians did vote for a change in economic policy by supporting the Conservatives in 1984, it was certainly not because of the Conservatives' campaign. Mr. Mulroney spent his time explaining that social programs were a "sacred trust," free trade was not mentioned, Mr. Wilson kept carefully hidden his plan to raise taxes ("We would not raise taxes. Tax levels are already too high," Wilson told the House of Commons on March 6, 1984) and deficit reduction was not a major theme. There was no popular mandate for any assault on the mixed economy and the welfare state. In this one respect Mr. Mulroney was different from British Prime Minister Margaret Thatcher and U.S. President Ronald Reagan, who at least told their electorates what they planned to do. In other particulars, however, the November 8 document was more accurate. It did herald a new direction. Eight years later we see the results.

The onslaught of the Mulroney Conservatives on Canada's mixed economy – social welfare tradition, is a striking example of branch-plant ideology. There is little party history to support the anti-statist, continentalist and decentralizing tendencies of present-day conservatism. Brian Mulroney has simply turned conservative tradition on its head. John A. Macdonald used the state to build the railway and tariffs to build a national east-west economy. R.B. Bennett increased the government's participation in Canada's cultural life by creating the Canadian Broadcasting Corporation, John Diefenbaker expanded the welfare state. Robert Stanfield called for a guaranteed annual income. Peter Lougheed and William Davis had no qualms about using public ownership to develop their provinces. Until the 1980s, conservatism was part of the Canadian consensus.

In repudiating both his party's traditions and Canada's post-war public philosophy, Brian Mulroney travelled down a path already trodden by the heavy boots of Margaret Thatcher and Ronald Reagan. Margaret Thatcher won her leadership in a 1975 "Peasant's Revolt" against the style and interventionist legacy of Edward Heath. Ronald Reagan failed narrowly in a right-wing revolt against Gerald Ford in 1976 but led his anti-détente, anti-state, anti-choice coalition to victory in 1980. Brian Mulroney ran as a moderate in 1976 but failed in his bid to succeed Robert Stanfield. From this he learned a lesson. By the end of the 1970s the volunteers and militants who made up the constituency wing of the party had turned significantly rightwards in their views, and in 1983 Mulroney won the leadership he had failed to gain in 1976 by appealing to this wing of the party. The *Agenda for Economic Renewal* stunned many casual observers of Canadian politics but it came as no surprise to those who had followed the transformation of the Conservative party. The far right wing had captured the party and through the electoral success of Brian Mulroney in 1984, they succeeded in capturing Canada as well.[54]

Conservatism's successful revolt against the post-war liberal order in Great Britain, the United States and Canada has many origins but one of the most powerful has to do with liberalism's failure to adapt the Keynesian paradigm to a changing world. Two of the pillars of the post-war consensus – a mixed economy and the welfare state – are as relevant today as they were in 1945. The third–the Keynesian theory of demand management–is now very difficult to implement. To stabilize the economy and create full employment, the theory requires the government to inject the proper amount of stimulus or restraint into the system. Fine tuning it is called. The assumption of the theory is that national actions can determine local results because we are working within a closed economy.

By the 1970s, however, the integration of the world economy was already so well advanced that any local actions could be overwhelmed by outside forces. It was difficult enough to assess with any accuracy how much additional demand a national economy needed, but even if you got it right, the world economy could defeat the whole purpose of the exercise. In 1981, for example, President Mitterand found that he could not stimulate his economy on his own and our Liberal government discovered in the same year that the U.S. policy of raising interest rates to stratospheric levels (Volckerism), could deal a devastating blow to our economic strategy. The nation-state was no longer powerful enough to do this particular job.

Conservatives leaped on this one failure and proclaimed that since the state could not manage demand right, it could do *nothing* right. Keynesianism, and along with it the liberal consensus as a whole, was blamed for inflation and declining growth rates. As faith in government declined, the pursuit of personal gain became the driving force not only in the economy but in society as a whole. The public-choice school of economics lauded the magic of the marketplace and held that all government activity was coercive interference in the natural and voluntary transactions of the market. They failed to note that government must precede the formation of markets because someone has to enforce the obligations of contracts!

Monetarists, led by Milton Friedman, led the attack on Keynesianism and announced that inflation could be reduced only by controlling the money supply. If managing demand was difficult for Keynesians, controlling the money supply soon proved to be impossible for the monetarists. Monetary targets were rarely if ever reached. When they were, the results were often opposite to the theory, and in a world of credit cards, millions of bank accounts and world financial flows, it became difficult even to define money. Conservative social theorists like Charles Murray and George Gilder opined that welfare assistance actually hurt the interests of the poor.[55] Supply-siders threw in the cheery thought that government revenues would magically increase if taxes were cut – especially taxes on the incomes of the wealthy. Businesses and their supporters were only too happy to endorse movements that cut environmental regulations, limited the power of labour and reduced their taxes. British Labour Party leader Neil Kinnock spoke for many outside his own party when he condemned Thatcherism with words that apply equally well to Reaganism or Mulroneyism: "No obligations to the community, no sense of solidarity . . . no neighbourhood, no number other than one, no time other than now, no such thing as society – just me! and now!"[56]

An Agenda for Economic Renewal proclaimed most of these new conservative views. The economic priority problem for Canada was to be the deficit. The market was to be our salvation. The previous Liberal government and all its works were lambasted: "Through excessive regulation and intervention it has substituted the judgement of politicians and regulators for the judgement of those in the market place."[57] Privatization, deregulation, financial incentives for the private sector and, above all, deficit reduction, made up the core of the plan. Higher taxes, of course, were *not* supposed to be the principal means to reduce the deficit. Supply-side ideology opposed higher taxes and Mr. Wilson had joined the chorus of those who complained in 1984 that taxes were already too onerous. These policies were supposed to restore growth, increase investment (especially on research and development) and reduce inflation.

_____ The Good, the Bad and the Ugly_____

The economic results after eight years of Conservative rule mock these aspirations. The one indisputable gain is that through the stringent policies of the Bank of Canada, inflation has been reduced to levels not seen since the 1960s. But apart from this, the conservative world has not turned out as it should

have.[58] For two years now we have been in a steep recession
that shows little sign of abating. Since the recession began in
April 1990, 415,000 jobs have been lost; 1991 saw a record
number of bankruptcies (75,773); and corporate pre-tax profits
have fallen 50 percent since 1988. Well-known corporations
like Lavalin have gone under, and even mighty Olympia and
York is under siege. Food banks have mushroomed, with nearly
400,000 Canadians using such facilities once a month. The
unemployment rate in June 1992 was 11.6 percent, the highest
rate since September 1984 when Brian Mulroney stumped the
country crying, "Jobs, jobs, jobs." Despite the success in
bringing down the inflation rate, a recent report of the Bank of
Nova Scotia declared that "1990–93 will nevertheless mark the
worst four-year performance of the Canadian economy in the
post-war era."[59]

The *Agenda for Renewal* harshly criticized the economic
record of the previous Liberal government, but in many particulars the Conservative record does not bear comparison. Real
annual growth in the GNP averaged 4.0 percent in the previous
sixteen years of Liberal government, compared to 2.6 percent
from 1985 to 1991. Savings rates were 14.8 percent in 1984 and
only 10.3 percent in 1991. Canada was in tenth place in OECD
research and development spending in 1984, but we had
slipped to seventeenth place by 1990. Despite all the Conservative rhetoric about free trade and promotion of Canadian
exports, in 1984 Canada enjoyed a current account surplus of
$1.7 billion in its dealings with the rest of the world, but this
had fallen through the floor to the astonishing level of a $26.7
billion deficit by 1991.

Higher taxes were not part of the Conservative program in
1984 but they may prove to be one of the most enduring aspects
of the Conservative legacy. Canadian families paid 15.9
percent of their income in taxes in 1984, but after thirty-two tax
increases since 1984, taxes ate up 19.8 percent of income by
1990. The tax burden of a poor working family of four, for
example, increased from $175 in 1984 to $822 in 1991, an
increase of 370 percent. A middle-income family's tax burden
went up 17 percent over the same period, while upper-income
families earning more than $120,000 saw their tax burden drop
by 6 percent. Because of slower growth and higher taxes, the

real income of families failed to increase at all in the decade of the 1980s; average family income after taxes in inflation-adjusted dollars was $40,400 in 1989, compared to $40,000 in 1980. Four hundred dollars after a decade of work! Canadian families have been running harder than ever before, only to find themselves in the same place.

But in the cruellest cut of all, net public debt, which stood at $206 billion in 1984/85 had more than doubled to $420 billion by 1992. The economic legacy of the Mulroney government includes more than half the total debt accumulated since Confederation! Despite all the promises, all the tax increases and all the spending cuts, Canada's budget deficit stubbornly stayed at over $31.4 billion in 1991/92. It is enough to make a conservative idealogue weep!

_____ The Race among Nations _____

In fact, the Conservative agenda so boldly proclaimed in 1984 has now begun to look tattered. Torpor has replaced activism as the order of the day. The current recession hit Canada like a thunderbolt in the winter of 1990 but the government's reaction to it has been strangely listless. The Conservatives are at an impasse. Having moved to correct what they regarded as the excesses of the Keynesian welfare state, they are without ideas now that the pruning has been done.

This stasis results from internal contradiction as much as from exhaustion. Conservative ideology now prevents the attainment of conservative goals. In Canada, Great Britain and the United States, the three current conservative administrations repeat the buzz words "global competitiveness" like a mantra, but their animus against activist government and public investment is now the largest single obstacle to developing competitive economies. Conservatives have seen the mountaintop, but their ideological baggage prevents them from ever leading us to the summit.

Unfortunately, Canada's key competitors on the world market have been on the mountaintop for quite some time, and they are benefitting from their position. Germany practises a "social" market with high welfare expenditures and a banking system that organizes and energizes the economy. Germany will invest between $600 and 700 billion over the next decade in the former East Germany, giving it Europe's most modern plant and equipment.[60] If Germany will be investing vast amounts in the future, Japan has already invested huge sums in the recent past. It is a "development" state with an activist government that works to produce and enforce national consensus. Between 1986 and 1991, Japan invested $3.5 trillion in new plant and equipment, out-investing North America on a per-capita basis by 250 percent! These are the nations Canada will have to compete against if we are to succeed in the new world economic order.

In Japan and Germany the state is not an alien force. Government, in these societies, helps individuals and companies adapt to the changing world. Risk, in other words, is socialized. In Canada, the United States and Great Britain, conservative administrations have said to workers, You are on your own; markets alone will do the job of adjustment; markets alone will direct investment. Naturally enough, since Canadians have to cope alone with job loss, global competition and technological innovations, many will turn against the process of change itself.

This conundrum becomes clear in the aftermath of the great free trade debate. Free trade was not just about reducing tariffs to give consumers a break. One of its essential purposes was to use enhanced American competition to force the restructuring of the Canadian economy. Yet markets destroy at the same time as they create. Having introduced free trade, the Conservative government did nothing to help Canadians take advantage of it. The Canadian dollar was allowed (some say encouraged) to rise, which took away the exchange-rate advantage that Canadian exporters had formerly enjoyed. Since Canada's was the smaller economy, one would have expected the government to encourage industry or private-sector working groups to put plans into effect to maximize Canada's locational advantages and minimize our disadvantages. Nothing was organized.

In the 1988 campaign the Conservatives promised adjustment assistance and appointed a blue ribbon task force, headed by Jean de Grandpré, to advise them on the issue. In 1989 de Grandpré recommended a training levy to be imposed on business. That was the last thing heard about worker adjustment assistance![61] Faced with rising unemployment and training needs, the Conservatives actually cut the budget of Employment and Immigration by $100 million in 1991 and by $100 million again in 1992. Markets do force adjustment, but the burden of sacrifice often falls unfairly on those least able to cope. Our task must not be to impede adjustment but to assist it by bringing equity to market outcomes.

To be successful, the Canadian economy needs more than the private investment of motivated capitalists. Success also depends on a well-trained workforce that is able to adjust to a world economy, and it is government that has a comparative advantage in helping to bring about this desired outcome. Governments can concentrate the resources, create a framework of incentives and penalties and focus the national will on priorities.

By ignoring the productive elements of government intervention, the Conservatives ignore the lessons of Canada's past as well as the successes of Japan and Germany in the present. Canada is a success story today because of the strength of past public policy. Lester Thurow makes the point that North America moved ahead of the economic pack at the end of the nineteenth century because it combined great natural resources with a great public policy innovation–mass education: "We had one hundred years when we were educating our population and the rest of the world was not. In 1950 North America had a workforce that was better educated from top to bottom than any other workforce on the face of the globe. We in North America put national resources together with education, skills, and we became the most successful economy in the world."[62] Investment in people was complemented by investment in infrastructure–from the time of Sir John A. Macdonald and Laurier through to C.D. Howe, Canada invested in roads, railways, ports and airports. In 1960, for example, 13 percent of the total investment of all governments in Canada was in infrastructure. Today it is only 5 percent.[63]

To succeed economically in today's world Canada must compete with Europe, Japan, the United States and the developing world. There must be a reason to locate and produce *in* Canada. Business will not do so for sentiment. We have to engineer our own advantages. Although they never used that language, that was precisely the approach of Macdonald, Laurier and Howe. Each of these nation-builders used the state as a catalyst to nudge the market towards public ends. Conservative reluctance to use our government intelligently, as the Japanese and Germans are using theirs, is simply perverse.

___ The Politics of Stealth _____

The *Agenda for Economic Renewal* promised "not to weaken the basic income support programmes that have served Canadians well"[64] but no important social advance has occurred since 1984. Instead the Conservatives have practised what one observer has called "social policy by stealth"[65] by changing benefit levels and tax percentages, by reducing inflation indexation and by putting a cap on transfers to the provinces. In 1985 Michael Wilson attempted a frontal attack by cutting old age pensions, but he was forced to retreat in humiliation. In subsequent budgets he achieved the same goal by confusing Canadians rather than confronting them.

According to Ken Battle, the former director of the National Welfare Council, the Conservatives shaved $3.5 billion from the child benefit system between 1986 and 1991. It is estimated that federal transfers for health and post-secondary education will be cut by nearly $100 billion from 1986 to the year 2000 (assuming policies do not change). What cannot be debated is that federal social spending has fallen from 10.4 percent of GNP in 1984 to 8.4 percent in 1991/92.

This reduction in social transfers was accompanied by increased tax burdens on the working poor and middle-income families, while upper-income Canadians enjoyed a $100,000 exemption from the capital gains tax. Canadian Tories, like their cousins in the United States and Great Britain, practise what John Kenneth Galbraith calls the "sparrow" theory of economics: if the horse is fed enough oats, some will pass through to the road for the sparrows. "To this end, the rich needed the spur of more money, the poor the spur of their own poverty."[66]

The Conservatives' policy of weakening social security is as misguided as their reluctance to make our government as much a partner of the private sector as the Japanese Ministry of International Trade and Industry is for Toyota. In our view equity is not a luxury – it is an essential component of economic productivity itself. Public goods like education, health care and social security do not merely distribute wealth, they help create it by allowing individuals from every income stratum to have the chance of a productive life.

In Japan, for example, only 5 percent of young people fail to complete high school, while in Canada one-third of our students drop out before finishing their secondary education. In Canada, one million children – 16 percent of the youth population – live in poverty, compared to 5 percent in Sweden. And if a dropout does succeed in getting a job in Canada, only one in four firms engage in worker training: on a per-employee basis, the United States spends twice as much as Canada, the Japanese five times as much and the Germans eight times as much.

Canada cannot afford a lost generation. One million Canadian children live in poverty, children under eighteen account for 40 percent of the 400,000 people who use food banks regularly and 51 percent of aboriginal children live in poverty.[67]

It is a matter of simple, human decency to help the blameless – our children – and it is an urgent economic priority not to turn our backs on such a large part of the future labour force. The poor child of today will be the dropout of tomorrow. Canada cannot afford the waste of having one-third of its young people drop out of school. By failing to invest now, we are committing future generations of Canadians to an economic race they cannot win.

There are solutions to this problem, just not easy ones. The first task is to get our priorities right. In the last Liberal government, for example, we made poverty among the aged the overarching social priority. Resources devoted to income security increased from 5.2 percent of GNP in 1968/69 to 10.4 percent by 1984/85. The old age pension was increased and the guaranteed income supplement steadily raised. Other social assistance suffered; we could not do it all. But to govern is to choose, and the Economic Council reported recently that poverty among the aged had declined from 43 percent in 1973 to 9 percent in 1989.[68] This is a societal achievement of immense proportions. It also proves that government can work.

Canada must now do for children what has already been done for the elderly. Fiscal prudence, of course, requires that Canada must not spend with abandon. And given the spate of

Conservative tax increases, including the GST, there is now little room for additional revenue enhancement.

But recognition of the realities of the need for tighter fiscal policies does not mean we are reduced to immobilism. Priorities can change. There can be readjustments from within. The burden of sacrifice and benefit can be altered. At a minimum, a government that commits $4.5 billion to new helicopters while cutting job training has its priorities all wrong. With one-third of Canadians likely to experience poverty at least once during their working career, as soon as the economy allows, the social safety net should be strengthened by returning to full indexation of benefits. Having a floor beneath which no Canadian can fall is an entitlement every citizen needs. Our social security system is not a luxury – it is part of the social contract.

Parental leave, maternity benefits and flexible working hours should become part of a family policy that places a premium on improving the home environment for our children. Like medicare in the 1960s, a national day-care policy should be Canada's next great social advance. Simply raising the child-care exemption (which helps the wealthy) as the Conservatives have done, is not enough.

In 1983/84, before we left office, we examined the possibility of turning the federal government's block grants on higher education into student vouchers, thereby creating a "market system" to bring competition to universities. We also looked at the creation of a voucher system in training so that young people not going to university would still be encouraged to upgrade their skills. To create a real learning society in the 1990s, similar policies will have to be implemented.

Conservative antipathy to activist government must be overcome if Canada is to have a decent human resources policy for the 1990s. But even if a national consensus did emerge that it was once again time to try the liberal remedy, another roadblock has been thrown in the way. The recent federal-provincial agreement on the Constitution – if implemented – will transfer labour training to the provinces and limit the ability of the federal government to introduce new national programs like daycare. Canada is already the only country in the Western world without a national education policy. We will soon be the only country in the world without a national employment or training policy. The Conservatives' willingness to weaken Ottawa by appeasing the provinces means that Canada is giving up powers to influence employment policy at precisely the time that governments in the rest of the world are concentrating on human resources!

The Conservative attack on the Keynesian consensus forced liberals to take stock, re-evaluate our priorities and re-examine the efficiency of the state. The Conservative emphasis on markets is not mistaken, but it is not enough. Change must come, but the risk must be shared. True market efficiency requires social equity. To forget one is to ensure that neither objective will be achieved.

_____ The Thirty Years Constitutional War _____

> *"The doctor smiled and took his fees,*
> *There is no cure for this disease."*[69]

> –Hilaire Belloc

Faced with surging Quebec nationalism and intense international economic competition, the Mulroney Conservatives have responded to these threats by a third divisive thrust – the provincialization of Canada. In the constitutional negotiations which have been ongoing since 1987, the federal government's position has been all tactics and no vision. Get a deal, any deal, pretty well sums up the story. Mr. Mulroney has mediated between the provinces but has had no fixed views of his own. Conservatives still cannot answer the question "But who will speak for Canada?"

In 1967 Canadians were advised that entering into constitutional negotiations would be like "opening a can of worms." So it has proved. For over thirty years federal and provincial politicians have been engaged in a continuous merry-go-round of speeches, conferences, ultimatums and last-chance negotiations. Constitution making has consumed political and psychic resources out of all proportion to the intrinsic worth of the exercise. Rancour, discord, ennui and exasperation have been the inevitable result.

Constitution making is difficult because the stakes are so high. Once an item is written into the constitution, it is almost impossible to change because of the rigidity of our amending formula. Since 1982, on most topics, seven provinces representing 50 percent of the population must agree. In the normal course of deal making, the parties will compromise or experiment, because if the solution doesn't work it can always be fixed, but in constitution making, if it is a mistake, it is a *permanent* mistake. Therefore every clause and comma must be subject to rigorous analysis.

The constitution is also the highest law of the land: inclusion in the constitution has therefore taken on immense symbolic importance. Most of our bitter debate today is about status and symbol: Quebec is already a distinct society and has a considerable amount of autonomy in practice, but it wants its distinct status to be recognized in the constitution. Alberta wants an equal Senate because of the theory of provincial equality. Aboriginal Canadians want their rights as peoples acknowledged, although social advance and land claim settlements are at least as important as native self-government. Groups want affirmation of their status by mention in the constitution. Because of this, rather than engaging in the normal administrative and political method of give and take to solve problems, Canadians have developed a mania for putting things in the constitution that don't belong there. By trying for a constitutional settlement on every issue, we guarantee that nothing will ever be settled.

In assessing Canada's obsession with the constitution, one of the first of many ironies is that there is very little wrong with our existing framework. It can be improved, no doubt. The "notwithstanding clause," for example, is an affront and should be removed from the Charter. But as far back as the early 1960s, one of us wrote that "I am not in a frantic hurry to change the Constitution, simply because I am in a frantic hurry to change society."[70]

What was true in 1965 is even more evident today. Canada can move forward on a host of fronts without bothering to call federal-provincial conferences. Pilot projects in native self-government can proceed without constitutional sanction. Minority languages can be protected. Provinces can end trade barriers by mutual agreement without putting exemptions into the constitution forever. Federal administrative jurisdiction in a variety of fields can be delegated to the provinces, as we did in

1978 with Quebec over immigration, without changing our supreme law. Canada's constitution is already a flexible document that has stood the test of time. Constitutional failure or success should not be a metaphor for the failure or success of Canada. What is important is to make real changes in the conditions that affect people's lives. If we can put an end anytime soon to Canada's Thirty Years War, the constitutional file should be put on the shelf for at least a generation.

A second irony in the constitutional debate is the about-face the Conservative party has made in recent years regarding the division of powers. Despite the centralist legacy of its founder, Sir John A. Macdonald, the Conservative party has now become the provincialist party. Robert Stanfield advocated the *"deux nations"* theory of federalism in 1968; Joe Clark developed his community of communities approach in 1979; and since 1984 Brian Mulroney has been willing to discuss dealing away virtually any federal power in exchange for a constitutional settlement. No premier has asked for the Post Office yet, but if they do, mail your letters right away!

Why has present-day Conservatism so resolutely turned away from its heritage? Some of the reasons are given in the sections above. The Conservatives have made a tactical alliance with Quebec nationalism and for many nationalists, Ottawa is the enemy. Anti-government ideologues have become another important influence within the Conservative party, and for these people, while all government is to be abhorred, since Ottawa is the most powerful jurisdiction and has been an activist player on behalf of social welfare, it needs to be cut down the most. Politically, as the Liberal party became dominant at the national level between 1963 and 1984, the Conservatives began to rebuild their base in the provinces and strong premiers like Brian Peckford and Peter Lougheed were influential in moving the Conservatives into the provincialist camp.

Leading the anti-Ottawa coalition that is the present-day Conservative party, Brian Mulroney has placed more importance on the successful conclusion of a constitutional deal than on the substance of the deal itself. Since the provinces know that his bottom line is a deal, any deal, they have not had to bargain in a serious way over the distribution of powers. If enough provinces want a change, there is a good chance of success. If there is provincial disagreement about the wisdom of carving up Ottawa's jurisdiction, then federal responsibility is likely to endure, but in all cases the initiative is with the provinces.

In 1987, for example, Manitoba Premier Howard Pawley described how he and David Peterson had defended federal powers in the Meech Lake discussions while the prime minister was silent.[71] In the current round of constitutional negotiations, in September 1991, to great fanfare, the federal government announced that it wanted important new powers for the economic union. It would be willing to bargain away powers like employment policy that it felt could better be administered locally, but in exchange it wanted an end to provincial trade barriers. It did not turn out that way.

Like the grand old Duke of York, the idea of economic union was marched up to the top of the hill and then quickly marched down again. In the July 1992 Pearson Accord, the provinces won so many exemptions to the free economic movement of goods, capital and labour that the C.D. Howe Institute argued that "Canada would be better off with the existing, outdated common market clause than with the proposal that now exists."[72] Mr. Mulroney promised to do better. But in the next negotiating session in August, while Alberta won its equal Senate, Quebec gained its veto and natives won self-government, the federal government failed in its attempt to tear down domestic trade barriers. Initial reports indicate that the First Ministers agreed to a list of exemptions even longer than the thirteen exemptions granted by Mr. Clark on July 7, 1992.[73] The *Globe and Mail* suggested that "the gutting of the economic union does not suggest a great spirit of nation-building is abroad in provincial capitals."[74] Or in Ottawa.

_____ Executive Federalism Fights Back _____

In 1982, the provinces had gained greater control over national resources in the only division-of-power amendment in the repatriation package, but it was certainly not the feast that the provincial devolutionists had dreamed about. The Charter, too, had earned the support of women, the disabled and the civil libertarians, and the lash of public opinion had forced the premiers to agree to reinstate Charter provisions on equality and native rights that they had wanted dropped.

During the Meech Lake negotiations, however, the provinces launched their counter-revolution. They had lost an important bargaining lever when they could no longer use the desirability of repatriation to gain greater devolution of powers. Brian Mulroney, however, happily replaced this lost provincial advantage and then some. By accepting the fake nationalist thesis that Quebec had been deceived in the 1980 referendum and betrayed after the "night of the long knives" in November 1981, Mulroney gave Premier Bourassa operating room to revive the old strategy: Give me more powers and I will agree to the constitution. And to meet Quebec's demands, Mulroney had to gain the support of the other provinces. Thus, the Quebec round became the Provincial round. As proposed in the Meech Lake Accord, the provinces would gain the power to appoint the Senate and Supreme Court and receive fiscal compensation for opting out of national spending programs.

In a classic demonstration of executive federalism, the premiers met twice, consulted no one and then proclaimed that the deal was a seamless web that could never be changed. Citizen involvement – so important for the victory of the Charter in 1982 – was nowhere in sight. "Meech Lake was a powerful counterattack to reinstate the dominance of government," writes Alan Cairns, "and to reassert the primacy of federalism, and to do so entirely from a provincial perspective."[75]

Meech Lake failed. As this essay is being written in August 1992, the First Ministers have come to an agreement that enshrines much of the Meech Lake Accord plus: an equal, partially elected and not very effective Senate; an expanded House of Commons with Quebec perpetually guaranteed 25 percent of Commons seats; restrictions on federal spending power as well as the transfer of federal jurisdiction in areas like culture and labour-market training to the provinces; and the entrenchment of native self-government. It is not possible to comment directly on these proposals, since no legal text is available and many details are still unclear. The process leading to ratification is also unknown, although Quebec, Alberta and British

Columbia have all passed laws stipulating that provincial referendums should be held.

Whatever the details of the final agreement, we hope that the
prime minister will hold a national referendum. On constitution
making we place our faith in the people. People, not governments, are sovereign, so it is the people who should decide. A
national referendum is the only way to break our political deadlock and release Canada from its constitutional obsession. We
could do worse than follow the advice of Thomas Paine: "The
constitution of a country is not the act of government but of the
people constituting its government."[76]

If the prime minister tries to replicate the Meech Lake
process of playing the old game of executive federalism while
ignoring the very real desire of Canadians to play a part in their
country's future, we can only repeat about our prime minister
what one historian said of Philip II of Spain: "No experience of
the failure of his policy could shake his belief in its essential
excellence."[77]

_____ The Wisdom of the Mean _____

> *"The role of government is to*
> *represent the future to the present"*
>
> –Lester Thurow[78]

Heraclitus, one of the first philosophers of classical Greece,
believed that "everything is in flux." What was true of Greece
in 500 BC is even more apparent in our own age. The Soviet
Union is no more. The Cold War has been won. A revolution in
electronics and computers has transformed the world economy
and with it the very viability of the nation-state. Ethnic loyal-
ties are exploding in conflict at the same time as world popular
culture is becoming ever more homogenized.

This essay has made two points. First we have argued that
the response of the Mulroney government to our changed world
has been to make Canada's situation worse. Ethnic nationalism
has been appeased rather than combatted, government has been
derided rather than used as an agent to help individuals adjust
and Ottawa has been weakened at the very time that we most
need to mobilize the national will.

Second, we contend that a particular public philosophy – the concept of a just society where individuals are treated equally and have the opportunity and resources to live their own definition of the good life – is best suited to helping Canadians adapt to this world of change. Since our goal is to expand freedom by expanding choice, by definition our philosophy inclines toward moderation and balance. Nothing in excess, warned the Delphic oracle. That stricture is our guiding light. Individuals should not be deprived of their linguistic and cultural heritage. We therefore support minority rights, including language rights. But the quest for linguistic security should never go so far as to deprive other individuals of their civil liberties. If the goal is to promote cultural diversity as a *means* of extending individual choice rather than to establish cultural or ethnic identity as the primary good, then abuses are prevented. Moderation reigns. Similarly with economic and social policy: liberals want citizens to have both entitlements and provisions. The dynamics of the free market are allowed to flourish but not without counterbalancing government initiatives to ensure that fairness prevails as much as possible. Equality of opportunity is advanced, but not equality of condition. In federalism there must be a balance between the centre and the provinces. The goal is individual self-realization, everything else is a means to that end.

To provide the conditions for the free development of human capabilities, leaders must have a cold eye and a warm heart. A cold eye for the realities of our times, a warm heart for the potential of humankind – and modesty about what can be accomplished. As Camus wrote, "Perhaps we cannot prevent this world from being a world in which children are tortured. But we can reduce the number of tortured children."[79] Erode by inches the conditions which produce avoidable suffering. Expand by inches the capacity of every citizen to make meaningful choices. Every citizen can make a difference and all must try. We say with the poet Louis MacNeice:

> "By a high star our course is set,
> our end is Life: Put out to sea."

Thomas S. Axworthy
Pierre Elliott Trudeau

PART II
The Global
Transformation

In a celebrated 1960 speech announcing Britain's renunciation
of colonialism, Harold Macmillan called upon his countrymen
to recognize "the winds of change" sweeping over the world.
The British prime minister's metaphor was compelling, and in
the three decades since he spoke, "the winds of change" have
fundamentally altered the globe's power balance.

In the 1960s, the United States was at the zenith of its power. The only other superpower, the Soviet Union, had been
humiliated over Cuba in 1962. Despite early fears about a
"missile gap," the Americans enjoyed clear nuclear superiority
over any possible rival. Economic power went hand in hand
with military might. So much so, that J. J. Servan-Schreiber was
sufficiently alarmed to write *The American Challenge*, warning
Europe about U.S. economic domination.

Over the next twenty years the world witnessed a stunning
reversal of these bi-polar verities. At immense cost, the Soviets
achieved military parity with the United States. China emerged
as a great power in its own right, destroying all the old Cold
War assumptions about the Sino-Soviet bloc. Third World
countries like Vietnam and Afghanistan handed defeats to each
of the superpowers. The United States continued to be the
foremost economic power, but not the only power, as Japan,
the western Europeans and newly industrialized countries like

51

Taiwan, South Korea and Singapore carved out large market shares of world trade. Canada's response to these turbulent changes is outlined in Thomas Axworthy's chapter on foreign policy.

One of the primary lessons to emerge from the decades under review in this volume, is that economic prowess is a far more supple and critical ingredient of power than the traditional reliance upon arms. Indeed, since 1968, the world economy has changed almost beyond recognition: Japan has become an economic superpower; international capital moves across the world at the flick of a computer switch; regional blocs, especially in Europe, have realigned trading patterns; production and marketing strategies have become globalized.

International events like the OPEC shocks of 1973 and 1979 and the Volcker interest rate shock of 1981 feature prominently in the essays of Marc Lalonde on energy, Joel Bell on industrial policy and Ian Stewart on macroeconomics. Two of the shocks, the OPEC crisis of 1973 and the Iran crisis of 1979, sent the price of petroleum skyrocketing to a tenfold increase. Energy thus became a central preoccupation of Canadian politics throughout our time in office. The stakes were so high that energy policy became a battleground for radically opposed beliefs about economic development, regional fairness and the functioning of federalism itself.

As Marc Lalonde's chapter makes clear, Canadians, unlike Americans, did not have to wait in line for their gasoline. Despite the severity of the OPEC crises, Canadians suffered no interruption in supply. After intense conflict with Alberta, better balance was also achieved in the distribution of oil revenues. Viewing energy not merely as a commodity, but as an essential building block for regional and industrial development, we also favoured administered oil pricing. From 1961 to 1973, Ontario consumers paid $1.00 to $1.50 more per barrel than the world price to assist the Alberta industry by giving it a guaranteed market. After the OPEC crisis of 1973, Canadian consumers paid less than the world price as increases up to the world level were introduced gradually. The principle behind both the 1961–1973 National Oil Policy and the 1980–1984 National Energy Program was the same—a "made in Canada" oil price to develop and use energy, to give Canadians greater economic security.

Unlike energy, industrial policy in Canada was not affected by dramatic events like the two OPEC crises. But the rules of the industrial game were nevertheless transformed. As Joel Bell demonstrates in his contribution, developments in the global economy exerted a powerful cumulative impact on Canada's ability to produce good products at good prices. These changes had a particularly profound effect on resource industries, which have always been the staple of the Canadian economy. With growing global competition in agriculture, forest products and minerals, it was imperative to build an industrial structure that would allow Canadians to compete on the basis of technological skill and superior research. Since the Canadian market is so small, we believed that government could play a useful, though not a predominant, role in the necessary restructuring.

Many are skeptical about the ability of government to influence the economy. Yet through the use of a wide array of public policy instruments, foreign control of the Canadian economy fell from 37 percent in 1971 to 23.6 percent in 1986.[1] On foreign ownership, we helped turn the tide. Of course, in 1984 Mr Mulroney declared Canada "open for business," and there have been many foreign takeovers since that date.

Ian Stewart's chapter on the decline of the Keynesian consensus succinctly describes the sharp break in the world's economic fortunes that occurred after the first OPEC crisis. From 1947 to 1973, the world experienced a golden age of almost uninterrupted economic expansion. In the ensuing decade, however, the world grappled simultaneously with the twin evils of inflation and unemployment. Keynesian theory had no easy answers to the problems of stagflation. We learned, in particular, that inflation is a relentless foe: it destroys confidence in the future, sets one group of Canadians against the other in a desperate pattern of catch-up and wreaks special havoc upon the poor, the unorganized and the aged. We have no apologies to make for resorting to wage and price controls in 1975, for establishing the Six-and-Five voluntary wage program in 1982 or for condoning a strong Bank of Canada policy in fighting this disease. Inflation destroys any possibility of a Just Society. But even these measures paled in comparison with the anti-inflation zeal of Paul Volcker, head of the U.S. Federal Reserve, whose actions resulted in another external shock to the Canadian economy, one that was every bit as severe as the oil shocks of OPEC. In 1980–81, Volcker raised American interest rates to unprecedented levels, and as the Bank of Canada had little choice but to follow suit, Canadians were hit by the thunderclap of interest rates of over 20 percent. The Volcker shock inaugurated the recession of 1982, the only year during our four terms of government in which negative growth was recorded.

Yet, despite the impact of inflation and high interest rates, Canada advanced economically during our years in office. From 1968 to 1984, the Canadian economy expanded on average 3 percent a year, a growth rate above that of the United States.[2] But were Canadians materially better off in 1984 than in 1968? The answer to that question can be found in these figures: average real family incomes increased by 33 percent during that period—from $29,772 in 1969 (in constant 1986 dollars) to $38,721 in 1984.[3] In other words, average family income expanded by a third in real terms.

Most important, during our time in power, the Canadian economy expanded enough to provide jobs for most of the baby boom generation and women seeking employment. In the next section of the book the youth explosion and the women's movement are discussed at some length, but there can be little doubt about their economic impact. The new legions of young people and women gave Canada the fastest-growing labour force in the Western world: from 1969 to 1983, the labour force grew by 3.5 million, a 50 percent increase.[4] Women's participation in the labour force increased from 38 percent in 1970 to 50 percent by 1981,[5] and 60 percent of women over twenty-five were members of the labour force by 1983.[6] To meet the impressive challenge of providing employment for the women and young people who wanted it, Canada produced over three million jobs between 1969 and 1983, an employment record far above the OECD average.[7] Unemployment rates were still too high, yet the vast majority of Canadians were working.

Still, whatever our economic accomplishments, expectations

always exceeded results. In a democracy this is inevitable. But as Charles de Gaulle remarks in a melancholy passage in his memoirs: "I was reminded that economic progress, like life itself, is a struggle whose course is never marked by a decisive victory. Even on the day of an Austerlitz, the sun does not emerge to light up the battlefield."[8]

Thomas S. Axworthy
Pierre Elliott Trudeau

"To Stand Not So High Perhaps but Always Alone": The Foreign Policy of Pierre Elliott Trudeau

————by Thomas S. Axworthy————

Thomas S. Axworthy is Executive Director of The CRB Foundation and an Associate of the Center for International Affairs, Harvard University. He was Principal Secretary to Prime Minister Trudeau from 1981 to 1984.

THE TRUDEAU ERA in Canadian foreign policy began in a world of ferment; it ended in a world locked into the status quo. As Pierre Trudeau was taking the oath to become Canada's fifteenth prime minister on April 20, 1968, Parisian students were already filling the streets in an agitation that nearly toppled de Gaulle, Prague was in bloom as Czechoslovakia experimented with the human face of Communism and the American antiwar movement was drawing up plans to converge on the Democratic Party Convention in Chicago. As Prime Minister Trudeau left office on the morning of June 30, 1984, Ronald Reagan was sleepwalking his way towards a triumphant re-election, Helmut Kohl and Margaret Thatcher were congratulating themselves on the successful introduction into NATO of yet another generation of nuclear armed missiles and a sullen Eastern Europe lay inert under the dead weight of the post-Brezhnev Presidium.

For sixteen years, through word and deed, Pierre Trudeau sought to change the prevailing foreign policy attitudes and

---

The quotation in the title is taken from Edmond Rostand's *Cyrano de Bergerac.*

assumptions of his times. His first significant act as prime minister was to proclaim Canada's willingness to recognize the People's Republic of China—the initial step in a sweeping foreign policy review. His last important initiative as prime minister was to undertake a worldwide peace mission worthy of Woodrow Wilson. Trudeau's record in international affairs can be judged not only according to the traditional criterion of how intelligently he calculated the interplay between Canada's interests, commitments and capabilities, but also in light of the larger question of how a small or middle power can help bring about peaceful global change. For the enduring interest in Trudeau's conduct of foreign policy lies in the example it provides of liberal idealism at work in a conservative age.

The Two Faces of Foreign Policy

Throughout history, order versus justice, stability versus change, empiricism versus idealism, have been the central divides of political life. So too in foreign policy. Two distinct schools of thought, each grounded in differing assessments of human nature and heir to a long intellectual tradition, have contended for the allegiance of humankind. Both philosophies tell us part of the truth about ourselves.

The first approach originates with the ancient Greeks. Best expressed by Thucydides, this tradition of power politics, or realpolitik, starts with the proposition that fear, ambition and attachment to possessions are universal human traits which can be contained but never overcome. "The strong do what they can," Thucydides writes, "the weak do what they must."[1] Because anarchy is the condition, security is the objective, power is the means and military force is the instrument. Wars are caused by the perceptions of statesmen that hostile powers are increasing in influence: "What made war inevitable," writes Thucydides, "was the growth in Athenian power and the fear this caused in Sparta."[2] Power politics, then, is rooted in what Thomas Hobbes, the translator of Thucydides, described as the "war of every man against every man."[3] In such a primitive state of nature, only a balance of power can prevent war. Based on this pessimistic assessment of man, practitioners of realpolitik like Otto von Bismarck have drawn the conclusion that "the only healthy basis for policy for a great power is egotism."[4]

Contending with the view that man is inherently aggressive, that security through power is the only objective worth pursuing and that morality cannot be applied to the savage world of international politics is the approach of liberal idealism. Originating with the fathers of the Christian church, gaining momentum with Grotius's first formulation of international law and finding its fullest intellectual expression in Immanuel Kant's *Perpetual Peace* (1795), this view holds that humankind forms a community, that even princes should be subordinate to the rule of law and that reason can and must govern the use of armed might.

Like the adherents of power politics, liberals start with few illusions about the nature of man: "From such warped wood as is man made, nothing straight can be fashioned," writes Kant.[5] Therefore, in the international arena, "the desire of every nation (or its ruler) is to establish an enduring peace, hoping, if possible, to dominate the entire world."[6] But unlike the pessimistic proponents of realpolitik, liberals believe that humans can progress, that through the steady application of reason it is possible to move beyond the law of the jungle. The kernel of reason, writes Kant, "gradually reacts on a people's mentality, whereby they become increasingly able to act freely and it finally even influences the principles of government which finds that it can profit by treating men who are now mere machines, in accord with their dignity."[7]

Kant's eighteenth-century Enlightenment ideals were translated into a fully fledged foreign policy doctrine by the middle of the nineteenth century. English liberals like Charles James Fox, John Bright and Richard Cobden, and American idealists like Woodrow Wilson developed an Anglo-American school of diplomacy that promoted representative institutions, free trade and noninterference in the affairs of other nations against the then-dominant tides of elitism, militarism and empire.

The Anglo-American school had a riposte for all the central propositions of realpolitik: first, on the issue of whether states were inherently aggressive, liberals made the point that states with representative institutions acted differently. Free peoples do not fight each other. As Charles James Fox said about the enmity between Britain and France, "If our two countries have liberal governments at the same time, the cause of the human race is won."[8] Indeed, since the time of Kant, there has never been a war between two democratic states.[9] Second, while power politics emphasized military force, the liberal view was that economic strength, especially free trade, was more important. As Richard Cobden said in the famous Don Pacifico debate of 1851: "The progress of freedom depends more upon the maintenance of peace, the spread of commerce, and the diffusion of education, than upon the labour of cabinets."[10] Lastly, liberalism equally rejected the claims of the realists that state behaviour was not a fit subject for moral judgment. Without a higher purpose, liberals argued, the balance of power was only mechanics. People might seek security, but they also hunger for justice. As John Bright exclaimed, "We have the unchangeable and eternal principles of the moral law to guide us, and only so far as we walk by that guidance can we be permanently a great nation, or our people a happy people."[11] Reflecting the zeal, and perhaps the hubris, of the school of thought he came to personify, Woodrow Wilson gave voice to the idealistic article of faith that "If it [the League of Nations] cannot work, it must be *made* to work."[12]

Yet, however impressive the rhetoric, liberal foreign policy has never predominated in the international system. When Kant wrote, there were only three liberal republics. Charles James Fox may have preached reconciliation with revolutionary France but William Pitt sent troops instead; John Bright and Richard Cobden thundered against Britain's involvement in the Crimea but Palmerston went to war nevertheless; and even though Woodrow Wilson won the plaudits of the world for his democratic crusade, his own Senate rejected the League of Nations. In international affairs, liberal idealism has always been a minority faith.

The Trudeau Dissent

Never dominant, liberalism at least contended against realpolitik in the nineteenth and early twentieth centuries. Not so after World War II. Hitler offered horrifying new evidence of the depth of human depravity, and Wilsonian idealism was blamed for the unpreparedness of the Western democracies in opposing fascism. For a few brief months after World War II, the followers of Franklin D. Roosevelt hoped for a new internationalism, but the Cold War soon reduced the world to two armed camps. In a bipolar world bursting with nuclear weapons, pæans to the community of man and the inevitability of progress seemed hopelessly naïve. Practitioners and theorists alike paid homage to the precepts of power and interest, the *"froids monstres,"* in de Gaulle's phrase, of international politics.[13]

Few strayed from this postwar orthodoxy. One contrarian appeared in Canada. Pierre Elliott Trudeau has written that "the only constant factor to be found in my thinking over the years has been opposition to accepted opinions."[14] An intellectual steeped in the works of Acton, Newman, Mounier and Maritain, Trudeau is best known for his elegant defence of classical federalism—opposing federal centralization in the 1950s when the provinces were weak and just as stoutly opposing federal decentralization in the 1960s when the provinces were strong—but he swam against the tide just as consistently in his opinions on foreign policy.

Trudeau's third article in *Cité libre*, the review he helped to found, was devoted to the Korean war and in that early piece (May 1951) he sounded themes later to be central to his international approach. War, he declared, was not the greatest of evils, nor peace the ultimate good: "For the most important thing is justice; and we must sometimes take arms to defend it."[15] In calling for a foreign policy independent of the United States, he castigated the Liberal government of Mr St-Laurent for not recognizing the People's Republic of China and deplored the pittance spent on foreign aid compared to "the five-billion-dollar military budget and the amount of effort put into setting up an armed camp with the countries of the North Atlantic."[16]

In the years prior to his entry into politics in 1965, Trudeau continued to write frequently on international affairs, publishing articles on John Diefenbaker's foreign policy, foreign investment in Canada and the nuclear arms race.[17] More directly, he travelled around the globe. Few leaders, if any, had as much firsthand knowledge about the world as Pierre

Trudeau; invariably, during his later state visits abroad, the prime minister would meet someone who had been with him on the boat leaving Shanghai in 1949 or who had attended the same World University Service Conference in Nigeria in 1957. Free of racial stereotypes or ideological fanaticism, Trudeau quenched his thirst to know about the planet. He was a citizen of the world long before he became prime minister.

He was also willing to take chances. In 1952, at the height of the McCarthy scare in the United States, he accepted an invitation to attend an economics congress in Moscow. In 1960, he returned to China to assess the impact of the revolution. Travel to the Communist world was rare enough at the time, but in Quebec, the anti-Communist dogma of the day was a special article of faith for both the clerical establishment and the Union Nationale government of Maurice Duplessis. "The only fear that we might possibly have thought reasonable," Trudeau and Jacques Hébert ruefully recalled about their trip to China, "was that of being denounced and vilified by compatriots on our return."[18]

Through his writing and travel, Trudeau had already formed several clear ideas about Canada's foreign policy long before he ran for office in 1965. Three conclusions stand out:

- he was skeptical about the Cold War alliance structure and distressed by the Manichæan tendencies of the United States;
- he was struck by the vast diversity of the globe and impatient for Canada to open its eyes to the opportunities and problems of the Third World (recognition of the People's Republic of China was a case in point);
- he was horrified by the illogic and danger of nuclear weapons.

During his brief tenure as a member of Parliament and Cabinet minister before he moved on to the prime ministership in April 1968, Trudeau further consolidated his foreign policy perspective. He attended sessions of the United Nations General Assembly in 1966. In his role as parliamentary secretary to Prime Minister Pearson, he visited Africa in 1967 as part of the diplomatic effort to make Canada a charter member of la Francophonie and to ward off Quebec's attempts to achieve an independent international identity. The opportunity to work closely with Mr Pearson deepened Trudeau's appreciation of the complexity of foreign affairs, but his experience as a Cabinet minister also made him a profound critic of at least one aspect of the Pearson legacy.

Under Mr Pearson, Cabinet ministers ran their departments with little reference to the Cabinet as a whole. Canada's foreign policy was therefore largely determined by Paul Martin, the secretary of state for external affairs, after consultation with the prime minister. Few policy issues were ever brought to Cabinet, an omission that did not sit well with many of the ministers. In May 1967, for example, Walter Gordon, one of Trudeau's colleagues in Cabinet, became so exasperated with this procedure and with the Cabinet's consequent inability to influence Canada's policy on Vietnam that he publicly broke with his own government and called for the end of American bombing. Trudeau and many others sympathized with Gordon's plight. When Trudeau became prime minister, he broke down the Cabinet fiefdoms and made collective decision making the centrepiece of his structural reforms of government.

In April 1968, a new prime minister with a new style came to power. Elected leader of the Liberal party on April 6, Pierre Elliott Trudeau assumed the prime ministership on April 20, quickly called a federal election and won a smashing victory on June 25. Trudeau's election triumph, which saw the first majority government returned since 1958, capped one of the most meteoric rises in Canadian political history.

During his campaign for the leadership, Trudeau had told a Calgary audience that he "would tend to withdraw somewhat from NATO,"[19] and in his first press conference as leader, Trudeau gave notice that changes were coming: "Most of our foreign policy today is based on . . . pre-war premises or immediate post-war premises . . . complete re-assessment is needed and our participation in NATO is one aspect of it."[20]

True to his word, the new prime minister's first official policy initiative was the launching of a major foreign policy review. A May 29, 1968, statement announced that the government would undertake "a thorough and comprehensive review of our foreign policy which embraces defence, economic and aid policies."[21]

In this same detailed statement, which surprised many, except perhaps devoted readers of *Cité libre*, the government announced that it would take a hard look at NATO, relations with Latin America and the Pacific Rim, that Canada's relations with francophone Africa would assume a new importance, foreign aid expenditures would increase and, most importantly, Canada would finally recognize the People's Republic of China. The Trudeau era had begun.

___Power and Principle _____

Although Pierre Trudeau's foreign policy was based on a liberal international agenda, it would be naïve—and inaccurate—to say it was entirely idealistic. Any sensible foreign policy contains elements of both power and principle. Idealism without an accurate assessment of the underlying realities of power becomes mere preaching. Realpolitik, without a spark of moral commitment, becomes equilibrium for equilibrium's sake, and in time the structure crumbles. As Francis Bacon wrote, "He that will not apply new remedies must expect new evils, for time is the greatest innovator."[22] Statesmen must wear both faces of foreign policy.

Pierre Trudeau was a liberal who knew how to win power and how to use it. He understood that it was critical to differentiate between what was desirable in theory from what was attainable in practice. In April 1968 he modestly assessed Canadian capabilities in the following terms: "We begin by reminding ourselves that we're perhaps more the largest of the small powers than the smallest of the large powers."[23] Therefore, he concluded, "we shouldn't be trying to run the world, we should be trying to make our country a good place."[24] In the 1850s, Richard Cobden believed equally that the best way to promote liberalism was "by setting a good example ourselves."[25]

A sensible appreciation of the limits of Canadian influence, however, did not prevent Trudeau from undertaking initiatives that were outside Canada's sphere of control. In area after area—arms control, Third World development, environmental protection, new frontiers in international law—Canada took the lead in suggesting ideas based on different assumptions than those of our larger, more powerful allies. Trudeau knew that one of the essential strengths of a middle power is that it can afford to fail. We can try out new concepts because there is little to be lost. Great powers are so caught up in concerns of prestige and credibility that they are unduly sensitive to loss of face. "The role of the super powers cannot be denied," the prime minister told the House of Commons in 1981, "but it must not be exclusive."[26]

Having the intellect and courage to develop fresh approaches, then, is one means of influencing the international system. There are other avenues for a middle power to explore as well—most of them lying outside realpolitik's traditional military definition of power. The Trudeau government tried them all. Liberal idealists had long believed that economic progress was ultimately more useful than military might. Between 1968 and 1984 the Trudeau government oversaw a vast expansion of the Canadian economy, which, in turn, allowed new resources to be applied to the foreign domain: Canada's GNP increased from $75.4 billion in 1968 to $444.7 billion in 1984, the federal budget expanded from $12.3 billion to $109.25 billion during the same period and the average income per family jumped from $8,927 in 1969 to $35,767 in 1984 (in constant dollars, family income went up a still-impressive 33 percent). In 1976 Prime Minister Trudeau used Canada's economic clout to gain one of his greatest foreign policy victories when Canada was admitted as a fully fledged member to the Western Economic Summit. As one of the seven members of the summit, Canada has gained entry into one of the most exclusive forums in the world.[27]

Canada's economic growth enabled foreign aid to increase nearly tenfold, from $277 million in 1969 to over $2 billion in 1984, and the Canadian International Development Agency (CIDA) became a third arm of foreign policy, along with the traditional departments of External Affairs and National Defence. Diplomatic expertise was not neglected as Canadian public servants like Maurice Strong and Alan Beesley helped shape critical world forums like the 1972 Stockholm Conference on the environment and the 1974 to 1982 United Nations

Law of the Sea Conference. Canada's military continued to be a useful peacekeeping instrument.

Finally, an appeal to public opinion, the touchstone of liberal faith, was part of the Trudeau arsenal as Canada openly campaigned in the United States for a change in the Reagan administration's policy on acid rain and the prime minister undertook a peace mission in 1983 to restore political dynamism to faltering arms control negotiations. Comparing Canada's capabilities in the 1980s with our strength in the 1950s, when he was a senior diplomat in External Affairs, John Holmes has concluded: "Our power is, of course, infinitely broader and stronger than it was in the golden decade, but there is more competition."[28]

Like any state, Canada used its power to defend, to the best of its ability, the national interest. Three examples are explored later in this essay: the Canadian campaign to counter the efforts of France to encourage Quebec independence, Canada's defence of Arctic sovereignty and the Third Option policy of building counterweights vis-à-vis the United States. A liberal foreign policy, however, is not content with promoting national interest alone: liberals seek to change the international environment as a whole. Arnold Wolfers, the noted American theorist of international relations, calls such efforts "milieu" goals: "Nations pursuing them are out not to defend or increase possessions they hold to the exclusion of others, but aim instead at shaping conditions beyond their national boundaries."[29]

Pierre Trudeau's desire to shape the world—always tempered by the recognition of Canada's limited ability to do so—was evident in his initial "Canada and the World" statement of May 1968. And for the next sixteen years he never stopped trying.[30] His first mandate saw a blizzard of foreign policy activity: the 1968 decision to recognize the People's Republic of China; the 1969 withdrawal of one-half of the Canadian NATO forces from Europe; the 1970 Arctic sovereignty and environmental legislation; the 1971 Canadian-Soviet Protocol on co-operation; the re-orientation of aid and diplomatic priorities to reflect Canada's francophone heritage; and the freezing of defence spending accompanied by a sharp acceleration in development assistance.

Through the 1970s foreign policy continued in the same direction and a new priority arose. In 1971 President Nixon ended Canada's special economic relationship with the United States by imposing a variety of duties on imported Canadian goods. Canada had two choices: to accept American economic domination or to develop greater economic autonomy. By creating the Foreign Investment Review Agency (FIRA), the Canada Development Corporation (CDC) and Petro-Canada, the Trudeau government's Third Option attempted a more independent economic policy and this diversification strategy led to the successful negotiation of formal contractual links with Europe and Japan. The decade of the seventies also saw Trudeau's initial interest in improving development assistance broaden into a Canadian commitment to work toward a new North-South dialogue. Throughout the decade, Canada continued its efforts to bottle up the nuclear genie by imposing the world's strictest limits on the export of nuclear technology, and in 1977 Canada ended formal government support for commercial activities in South Africa.

By his fourth term as prime minister (1980–84), Pierre Trudeau had grown even bolder. The foreign policy agenda occupied an increasing amount of the prime minister's time, and ambitious designs tumbled out, one after the other. In 1980 Energy Minister Marc Lalonde unveiled the National Energy Program, which sought to achieve 50 percent Canadian ownership in the oil and gas industry, thereby provoking protests from the United States. In 1981 Prime Minister Trudeau used his position as chairman of the Ottawa Economic Summit to promote North-South negotiations, and Trudeau himself was elected co-chairman of the Cancun summit meeting between leaders of the affluent and the underprivileged. In the 1960s and 1970s the government had been forced to react to the designs of the United States in the Arctic and France in Quebec, but by the 1980s Canada was a leader itself in shaping the 1982 United Nations Convention of the Law of the Sea, and by working aggressively in la Francophonie to create a French summit similar to the Commonwealth. As for East-West relations, Trudeau announced in 1983 a peace initiative to decrease tensions and speed arms control. By 1984, the Trudeau government had also de-nuclearized the Canadian military by replacing with conventional systems all the nuclear weapons it had inherited in 1968. In the Trudeau era there were "milieu" goals aplenty.

A liberal state should provide a good example at home and do what it can abroad. As Walter Lippman writes, a successful foreign policy "consists in bringing into balance, with a comfortable surplus of power in reserve, the nation's commitments and the nation's power."[31] It remains to apply these tests to five aspects of the Trudeau legacy.

Thwarting France

The May 1968 announcement of the foreign policy review began with the premise: "Our paramount interest is to ensure the political survival of Canada as a federal and bilingual sovereign state."[32] This emphasis not only reflected Trudeau's overarching domestic priority but it responded equally to an extraordinary external threat posed by an erstwhile friend, the France of Charles de Gaulle. Saviour of France—not once but twice—de Gaulle's attention, once he had solved the Algerian crisis, turned increasingly to enhancing France's role in the world. His imperious gaze did not neglect the province of Quebec.

Two recent full length studies—*Vive le Québec libre* by Dale Thomson and *L'art de l'impossible* by Claude Morin—document at length the role of France in encouraging Quebec autonomy.[33] Long before de Gaulle, of course, Quebec had established missions abroad. Tourism, trade, industrial development, cultural exchanges and the like occupied most of the time of such delegations. In 1965, for example, Canada and France signed a framework agreement which encouraged such activities by the provinces, providing always that the federal government's sovereignty over foreign policy was respected. Quebec's activity provided a useful goad to a federal government that had too often ignored the French dimension of Canada in its foreign and aid policies.

Some individuals in Quebec wanted more. They saw an international role for the province as an indispensable asset in their quest to disintegrate the Canadian union and form a separate French-speaking state. If the world treated

Quebec like a state instead of a province, then the separatist option would attain new legitimacy at home.

Such an approach found an attentive audience in the Elysée palace. As early as 1963 President de Gaulle had made up his mind: ruminating on the eve of Prime Minister Pearson's visit to Paris, de Gaulle wrote: "We must establish special forms of cooperation with French Canada, and not allow what we do for and with it to be submerged in an arrangement involving the totality of the two Canadas [sic!]. At any rate, French Canada will necessarily become a state and it is necessarily in that perspective that we must orient our actions."[34]

Officials close to the president began to work actively with their counterparts in the Quebec government and with Quebec supporters of independence. De Gaulle himself went public when on an official visit to Canada in 1967 he uttered his famous cry, "Vive le Québec libre," the slogan of the separatists. René Lévesque, one of the dignitaries present at the Montreal Hôtel de Ville, records in his memoirs the impact of this declaration: "We turned around to face the rest of the guests. It is rare to have such an opportunity to see the two Montreals so clearly. In a state of shock, frozen in fury ... stood the Anglophone city. As for French Montreal, except for those constrained by office or acquaintance to reserve, they did not hide broad, complicit smiles."[35]

Personal expressions of support for independence were one thing, but more dangerous still were the actions of the French state. Early in 1968 de Gaulle followed up his "Vive" by engineering an invitation from its African ally Gabon to the Government of Quebec (addressed to the minister of foreign affairs of Quebec) to attend an international conference on education. No invitation was sent to the Government of Canada. This was a direct challenge to Ottawa's authority. A note of protest was sent to Paris and Ottawa showed its displeasure with Gabon in a direct way when Canada's new ambassador delayed presenting his credentials to the authorities in Libreville. In April France hosted a second conference on education. Again Ottawa was excluded, de Gaulle writing: "We have no concessions and no friendly gestures to make to Monsieur Trudeau, who is the opponent of the French fact in

Canada."[36] The Canadian ambassador to France was called home for consultations.

By deflecting France's immediate challenge to federal authority and through the long-term development of a new emphasis on francophone Africa, the Trudeau government demonstrated that it knew how to use power. France is a more powerful state than Canada, but support for Quebec independence was only one French foreign policy goal among many and it was probably not too high a priority at that. For Canada, defence of its national integrity was the "paramount objective," as Trudeau's first foreign policy declaration stated. Thus, Canadian efforts were sustained and concentrated; French interest was spasmodic and diffuse. By 1984, France's challenge to Canada was only a bad memory and it was now the Trudeau government that was mounting an initiative to establish a francophone summit.

Canada's response to de Gaulle's offensive was on several levels. First, French actions were protested and in strong terms. There was no question of being overly polite when a foreign state was interfering in our domestic affairs. The prime minister publicly castigated French officials who came to Canada looking to create trouble. France was made to understand that it would pay a price for its actions. Given that de Gaulle was severely criticized at home for what was regarded as bizarre behaviour, Canada's willingness to kick up a fuss meant that French officials had to be careful. And just as important, Canada did not overreact by breaking off relations with France or embarking on economic boycotts (although these options were discussed by Cabinet). De Gaulle was an old man in a hurry. As much as possible, the government made a distinction between the policy of de Gaulle and the policy of France. This made it easier for de Gaulle's successors when it came time to shelve his policy.

Second, the African allies of France were patiently educated as to why the federal government could not take lightly Quebec representation at international conferences, and it was impressed upon the African countries that it was dangerous to encourage secessionist movements. "Politics," Max Weber has written, "is the strong and slow boring of hard boards,"[37] and never more so than in international diplomacy. As a parliamentary secretary, Pierre Trudeau had toured Africa in 1967 to inform the continent's leaders about the francophone dimensions of Canada, and he was but the first in a long line of Canadian ministers and officials to work on the francophone Africa dossier. Diplomatic attention to French Africa was also bolstered in more tangible ways. In 1963 francophone Africa had been allocated only $4 million of Canada's aid budget; by the early 1970s this figure had been increased to $100 million, equal to the amount spent on the Commonwealth African states. Under the Trudeau government la Francophonie became a magnet for Canadian aid and diplomacy instead of the placid backwater it had been previously. France is still at the epicentre of la Francophonie but Canada has become a player of note in that association. This positive development is part of the legacy of the intricate France-Quebec-Canada triangle of the late 1960s.

The third component of Canadian success was the remarkable transformation of domestic attitudes toward bilingualism and the French fact. Ultimately, the skill and persistence of Canadian diplomacy and the usefulness of Canadian aid to the economies of French-speaking African nations could not have helped the federal government to win its case if it did not have a valid case to present. And the Trudeau government did more than any previous Canadian government to ensure that policies and funding supported the principle that Canada as a whole, not just Quebec, is the home of French-speaking Canadians. French and English language rights were guaranteed in the federal public service, in federal government services and throughout Canada's educational systems. The inspiration for such reforms was simple justice and the necessity of keeping Canada united—not foreign policy. But the validity of the case Canada was making in Africa was reinforced when its proponents were a French-speaking Canadian prime minister, French-speaking Canadian ministers and French-speaking Canadian public officials. With some asperity, Claude Morin notes: "The federal politicians and bureaucrats associated with External Affairs—at least those who were French-speaking and from Quebec—thus became the most stubborn adversaries of

Quebec's advances onto the international scene."[38] Reform at home made for coherence and credibility abroad.

In 1968 France had induced Gabon to do its bidding by excluding Canada from its international assembly. In January 1969 the Congo, which was less subject to French influence, invited the federal government to assemble a Canadian delegation that would include representatives from Quebec. France continued to promote the independent right of Quebec to have international representatives. In 1970 the matter was settled. At a conference in Niamey, Niger, Gérard Pelletier, Canada's secretary of state, negotiated a solution in which the French demand for independent Quebec status within l'Agence de coopération culturelle et technique was denied but the province was admitted as a "participating government." So, too, was New Brunswick. To sweeten the compromise, Canada agreed to pay 33 percent of the cost of the initial budget of the new organization. (France agreed to contribute 45 percent.)[39]

De Gaulle resigned the French presidency in 1969 and although his successor, Georges Pompidou, continued the Gaullist policy towards Quebec (as did Jacques Chirac, the Gaullist mayor of Paris), the fires began to die down. In 1974 Valéry Giscard d'Estaing became president of France and Pierre Trudeau made his first official visit to Paris. The French formula for dealing with the triangle now became: noninterference in Canadian affairs while maintaining special ties to Quebec. The election of the Parti québécois in November 1976 gave hope to Claude Morin, now a minister in the Lévesque government, that Quebec could again have independent influence in Africa, but there was no repeat of the Gabon incident.

Instead, throughout the period, Quebec was largely on the defensive. Prime Minister Trudeau joined forces with President Leopold Senghor of Senegal to promote a new organization of la Francophonie with an annual francophone summit of heads of government. France did not want to participate in a summit that excluded Quebec, but at the Williamsburg Economic Summit of 1983, Prime Minister Trudeau and President Mitterrand discussed the possibility of a two-tiered summit with heads of government meeting at one level and other participants meeting on more technical issues. Agreement in principle seemed to be within reach, but the initiative eventually stalled. Trudeau's promotion of the francophone summit, the support given to this idea by the Africans and his near success in persuading France to join the project demonstrate vividly, however, how much the rules of the game had been transformed since the intoxicating days of *"Vive le Québec libre."*

___Protecting the Arctic_____

In reacting to France's promotion of Quebec secession, the Trudeau government turned the tide by actively promoting la Francophonie as a central goal of its foreign policy. A problem was turned into an opportunity. So, too, with protection of the Arctic. An initial threat was creatively managed by expanding the frontiers of international law, and this initiative, in turn, led to Canadian advocacy of a new international regime to govern the Law of the Sea. John Holmes writes that Canada's Arctic policy "asserted the right of a lesser power not only to challenge but also to push along international law when the great powers were intransigent . . . it launched the Trudeau administration on its most effective and laudable international enterprise, a leading and highly constructive role in the most important contribution to world order since [the founding of the United Nations at] San Francisco."[40]

De Gaulle's threat to Canada was in the traditional mode of state-to-state behaviour. Thucydides would have recognized instantly the manœuvres of Quebec to gain French backing and the French president's subsequent manipulation of smaller allies. The threat to the Arctic was more typical of late-twentieth-century statecraft: it arose from actions by the private sector and included a host of issues—environmental protection, native rights and transit rights over polar regions—that would perplex any classical scholar.

In 1968 vast amounts of oil were discovered at Prudhoe Bay in Alaska's North Slope, and soon thereafter, Humble Oil, a private American company acting on behalf of Exxon, announced that it would send the tanker *Manhattan* through Canada's Northwest Passage in the summer of 1969 to test the passage's feasibility as a delivery route.

Humble's project presented Canada with multiple problems. The Arctic is one of the world's most fragile ecosystems. An oil spill would damage the environment for generations, destroying local food sources and wiping out the livelihood of the Inuit. The issue of Arctic transportation is connected with many of the difficult trade-offs of our time: economic development versus ecological demands, native rights versus property rights, the energy needs of the South versus the heritage of the North. But in the case of Humble Oil, there was a complicating international factor of immense importance. Canada's sovereignty over the Northwest Passage and therefore its legal right to impose standards and regulations on Humble Oil was contested by the United States, whose government contended that the passage was an international strait, not subject to anyone's national jurisdiction. Even though Canada was a close ally, the U.S. Navy fretted about the precedent of Canada closing off an "international" strait. Jousting with France about Quebec was one thing, combatting with a superpower about sovereignty over the Northwest Passage was another.

Opposition parliamentarians and editorial writers across the land urged the government to confront the United States by making a bold declaration of sovereignty. Such proposals bring to mind H. L. Mencken's adage, "For every human problem there exists a solution that is simple, neat and wrong." In April 1970, before the *Manhattan*'s second voyage, the government announced its strategy. Rather than focusing on sovereignty, it emphasized the need to control pollution. (In March 1970 the tanker *Arrow* had sunk, spilling one million gallons of oil off the Nova Scotia coast.) Instead of beating the nationalist drum for territorial possessions, it spoke about Canada's responsibility as a "custodian" of the North. Canada's three-mile territorial limit was extended to twelve miles, thereby increasing the size of Canadian territory by one-eighth and asserting additional control over the Prince of Wales and Barrow Straits. Although the extension was controversial at the time, seventy-eight states have since followed suit with a twelve-mile limit. The Arctic Waters Pollution Prevention Act was also passed, establishing the new concept of a pollution zone of one hundred miles in the waters around the Canadian Arctic archipelago within which Canada would enforce strict standards. The Nixon administration protested, but Humble Oil immediately agreed to abide by the new rules.

Canada moved swiftly to gain international support for its policy. Sweden and Iceland quickly came on board. In June 1970, the other Arctic superpower, the Soviet Union, announced that it was opposed to the American stand. Malta, which had originally proposed the "common heritage of mankind" concept of the Law of the Sea to the United Nations, and the Latin American coastal states were sympathetic as well. John Kirton and Don Munton conclude that "by the summer of 1970 it became clear that the United States no longer had an international constituency for its efforts to shape the development of international law in this area. And despite the formidable array of unilateral economic, military and political instruments at Washington's disposal, it chose not to deploy them alone on behalf of the old regime. By 1970, the United States was unable to define the new and unwilling by itself to defend the old international order."[41]

Further, Canada took the concepts of pollution zones, custodianship and the extension of international law that it had applied in the Arctic and made them the centrepiece of Canada's approach to the United Nations–sponsored Conference on the Law of the Sea—the forum that had been established in 1974 to explore Malta's concept of the Law of the Sea as a "common heritage of mankind." The Law of the Sea Conference became a centre of Canadian diplomatic activity for nearly a decade from 1974 to 1982.

At the first session, the Conference elected Canadian diplomat Alan Beesley to be chairman of the drafting committee. The principle of a twelve-mile territorial sea and a two-hundred-mile economic zone was accepted at the first substantive session in Caracas in 1974. The Arctic Waters Pollution Prevention Act was vindicated when the conference passed Article 234, which permits coastal nations "to adopt and enforce non-discriminatory laws and regulations for the prevention, reduction, and control of marine pollution from vessels in ice-covered areas."[42] Canada also advanced the idea of a voluntary international development tax on continental shelf mineral resources and supported the demands of developing countries for revenue sharing. Such an extension of international law was anathema to the Reagan administration, which came to power in 1981. Under pressure from the American mining industry, which saw potential gains in the deep sea being distributed to the Third World, President Reagan announced in July 1982 that the United States would not sign the treaty. Great Britain's Margaret Thatcher followed Reagan's lead.

The Law of the Sea Conference took a decade to negotiate and it produced a convention of 320 articles governing nearly all uses of ocean space, which has been signed by 159 states, Canada being among the first to do so. To the conservative governments of the United States, Great Britain and West Germany, the interests of the mining industry may weigh more heavily than the "common heritage of mankind" but ideas sometimes take on a life of their own. The United Nations Convention of the Law of the Sea was a turning point in the history of international law. Canada was a midwife to its birth. In time, even the status quo powers may come to see that the common good should take precedence over economic greed.

Building Counterweights

Before entering active politics, Pierre Trudeau commented that 70 percent of Canada's foreign policy was predetermined by the Canada-U.S. relationship, so the Department of External Affairs had to work hard to maximize Canada's freedom of manœuvre in the remaining 30 percent.[43] This early recognition of the centrality of the United States led to some of the boldest and most controversial policies of the Trudeau government. While recognizing the basic ties of interdependence and mutual interests that made the two countries friends and allies, from 1968 to 1984 the Liberal government systematically put into place policies designed to promote Canadian ownership in the domestic economy, diversify Canada's trade with the world and protect Canadian culture from the overwhelming pull of the American entertainment industry. Interdependence was a given, but vulnerability could be reduced. The Trudeau government sought to strengthen Canada's ability to travel down a different path.

By no stretch of the imagination could Pierre Trudeau be considered anti-American. He had studied at Harvard, he had a genuine love for America's contribution of the concept of checks and balances to political theory and he could quote from memory the writings of American statesmen like Thomas Jefferson. But he also recognized that because the United States dominated so many facets of Canadian life, it was necessary for the national government to try to counter the market forces that led inevitably to greater north-south integration. "My political action, or my theory—insomuch as I can be said to have one—can be expressed very simply:" he wrote in *Federalism and the French Canadians*, "create counterweights."[44] During the Trudeau years, "creating counterweights" was what Canada's policy towards the United States was all about.

Canada's vulnerability to shifts in American policy was dramatically revealed on August 15, 1971, when President Nixon destroyed the Bretton Woods system by announcing a 10 percent surcharge on all goods entering the United States, an end to the convertibility of the U.S. dollar into gold or other reserve assets and the creation of the Domestic International Sales Corporation (DISC) to provide export subsidies to American firms by deferring taxes on export sales indefinitely. With over 20 percent of Canada's GNP in 1970 dependent on exports and with 65 percent of that total being exported to the United States, Nixon's actions directly threatened Canada's prosperity. At one stroke, the "Nixon shock" transferred the largely academic debate about foreign investment and Canada's independence into a pressing economic crisis.

Within a few months, under pressure from the international community, including Canada, most of the August 1971 measures were rescinded. But Canada had received a real scare. In October 1972, the Trudeau government announced a far-reaching new policy to enhance Canada's autonomy.

External Affairs Minister Mitchell Sharp told Canadians that they had three options: first, maintenance of the status quo; second, closer integration with the American economy; and a third option—"to develop and strengthen the Canadian economy and other aspects of its national life and in the process to reduce the present Canadian vulnerability."[45] The strategy, Mr Sharp explained, "will have a permanent test for each policy instrument we devise. What will it do to strengthen our economy and reduce its vulnerability . . . the emphasis of the Third Option is on Canada— on decisions that have to be taken in this country by Canadians rather than matters to be negotiated with the United States."[46]

The Third Option approach to Canadian-American relations had three main components: strengthening Canadian ownership of the economy, diversifying Canada's trade abroad and protecting Canadian culture. The Third Option paper discussed the growing American presence in Canada caused in part by "the large flows of U.S. capital, mostly in the form of direct investment."[47] In 1971, foreigners owned 37 percent of Canada's assets and American direct investment formed the largest portion of this total (28 percent of Canadian assets were owned by Americans). No other country in the Western world had nearly 40 percent of its economy controlled from abroad, and in certain sectors, the proportions were even more startling—90 percent of the petroleum industry, for example, was foreign-owned. Foreign-owned corporations occasionally took actions directly against Canada's interests—such as Ford Motor Company's decision not to export trucks to the People's Republic of China and Exxon's diversion of oil intended for Canada to the United States during the 1979 OPEC oil crisis. In other cases, foreign-owned subsidiaries were the reluctant agents of American foreign policy. In 1981-82, for instance, the Reagan administration tried to prevent American-owned subsidiaries located outside the United States from bidding on gas pipeline projects in the Soviet Union. The dividends of foreign subsidiaries that were paid to investors also exerted constant pressure on Canada's balance of payments.

Enormous political will was needed to reverse the process of growing American ownership of the Canadian economy. Each stage in the process led to disputes with the United States government—and as these disputes intensified, the Canadian business community became more upset. Positive measures to encourage Canadian savings and capital formation, however, formed the core of the policy. Canadians were given generous tax incentives to save, through the Registered Retirement Savings Plan provision (RRSP), dividend tax credits and corporate and individual tax cuts. Reflecting the impact of these policies, in 1983 the personal savings rate in Canada was 14 percent compared to 4 percent in the United States. Starting in 1975, Canadians became net exporters of equity capital, investing more in the United States than Americans were investing here.

Regulation was also used to control American ownership of the economy. In 1973, the Foreign Investment Review Agency (FIRA) was created to screen foreign investment and to bargain with foreign investors for the maximum possible benefits to accrue to Canada. Direct government ownership was also not shunned. In 1971, the government created the Canada Development Corporation, which bought foreign assets in mining and manufacturing, and in 1975 Petro-Canada was established to give Canadians a "window" on the oil industry. In 1980, the National Energy Program (NEP) called for 50 percent Canadian ownership in the petroleum industry.

By the mid-1980s, the tide had turned. Statistics Canada reports that foreign control of the Canadian economy fell from 37 percent in 1971 to 23.6 percent in 1986—and American ownership fell from 28 percent to 17 percent during the same period.[48] The petroleum industry, once 90 percent foreign-owned, was 49 percent Canadian-controlled in 1986, nearly reaching the NEP goal.[49] The decline in foreign control of the Canadian economy and the growing export of Canadian capital to the United States meant that Canada's investments in the United States represented 60 percent of the amount of American investments in Canada by 1985 (a dramatic rise from 10 percent in 1973).[50] By the end of the Trudeau era, Canadians owned more of their own economy and they owned more of the American economy. After World War I, the United States repatriated ownership of large portions of its economy from Britain; in the late twentieth century, Canada achieved a similar feat by reducing the American investment stake. Both transformations are examples of growing economic maturity.

If investment policy was one major priority for the Trudeau Liberals, commercial policy was another. The Trudeau government believed in both trade liberalization and trade diversification. It was singularly more successful in reducing barriers, however, than in reducing dependence on the American market. Writing in 1958 in *Cité libre*, Trudeau made the point that "political and economic domination are inextricably linked."[51] Prior to World War II, Canada had been able to balance its trade between the United States, Great Britain and the rest of the world. In 1938, for example, 40 percent of Canada's exports went to Great Britain and 23 percent went to the United States. As late as 1960, Britain took 17 percent of Canadian exports. By 1970, however, the United States now took 65 percent of Canada's exports and Great Britain only 9 percent. Most of the trade eggs were in one large basket. As Trudeau had forecast in *Cité libre*, Canada's dependence on a single market made us exceptionally vulnerable to the Nixon shock of 1971.

Trade liberalization and diversification became the goals; the basic approach was to strengthen multilateral trade links through the General Agreement on Tariffs and Trade (GATT). In 1969, for example, the budget of that year immediately implemented the Kennedy Round of tariff reductions, which had originally been scheduled to take place in stages. Canada then became an active participant in the Tokyo Round of trade negotiations (1973–79). After GATT's formation in 1947, Canada's tariffs declined from 22 percent before World War II to 16 percent in the 1960s. By implementing the cuts of the Kennedy and Tokyo Rounds, the Trudeau government further reduced this to 9 percent. From 1968 to 1984, exports as a percentage of GNP increased from 23 percent to nearly 30 percent, manufactured end products increased from 33 percent of exports in 1970 to 42 percent in 1984. Canada ran a persistent trade surplus with the rest of the world ($20 billion in 1984), and in the 1980s this trade surplus was so large that Canada even ran a modest current account surplus. (Since 1984 the trade surplus has been cut in half and the 1989 budget of Michael Wilson therefore forecasts a current account deficit of

$11 billion in 1988 compared to a surplus of $3.4 billion in 1984.) By the conclusion of the Tokyo Round, Canada's negotiators had succeeded in obtaining free access for 80 percent of Canada's exports to the United States, with only a small average tariff of 5 percent on the remaining 20 percent. This was virtually free trade—without Canada giving away bilateral concessions in energy and investment as the Conservatives agreed to do in their Canada-U.S. Free Trade Agreement, which came into effect on January 1, 1989.

In the Trudeau years, trade certainly expanded, but it did not diversify. In 1970, the United States was the destination of 65 percent of Canadian exports; by 1984, despite the Third Option, 75 percent of exports went south. The question is, Why?

Prime Minister Trudeau made a definite personal commitment to expanding Canada's contacts with the world outside the United States. Before the Third Option was announced in 1972, he had already given high priority to relations with Asia, Africa and Latin America. In 1976, he travelled to Europe to sign a contractual link with the European Economic Community and in the fall of 1976, he successfully completed a similar mission to Japan. The Third Option was forward-looking in recognizing the rising power of Japan and the significance of the European market (the EEC has grown from six nations with 165 million people in 1960 to twelve countries with 320 million citizens in 1988), but it did not contain policy prescriptions strong enough to change Canada's ingrained export habits. Trade did not follow the political gesture of the contractual link.

To change the individual decisions of thousands of exporters may, in fact, be beyond the power of any government. By direct acquisition of foreign assets through agents like Petro-Canada, the government of Canada could increase Canadian ownership in the petroleum industry. By cutting tariffs, the government could liberalize trade. But the ability of government to redraw trading patterns was too limited to turn the diversification goal of the Third Option into a reality.

Yet some of the predictions of the Third Option paper have, unfortunately, come true. In 1972, Mitchell Sharp made the point that if Canada did not diversify its trade portfolio, it would have to depend upon the goodwill of the United States. If this goodwill ever faded, we would be in trouble. This is precisely what happened. In 1983, the Trudeau government successfully beat back an attempt by American competitors to restrict Canadian softwood exports to the United States, but many other petitions against Canadian products were filed. In the subsequent free trade negotiations, the Mulroney government gave up Canada's sovereignty in energy and investment policy in exchange for a weak mechanism to settle trade disputes. By failing to diversify, Canada made itself hostage to American special interests and their ability to influence the U.S. Congress.

Cultural policy was a third component of the Liberal approach to Canadian-American relations. John Kenneth Galbraith, a native Canadian and distinguished Harvard economist, once replied to a question about the priority of culture vis-à-vis foreign investment in the following way: "I would be much more concerned about maintaining the cultural integrity of the broadcasting system and with making sure that Canada has an active, independent theatre, book publishing industry, newspapers, magazines and schools of poets and painters. . . . These are the things that count."[52] The Trudeau government made sure that they counted. Under the leadership of Pierre Juneau in 1968, the Canadian Radio and Television Commission (CRTC) prohibited foreign ownership of broadcasting outlets, and in 1970 Canadian content regulations for television and radio were increased. In 1976, *Time* magazine lost its special exemption from Canadian tax laws, thereby putting Canadian publications like *Maclean's* in a better position to compete. Canadian advertisers lost the right to declare advertising spots on U.S. border stations as legitimate business deductions, thereby giving a boost to Canadian broadcasters. A book publishing policy and the Broadcast Development Fund followed in the 1980s. Throughout the Trudeau years, public broadcasting was given strong support.

In Canada, the private market alone cannot develop a cultural industry. It is so profitable to import cheap American product that government must regulate the private sector to give Canadian artists any opportunity for exposure at home.

The government must attempt to provide Canadian options even under the overwhelming pressure of American popular culture. As Graham Spry said long ago about the need for Canadian public broadcasting, it is the State or the United States.

There are easier things to do than create a counterweight to the power of the United States. The Trudeau government used every tool in the public policy arsenal to encourage Canadian ownership of business; the tide of American ownership of Canada's economy was first halted and then reversed. An activist cultural policy regulated the private sector to ensure that higher levels of Canadian content were reached in the cultural industries. But the Canadian government's ability to influence the decisions of thousands of Canadian exporters to add Europe and Asia to their list of target markets was limited. Trade increased but so did the concentration towards the United States. In defending its policy of autonomy, the Trudeau government opted for Canadian independence. It successfully withstood the protests of the U.S. government, but it was less successful in persuading the Canadian business community of the wisdom of this course. Writing in 1973, John Halstead, a former assistant under-secretary of state for external affairs, asked several tough questions about the Third Option: "Can we take the measures necessary to support a long-term strategy along the lines of the Third Option? Does our federal system or our geopolitical situation allow us to? Do we want to?"[53] Many years after the Third Option policy was announced, and particularly in the aftermath of the 1988 free trade debate, we are still no closer to having a definitive answer to Halstead's inquiries.

____Beyond the National Interest _____

In both francophone Africa and the Arctic, Canada was able to husband its resources, concentrate on a key objective and ultimately prevail over much stronger adversaries. Francophone Africa chose Canada's interpretation of Quebec's international role over that of France. Most of the international community chose Canada's interpretation of Arctic jurisdiction over that of the United States. Had either of these major powers felt that their core interests were affected, the results may have been different, but since the issues were only secondary to them (though vital to Canada), the less powerful state carried the day. Similarly, the Third Option proclaimed a set of objectives that the Trudeau government successfully maintained despite the protests of the United States, though at the cost of considerable domestic controversy.

This matrix changes in the two issues we examine below. On North-South relations and East-West arms control, the interests of the great powers were paramount. The Trudeau government tried to change the stance of its allies, but Canada's leverage was limited. On issues directly affecting the national interests of Canada, Trudeau's foreign policy was largely successful; on issues affecting the international community as a whole, where the key variable was not what Canada did, but what it could persuade its friends to do, the record is less clear. Two recent studies of foreign policy in the Trudeau years, for example, conclude that the "era, in retrospect, was one of frustrated designs"[54] and "like the North-South initiative in 1981, the peace mission ended abruptly in failure."[55] Neither of these initiatives, it is true, succeeded in the short term. But there is value in raising issues and forcing nations to confront international problems. Trudeau used his position to promote a liberal agenda during a conservative age. The greatest failure of all would have been to remain silent.

___Sharing the Wealth_____

Writing in 1951, Pierre Trudeau asked rhetorically, "Will Canada never be able to take advantage of its position as a small power to develop and disseminate a foreign policy oriented towards mutual aid, rather than one based on domination, exploitation and the pursuit of commercial opportunities?"[56] Campaigning in his first election as prime minister, he quoted with approval Pope Paul VI's belief that "the new name of peace is development."[57]

The record of the Trudeau government in Third World development never matched the prime minister's sometimes soaring rhetoric, and for that reason critics of the policy have given praise only grudgingly if at all. But in fact, under

Trudeau, Third World issues became one of the dominant concerns of External Affairs and this represented a profound change in Canada's foreign policy tradition. In 1950, Canada had begun its aid program in the Colombo Plan, and through the Commonwealth connection, Canada kept in touch with important Third World nations like India. The real focus of Canadian policy, however, remained almost exclusively on Europe and the United States. Trudeau changed this. Third World leaders like Michael Manley of Jamaica, Julius Nyerere of Tanzania and Lee Kwan Yew of Singapore had ready access to the prime minister. The new priorities of the Pacific Rim and Africa, announced in the May 1968 statement, were soon reflected in the prime minister's official travel. In 1970, two years before the Nixon-Kissinger opening to China, Canada completed the negotiations to recognize the People's Republic and the formula used (Canada "took note" of China's position on Taiwan) was later adopted by such countries as Belgium, Italy and Peru in their negotiations on recognition. If an initiative affecting Asia was one of the first acts of the Trudeau government, it was also one of the last: just before leaving office, the government created the Asia Pacific Foundation of Canada, a body devoted to strengthening the ties between Canada and the Pacific Rim.

Before 1968, Canada's modest foreign aid program was the responsibility of an External Aid office, jointly directed by the Departments of External Affairs and Trade and Commerce. In 1968, a new institution, the Canadian International Development Agency (CIDA), was formed and Maurice Strong, a dynamic businessman, became its first president. CIDA has since become the key engine of Canada's aid effort. In 1970, the International Development Research Centre (IDRC), the jewel in Canada's foreign aid crown, came into being with an international board of directors, complete freedom to distribute untied aid and a mandate to promote research by Third World scientists. The institutional structure was completed in the 1980s when the Petro-Canada International Assistance Corporation (PCIAC) was formed in 1981 to help train geology crews, seismic experts and oil exploration teams in Third World countries, and in 1985 when the International Centre for Ocean Development began its work of transferring technology between Canada and the Third World in the field of ocean resources. From a single office, the bureaucratic structure behind Canada's development effort has grown into a sophisticated and powerful force.

In 1969–70, Canada allocated $277 million, or 0.34 percent of GNP, to Official Development Assistance (ODA). By 1975, this amount had been increased to $760 million, or 0.54 percent of GNP. In 1984–85, ODA was over $2 billion, or 0.49 percent of GNP. While Canada never met its aid goal of 0.7 percent of GNP during the Trudeau period, it did become the fifth-largest aid donor among countries belonging to the Organization for Economic Co-operation and Development (OECD). And perhaps as important as the amount of aid was the quality of aid. In 1977, Canada forgave all its ODA loans to the least developed nations. In 1980 it transformed CIDA's program by allowing 100 percent of its assistance to take the form of grants. As the content of aid was improved – from loans to grants – so, too, was the direction: in 1970 only 5 percent of Canada's aid went to the least developed nations – the poorest of the poor – whereas by 1980, about 30 percent was directed to the most destitute nations.

Canada's aid giving, if not as generous as that of the Scandinavian countries, improved dramatically in quantity and quality during the Trudeau years. But in one area, the record is less admirable. When confronted by trade-offs between domestic economic interests and the needs of the least developed nations, domestic interests too often prevailed. Tied aid is a case in point – the requirement that the recipient country use the donor's grant to purchase the donor's goods. The Trudeau government made important moves in reducing the amount of tied aid: it early decided that all aid to multilateral agencies would be untied, and it reduced the portion of CIDA's bilateral tied aid to 80 percent. But even with this move, about 60 percent of Canada's total aid package continued to be tied – a high percentage among the OECD countries. Textile protection was another problem: in 1973 Canada signed the Multi-Fibre Agreement (renewed in 1981 and 1986), which restricted the import of low-cost garments and textiles from the Third World. The influence of power – whether it be that of a domestic manufacturing lobby

or that of an international competitor—is rarely absent from
foreign policy.

In 1973 the Third World nations issued a call for a New
International Economic Order (NIEO) and a single-minded
concentration on aid transfers was replaced by attention to a
more broadly based set of concerns about trading relationships, commodity funds and energy affiliates. By this time,
Canada had already reformed its aid practices, and from the
mid-1970s to the end of the Trudeau period, Canada used its
position to help bring Third World concerns to the councils of
the West. The general esteem in which Third World leaders
hold Pierre Trudeau is due at least as much to this personal
advocacy on their behalf as to Canada's increases in aid flows.
This esteem was soon reflected in new opportunities for
Canadian leadership. In 1976, for example, after making an
eloquent address to the Nairobi United Nations Conference on
Trade and Development, Allan MacEachen, the minister for
external affairs, was elected as co-chairman of the 1976–77
Paris Conference on International Economic Cooperation. In
1981 Pierre Trudeau used his position as chairman of the
Ottawa Economic Summit to put North-South issues high on
the agenda. At that same meeting, Trudeau urged U.S.
President Ronald Reagan to attend the October 1981
International Meeting on Cooperation and Development in
Cancun, Mexico. Reagan did so and Trudeau was subsequently
asked to be chairman of the conference. The Third World
nations hoped to persuade the United States to support a
process of North-South negotiations on the NIEO agenda.
They failed. Any blame, however, must be shared equally by
the North and the South. The Group of 77—the key organizing
group of the South—was so influenced by some radical nations
that they proposed an agenda that had no chance of being
accepted by Reagan and Thatcher. Interlocutors like Trudeau
simply could not bridge the gap.

Cancun was more than a missed opportunity. It was a symbolic
turning point in the relations between North and South.
Throughout the 1970s Third World nations had been
advancing economically (fuelled by recycled petro-dollars
from Western banks) and this progress led to exaggerated

demands. The 1981–82 recession, which burst onto the world simultaneously with the Cancun conference, provoked a debt crisis which has reduced the bargaining power of the Third World and made its economic future even more problematical. In the 1970s, there was a net annual capital flow of $20 billion to the underdeveloped world: in 1988, there was a net flow of $50 billion from the Third World to the West to repay old debt. The South is running faster only to fall farther behind. The "marginal men," to use the phrase of Robert McNamara, former president of the World Bank, are becoming even more marginalized.

Rhythms of Crisis

"Twisted, charred, liquefied, volatilized.... Of an entire humanity there will remain only traces of shadows imprinted on the concrete debris, on stones in the fields, on cliffs overlooking the sea—like so many blotches on a bad photographic plate."[58] Written in 1961, this graphic description of the effects of nuclear war expresses the horror that Pierre Trudeau felt about the prospects of mass incineration. He spent a good part of his career trying to do something to avoid it.

Trudeau understood the realities of great power politics and recognized that each superpower had a regional zone of influence that it was determined to control. He made sure that Canada was never regarded as a threat to the security of the United States (the North American Aerospace Defence Command [NORAD] agreement was renewed in 1975 and again in 1981) and Canada did its part to ensure alliance solidarity by agreeing to allow the testing of cruise missiles over its airspace in 1983. He had no illusions, either, about the repressive nature of Communist regimes: Canada developed the Western position on the human contacts section of the 1975 Helsinki Accord, aid was cut off to Cuba after the Soviet-Cuban adventures in Angola, thirteen Soviet spies were expelled from Canada in 1978 and Canada boycotted the 1980 Olympics because of the Soviet invasion of Afghanistan. Whatever initiatives Trudeau took to relax East-West tensions, he did so as a committed member of the Western alliance.

But Trudeau did have definite views on the value of détente. He believed that the Soviet Union and the People's Republic of China had to be encouraged, enticed or cajoled into becoming full participants in the community of nations. The way to reduce their revolutionary zeal was to bind them to the world, not to cast them beyond the pale. Trade, scientific exchanges, tourism and culture were all threads to be spun into a web. The nonrecognition of China and the 1981–82 attempt of the Reagan administration to stop the construction of the Soviet-Europe gas pipeline were simply madness. Trudeau practised the politics of inclusion, not exclusion.

Military power was necessary to contain Soviet adventures while this long-term process of normalization was at work, but for Canada military power could rarely be used. Canada's ability to mount military peacekeeping operations occasionally contributed to stability—as in 1974 when Canada helped Henry Kissinger create the United Nations Disengagement and Observer Force on the Golan Heights between Syria and Israel—and our military participation in NATO and NORAD was part of the alliance dues. But with financial resources being scarce, the Trudeau government did not overly invest in military preparedness.

In 1969, Canada's contribution to NATO's central European front was halved to five thousand troops and defence spending was frozen for three years. In 1975, as détente receded, defence spending was increased, and in the early 1980s Canada met the NATO target of a 3 percent annual increase in military spending. From 1968 to 1984, however, defence spending as a whole declined from 2.6 percent of GNP to 2 percent, and troop levels fell from 101,676 to 80,838. More importantly, Canada divested itself of four nuclear weapon systems. In 1968, under a dual-key arrangement with the United States, Canada's troops manned the nuclear-armed Honest John missile in Europe and the Bomarc nuclear anti-aircraft missile in Canada; the CF-104 Air Division in Europe had a nuclear bombing role; and Canadian CF-101 interceptors were armed with the nuclear-tipped Genie rockets. The Honest John and Bomarc missiles were soon retired, the NATO air division was given a conventional bombing role, and with the arrival of the conventionally armed CF-18s in 1984 to replace the nuclear-armed CF–101s in NORAD, Canada once again had a nuclear-free military.

Nuclear nonproliferation became a central concern in the 1970s after India's explosion of a "peaceful" device in 1974. Canada is a major exporter of both uranium and sophisticated nuclear technology like the Candu reactor, and in 1956, as part of its aid program, Canada had sent a research nuclear reactor to India. The United States supplied the heavy water to charge it, West Germany supplied the design for the heavy water plant and France built the reprocessing plant for the spent fuel rods. There were strict prohibitions on such aid being used for weapon development. This reactor, however, made the plutonium used in India's nuclear explosion. India's duplicity shocked Canadians.

After the explosion, Canada imposed unilateral restraints on its uranium exports and announced that safeguards on exports of nuclear material to states not party to the Treaty on the Non-Proliferation of Nuclear Weapons (like India and France) would be as stringent as the safeguards required by the Non-Proliferation Treaty. Although it was too late to affect India, Canada was now in the vanguard of supplier states in imposing stricter regulations on the export of nuclear technology. In 1983, as part of his peace mission, Prime Minister Trudeau proposed a strengthening of the Non-Proliferation Treaty and urged nonadherent states like India to join. (Mrs Gandhi refused.)

Following the difficulties with India, Prime Minister Trudeau continued to confront the problem of nuclear proliferation. In 1978 he suggested a broad "strategy of suffocation" to impede the arms race by limiting research and development of nuclear weapons through a comprehensive Test Ban Treaty. By 1980, the chances of gaining approval of such a treaty had withered to zero with the Soviet invasion of Afghanistan and the coming to power of the Reagan administration. Instead, the Cold War went into its deepest freeze since the Cuban missile crisis of 1962. Prime Minister Trudeau increasingly became preoccupied with three inter-related threats: the spread of nuclear weapons, the increasing use of force and the lack of any meaningful political dialogue between the Eastern bloc and the West. While dangers were multiplying, our leaders were shouting past each other.

In 1983, these ominous trends were coming to a head. The Soviets withdrew from all arms control negotiations. No summit between Soviet and American leaders was in the works. NATO summits to discuss Western strategy were a farce, with pre-cooked communiqués and events stage-managed to prevent any meaningful discussion. Prior to 1968, Pierre Trudeau had felt frustrated because of the lack of opportunity for Cabinet ministers to contribute to Canadian foreign policy. Similarly, by 1983, he felt frustrated by the lack of opportunity for the Allied nations to put forward their perspective on Western strategy. One option was to go it alone.

In September 1983, the Soviets shot down a Korean airliner. In October, the United States invaded Grenada. A whiff of Sarajevo was in the air. Trudeau decided to act. A task force of officials feverishly began to work on a set of proposals and on October 27, 1983, Trudeau told the world that he would attempt to inject a "jolt of political energy" to reverse the "trend lines of crisis." "What made the Trudeau initiative unique in contemporary international politics," according to two respected Canadian analysts, "was the effort by one senior statesman to reach out directly to other political leaders to engage their own personal involvement in trying to alter the prevailing directions in the management and control of nuclear weapons."[59] Trudeau visited the capitals of Western Europe in early November 1983; India and China in late November; Washington in December; East Germany, Czechoslovakia and Romania in January 1984; and the Soviet Union in February 1984. He carried with him five proposals: renewed dialogue between East and West starting with the Stockholm Conference on Disarmament, a strengthened Non-Proliferation Treaty, a new emphasis on conventional force reductions in Europe, a five-power nuclear disarmament conference and a ban on high-altitude antisatellite missiles.

Some of Trudeau's proposals had immediate impact; most did not. NATO did agree to send foreign ministers to the Stockholm Conference. The rhetoric of Western leaders, especially President Reagan, also became much more conciliatory. Reagan even began to express publicly one of the basic principles of the Trudeau peace mission: that "nuclear war cannot be won and must never be fought." The countries participating in the London Economic Summit in June 1984 jointly declared that "each of us will pursue all useful opportunities for dialogue."[60] The lagging Mutual and Balanced Force Reduction talks in Europe did receive more attention. But India rejected the nonproliferation proposals and Britain rejected the idea of a five-nation forum. The antisatellite proposals are still being examined in various arms control negotiations. Within Canada, the peace mission was widely supported and the last piece of legislation to be passed by the Trudeau government created the Canadian Institute for International Peace and Security, a body devoted to research and public discussion of issues affecting peace and war.

Academic and media critics, however, have railed about the peace initiative. How could Canada dare to give advice to the superpowers? Was it not doomed from the start because of American opposition? Yet the fact remains that while in the fall of 1983, no major Western power apart from Canada had any initiative underway to improve East-West dialogue, by the summer of 1984, virtually all of them had gotten into the act. Trudeau was the first to realize the necessity for speaking out—whatever the political cost in criticism or ridicule. As Geoffrey Pearson, Canada's former ambassador to the Soviet Union, writes: "By taking a global approach to security, Mr. Trudeau ran the risk of aiming too far and too high. But to aim high and far is not necessarily to miss the mark."[61] The lesson of the Trudeau peace mission can be stated quite simply—he saw a crisis and did what he could.

The Legacy of Liberalism

If one test of a middle power's foreign policy is to provide a good example at home, the Trudeau government surely gets high marks. Whatever sins it may have committed, hypocrisy was not among them. It campaigned for francophone rights at home and in francophone Africa abroad. It emphasized a North-South dialogue but also increased its own foreign aid tenfold. It opposed the escalation of the superpower arms race while reducing military spending at home and retiring the four nuclear weapons systems of the Canadian Armed Forces.

If a second test of success is an adequate balance between power and objectives, the results are more mixed. Canada's power during the Trudeau years did increase: foreign aid became a third arm of foreign policy and economic development led to a seat at the Western Economic Summit. Canadian ownership of the domestic economy expanded, as did international trade. Canada acquired new influence with Third World nations, and the professionalism of the country's diplomatic corps remained high. Canada had enough power to prevail in contests with larger powers like France and the United States. But as a middle power, Canada did not have enough influence to move its Western allies in significant ways on North-South issues or arms control.

That being the case, the question remains, Is it worthwhile for a state like Canada to even try to exert influence on the international scene? Liberal values say yes, and so does Canadian tradition. Lester B. Pearson set the standard for the Canadian variant of liberal internationalism. During Pearson's golden decade, Canada helped build institutions like the United Nations and NATO, and Pearson himself invented the concept of international peacekeeping. Trudeau worked on a different agenda than his predecessor—the environment, arms control and the Third World—but both men shared the same type of commitment to the international community and both were willing to have Canada take chances.

What is the legacy? In his final speech on the peace initiative to the House of Commons on February 9, 1984, Trudeau praised his fellow countrymen, but the words also serve as a fitting memorial to his own career:

> Let it be said of Canada and of Canadians, that we saw the crisis; that we did act; that we took risks; that we were loyal to our friends and open with our adversaries; that we have lived up to our ideals; and that we have done what we could to lift the shadow of war.

CHAPTER 2

Riding the Storm:
Energy Policy, 1968–1984

—————————by Marc Lalonde—————————

Marc Lalonde was Principal Secretary to the Prime Minister of Canada between 1968 and 1972 and was a minister of various departments in the Trudeau government between 1972 and 1984. He is currently a senior partner in the law firm Stikeman, Elliott.

THE STORY OF energy during the Trudeau years is essentially the story of oil and gas during that period, and even though this chapter will deal with energy policy and the oil-producing provinces as a whole, the story of government relations in this sector is largely the story of the relations between the Alberta government and Ottawa.

When the Trudeau government took office in 1968, supplies of coal, uranium and hydro resources had been ample enough to meet Canadian needs for many years, and they had gradually been developed to fill a growing foreign demand. Canada also had a safe and reliable nuclear generating capacity to supplement its traditional energy supply, which had been established with none of the controversy and hostility the nuclear industry had encountered in many other countries.

Oil and gas, on the other hand, had been a contentious subject since the 1950s and it remained so, right through the 1980s. Several factors came into play. First of all, Canada's share of that energy source was overwhelmingly concentrated in a single province—Alberta—which during this time relied increasingly on oil and gas for its economic development. Next, large and sudden price increases were generated by OPEC in 1973 and 1979, and prices remained high until the subsequent market decline in energy prices following the 1981 recession and the increases in non-OPEC supply starting in the early eighties. The whole situation was made worse by the fact that the "energy crisis" in Canada was largely the result of foreign events over which Canadians had no control. Finally, the implications of rising energy costs put severe pressures on the federal fiscal situation. All these things combined to make energy a central and controversial issue throughout the Trudeau years.

Reflecting on the history of energy policy in Canada, it is fair to say that since the 1950s,[1] energy policy has evolved as a continuum of adaptations to political and economic change at home and on the international scene. Since then, with varying degrees of emphasis dependent on the circumstances of the day, the Liberals pursued four broad objectives. There was, first of all, the development of western provincial economies and the petroleum industry through aggressive production and marketing of Western Basin oil and natural gas. Then, as OPEC restricted supply and increased prices dramatically, energy policy had to ensure security of supply for Canadian needs and address the implications for the Canadian economy of rapidly rising petroleum prices. Thirdly, bearing in mind the strategic nature of the oil and gas industry, the maintenance of a significant degree of Canadian ownership, whether pursued through private or public means, was considered a priority. The last objective had to do with ensuring that the federal government received a share of tax revenues commensurate with the additional burden imposed upon it by programs set up to mitigate the effects of rising petroleum prices. That increased burden resulted from the need to facilitate the adjustment of the Canadian economy to the new energy environment as well as from the increasing equalization payments that the federal government was required to make to the non-petroleum-producing provinces.

Although Canadian energy policy has always been part of an evolutionary continuum, its development since the 1960s can be divided into three distinct time periods: the sixties and early seventies (1960–1973), the mid- to late seventies (1973–1979) and the early eighties (1980–1984).

___ 1960–1973: The National Oil Policy _____

In 1959 the Royal Commission on Energy tabled a report that

was to become the cornerstone of domestic policy for the years 1960 to 1973. Following the Borden Commission's recommendations, John Diefenbaker's Conservative government made two significant moves: it established the National Energy Board as energy policy regulator and advisor late in 1959 and set up the National Oil Policy (NOP) in February 1961.

The aim of the National Oil Policy was to promote the Alberta oil industry by securing for it a protected share of the domestic market. Under the policy, Canada was divided into two oil markets. The market east of the Ottawa Valley (the Borden Line) would use imported oil, while west of the Borden Line, consumers would use the more expensive Alberta supplies. For most of the 1961–73 period, consumers to the west paid between $1.00 and $1.50 per barrel above the world price, which, just before the 1973 OPEC oil embargo and price increase, stood at around $3.00. They also paid proportionately higher prices at the pump than Canadians east of the Borden Line.

___ Trudeau in Power _____

When the Trudeau government took office in 1968, the National Oil Policy was evaluated on the basis of the major changes that had taken place in the market in the seven years since the NOP's implementation. Canadian exports were regularly exceeding the quotas established under the U.S. overland exemption for Canadian oil and gas. Meanwhile, foreign oil was illegally making inroads into the territory west of the Borden Line. The Canadian oil industry was facing extreme pressure just as production had exceeded the NOP goal of one million barrels a day.

In its 1969 report on the NOP, the National Energy Board concluded that, in spite of the market changes, the basic problem had not changed since 1961 – namely, we had more resources than markets. Although the NEB pointed out that the resources were relatively expensive to explore, develop and transport, it concluded that the policy had benefited the economy in general and oil industry growth in particular. There was therefore a renewed commitment to the NOP and to finding more export markets.

Without co-operation from the United States, however, little could be done to improve conditions in Canada's main export market. And that co-operation was not forthcoming. In 1970, the United States re-evaluated the 1959 overland exemption for Canadian gas and oil, which had by then reached export levels nearly double the 230,000 barrels a day allowed under the exemption. Despite increasing demand in the northeastern United States, President Richard Nixon imposed import controls and an import tax on Canadian oil.

At the same time, western producers and Ontario refiners protested continued incursions of imported non-western oil into markets west of the Borden Line. New oil-refining capacity in the Maritimes and Quebec, funded by regional development grants, was securing a foothold in the markets traditionally served by Ontario refineries, which used higher-cost western oil for feedstock. This practice was clearly illegal but Ontario refiners could not compete against products produced with oil from sources that were declining in price.

___ The End of the Surplus Era _____

Between 1970 and 1973, OPEC member states moved decisively to end the oil-company practice of generating profits by depressing well-head prices and to combat the declining balance of payments they were experiencing as a result of the devaluation of the U.S. dollar. Frustrated by oil company intransigence against increased prices for its oil, Algeria nationalized its oil and gas production in June 1970. Libya followed suit by increasing well-head taxes and nationalized its major producer, Occidental Petroleum, in 1973. Combined OPEC negotiations with oil companies had resulted in the Teheran Agreement of 1970 to increase well-head taxes, encourage government participation and institute collective pricing. However, the agreement quickly unravelled as the U.S. dollar continued to depreciate and oil companies dragged their feet on several provisions of the agreement. Another development also tolled the bell for the era of surplus markets. After 1970, U.S. domestic oil production began to decline and the United States became a net importer; that foreign dependence increased continuously over the 1970s.

The first effects of these changes on Canadian oil and gas policy were seen in an August 1970 decision by the National Energy Board not to allow a gas export application, on the grounds that it exceeded current supplies. Exports were discouraged further as the NEB began its first comprehensive examination of what constituted a reasonable export price. From that point on, export applications were assessed not only on the basis of supplies available for export, but also according to contract price. The NEB had concluded that it should ensure that Canada received the best possible price for its exports, as well as making sure that enough reserves would be available to meet future Canadian needs.

In December 1972, the National Energy Board issued a report stating that there would be a shortage of oil and gas for domestic consumption by the end of the decade if exports continued at their current rate. By August 1973, the price of oil had risen from $2.00 a barrel to $3.00 a barrel in one year.

Until 1973, the Trudeau government had been implementing an energy policy very similar to the one established in 1961. At the same time, it strengthened and improved the quality of the regulatory and administrative institutions that affected oil production and actively supported exploration in frontier areas, in the face of a forecast levelling-off of Alberta's production by the late 1970s. The federal government also continued to lobby to prevent American markets from closing up even more. Between 1962 and 1972, Canada had more than doubled its domestic oil production (1,700,000 barrels a day versus 700,000 barrels a day), and its exports to the United States had quadrupled (995,000 barrels a day versus 236,000 barrels a day).

___ 1973-1979: The First OPEC Oil Shock ___

Even before the OPEC oil embargo, which is usually considered to have marked the beginning of the "energy crisis," Canada was experiencing an energy crisis of its own. In fact, by 1973, the future of Canadian oil supply was in worrisome shape. The United States was increasingly dependent on imported oil and gas, and as the Canadian industry was exporting an average of 825,000 barrels a day, it was liquidating easily accessible reserves at a fast rate but doing little exploration for new ones.

In March 1973, the government acted to restrict oil exports. In September, as part of a national voluntary wage and price restraint program instituted in the face of mounting inflation, the prime minister requested industry to freeze oil and gas prices until January 30, 1974. In October, an export tax was instituted. The export restrictions, price freeze and export tax were established partly in response to conditions in the United States. Demand surges south of the border, coupled with regulated prices, could have siphoned off much of Canada's supply at fire-sale prices, if export restrictions and the export tax had not been imposed. Without these policy changes, Canadian reserves would have been rapidly sold into a price-controlled down-market, thereby robbing producers and governments of rents and threatening Canada's security of supply.

___ New Rules: December 1973 _____

The combined pressures of increasing demand from oil-importing countries and the effects of the OPEC cartel actions (culminating in the October oil embargo) resulted in a doubling of oil prices between January 1 and October 16, 1973 (from US$2.59 to US$5.11). The dramatic consequences of the embargo led to another doubling of prices on December 22, 1973 (from US$5.11 to US$11.65). In response to the October price increase and embargo, the prime minister announced on December 6, 1973, decisions that marked the end of the 1961 National Oil Policy. The aim of the initiatives was to increase Canada's self-reliance in oil and gas, and so reduce the country's exposure to the detrimental effects of volatile international events.

The Borden Line was abolished to form a single national oil market operating under a one-price policy, which was instituted for all oil and natural gas, subject only to transportation differentials. The difference in the prices of imported and domestic oil was offset by payments to importers through the Oil Import Compensation Program (OICP), which was, in turn, partially funded by the export tax instituted in October 1973.

Petro-Canada was established in July 1975 as a Crown corporation, its main objectives being to accelerate (in co-operation with existing companies) the exploration for and development of new oil and gas resources in the Arctic and offshore and to undertake the extraction of oil from the Alberta tar sands. The federal government also decided to extend the interprovincial oil pipeline from Montreal to Sarnia; this was completed by 1976.

As in 1961, the question arose in 1973 as to whether the price of oil and gas in Canada should be allowed to move freely or whether it should be administered. If the price moved freely, Canadians would immediately pay the higher world price; if it was administered, they would gain a comparative advantage by paying lower prices for their own oil and gas resources at home, while charging world price for exported oil and gas. The reverse of this sort of two-tiered system had been in operation since 1961: most Canadians had had to pay more than the world price for their oil products, in order to support the Canadian oil industry. This system was not even exclusive to the oil industry. Such a regime had been established in support of Canadian wheat farmers in the late 1960s, when the domestic price for wheat was set at a price level higher than the international price. That regime remained in effect during the 1970s with adjustments such that if the international price exceeded a certain level, Canadian consumers would then be benefiting from lower domestic prices. Such an event did in fact occur for a while. As for petroleum products, the Canadian government's answer in 1973 was the same as in 1961. It opted for administered pricing, except that this time Canadians would be paying less, not more, than international prices. That decision was further influenced by the fact that the United States also ran a two-price market for domestic and imported oil.

Revenue Sharing

The need for price restraint in domestic markets reflected a systemic flaw in the structure of energy revenue sharing in Canada: the country did not have a system already in place to ensure that windfall gains from oil price increases were shared equitably. This basic flaw was at the root of much of the debate

and acrimony that surrounded oil and gas policy throughout
the seventies.

As long as the differential between Canadian and world
prices was only a few cents per barrel, the matter of revenue
sharing remained secondary. In fact, in the early fall of 1973,
the federal government encouraged Alberta to raise the
royalties it collected from the industry and indicated that, if it
did so, the federal government would lift the price freeze
announced in September. Alberta then proceeded to raise its
royalties in November 1973.

OPEC's Christmas week doubling of oil prices radically
changed the situation. With the new higher prices, the potential
take of the new Alberta royalty regime was enormous. The
federal government was faced with a proportionate loss of
revenue because oil extraction companies could deduct
royalties from their federal taxes. At the same time, the federal
government had to absorb a significant increase in expenditures on two sides: (1) an increase in normal equalization
payments to qualifying provinces (under the existing formula,
even Ontario would eventually qualify for equalization
payments but fortunately, when it came to this, Ontario agreed
to amend the formula) and (2) more funds to compensate
consumers who depended on imported oil. The issue was
emphatically not one of reducing the wealth of the people of the
oil-producing provinces; for years, the federal government had
been promoting production in order to increase prosperity in
those regions. The question revolved around the need to
cushion the impact of the price bonanza on the federal
government and on Canadian consumers. In the absence of a
sensible revenue-sharing system, price became the mechanism
of last resort.

Several federal-provincial conferences were convened in
1974 to tackle the energy-pricing issue. In a January meeting,
the first ministers agreed to maintain the freeze on oil prices
introduced in September 1973 and endorsed the single
domestic price concept. The meeting reconvened in March and
an agreement was reached to raise the domestic price to $6.50
from $3.80 a barrel (at that time, the international price stood
at about US$12.00). Yet no agreement could be reached on
the revenue-sharing issue, as Alberta insisted on its right

to establish royalties at whatever level it felt appropriate—although higher royalties led to greater erosion of the federal tax base.

When later that year Alberta raised royalties to 65 percent of price increases over $3.50 a barrel, the federal government decided to take steps to protect its tax base. The November 1974 budget eliminated the deductibility of provincial royalties from federal income tax and increased corporate income tax on resource profits. Although the federal budget of 1975 allowed for some deductibility of provincial royalties, years of acrimonious negotiations followed, with Alberta and the federal government arguing about what would constitute appropriate revenue sharing. The issue was to dominate federal-provincial relations until the 1981 Canada-Alberta Energy Pricing and Taxation Agreement was reached.

___ Exploration Incentives _____

To counter the possibility that Alberta's royalty increases and the federal government's elimination of royalty tax deductions would stymie companies who wanted to invest in exploration for new Canadian oil and gas deposits, both governments, from 1973 on, made special efforts in other ways to encourage the discovery and exploitation of new reserves. This was particularly the case for high-cost and risky ventures such as the development of the oil sands projects and exploration for oil and gas in the Arctic and eastern offshore areas (all part of what is called the "Canada lands").

In February 1975, for instance, the federal, Alberta and Ontario governments acted as equity partners with a three-member consortium in negotiations for the development of Syncrude's oil sands plant in northern Alberta. Together the three governments put up $500 million for a 35 percent interest in the project. The consortium was also exempted from the non-deductibility of royalties, was allowed to charge world prices on all its production and was given several guarantees relating to performance.[2]

For the industry as a whole, the supply emphasis meant the beginning of extensive subsidization, through the federal tax system, of exploration on Canada lands. Super-depletion allowances for exploration announced in February 1978 were so generous that companies could, in certain circumstances, make money on their exploration programs alone. Dome, Esso, Gulf and Mobil, who benefited from these tax subsidies, were the most active players in exploration on the Beaufort Sea and the Atlantic coast off the shores of Newfoundland and Nova Scotia.

___ Self-Reliance _____

In keeping with the emphasis on supply, the major policy initiative of the period encouraged self-reliance; by using domestic resources to the greatest possible extent, Canadians would be less vulnerable to arbitrary changes in the supply or price of imported energy. As described in the April 1976 policy paper, *An Energy Strategy for Canada: Policies for Self-Reliance*, self-reliance was different from self-sufficiency in that it did not emphasize producing resources that were more costly than foreign sources or which required government assistance to come into production. In a way, that paper was preparing the ground for a gradual reduction of the heavy subsidization programs that had previously been established for the oil sands and Canada lands projects in the wake of perceived shortages of oil and gas.

By 1977, energy programs were successfully meeting the requirements of Canadian consumers, and several policy developments were taking place that would stabilize Canadian energy markets for the remainder of the decade. Eastern refineries were being supplied with Alberta oil through the Montreal pipeline extension, tar sands production was underway and the production of conventional oil and gas was increasing. In June 1977, the federal government made an oil-pricing agreement with Alberta, whereby prices would be allowed to move towards world levels in six-month instalments of one dollar per barrel starting July 1, 1977, provided that any increase did not take the price above the average price of oil delivered in Chicago. (That city was chosen as the American mid-continent reference point which was most appropriate to ensure Canadian competitiveness.) American oil prices were also regulated and it was agreed by the federal and provincial governments that Canadian oil prices should not exceed American ones.

Under the two-year pricing agreement, Canadian prices moved up so that they were on a par with the average price of oil in Chicago by June 30, 1978. The price increase was complemented by a $0.10-per-barrel Syncrude levy raised by the federal government on all domestic and some imported oil; that levy was to pay the Syncrude consortium international prices after its start-up in the third quarter of 1978. In November 1978, the increase scheduled for January 1979 was postponed, since it would have raised Canadian prices above the Chicago price, although Alberta pressed for immediate moves to the increased price, should the average Chicago price increase occur before the next scheduled Canadian price increase.

By the end of 1978 it thus appeared that, despite continuing financial quarrels between the producing provinces and the federal government, Canada was reaching a plateau where Canadian prices closely matched world prices and a certain degree of stability could be expected in the energy field for a few years. In fact, the price of oil in real terms had declined since the 1974 increase, and the federal government could foresee the possibility of eliminating oil import subsidies and a stabilization of equalization payments resulting from high energy prices.

___ The Shock from Iran ___

The Iranian Revolution of February 1979 illustrated the volatility of oil markets and brought about a radical change that destroyed, overnight, the stability of the previous few years. In the space of a few months, the price of a barrel of oil more than doubled, going from less than US$14.82 in January 1979 to US$34.50 by January 1980. Canadian energy policy was back to square one, but starting this time from a much higher price plateau and subject to a much more inflationary environment.

Price and revenue sharing issues were once more in the spotlight on the political stage. Producing provinces, Alberta in particular, felt that since Canada had finally reached the range of international prices, it would be better to move up to the new international price. The consuming provinces argued that it was unconscionable to let OPEC arbitrarily impose a huge burden on Canadians when the country had a positive trade balance in petroleum products. As for the federal government, it could see that further large increases in petroleum prices would accelerate already significant inflationary pressures on the economy and increase the likelihood of a deep recession; at the same time, greater revenue for the government of Alberta meant increases in the cost of equalization payments to other provinces. On the other hand, keeping the price of oil below the international price would necessitate further subsidization of imports. In the circumstances, the federal government decided to continue with gradual and regular increases in the price of oil in Canada, rather than jumping immediately to the new international level.

The bright spot in the crisis of 1979 was that there were few actual troubles with supply. The policies and initiatives of the previous five years—the Montreal pipeline extension, increased reserves resulting from exploration, Syncrude oil sands production, conservation measures and oil import subsidization—were proven to be unqualified successes that helped all Canadians weather the crisis in a way that other import-dependent countries did not. Canadians did not have to endure the line-ups for motor fuel and the closing of schools, factories and public facilities that occurred in Europe and the United States.

The issue of scarcity south of the border was epitomized by the actions of Exxon when it ordered a tanker of Venezuelan oil bound for the Montreal refinery of its subsidiary, Imperial Oil, to be diverted to the United States.

___The Clark Government Negotiations___

When the Clark government came to power in May 1979, it attempted to reduce or reverse some of the programs and policies of the previous six years. Central to their platform was the elimination of Petro-Canada's primary role in national energy matters and, if possible, the privatization of the company. The new government also held a "community-of-communities" view of federalism, which entailed giving federal management powers over offshore oil resources to the adjacent provinces.

By June 1979, Canada's oil price was $8.50 per barrel below the average Chicago oil price, which had just undergone deregulation, and was at its lowest level in relation to international prices since 1973–74. In September, the National Energy Board reported that Canada's oil supply situation was very tight. Although Canadian production was running at 100 percent capacity, much of this was being used to fill demand raised by the Iranian oil shut-down and to meet Canada's obligations under the 1979 International Energy Agency emergency sharing agreement.

Numerous meetings took place between the government of Alberta and the federal government, but negotiations were as difficult as they had been at any time before. Minister of Finance John Crosbie summed up the atmosphere of the negotiations by publicly referring to Premier Lougheed as "Bokassa II," after the infamous Emperor of the Central African Republic.

In the final analysis, the downfall of the Clark government can be directly attributed to its inability to reach a reasonable and balanced energy pricing agreement with Alberta. By December 1989 federal and Alberta officials had only managed to agree in principle on pricing conventional oil and gas at 85 percent of Chicago prices and synthetic oil at international price levels, but they had yet to conclude an agreement by the time the Clark government was defeated in the House of Commons on December 13, 1979.

As for the Liberals, they felt that one of the main reasons for their defeat had been that, during the last couple of years of their mandate, they had lacked a sense of direction and had tried to accommodate too many contradictory positions. The government had ended up projecting an image of fuzziness and aimlessness. They were determined that if they came back to office, they would make sure that that kind of reproach could not be addressed to them.

The unexpected defeat of the Clark government accelerated the Liberal policy development process started by the Liberal caucus energy committee in the summer of 1979. Clearly, the election was going to bear on the energy issue and the Liberals could not just spend sixty days blasting away at an $0.18 a gallon gasoline price increase proposed in the defeated Crosbie budget. The Liberals had to offer an alternative. On January 25, 1980, in a speech before the Halifax Board of Trade, Pierre Trudeau released a seven-point energy platform, which was eventually to become the backbone of the National Energy Program. The platform promised a made-in-Canada price; energy security through accelerated development of domestic potential, particularly from the Arctic and the Canadian offshore; replacement of oil with natural gas and other energy forms; the strengthening and expansion of Petro-Canada; emphasis on conservation and alternative energy; increased Canadian ownership of the energy sector; and energy as a major element of any industrial or regional development strategy.[3] In policy terms, these principles translated into policies on self-sufficiency, pricing and revenue sharing, and Canadianization.

___ 1980–1984: The National Energy Program___

After taking office in February 1980 with a majority mandate from the Canadian people, the new government immediately began negotiations with Alberta for a pricing and revenue-sharing agreement. But it was clear from the beginning that the Alberta team would not move one inch from what it thought it had exacted from the Clark government.

A series of futile meetings of officials and ministers went on until the early fall of 1980 but it soon became obvious that the respective positions of Alberta and the federal government were irreconcilable at that stage. Prices were continuing to rise and nearly all forecasts pointed to still much higher prices. Armand Hammer, the president of Occidental Petroleum, was predicting prices of $100 a barrel by 1990, and the International Energy Agency, while not going quite that far, was forecasting shortages and fast-rising prices for the rest of the decade.

Given the potentially disastrous consequences of such developments, the Liberal government felt that it had to act quickly to make sure that the stand-off with Alberta did not continue for years to come. Bearing in mind the shabby treatment given the Clark government by the Alberta government and the futility of the discussions immediately after the 1980 election, it became clear that the issues of price and revenue sharing could not be resolved unless the rules of the game were changed. It was in this spirit that the National Energy Program (NEP) was developed.

Introduced in October 1980 as a budget document, the NEP brought about a significant change in intergovernmental relations over principles of pricing, revenue sharing and resource management. Oddly enough, compared to the energy policy that was in place from 1973 to 1979, the NEP was closer to the policy that had been articulated by the Diefenbaker government in the early sixties. That is, it was closely linked with economic development policy and was led by federal initiatives. Under the NEP, energy would be governed by a strategic nation-building policy guided by federal initiatives and with taxation issues at its core.

Faced with the challenge of negotiating in public, the government ensured that the NEP was not to be perceived as the opening gambit in federal-provincial negotiations, by presenting it as a firm budgetary decision.

The National Energy Program was based on three precepts:

1. Self-sufficiency through increasing domestic oil production, energy substitution and conservation programs (in light of the 1979 international oil crisis, the previous policy of self-reliance was considered inadequate);
2. Giving Canadians the opportunity to participate in the petroleum industry through a Canadianization program aiming at 50 percent of Canadian ownership by 1990;
3. A petroleum pricing and revenue-sharing regime that would be fair to all Canadians, as well as to the federal and provincial governments.

Of these three precepts, price and revenue-sharing were the most critical issues for a policy that sought to manage energy as a strategic commodity for nation building.

Internal cash flow in the industry had risen in 1979 to more than $7.1 billion from $4.9 billion in 1978, and those revenues were expected to rise by another 40 percent in 1980, with significant annual increases in subsequent years. The federal government recognized the need for large increases in revenue within the industry in order to encourage companies to proceed with high-cost developments in the oil sands and the Canada lands. Indeed, the system proposed by the federal government was designed to achieve such increases, and despite the hue and cry from the industry, the federal government had decided to leave the petroleum industry with roughly the same percentage of revenues as had prevailed during the previous decade. In effect, the industry would receive the same share of a much larger pie. True, the federal government wanted to change the tax system so as to give a comparative advantage to Canadian-controlled firms, and this meant that some benefits would be reallocated from foreign multinationals to Canadian firms. (The existing tax system was clearly favourable to the large, established firms, which also happened to be overwhelmingly foreign firms. They owned most of the existing fields and they could use the tax system effectively to continue tightening their grip on the Canadian oil and gas sector.) As it was impossible under our tax treaties to discriminate between Canadian and foreign firms, the only alternative was to replace most of the tax write-offs, which were of very little use to most Canadian firms, with a system of grants that would be related to a company's level of Canadian ownership.

Overall, industry revenue was therefore not adversely affected by the NEP, but the issue of federal revenue had become even more critical, and in order to achieve a fairer balance, the Alberta government had to make room.

Throughout the 1970s, the federal share of revenue from oil and gas stagnated and eventually declined to a 1979 low of 8.8 percent, with the remainder divided between the industry and Alberta. At the same time, however, the provincial share of revenues increased from 38.2 percent in 1974 to 50.5 percent in 1979: in fact, of all the oil-producing countries with a federal regime, Canada had the dubious distinction of having by far the lowest federal share of resource revenues. At the same time, with every increase in prices and corresponding increase in provincial royalty income, the federal government faced an increasing fiscal burden in the form of equalization programs, economic adjustment for damages caused by increased prices on other sectors of the economy, conservation programs and consumer protection.

The scenario for the 1980s appeared even more problematical. If the previous pricing agreements were to be continued, Alberta's share would continue to increase while the federal share would shrink dramatically and its energy-related expenditures would continue to increase.

New Tax and Expenditure Instruments and Canadianization

The National Energy Program introduced new federal revenue and expenditure instruments, which would increase the federal share of the revenue split. That money would then be recycled throughout the country to fund energy conservation and renewable energy initiatives, subsidies to switch away from oil to other energy sources, further price protection of consumers through the Oil Import Compensation Program and the Canadianization of the industry through the Petroleum Incentives Program (PIP). Energy revenue and expenditure were expected to balance for the first few years of the program, but it was clear that, in the longer term, it would generate substantial funds that could be used to reduce the federal deficit.

To increase its revenue, the federal government modified the tax system. Exploration and development expenditure deductions were eliminated and replaced by a grants system, the Petroleum Incentives Program (PIP), which was designed to Canadianize the petroleum industry. It provided for proportionately larger grants to the smaller companies, which happened to be mainly Canadian-owned, and allocated exploration grants to firms working in frontier areas on a pro rata basis, depending on the extent to which they were Canadian-owned and -controlled. It also provided higher grants for companies working in the Canada lands, in order to compensate for the higher costs of exploration in those areas and to fulfil the government's need to know what potential reserves existed there. Non-Canadian firms that held the largest and most highly prospective lands would be encouraged in their exploration agreements to farm out parcels of their interest or actual lands to Canadian companies, thus increasing the Canadian ownership ratio on lands already held by non-Canadian firms and focusing activity on the Canada lands. PIP grants would also help limit the amount of exploration expenditures that foreign-owned multinationals could deduct from taxes, thus counterbalancing to some extent the extensive capital exports that these companies were making through dividend payments to their owners.

Accompanying the decision to reduce deductions for companies were new taxes, introduced to capture part of the difference in rents between the pre-1979 price of oil and the higher international prices now being charged. The two most significant taxes were the Petroleum and Gas Revenue Tax (PGRT) and the Natural Gas and Gas Liquids Tax (NGGLT). The PGRT was a revenue tax without deductions originally assessed at 8 percent of revenues at the wellhead and the NGGLT was both a domestic and an export consumption tax. The other new taxes were the Petroleum Compensation Charge (to replace the Syncrude levy), the Canadian Ownership Special Charge (to finance increased public ownership) and the Special Compensation Charge.

The most contentious aspect of Canadianization was the reservation of a 25 percent Crown share in frontier lands. Through this, the federal government sought to emulate similar, albeit more comprehensive, programs to assert the national interest in resource ownership that existed in Britain, Norway, Australia and The Netherlands. The Crown share was immediately branded by the multinationals and the American government as expropriation without compensation, although how one can expropriate what one already owns is difficult to envisage. Contrary to the belief of some, this matter was never considered an essential part of the NEP, and on several occasions, the government came close to abandoning it. However, U.S. multinationals—especially Mobil Oil—overplayed their hand by exercising excessive pressure directly and through the American government, which resulted in the Canadian government standing firm on the issue.

___ Agreement with Alberta _____

The Alberta government reacted to the National Energy Program with outrage—partly because it had been misled about federal needs by the vacillation of the Clark government but mainly because it had unreasonably high expectations about its entitlements and constitutional role in energy matters. That outrage translated into concrete retaliatory measures: the gradual reduction of 180,000 barrels a day of oil supply from Alberta to the rest of Canada and a freeze on the Alsands and Cold Lake oil projects. For the industry, the period between November 1980 and September 1981 proved to be most difficult as it found itself caught in a tug-of-war between the two governments. The stalemate could not last forever, however, and some informal discussions eventually took place between senior officials, which led to formal official and ministerial meetings. Finally, an agreement satisfactory to both parties was signed in Ottawa on September 1, 1981, by Prime Minister Trudeau and Premier Lougheed. At a joint press conference after the signing ceremony, the premier of Alberta called the Energy Pricing and Taxation Agreement (EPTA) "a fair deal for the people of Alberta but . . . also a fair deal for the people of Canada. And I think," he went on, "after a lot of work and a lot of effort, that is what we have come up with . . . a balanced agreement."[4]

Under the agreement, many aspects of the NEP relating to pricing, taxation and exploration incentives were amended. In particular, the federal government had agreed to faster and larger increases in the price of conventionally produced oil. The federal share of oil revenue would also increase from about 10 percent to 26 percent of total revenue, while the industry share would move down from 43 percent to 37 percent of a much larger pie. The Alberta government agreed to see its share decline by about 10 percentage points, to 37 percent. For the first time since 1974, the federal government and Alberta had reached a long-term, comprehensive taxation and revenue-sharing agreement that appeared to leave behind the acrimonious battles of the past and established a predictable and financially attractive environment for the industry for years to come. Moreover, it entrenched the Petroleum

Incentive Program and the Canadianization philosophy—a dramatic breakthrough for Canadian energy policy.

Soon after the signing of the EPTA, similar agreements were reached with Saskatchewan and British Columbia.

____The Reversal of the Tide _____

While most of the expenditure programs included in the National Energy Program were launched as announced, the pricing, taxation and revenue-sharing regimes were greatly modified. In fact, these aspects of the EPTA, to the great disappointment of both federal and provincial governments, soon became the subject of constant revision (such as those contained in the 1982 NEP Update), as anticipated international oil price increases did not materialize and it became necessary for both Alberta and the federal government to leave increased financial room for the industry.

By the beginning of 1983, the international energy market was softening as a result of increased production of non-OPEC supplies and the continuing willingness of countries like Norway and Britain to charge prices below OPEC levels. The higher oil prices of the past decade had generated funds to pay for extensive exploration and development around the world, which had resulted in a glut of reserves. Pricing OPEC oil at $40.00 per barrel made alternative supplies and oil substitutes comparable to or cheaper than importing oil. Moreover, to a degree totally unexpected by energy analysts, oil demand went down in response to the oil price increases of the late seventies and this, in turn, put downward pressure on prices. In addition to increased energy conservation, the recession of 1981–82 had led to lower domestic and international sales.

As industry revenues dropped, exploration declined, so Alberta and the federal government took initiatives to help the industry weather the exploration slump. In fact, barely a month went by without new arrangements being worked out between the federal government and the producing provinces. Meanwhile, companies that had moved some of their exploration programs to the United States in response to the NEP began to return to Canada after finding that drilling for oil in the U.S. was not necessarily more lucrative.

At the same time, the NEP was promoting regional economic growth via oil and gas development in the Canada lands. The March 1982 Canada–Nova Scotia Agreement, for instance, provided for shared federal and provincial management of gas resources offshore from Nova Scotia. The province was given grants to help build the economic infrastructure associated with energy development, as well as federal royalty revenues simiar to those it could have claimed for itself onshore. Unfortunately, in spite of efforts made repeatedly until 1984, no similar agreement that was finally reached in 1986 is generally considered to be less advantageous to the province in revenue terms that the agreement proposed in 1983–84.

___ Looking Back _____

The National Energy Program was welcomed by many Canadians, and the general thrust of the policy found favour with most provincial governments. In fact, only Alberta expressed radical opposition to it. There is no doubt, however, that the oil industry was not pleased with the program, particularly between November 1980 when it was initiated and September 1981 when an agreement was reached with Alberta, as some of the industry's expected profits were channelled to both the Alberta and federal governments.

Many oil executives privately agreed that the federal government was entitled to more revenue from the oil industry, but they argued that they should not have become hostages in the quarrel between two governments. And they could not risk offending the government of Alberta by publicly supporting the federal position, since most of them were dependent on provincial authorities for all kinds of regulatory and administrative decisions. They had much more to gain by siding with the Alberta government. In fact, the most the federal government could hope to have from them was silence.

In the end, the NEP's opponents used the program as a scapegoat for all the problems the oil and gas industry faced during the eighties—even though the industry in Texas and elsewhere in the U.S. suffered as much as in Canada, if not more. And I leave aside the paranoid behaviour of a few individuals in the industry who campaigned against the NEP as the great socialist conspiracy to take over the industry.

A more rational analysis of the period would indicate that the greatest flaw in the National Energy Program and the Energy Pricing and Taxation Agreement with Alberta was the scenario of increasing international oil prices upon which it was based. It had been assumed that the international price would continue to increase at a rate of 2 percent per year in real terms, which would have resulted in a price of $79.65 a barrel by January 1990. One winces today at how wrong that forecast was, but in 1980 most analysts, including those from the industry, considered that those price projections were not excessive.

Had prices moved within a reasonable range of the projections, the Canadian consumer would be paying a lot more today for petroleum products, but the oil and gas industry would be very prosperous, the governments of producing provinces would have large Heritage Funds and the federal government would probably have no deficit.

This is not the way events unfolded, however, and as oil prices dropped to $15.00 a barrel, the federal government ended up again with the smallest share of income net of expenses (see Figure 1). As the NEP was coming out, the world entered the most severe recession since the thirties, with a resulting slump in demand for oil products. The United States unexpectedly found itself in a situation of excess gas supply—the famous "gas bubble" that kept on moving with the years until quite recently—thus curtailing U.S. demand for Canadian natural gas. At the same time, conservation measures adopted by various countries in the late seventies and early eighties were reducing demand, and non-OPEC oil production kept increasing. Scenarios built upon rapidly increasing prices for petroleum products came crashing to the ground.

A second flaw in the NEP was the administrative complexity of the program, resulting particularly from the replacement of tax incentives by grants, in order to encourage the Canadian-ization of the industry. While this was the only way to achieve that objective without contravening international tax treaties, it imposed upon the industry a complex new system and this burden appeared particularly heavy to the small producers

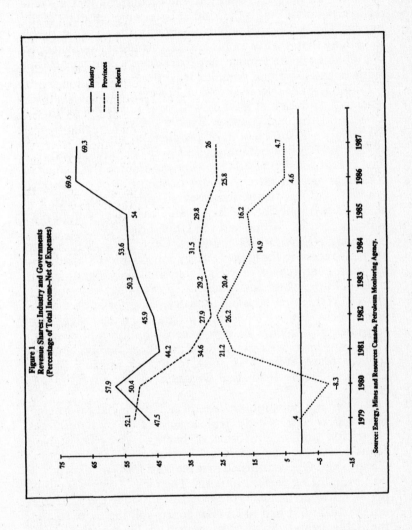

Figure 1
Revenue Shares: Industry and Governments
(Percentage of Total Income–Net of Expenses)

Industry
Provinces
Federal

Source: Energy, Mines and Resources Canada, Petroleum Monitoring Agency.

whom the NEP was trying to favour but who were not equipped to handle all the paperwork and the accounting that the new regime required. This is the kind of issue which drafters of the Income Tax Act perpetually face—that is, the choice between something that is fairly simple and easy to understand but open to loopholes or something that covers every contingency but requires extensive and complex legal drafting.

Looking at the overall situation, however, Canada managed its energy situation at least as well as, if not better than, any other industrialized country. By 1984, Canada had become practically self-sufficient in oil production, while in 1977 and 1978, it had been a net importer of over one million barrels a day. It had accomplished this while cushioning the Canadian consumer against extreme jumps in the price of oil, through gradual and moderate increases in prices; this was also achieved without the shortages and the queues at service stations seen in Europe and the United States.

Among all the OECD countries, Canada also had a most enviable record in the area of energy conservation. Canada had the most comprehensive energy conservation program of any country in the world and it quickly showed its effectiveness. It covered residential housing, industry, transportation and the government sector. While this program entailed significant subsidies, the savings in energy consumption and costs for Canadians have been tremendous and those savings continue to take place every year, as a result, for instance, of the Canadian Home Insulation Program of the seventies and eighties.

As to energy substitution, federal and provincial government programs encouraged the replacement of oil by natural gas, electricity, and other forms of energy, wherever it made economic sense. The subsidized extension of gas pipelines in Ontario and Quebec opened new markets for Canadian gas, as well as reducing fuel oil imports. The lack of increases in oil prices, however, made the projected extension to the Maritimes unrealistic and it had to be abandoned—all the more so after the Sable Island discoveries opened up the possibility of a source to serve the Maritimes and the northeastern United States.

As to Canadianization of the industry, the goal of 50 percent Canadian ownership by 1990 was a realistic one. By 1984 we were well on our way to achieving it. That figure had gone from 26.2 percent of the industry in 1979 to 41.3 percent in 1984. This goal had such broad national support that the subsequent Conservative government had to endorse it, even though its pursuit of it seems to have been lackadaisical.

The pricing arrangements made under the NEP and the EPTA protected consumers from sudden increases in oil prices while allowing the industry to charge near-international prices for nonconventional oil and to move relatively quickly to international price levels for conventional oil. Tax incentives and grants also encouraged the industry to pursue aggressive exploration and development programs. Unfortunately for the industry, during the last few years, it is not the Canadian price that has moved up but the international price that has moved down.

The 1974–84 period was one of major new discoveries and projects: oil and gas discoveries in the Arctic and offshore; the construction of mammoth oil sands plants; heavy oil projects; the extension of pipelines in Canada and to the United States; and the creation of Petro-Canada, the largest Canadian-owned integrated oil company, which ensured that exploration on Hibernia was continued and which was able to compete with foreign multinationals that practically owned the Canadian market.

Finally, the NEP established a modern, sensible land-management regime—the Canada Oil and Gas Lands Administration (COGLA)—for the Canada lands, and the fundamentals of that regime are still in effect today. With the decline in oil and gas prices, industry interest in the Canada lands has waned to some extent, but as prices rebound, exploration and development activities will surge again. Applications have already been put before the National Energy Board for the exportation of huge quantities of natural gas from the Mackenzie Delta. The Arctic and the eastern offshore still contain Canada's largest reserves of conventional oil and gas. If the COGLA is allowed to play its full role as these areas are developed, the national interest will be protected—and this in the broadest sense: environmental protection, windfall profits for native and other proximate communities, Canadian participation.

All this being said, it is a point of lasting regret to me that Alberta's sense of alienation deepened almost immediately after the introduction of the NEP and to some extent persists to this day in spite of the fact that a mutually satisfactory agreement was reached between Alberta and Ottawa in September 1981 and that close co-operation continued subsequently. Yet the battle for the hearts and minds of Albertans was probably lost from the start. There are substantial tactical disadvantages whenever the federal government tries to argue a case of national benefit against the government of a province which is particularly affected by a new policy. Coming from Quebec, I can certify that that situation is not exclusive to Alberta. It was inevitable that there would be substantial criticism from Alberta when the federal government endeavoured to redistribute large amounts of wealth from that province where the oil and gas industry was heavily concentrated. I am sorry, however, that we could not persuade Albertans that the NEP had sufficient national merit to warrant their support and endorsement.

After the NEP

What has been accomplished since 1984 to compare with the record of the preceding period? The main development in recent years under the Conservative regime has been the abdication of sovereignty in the energy field contained in the Canada-U.S. Free Trade Agreement that came into effect on January 1, 1989. For the first time in our country's history, we have embraced a continental energy policy. According to excellent U.S. administration sources, the provisions on energy contained in the Agreement were included mostly at the instigation of the Canadian government, which wanted to prevent future Canadian governments from resorting to nationalist energy policies. There must be few countries in the world where a government can see virtue in tying itself to a foreign power because it does not trust its electorate and future Parliaments to make decisions in the national interest.

As to the Conservative commitment to Canadianization, it is questionable. After having reached a high of 48.2 in 1985, the percentage of Canadian ownership will likely fall to the low forties in 1990 (see Figure 2). As to the important upstream sector alone, the situation is even more worrisome, Canadian control having gone from 47.9 percent in 1985 to 37.6 percent in 1988, a decline of 10.3 percent in merely three years.

Meanwhile, the average wellhead price of Canadian oil in 1988 was lower than it was in 1982. In spite of the fact that the industry has been receiving a larger share of the pie than ever, the total number of wells drilled between 1985 and 1989 has not been significantly higher than between 1981 and 1985. In fact, the total number of wells drilled was lower in 1986 than at any time during the eighties. And that was at a time when the federal minister of energy, mines and resources was boasting across the country that she had done away with the "ravages" of the NEP. In the last three years for which we have figures (1986-88), the total number of wells drilled barely surpassed the number drilled during the first three years of the NEP (1981-83), (21,215 vs. 20,423) and the average drilling rig utilization during those later years was significantly lower than in the period 1981-83 (38.2 percent vs. 48.3 percent), indicating a significant excess capacity. In addition, a recent report indicated that for the first six months of 1989, large oil and gas companies involved in recent acquisitions drilled about 70 percent fewer wells than in the first half of 1988.[5]

Yet we hear no outcry from the industry that it is being "decimated." The experience of the last few years has no doubt brought a good dose of realism to the industry and has tempered the outlandish expectations that prevailed in the oil patch in 1979-1980. This new mood was reflected on a Calgary bumper sticker that was popular a few years ago. It said, "Oh God, give me another oil boom; I promise I will not piss it away."

But current government policy does not reflect that mood. The prevailing attitude seems to be that oil and gas supplies are virtually endless.

In the United States, domestic crude oil production is at a lower level than at any time since the sixties, and imports are nearly back to the high levels of 1975-1976. Meanwhile,

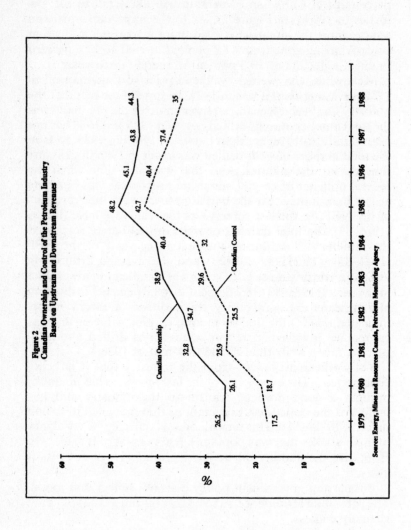

Figure 2
Canadian Ownership and Control of the Petroleum Industry
Based on Upstream and Downstream Revenues

Source: Energy, Mines and Resources Canada, Petroleum Monitoring Agency

Americans are buying more and more gas guzzlers. The International Energy Agency is forecasting increases of about 1 percent a year in oil consumption in all Western countries. As stated recently by the U.S. energy secretary, American vulnerability to oil-supply disruptions is greater today than it was at the time of the 1973 oil embargo. The energy provisions of the Canada–U.S. Free Trade Agreement put us exactly in the same boat as the Americans, and Ottawa's motto is, "Let us sell off everything we can," without any consideration for future Canadian needs. There is black humour in the scene of the Conservative government getting Parliament to enact on December 23, 1988, a specific provision excluding water (a renewable resource of which we have ample supply) from the application of the Canada–United States Free Trade Agreement Implementation Act, while in the same Act it hands over to the Americans our current and future oil and gas reserves (by definition nonrenewable resources with finite supply), by guaranteeing them an access to those reserves equal to that of Canadians.

We have the makings of another energy crisis before the end of this century. Meanwhile, Canada and the rest of the Western world are "pissing away" the period of grace given to them by the increased oil supply and lower prices of the eighties.

CHAPTER 3

Canadian Industrial Policy in a Changing World

———————— by Joel Bell ————————

Joel Bell served as an advisor to several departments and agencies of the federal government over a period of ten years, latterly as Economic Advisor to the Prime Minister. Subsequently, Mr Bell was Executive Vice-President of Petro-Canada and President and Chief Executive Officer of Canada Development Investment Corporation.

All governments, even those preoccupied with nonindustrial matters, recognize the fundamental importance of industrial success in maintaining high employment levels and standards of living and in creating wealth with which to pursue other interests. They also learn very quickly, if they do not start out with such an awareness, just how central these factors are to the political success and survival of a government. The Trudeau government was no exception. Early on, it identified industrial issues as an area in which it would like to make an impact. It initiated a series of high-profile programs in regional development, foreign investment and competition and made efforts to devise an "industrial strategy."

Industrial policy consists of more than a few prominent initiatives, however. It is made up of the combined influences of a great number of general and specific policies and programs: tax incentives; commercial or trade policy; government programs; policies affecting capital markets, science and technology; procurement practices; manpower training; and such key sectors as energy, resources, housing, agriculture, transportation, communications, culture and defence. All of these combine to mobilize large sums of money and to influence the structure and performance of an industrial economy.

This essay can only give an overview of the industrial setting in which the Trudeau government operated, a very brief description of the government's policy responses and a preliminary assessment of the extent to which those policies fulfilled the government's objectives.

___The Industrial Economy of the Late 1960s_____

The Canadian economy has always been heavily dependent on the country's rich store of natural resources, an emphasis that has been heightened by Canadian industrial policies, including tax policy and provincial practices in making Crown-owned or -controlled resources available for exploitation. Based on these activities, our relatively small population has enjoyed a high standard of living but has also felt limited pressure to generate indigenous, technology-based industries. This narrow base and the volatility of world prices for resources has made our economy vulnerable, and over a period of decades leading up to 1968, the prices paid for resources relative to technology-based goods and services had eroded. (OPEC-type energy price run-ups that occurred later are aberrations.) Economies like those of Germany and Japan, which focused more on technology and related manufacturing, had fared better than those of countries like Canada.

The context for Canadian industrial development was quite different from that of many of the countries to which we might compare our progress. We lacked the large local market of some. We were facing the loss of the British preferential tariff for Commonwealth countries which had benefited our manufacturing to a certain extent. And a high level of protectionism still existed.

We did not have the low labour costs that had given a number of countries their start; the wealth that had been developed in Canada had originated largely in resources; and the capital pools that we did possess lacked experience in and the traditions of risk taking in manufacturing and technology – with a few exceptions, such as the ones behind agricultural machinery and pulp and paper manufacturing. In common with our neighbours to the south, we faced a need to restructure and modernize some of our traditional industries – such as clothing, steel, automobiles and farm machinery—as new products were entering the market from recently emerging, lower-cost sources.

While some suggested that Canadians were not as willing to take investment risks as the savers in other countries, the shortfall lay more in the fact that our wealth pools were more limited and younger, and as just noted, inexperienced in manufacturing. Even some of our resource successes had historically produced their wealth results outside the country for colonial or foreign investors. We continued to experience a uniquely high level of foreign ownership for an advanced country, a fact which by this time was causing public concern.

In addition, the regional disparities caused by the historic location of industry were increasingly being seen as "unfair."

Meaningful changes in our industrial situation would occur only with the stimulation of our private industrial sector. However, our past history meant that change would have to occur in the face of challenges that were different (and greater) than those faced by the successful manufacturing economies to which we like to compare ourselves.

When the Trudeau government came to power in 1968, it expected further challenges to our limited manufacturing base through the reduction of the protection afforded by distance- and policy-based trade barriers—both changes being driven in good part by modern technology as policy pressures would build to respond to new technological realities. Already, only a small number of the new jobs being generated in our economy were in manufacturing, the trade deficit was actually worsening and our productivity gains were not strong compared to those of other industrial countries. However, our success in manufacturing and higher-value services would be important to our future prosperity.

The Need for Change

Holding our own in the face of the challenges to our manufacturing sector would require structural changes—that is, changes in the kind or organization of manufacturing that would locate in Canada.

Manufacturing activity occurs in a particular location because of a new idea or technology; a need to get around the problems of distance or policy barriers; or low costs of production. Each of these reasons represents a later stage in the life cycle of a product and involves lower margins. Canada had few examples of newly developed technology and was not a low-cost environment.

Much of our manufacturing had been based on foreign-developed products, frequently introduced into Canada through foreign-owned subsidiaries that had located in Canada for the second reason. These "branch plant" operations often had no responsibility for ongoing product development or process modernization, and this reduced their control over their own futures. They were also less likely to pursue additional export markets (where they might compete with the parent or an affiliate) or to seek out Canadian sources for the goods and services they required for their operations. Furthermore, Canadian branch plants often produced too wide a range of products or models to be efficient in comparative international terms. Without changes, they would be vulnerable to the more open and competitive world environment that was expected.

It became a priority for the new Trudeau government to examine the ingredients of industrial and particularly manufacturing success: the development of applied technology (including manufacturing-process technology for cost competitiveness) and product innovation; capital pools and intermediation to support the needed investment; market access to permit Canadian production to reach minimum economies of production scale and support research and development, with the prospect of a large enough market to recapture the front-end risk investment; and rationalization of production in Canada and between Canada and other markets, to permit competitiveness and to ensure that a fair share of the activities and benefits of industrial activity went to Canadians. On the resource front, costs of raw-material extraction would continue as the dominant factor, but it would be worthwhile to attempt to have the foreign barriers to upgraded products reduced and to insist on such further activity as was viable and realistic in Canada. Services, or at least the higher-value ones, would continue to depend heavily on the requirements of local industry or the demands of a higher-income population.

The overall picture, while one of concern, was by no means all bleak. The domestic market and local resources had generated success in a few manufacturing sectors, such as agricultural machinery, pulp and paper manufacturing and steel—even though some restructuring would be necessary to meet new competition. Public policy had helped support several notable ventures:

- Northern Telecom had prospered with the help of public policy, which gave its parent company, Bell Canada, a monopoly position and therefore protected its market.
- The Autopact, a free trade deal, allowed for rationalized production but also contained conditions negotiated with the U.S. government and the auto industry to ensure a reasonable level of Canadian production in the sector—even if it did not secure product development in the country.
- Government or directed procurement grants and loans and directed foreign aid had permitted many firms to capitalize on local market needs or to build on a shared-risk basis, to achieve competitive industrial performance, including performance in high-technology fields. The Canadian operations of many familiar names had benefited from these programs: CAE, Canadian Marconi, Bombardier, Lavalin, SNC, Pratt and Whitney, McDonnell-Douglas, IBM and Michelin are a few examples.

Governments of all stripes in Canada (as was the case in many other countries facing similar needs) had established Crown corporations and participated in a "mixed" economy, not for reasons of political philosophy, but for pragmatic reasons—to help a small economy undertake the large projects considered necessary for high living standards.

Although Canadian capital markets were concentrated and not always as accessible to small or venturesome projects as might have been desired, savings in Canada were high, producing adequate funds in the aggregate to handle all our requirements in the years immediately preceding Trudeau's first government. The gap lay in "industrial intermediation," whereby the risk capital is brought together with the technology, production skills and management expertise needed to launch a project (particularly in the manufacturing field) and a market around which to justify the development. Our pools of capital of any size (apart from those in financial institutions) were few and focused on resources, transportation and real estate, not manufacturing, and, as in the case of U.S. business, they were focused on performance against short-term measures. But there were savings and, as a result, investment funds in the country. In fact, the foreign industrial companies were able to make use of Canadian capital markets for a good deal of their funding.

___ Foreign Practices _____

Historically, many countries had placed a strong emphasis on domestic industrial development by erecting protective trade barriers and/or, increasingly, by using positive support methods. The political and social commitment of these countries to industrial development was such that much of the government-funded activity did not have to meet the test of financial returns, at least not against short-term measures. For instance, the U.S. targets of putting a man on the moon or defending the country were not tested on rate-of-return measures. The postwar reindustrialization activities of Japan and Germany were also dominant national purposes which escaped cost-benefit measures. These were tough competitive challenges to meet.

To cite a few facts from a longer and continuing list of examples:

- Half of all R&D spending in the U.S. continued to come from government; public or publicly assisted procurement and tax-free municipal bonds also produced significant advantages.
- Japan had long been mobilizing government and corporate funds for R&D and product development in targeted areas: protecting domestic markets for its own companies; encouraging new manufacturing processes (by absorbing, for

instance, virtually all the risk on new robotics initiatives); tying certain of its foreign investments to Japanese procurement; and using domestic demand to secure significant new manufacturing commitments from would-be suppliers (e.g., aircraft). Beginning as a "copier" environment after the war, it quickly moved beyond that stage.

- In Europe, governments combined to put massive support behind major industrial developments such as the Airbus aviation initiative, joint military aircraft development and the European space agency. Norway tied some North Sea oil permits to unrelated industrial commitments. France put considerable national support behind the development of the Concorde, the high-speed train and a computer industry, favoured "chosen" corporate vehicles in procurement to ensure their development and tied some oil imports to certain high-technology exports. German governments made equity investments to develop a petrochemical sector and the aircraft industry. Some of these efforts represented poorly spent monies on such struggling industries as steel and shipbuilding, but increasingly the focus became the technology gap, which was of significance to a more forward-looking selection of industries, and the restructuring or adjustment out of poorly performing sectors. Initiatives at the level of the European Economic Community have been concentrated in the area of research and development and in selected sectors of future importance.

While no assurances of profitable results can be given for research and related product development expenditures, it is not by accident that the economies in which R&D grew substantially in the 1960s and 1970s (doing so as it happens with government support) experienced dramatic industrial growth in the 1980s (Japan, Germany and France), while those that stalled have lost ground comparatively (the U.S. and the U.K.). Joint public-private ventures and spending through private firms were frequently the chosen routes, thereby mobilizing additional funds alongside the public-sector support, helping to test the industrial practicality of an expenditure and increasing the discipline and industrial spinoff of successes. In some cases, the government was itself the buyer; in others, the venture identified a market opportunity, perhaps with the help of government policy and protection, to ensure a market for the resulting product or service.

Before and during the first Trudeau administration, there were also indications that the U.S. was acting to deal with its own problems, which served to remind Canada that it should not rely on U.S. friendship to carry it through the emerging international environment:

- Oil imports from Canada were resisted periodically in the years prior to the early 1970s, in order to support local producers. With effort, some exemption was obtained, because the United States recognized that Canadian supplies would be part of their long-term security.
- Uranium imports were blocked in 1964.
- An interest-equalization tax was established in 1963 and Canada had to seek and secure an exemption, pointing out that U.S. entities would be hurt if the exemption were not put in place and promising supportive behaviour on capital movements.
- In August 1971 "Nixon Economics" resulted in an import surtax, a tax-related export incentive to recapture some foreign branch production, new countervail measures and the claim that we should reduce our manufactured goods exports to them, despite our substantial current account deficit when services were included.

These were not unfriendly, anti-Canadian moves on the part of the United States. They were simply national responses reflecting their view of the new industrial setting and the fact that their own problems were making the country less capable of accommodating Canadian interests, despite a good bilateral relationship.

Once again, certain conclusions were reinforced:

1. Neo-classical economics, which are based on the market system, would not alone explain the industrial performance of countries like Japan and Sweden. Similarly, American

defence and space activities were outside that economic model. Governments were influencing the pattern of industrial development and location.

Canada would need to deal with this type of competition in international negotiations and establish its pragmatic responses in the meantime.

2. Since the leading exports of a country are a reasonable measure of its strengths, the impact of the "protectionist" practices of foreign governments was evident in the fact that their leading exports were dominated by industries that had received the benefit of government policy and financial support.

If we were to participate in the growing value of manufacturing and services, we needed to stimulate domestic technological capacity, not only to develop Canadian innovations for industrial spinoffs, but also to make timely and effective use of technology to which we could gain access through international sources. Our R&D would best be linked to industry to ensure practicality, industrial implementation, market relevance and market access for the results.

3. While U.S.-Canada trade and industrial links would dominate, our economy would benefit from international market access and dealings with the emerging industrial strengths of Europe and the Pacific.

___ Policy Responses _____

1. Taxes, Grants and Loans

In an effort to increase investment in manufacturing and processing, corporate taxes were reduced and write-offs were introduced. The same response was used to encourage R&D. Later, the Scientific Research Tax Credit, for instance, was implemented in an attempt to carry this approach further and make the benefits of the general R&D tax incentives available to entities that were willing to invest but not currently taxable and to draw on general private investment funds for the support of work on technology. Although the idea behind this credit was good, it was badly flawed in its implementation. Abuses were committed by entities that claimed the benefits but were not later accountable for the performance of the research. Tax credits were also used in slow-growth and high-unemployment regions, as well as in some key industries (including resources, housing and culture). Some of these credits, when combined with other tax provisions, proved too generous, blunting good investment judgment by providing a large enough tax saving to render investments profitable to the taxpaying investor regardless of their fundamental merits or results. Tax measures succeeded in directing far more financial support to targeted activity than did the more visible direct spending and grant programs.

With international economic slowdown came a reduction in corporate liquidity and limits on the capacity of companies to act aggressively when growth opportunities returned. Efforts were made through the tax system to reduce the impact of these phenomena, to cushion the damaging effects of inflation on corporate finances and overall savings and to encourage equity investment (including interest deductibility for share acquisitions to encourage Canadian purchases). Savings to support investment needs were also very much encouraged through tax measures. Together the strategies represent a reasonably strong supply-side support.

Grant and loan programs were used to advance industrial projects, partly because they assisted firms that could not make use of tax incentives as they were not currently taxable and partly because the grants and loans could be less costly if focused on a particular project. Export financing support, as well as new-venture or product-development and industry-modernization programs like the one directed at the pulp and paper industry in the 1970s, are examples of expenditures made in response to a situation which required competitive governmental assistance to bolster an important Canadian industrial position or opportunity. While any mix of investment decisions will produce a range of results, some of the prominent survivors in industry today were beneficiaries of such funding.

2. Trade Barriers

Trade barriers were considerably reduced in the process of securing larger markets and pursuing rationalization. The first step in this area was the implementation of the Kennedy

Round of the General Agreement on Tariffs and Trade (GATT) implemented in the early years of the government. Under this round, negotiated by the preceding government, Canada had reduced barriers by less than its trading partners, and in the early 1970s the government undertook some unilateral reduction, induced in large part by an effort to reduce inflation, which in fact went a good deal of the way in catching up with the other countries. The government also introduced a program to remit import tariffs in situations where the companies involved were entering into international rationalization arrangements with foreign affiliates. The government went into the Tokyo Round of 1974 to 1979 giving strong support to further tariff reductions, making a concerted effort to reduce barriers on upgraded resources and actively promoting the first major effort at the reduction of nontariff barriers, which had taken on increasing importance among the new forms of protectionism that were arising in a lower-tariff world.

These initiatives provide some evidence that the Trudeau government would have preferred to remove market distortions caused by the intervention of governments around the world than to compete by introducing interventionist countermeasures of its own. Given Canada's relative size and clout in international terms, the country would be at a disadvantage if it had to compete on support measures with determined countries like the U.S. and Japan and the emerging European community, which were willing to dedicate substantial resources and use potent tools in the industrial cause.

When the government took office in 1968, the average tariff on all Canadian imports was 16 percent. By 1987, which corresponds to the end of the phasing-in of the tariff reductions that were agreed to during the Tokyo Round, the average tariffs on all imports had been reduced to 4 to 5 percent. Looking at dutiable products only, on a trade weighted average, the protection was 9 to 10 percent by 1987, compared with 15 percent in 1979 and 22.5 to 25 percent in 1968. On the export side, the average tariff on dutiable Canadian exports to the United States was 5.7 percent by 1987, with the average on all manufactured goods being 4 percent (some of the manufactured goods were duty-free: automotive products, aircraft, engines and parts). Raw materials were also duty-free. Exports from Canada to the European Economic Community faced a 4 to 7 percent barrier, with 40 percent being duty-free (primarily industrial materials in their least processed form).

Late in the mandate, discussions were initiated with the United States on sectoral free trade—to permit rationalization in combination with the appropriate domestic or bilateral arrangements to support growth in a particular sector. These discussions were to address government-support programs on each side of the border in a practical manner. It was felt that this would produce the market benefits without establishing a U.S.-Canada "bloc" approach, as this might prejudice the multilateral initiatives that the Canadian government favoured over regional international groupings. A U.S.-Canada bloc might also prejudice Canada's independent dealings with the emerging industrial strengths in Europe and the Pacific. Other countries were welcome to join in any particular sectoral discussions that were relevant to them.

This sectoral free trade initiative failed for several reasons. First, the government had too little time left in its mandate to follow it through. Second, the United States would have its price in terms of the sectors or issues to which it attached priority but which would pose problems for Canada and force a broader negotiation (e.g., entertainment, U.S. investment and pharmaceutical patents). Finally, within the government, views differed as to whether this largely bilateral initiative was compatible with the desire to progress on multilateral trade initiatives. In all, however, the government was an early and continuing advocate of the level international playing field (on a multilateral and bilateral basis), and it moved Canada some distance along the path to a freer trading environment.

The Trudeau government saw trade policy as the servant of industrial objectives and not as an end in itself. It was not a substitute for an effective industrial policy that would support Canadian performance in the more open but competitive relationship among industrial nations.

It is noteworthy that the Free Trade Agreement subsequently worked out with the U.S. included a five-to-seven-year deferral of the very important question of industrial development practices—the modern protectionism of industrial policy.

Neither did it give Canadian suppliers access to much of the U.S. defence sector—a sector that is the principal American vehicle for supporting industrial development and to which access would have provided an important manufacturing and technology stimulus for Canada. At the same time, Canada's negotiating strengths (access to its resources and the policy concessions sought by the U.S.) were included.

3. Research and Development

To advance its policies on science and technology, the government established the Ministry of State for Science and Technology in 1971. It encouraged all government ministries to turn their attention to this subject and helped co-ordinate their efforts.

During the 1970s, a considerable amount of government-funded research was contracted out to the private sector, but this stagnated somewhat in the 1980s. The Department of Communications also carried out research alone and in co-operation with industry as part of an industrial development mandate in this sector of the future.

The results of these R&D and technology objectives were mixed. Specific success stories can be cited, but the aggregate spending on R&D as a proportion of GDP fell well short of the dedication shown by our trading partners. While the successful countries now allocate 2.5 to 3 percent of their Gross Domestic Product to research and development (Japan is now targeting 3.5 percent), Canada reached between 1 and 1.5 percent during the Trudeau years. (The level has actually fallen since.)

The record of the industrial application of programs that were successful in government laboratories is also spotty. Although some results were helpful to certain private industrial initiatives where co-operation developed (such as Spar working with the Department of Communications lab), others (such as Telidon in the same department) languished in government bureaucracies or did not contain the essential ingredient of market access.

Joint efforts of government and business on the R&D front and the commitment of the most senior people in both sectors to such efforts characterize the more successful examples in other countries, but with a few exceptions, this kind of co-operation seems to elude Canada.

4. Regional Development

Regional development, dealt with in a separate essay, led to substantial funds being allocated to industrial installations – and a constant tension between the efficiency dictates of industrial development and the price to be paid for a more even regional distribution of activity. In the end, however, the government came to feel that projects were being carried out whose justification lay too much in the virtue of their regional location and not enough in their industrial logic. In the final analysis, this regional focus did reduce the disparities in infrastructure across the country – but made little real impact on income-level disparities. Future researchers will have to determine whether the gap might have widened in the absence of these efforts.

5. Government Purchases

Procurement was used in defence, transportation and communications – perhaps not as widely or as well as might have been possible – to support the establishment of Canadian capacities. One notable and successful initiative was the purchase of Canada's first communications satellite (ANIK I). The foreign supplier, Hughes, was required to take on a Canadian partner in that project and to transfer the technology to the partner, so that the Canadian firm could develop a second generation of technology and lead the next bid to supply Canada with a communications satellite. With this and other government support and co-operation from the Department of Communications lab, Spar Aerospace became this partner. Spar was able to take on the role of lead company in the next project and to work around the world, first with Hughes and later on its own.

6. Other Initiatives

There is much in the area of industrial initiatives by the Trudeau government which space prevents this essay from addressing: industrial spinoffs from energy policy, resource upgrading, use of oil and gas for petrochemical developments, support of the cultural industries, efforts in capital markets and intellectual property (patents, copyright and trademarks).

However, before turning to certain prominent industrial policy initiatives, it should be observed that some of the policies touched on just briefly here went through different phases involving changes that were confusing for the business community. Research and development, for example, was initially supported primarily through the tax system. Then the government used grants for a part of the incentive, only to revert again to a tax-delivered support as it tried to find the key to a more effective stimulus.

At the same time, the pursuit of other legitimate social objectives gave rise to regulatory burdens and distortions in the industrial area that were not always as efficient or as reconciled with industrial objectives as they could have been. The government tried to deal with some of these complaints by establishing co-ordinating ministries aimed at reconciling and simplifying the various policies and programs.

This "rational" policy analysis must also be tempered by acknowledgement of the realities that face every government—dealing with industrial crises not of their own making, provincial project initiatives, and companies confronting government with the choice of financial support or closure. Not every specific decision to support a venture or company would be seen to fit neatly into the policy aims summarized here. Some proved to be good decisions, some produced disappointing results and others were regrettable, probably even in the view of those who made them. (These were sometimes failures of the political process more than of the policy, if one can separate them in such cases.) It is easy in a political setting to remember the mistakes and forget the successes—the government had both.

_____ Prominent Policy Initiatives _____

A little more attention should be given to a few significant industrial policy initiatives with which the Trudeau government is identified: competition policy, foreign investment policy, Canada Development Corporation (CDC) and Canada Development Investment Corporation (CDIC) and the attempt to develop an "industrial strategy."

1. *Competition*
The government proposed early in its term to remove the criminal behavioural focus of the Combines Investigation Act and replace it with an economic performance test of acceptable transactions, to be administered by a specialized tribunal.

Transactions such as mergers and rationalization agreements that would improve efficiency were to be allowed—provided only that these improvements would make it through to the market in the form of lower prices than otherwise or that they would result in the survival of a business that would otherwise fail. Arrangements that allowed a Canadian company to have market domination or even a domestic monopoly could be justified in cases where the company could point to current or poised foreign competition that would provide enough competition to protect Canadian customers from unfair treatment. The company seeking to gain a domestic monopoly could propose a Canadian tariff reduction on competing foreign imports to strengthen its argument in this area.

This line of thinking represented a sharp departure from the past Canadian and contemporary U.S. thinking that had long dominated the field, according to which percentages of market share were far more important factors for determining acceptability or illegality. It can be understood in light of the earlier discussion of the perceived need for improved efficiency, international competitiveness and rationalization. It would, however, involve a different kind of governmental scrutiny and, in the eyes of the business community, an excessive one. Business was not confident that the policy would have permitted the pragmatic business responses to market challenges that it was intended to make possible.

This shift to economic performance principles was not implemented immediately, but did gradually enter the competition legislation in stages over a period of several years. Experience with this more economics-oriented approach is only now being built up.

2. Foreign Investment

When the government came to office, foreign control was high, having reached 58 percent of manufacturing, 65 percent of mining and smelting, 64 percent of oil and gas production, 95 percent of rubber products and 99 percent of petroleum and coal products. Furthermore, one-third of all corporate capital in Canada was governmental, one-third private Canadian and one-third foreign (80 percent of that being held by residents of a single country—the United States). The government's analysis was that the country would not have been well served simply by blocking foreign investment, but it was true that foreign subsidiaries often, but not always, acted differently from their Canadian-owned counterparts or Canadian-based multinational companies in such areas as product development, exports and procurement. Many of the foreign-owned subsidiaries did not benefit fully from their involvement in an international structure, since rationalization often did not occur. Overall, Canada did not attract as great a share of the total spinoff or proceeds available from an industrial activity as was believed possible—and best for Canadians.

The purpose of any policy response was not to make a moral judgment on a company's foreignness, and in fact, the government continued to extend its full industrial support policies and programs to all companies, regardless of their ownership. The objective was to achieve a more rational and healthier industrial structure, the superior performance that sensible international integration could provide and prospects for future development on that base.

As a result, the means chosen was that of negotiating with the foreign proponents of "significant" takeovers and new investments to achieve these results in individual cases. The government's bargaining position lay in its ability to offer the applicant access to a reasonably lucrative Canadian market. The "world product mandate," or the more complete scope of activity for Canadian subsidiaries, that FIRA sought from such deals, would, of course, make for a different split of the activities and spinoffs of the undertaking between its home and the Canadian industrial environment and was intended to help deal, for Canada's benefit, with the reality of pressures being exerted elsewhere by governments for more of these activities to be undertaken in their jurdisdictions. If FIRA was successful, Canada would see more jobs, more technology, lower costs and a more secure industrial future.

It was the intention that the government would involve itself in the important cases where a lot was at stake and where it could hope to make a difference, as well as in sensitive sectors such as the cultural industries and certain technologies and resources. FIRA was also expected to learn why the activities or structure it sought in particular cases were not readily achievable and to give the government advice on policy changes or things it could do to make it economically possible and realistic for the company and the industry to perform as hoped. This input, over time, would be used to shape pragmatic industrial policies and practices and to influence industrial programs as well – a sort of series of Autopacts. In combination with the range of industrial policies noted earlier, it was hoped that new Canadian players and existing operations would grow to be significant, world-competitive entities.

In fact, the administration of the policy failed to meet these two objectives. It failed to simply record and pass over the cases of minor significance. The legislation provided broader technical coverage in order to allow FIRA to secure information and find the sensitive cases – but the government envisaged automatic approval after notice had been given by the company to the agency in the greatest number of cases – in much the same way that U.S. anti-trust notification operated. In practice, however, FIRA's administration negotiated almost every case, causing unnecessary antagonism and excessive delay – and a raising of the thresholds did very little to correct the problem.

As for the use of negotiations to influence industrial policies and programs, the administrators of the Agency wanted no part of this more complicated process and chose to adhere to a narrow fulfilment of their legislative mandate. An opportunity was missed.

It would be interesting to see some research analyzing whether the managements of foreign subsidiaries in Canada made use of FIRA's review to pursue opportunities they wanted to promote with their head offices; whether superior structures for Canadian performance and benefits resulted; and whether Canadian entrepreneurs were able to capture opportunities that would not have been available to them if the investment review legislation had not existed.

By the time the government left office, foreign ownership levels had nonetheless changed. Likely as a result of both economic maturation and policy, the level of foreign control of nonfinancial Canadian corporate assets fell from 35.3 percent in 1968 to 23.8 percent in 1984, manufacturing declined from 58 to 44.1 percent, mining and smelting from 65 to 35 percent; oil and gas from 64 to 57 percent, rubber products from 95 to 92 percent, and petroleum and coal products from 99 to 59 percent.

3. Canada Development Corporation
and Canada Development Investment Corporation

The Canada Development Corporation (CDC) was created in 1971 to add another pool of industrial capital and capacity to the Canadian marketplace, with emphasis on manufacturing. Polymer, a Crown corporation, was transferred to CDC, marking the first significant privatization of a Crown industrial corporation when, shortly afterwards, as planned, shares of CDC were sold to the public.

CDC was to be a forward-looking company that instigated promising operations either as a joint-venture partner with industry or alone as a Canadian presence in important new industries. It was not to be a vehicle for buying back the past. The government understood that the corporation's ownership structure of private- and public-sector shareholders would preclude its use as a tool of industrial policy to respond to specific government concerns. It believed, however, that as the largest shareholder, it would have an open relationship with the company and benefit from the company's advice when it encountered specific industrial problems and needed some experienced views on the viability of a proposal. The CDC would not be looked to for funds where it did not see a strategic or commercial shareholders' interest for itself.

In fact, the relationship between the CDC and the government was very tense as the corporation feared too much government influence, despite assurances to the contrary, and its holdings evolved heavily into resources instead of manufacturing. Its heavy debt leveraging and problems with some of its acquisitions created further difficulties. The government was not an active shareholder; it left the company to make its strategic and financial decisions on its own. The CDC initiative had failed to live up to the government's expectations.

To resolve the tension, an agreement was reached in the spring of 1982 for the government to divest itself of this holding in a manner which was best for the corporation and its shareholders. CDIC was activated to handle this and certain other government industrial holdings when it became obvious that they required urgent attention as well.

One of these was Canadair, which for many years had been the principal airframe manufacturer in Canada, but whose U.S. parent, General Dynamics, was about to remove capacity and equipment from this facility in 1975 — for its own strategic reasons and as a result of changes in the industry from planes that Canadair could produce under licence to more sophisticated aircraft, which, as complete aircraft, were beyond the production capability of the company.

Canada is a significant market for aircraft, and offset (whereby some part of the value or components of Canadian government purchases from a foreign aircraft manufacturer had to be produced by Canadian operations) remained an active government policy tool. Canadair's Canadian management convinced the government in 1975 to purchase the company on the grounds that it was commercially viable in the hands of a shareholder that did not want to see it closed and that it could be resold before too long. Cut loose from its parent and their strategic and commercial disciplines, the management proposed a new strategy of designing and building an entire aircraft — a business jet, to be called the Challenger. The company projected a development cost of just over $106 million over a two-year period and a peak cash requirement, including tooling and production build-up, of some $128 million, to be reached one year later. The government's disappointment and anger was evident by late 1982 when these cash amounts crept up toward $1.5 billion, including interest, and the schedule stretched to six or seven years. The problem had not been communicated to the government in a timely way and something now had to be done urgently. CDIC was activated to deal with the situation. No comfort could be taken from the fact that this industry in other countries had gone through similar loss experiences and their governments had provided substantial financial support.

A similar situation had developed at de Havilland, where the government had funded a large part of the design of a new aircraft, the Dash 7, to follow on the success of de Havilland's Twin Otter. The parent, Hawker Siddeley of the U.K., had a commuter aircraft in design at home and concluded in 1974, when the Dash 7 was well into its development, that it did not want to proceed with the project. Once again, with commercial logic similar to that used in the case of Canadair, and supported by a Boeing study predicting an attractive market for the product, the government acquired the company in 1974 and continued the development. The Dash 7 was a technical success, but the predicted market did not materialize and the company turned its good design capacity to the Dash 8, on which it placed virtually all its hopes. The de Havilland plant had not been modernized for some time, so production costs were not particularly good. The cash requirements also mounted as the Dash 8 design and build-up had to be supported without the benefit of good cash flow from the Dash 7 or from earlier products whose principal markets had by then been satisfied. To complicate matters, the industry went into a deep cyclical trough as a result of the recession in the early 1980s. By late 1982 de Havilland was also in real difficulty and CDIC was given responsibility for the situation.

After the Canadair and de Havilland difficulties, the government concluded that its existing machinery had not worked to monitor its industrial investments, advise on the risks involved or control the companies as an active shareholder should. These two and other companies held by the government had strayed from commercial disciplines. Even businessmen on the boards of government companies seemed to feel that they should respond to more than commercial considerations once government was involved. The government, on the other hand, had participated in order to permit something of industrial importance to proceed – but according to commercial criteria.

CDIC was mandated in November 1982 to perform the monitoring task, ensure full public disclosure on an ongoing basis, correct the troubled situations, establish a commercial environment for these and other holdings transferred to its responsibility, establish a sense of direction for these companies under which they would have good value to a commercial shareholder and divest of them in a sound commercial way, consistent with the industrial purpose for which the commitment had originally been made. The government had become involved in shareholdings for what it believed to be good reasons at the time, but no one had the job of reviewing the need to continue to hold the investment or of promoting the idea of a sale—freeing up funds and permitting attention to be given to a new priority or requirement. CDIC was to fill this role.

In addition to the government's shares in CDC and the two aircraft companies, CDIC was given responsibility for other government holdings, for which there was no longer any policy need for government ownership (if such a reason had ever existed). Among these were Eldorado Nuclear Limited, Teleglobe Canada and Massey-Ferguson Limited. Eldorado had originally been acquired in wartime in light of the sensitivity of uranium and nuclear activity; Teleglobe had been purchased when the Commonwealth governments concluded after the war that international telecommunications should be government-controlled for security reasons; and a partial shareholding in Massey-Ferguson had been acquired in the early 1980s when the company would have faced bankruptcy without restructuring and refinancing. CDIC was expected to build up a capacity that would be available to government to handle future problems of this sort, which it was felt would inevitably arise. Its role was to advise, to help attract commercial partners (in order to minimize government costs and increase commercial or market tests of decisions), to hold and monitor, to report and to divest. The corporation would be well aware of government thinking, but it would operate in a commercial manner—deviating from this only in cases of written, public government instruction and specific funding.

The government did not have to wait long for the next CDIC assignment. The East Coast fisheries—like Chrysler and Massey-Ferguson a few years earlier—required restructuring and financing to survive. This led, in 1983, to the creation of Fisheries Products International in Newfoundland and a restructured National Sea Products in Nova Scotia and Pêcheries Cartier in Quebec.

CDIC made considerable progress on the first part of its mandate—returning Canadair to a profit by April of 1984, a profit that continued to increase. (Comparing pre-financing charge operating results, the company went from a loss of $25 to 30 million per month to a $1 million monthly profit by that date.) Losses at de Havilland were reduced considerably, and similar steps were taken with CDIC's other holdings. Strategic reviews were carried out with each company, evaluations done, divestiture plans prepared and discussions begun with prospective buyers.

The government felt that it had begun to rationalize its direct involvements in industry and to ensure a continuing reassessment of any involvement it did have, in order to provoke divestiture when policy reasons no longer required its participation or where, in nonpolicy involvements, it could dispose of its holdings and turn its attentions to new priorities. Whether the approach might reduce the involvements of government, diminish the number of situations in which it "backed into" those involvements and achieve more effective and financially disciplined participation remains only partially answered by the limited experience. The general direction was continued by the new government but through a CDIC that was at least for a time substantially cut back.

4. Industrial Strategy

The government's desire to develop an industrial strategy was precipitated by a number of factors: the maze of competing demands for government support of one kind or another in different industries; the fact of governments around the world intervening to capture their own shares of industrial activity and benefits—whatever their rhetoric; and the pressures to respond to various crises or to manage various support programs. All called out for some road map or industrial strategy. Some of the more successful countries did, in fact, selectively target certain industries for their support, for at least a period of time—not closing down the other industries but actively supporting some while leaving others to the vicissitudes of the marketplace. Concentrating limited resources in this way, especially in a middle-sized country that could not be all things to all people, had obvious appeal. Good investment strategies always involve selectivity.

As the effort progressed, the government had difficulty coming to grips with conflicting views. According to the one, the government's role was to foster a healthy economic environment that would be conducive to efficiency and competitiveness—domestically through sound macro or general economic policies and internationally by promoting freer trade, along with international economic co-ordination. Then it should stand back and let the marketplace work to produce competitive industrial activity in its jurisdiction. Direct involvement by government would be "reactive" to demands or problems.

According to the other view, the above action was necessary but not sufficient to do justice to the country's opportunities or to deal with the reality that governments around the world were making intense efforts to attract and support industrial activity within their borders. We needed techniques of our own, which was regrettable perhaps, but necessary. This view was not incompatible with the fact that market forces, inherent competitiveness and technology dictates would be the major determinants of industrial success. The debate was over the degree to which a well-analyzed, supportive effort of government could help develop an edge for some activities, sectors or firms. The majority of Trudeau's Cabinet ministers belonged to the second school of thought. In retrospect, it is apparent that the ingredients for an active plan were missing. In the oft-cited examples of Japan, Germany and the United States, conditions were different. Japan and Germany were caught up in the national will to rebuild a postwar economy, the U.S. in its commitment to defence and space. These phenomena had no counterparts in Canada, which would have led to a consensus and setting of priorities for particular industrial initiatives—certainly the esoteric appeal of an "industrial strategy" would not do that job.

In Canada the corporate sector did not share the desire to be focused on a few priorities as a way of achieving some new industrial progress—perhaps, in part, because much of our industry drew its costly technology and innovations from foreign corporate parents so that Canadian industrial generating or innovation capacity was not particularly important to product or corporate development. Canada could afford to be less selective or specialized if indigenous industrial development was not a prominent concern—we had the whole world to draw on.

Our government departments were largely reactive—responding to problems and backing into involvements, and consequently often dealing with the weak in our industries. It was hard to say "no" to a rescue in the absence of community confidence that new, sustainable activity was in the offing. Trade policy was far more important than industrial policy in such a context, as a means of both creating the desired market environment and affecting the way in which a company would deal with its parent and affiliates.

The government nevertheless went through a series of efforts on industrial strategy, looking variously at overall approaches to technology stimulation; the fostering of other key ingredients to industrial success such as risk capital, market access and industrial intermediation; and policies aimed at developing particular industrial sectors. It consulted extensively and built up a better data base than it ever had before on Canadian industry—along with a wish list from each sector for the support the government might give it to permit it to do more and for the ways in which government might reduce the constraints its various policies imposed on the freedom and action of business.

In pursuing the idea of developing an industrial strategy, the government was not seeking a centralized planning system by any stretch of the imagination—but it did not get what it was after: a sensible framework within which it could respond to requests for support and restructuring; a notion of where and how it might usefully concentrate or apply its muscle; a forward-looking alternative to backing into crisis responses, where money was being spent and government was getting involved or intervening in any event, but less constructively, it seemed. The business community, on the other hand, feared a more *"dirigiste"* strategy. It did not perceive or share the government's vision of risk-sharing joint efforts that would, through shared financial involvement, presumably be market-tested pursuits of commonly identified projects and priorities.

Canada also had to deal with the fact of a fragmented industrial policy setting—involving both federal and provincial governments. Interestingly enough, there is some evidence of a concerted approach in Quebec, which resolved to build a stronger economy and mobilized public resources. The Caisse de Dépôt et Placement du Québec, for instance, uses some part of the government's pension and insurance funds it manages, to support the development of Quebec-based business, and hydroelectric development was undertaken with clear preferences for local companies, which became world-class players with this experience behind them. Where the Quebec government has become involved, it has generally restricted itself to financial risk sharing and refrained from taking full ownership and operating responsibility.

Whether attempting to develop an industrial strategy was a wise and practical idea for Canada or not, the government's hopes in this area ended in frustration.

___ An Overview_____

The Trudeau government's assessment of the strengths and weaknesses of the domestic and international economies would appear to have been accurate. Governments around the world have continued to play an active role in trying to attract industrial activity in markets that have become more open and globalized through modern technology and the reduction of traditional trade barriers; technology has played an increasingly important role in industrial and income growth; and industrial strength is often found in sectors in which concerted efforts have been made by business and government working together.

The government believed that success would require an economy kept healthy through sound economic management and exposure to market forces, including those on the international level; supportive general or framework policies; and, where necessary or helpful, although not by preference or philosophical bent, a willingness on the part of government to go further and use more direct measures. In fact, the government did use direct measures where it saw no alternative, but preferred to reduce protectionism around the world through international negotiations to which it gave a new emphasis.

Too much direct involvement was undertaken in response to crises put to the government and in shoring up weaknesses. This contributed to a discrediting of governmental policies in industrial matters. These experiences demonstrate that government was a poor shareholder. Where its reason for participating is industrial development, the government should avoid situations where it has complete ownership and responsibility for operations, without the benefit of a business interest that is also at risk, to apply commercial standards to the investment and to watch over operations—an approach for which one might also find support in the Quebec experience.

On balance, the country held its own industrially through the turbulent and challenging world environment of the late 1960s to the early 1980s—not a bad comparative international performance—although it did not make any quantum leap forward. The period saw an energy crisis with sustained industrial spillover effects—a crisis with particular significance for Canada which, by reason of its geography, climate and industry mix, is energy-price sensitive. It saw a substantial reduction in trade barriers (to which Canada made a real contribution); the emergence of effective new competitors for many traditional North American industries; and a more rapidly changing technology environment—all challenges to holding one's position in industrial and manufacturing terms as a middle-sized economy with Canada's particular historical context. In fact, Canadian exports of finished manufactured goods (end products)—excluding edible items—nearly tripled in volume between 1971 and 1984. That was the largest relative increase of any sector in the Canadian economy by a significant margin. At the same time imports of manufactured goods increased considerably, without adversely affecting self-sufficiency in such items, thus demonstrating a significant increase in the specialization or rationalization of Canadian manufacturing production in international terms. And Canadian production of manufactured products rose between 1968 and 1984 from $42 billion to $230 billion—a rate which, in common with other developed nations, was not as high as that for services, but exceeded that of the primary or resource sector. Through this period, much of the manufacturing sector (e.g., steel, automobiles, commodity chemicals and many small businesses) would appear to have become confident and rationalized enough to support the Free Trade Agreement with the United States—something widely opposed in earlier times. Other sectors remained concerned about their readiness or the implications for their activities in Canada in comparison with ventures elsewhere (e.g., food, furniture, textiles and appliances).

In sum, not a bad performance, and results which do tie in with the targets the government set for itself – although everyone involved in the industrial economy and in government efforts in this area would understandably aspire to more.

The government may have started its term with too much faith in government industrial policies, but concluded its years in office with the view that wise government policy alone will not produce the desired results. At the same time, it felt that the evidence in Canada and around the world suggested that the marketplace alone, without deliberate government policy and involvement and the working together of government and business on common goals or projects, would also leave Canada with fewer tools than other countries have – and less than our potential share of industrial activity and benefits. Neither extreme would seem best for Canada. Mobilizing a national will and effort for industrial objectives would have to precede any dramatic advance, however, and that national will simply was not strong enough or stimulated sufficiently for that kind of advance to occur.

The industrial challenges that the Trudeau government faced have not gone away. The rivalry from the external environment is even stronger, Canada can increasingly be supplied from abroad, our R&D is falling as a proportion of GDP, our productivity improvement is low, labour costs per unit of output are actually rising and the challenges for Canadian companies to represent a reasonable share of the leadership of industry is evident in the spate of mergers which is internationalizing business structures.

The challenges will, furthermore, be faced in an economic and political climate that makes concerted action difficult. The competitive success of Japan and the newly industrialized countries and the lagging technology and manufacturing productivity of North American manufacturing in consumer goods in particular has caused serious and continuing trade and payments imbalances for the U.S. and Canadian economies. Oil-shock-inspired inflation, followed by dramatic worldwide monetary restraints and recession, combined with continuing public-sector spending (much of it under statutory support program provisions) generated entrenched deficits due to accumulated debts, which a sustained period of growth and some tax increases have not yet reversed.

These circumstances have limited the financial and policy capacity of government to respond to new challenges and damaged the credibility of public-sector responses. Globalization restricts the capacity of any one government to deal with some of the problems and pits our development against the best technology and lowest costs others can manage. The international industrial shifts have had very different impacts on different regions of the country, exacerbating regional tensions. However, reinforcing Canadian economic ties in the face of the stronger north-south forces under free trade is important if the country is to maintain the kind of national clout it needs to deal with global industrial competition and achieve goals that go beyond economics alone.

In addition, the Canada-U.S. Free Trade Agreement imposes certain constraints, along with its market-access benefits. Under the terms of the Agreement, it will be more difficult to draw preferentially on Canadian market demand in general and public-sector spending and procurement in particular, as a lever for developing Canadian technology and industry.

Nevertheless, the same conditions that make the environment a difficult one in which to act also increase the urgency of our need to stimulate the country's best private-sector industrial abilities and to back them with effective public-sector support. The lessons drawn from our experience should guide us in selecting better and more effective techniques for combining the efforts of industry and government in a strategy for competitiveness. The price of failure is too high.

CHAPTER 4

Global Transformation and Economic Policy

by Ian A. Stewart

Born in Toronto and trained as an economist at Queen's, Oxford and Cornell (Ph.D.), Ian Stewart, after teaching in the United States, joined the Bank of Canada in 1966. Entering the public service in 1972, he served in a number of capacities in various agencies, including Economic Advisor in the Privy Council Office and Deputy-Minister of Finance and of Energy, Mines and Resources. Retired from the public service since 1986, he currently advises, researches and writes from Ottawa.

THERE ARE GOOD reasons to feel a little intimidated when asked to contribute some thoughts on economic policy to a volume on the Trudeau years. It is a little early, perhaps, to attempt to write good history. It takes time for the welter of specific circumstances surrounding any act of public policy to be sifted and weighed, permitting a more balanced assessment of the forces in play.[1] Even more critical—the Trudeau years became years of global transformation. While this characterization of the period is generally accepted, no consensus has yet been reached on the relative importance of the forces which forged that transformation. Continuing contention about the issues not only influences assessments of the nature and importance of economic forces affecting the world, but also influences views about what might or ought to have been done about them.[2] All of this makes the task difficult enough, but for one who continues to feel constrained, even after retirement, by the canons of Westminster, which state that public servants should exercise considerable discretion in commenting upon political events, the task is even more formidable.

The post–World War II period had seen a broad consensus

on the structures and policies of national and international economic management, but this consensus dissolved under the influence of the economic shocks of the late sixties and early seventies, to be replaced by sharply diverging schools of economic thought. Economic contention, in turn, gave rise to increasing political tension. Monetarism, the new classicism, the new Keynesianism, supply-side-ism—all had their corresponding political movements in various shades of neo-conservatism and neo-liberalism. As new classical economists questioned the role of the state in economic theory, political theorists sought to apply the economist's model of self-interest to the behaviour of politicians and public servants and questioned the capacity of government to serve the public interest. This view was only reinforced, and economic expectations dashed, when it became publicly apparent that the governments of industrial countries were having more and more difficulty controlling economic events. Respect for the institutions and processes of government diminished. While the forces of reaction seem clearly not to have been as extreme in Canada as in some other countries, much of the period was nonetheless marked by political tension and contention. Inevitably, these tensions were translated into the stuff of party politics—which makes all of this uneasy territory for a former public servant to be writing about. However, a public servant's rendering of events, though of very summary structure in these pages, may assist those whose historical responsibility it will be to come to balanced assessments of the era.[3]

_____ A Little Pre-History _____

In 1968, there was scant indication that the Trudeau years would see economic shocks, the acceleration of global change and the collapse of what had become known as the Keynesian consensus. That consensus had extended licence to governments, not only to seek to manage full-employment policies, but to intercede more generally in the market economy to repair its failings and to redistribute incomes and wealth. After a period of turbulence around the turn of the decade, the Canadian economy and the industrial world had generally grown robustly and steadily throughout the sixties. With issues of stabilization and full employment apparently conquered, the government could turn its attention even more intently to the quality and regional distribution of growth, and the regional and personal distribution of its benefits in incomes and wealth.

Though these issues had not been ignored by previous governments, Canada had come rather late in the day to put the pillars of its social security structure in place. Only in the years immediately preceding the first Trudeau government did the Canadian federation finally come to the constitutional understandings and provincial agreements that allowed for the initiation of the Canada and Quebec Pension Plans, the addition of the Guaranteed Income Supplement to the Old Age Security system, the introduction of medicare to create a comprehensive health insurance system, the creation of the Canada Assistance Plan to share welfare assistance with the provinces and the movement towards the principle of sharing the costs of post-secondary education.

There was a need to consolidate these developments and supplement them with further initiatives. Canada's evolving version of the welfare state did not alter the fact that, despite the rapid expansion of redistributional effort, poverty remained deeply embedded. The Economic Council of Canada and the Senate's Croll Committee on Poverty were about to bring these issues into sharper public focus.[4] A royal commission on taxation—the Carter Commission, appointed by Prime Minister John Diefenbaker—had produced a radical report with a central focus on equity, evoking a strong reaction from the business community[5] and emphasizing the fact that some form of tax reform was essential. At the same time, extended prosperity sustained a nationalist focus on the control, ownership and repatriation of foreign-owned assets in Canada. And concerns for the developing world seemed to demand that at least some part of the product of these assets be used in the worldwide dispersion of the growth process.

New issues were also emerging, along with confidence that government policies would be set up to deal with them. The Canadian baby boom was beginning to disgorge its first members from the schools into the labour force with a consequent rise in youth unemployment rates and a growing concern, as in the United States, for the economics of "opportunity." With the enormous transfer from rural to urban occupation that had occurred during the postwar years, attention was turning to the problems of cities, municipalities and urban development. Rachel Carson's *Silent Spring*, published in 1962, had begun a process of environmental awareness that seemed to demand response.

In short, despite recent accomplishments, the menu of issues that the "Just Society" had to address remained a rich and extended one, and no intractable obstacles, other than the inherent difficulties of the issues themselves, seemed to stand in the way of their resolution.

___ 1968–1973: The Last of the Postwar Order _____

With the benefit of hindsight, it may be claimed that most of the signs of impending economic shocks were visible as early as 1968. Certainly inflation, which, aside from a sharp burst at the time of the Korean war, had remained at negligible levels throughout the postwar period, had begun an ominous creep upwards through the sixties and was now the cause of the most gnawing macroeconomic management worry. The growing American involvement in Vietnam might have suggested to the prescient that careless war finance would both add liquidity to the inflationary fires and fundamentally disturb the international financial order. It was, however, too early for anyone seriously to imagine that the falling real cost of energy that had underpinned the rapid real growth of the postwar period was about to be sharply reversed. The stirrings of technological change, centred around the computer, were beginning to be evident, but the revolution built around microelectronics was not yet in sight. The emergence of a tier of newly industrializing countries led by a resurgent Japan, though visible, had not yet threatened the hegemony of the United States and its Bretton Woods industrial partners. There had been some internal debate in Canada, even within the Liberal Cabinet, about the pace at which the functions and expenditures of the federal government were expanding, but little fundamental questioning of the directions of economic and social policy had taken place.

This is not to say that some of the early initiatives of the Trudeau period failed to take into account these intimations of strain. The predominant innovations in these years were structural in nature. Some were reflections of emerging stress, some of commitment to the Just Society. Of the former, particularly notable were the creation of the Farm Prices Review Board with a mandate to investigate and recommend price restraint, and its successor, the Prices and Incomes Commission, created to seek accommodation between conflicting business and labour interests. Both sought to alleviate inflationary pressures through rational analysis of their origins and consensual agreements aimed at their abatement. Both underestimated the growing embeddedness and intransigence of the disease. Neither was particularly assisted by monetary and fiscal policy.

A short sharp fall-off in the level of economic activity in the winter of 1969–70, which monetary and fiscal authorities were inclined to tolerate to ease inflationary pressures, provoked such a sudden and sharp run-up in unemployment rates that restraint was quickly abandoned. Nor was Canada alone in applying stimulative medicine as the industrial world began the rapid and intense cyclical expansion leading to the fateful events of 1973. But more of that later.

A further structural innovation which might be said to have been prescient of the strain to come was the creation of the Ministry of State for Science and Technology (MOSST) in 1971. Intended to provide the government and the Treasury Board with overall advice on research and development policy and the allocation of government scientific expenditures, the creation of MOSST was an early recognition of technological revolutions aborning and Canada's relatively inadequate performance, compared to that of its industrial competitors. In a similar way, a major study of energy policy, commissioned in 1971 and published in 1973, provided Canada with some preparation for OPEC revolutions to come.[6]

These premonitions aside, however, most structural and policy initiatives of the early Trudeau years reflected the Just Society themes with which the era had begun. Principal among these were the creation of the Ministry of State for Urban Affairs, the establishment of the Departments of Regional

Economic Expansion (DREE) and of the Environment, the development of an extensive array of job creation programs, directed particularly at new entrants to the labour force, the extension of unemployment insurance to include a further elaboration of regional and extended benefits and the expansion of the Canadian International Development Agency (CIDA). Towards the end of this period came the publication of the Orange Paper on assistance to the working poor and the beginning of a set of negotiations with the provinces intended to put in place the next major step in the evolution of the welfare state.[7]

This period also saw the birth of the Canada Development Corporation (CDC) and the Foreign Investment Review Agency (FIRA), one to positively assist the Canadianization of industrial initiatives, the other to ensure that foreign investors would bring substantial benefits to Canadians. Though these initiatives may be said to have responded to intense nationalist sympathies in the country, they combined with the long and intense struggle to consolidate the tax reform process initiated by the radically equitarian Carter Commission proposals[8] to sow the seeds of unease between the government and segments of the business community, and this unease, along with restive industrial relations, foreshadowed the erosion of the Keynesian consensus in Canada. The phenomenon was not unique to Canada and indeed was about to occur in all industrial countries as the last great boom of the postwar era met with capacity constraints in all sectors, particularly in food and oil. For a short period in 1972–73, however, the dislocations of inflation and the increasing instability of the international monetary and payments system (as the United States first floated its dollar and then experimented with wage and price controls) were disguised in Canada as the revised tax system continued to deliver a fiscal dividend that supported continued expansion of federal expenditures.

____1973–1975: The Transition to Stagflation _____

There were two momentous price shocks in 1973: one well known to Canadians, the other, ironically, less well known. The better-known one, of course, was the dramatic increase in oil and gas prices. Less well recognized was the meteoric rise of food prices. The price of food in general, of grains in particular and of wheat among grains, had risen steadily during 1972 and 1973 under the direct influence of a rapid expansion of world economic activity and demand. Indeed, the appearance of impending grain shortages seemed to lend credence to predictions being made by the Club of Rome about limits to growth through resource shortages. The rising prices of food and wheat were the first indicators of the "supply shocks" about to undermine the world economy. For Canada, however, rising resource and grain prices meant a shift of the terms of trade in Canada's favour and provided a strong underpinning to economic growth and employment creation. Though inflationary pressures were intensified, the difficulties that the world economy was facing were, for a time, less apparent to Canadians.

The second supply shock, the quadrupling of crude oil prices, coming on top of the shock of food price increases, plunged most of the world into deep recession. Except for the oil-exporting nations, the recession brought a dramatic halt to a real growth process that had gone on with only minor interruptions since World War II. Although an upper tier of newly industrializing countries, benefiting from a massive recycling of petro-dollars, was to resume substantial growth, the industrialized world was to experience an inadequate recovery process, sharply rising unemployment rates and continuing, deeply embedded inflation. The postwar era was effectively over and the era of stagflation had been born.

Having a near-balance in its imports and exports of energy, Canada was sheltered from the more dramatic macroeconomic effects of the oil shock. Two policies sheltered it further. The emergence of a "one-price" policy for oil in Canada, which held oil prices well below the world price, cushioned the shock to both industry and consumers for a time. As immediately important were two extremely stimulative budgets, brought down in the spring of 1973 and the fall of 1974. In the first, the finance minister of the time, John Turner, indexed the personal income tax system to prevent inflation from causing bracket creep and real tax increases. In the second, major tax cuts supported consumer expenditure.[9] As a result of these policy

measures, Canada, alone among industrialized countries,
totally averted the 1974–75 recession. However, it could not
protect itself from the collapse in productivity growth that
afflicted the entire developed world. Nor could it stave off a
consequence of recession avoidance: more virulent inflation
than that of its industrial competitors. While recession was
helping bank the fires of inflation in most countries, Canadian
unit labour costs, a combined measure of wages and
productivity growth, were rising rapidly compared to those of
its trading partners.

In the fall of 1975, the Anti-Inflation Board was formed and
price and wage controls imposed, though the decision seemed
to have no strong support from any quarter. For much of the
business community, the prospect of a reduction in cost
pressures was tempered by its growing philosophical aversion
to government intervention. For the labour community,
relations with government, which had been characterized by
growing unease, degenerated into outright hostility. The
Canadian Labour Congress mounted open protests and
withdrew its representatives from government councils. For
the general public, the imposition of controls represented a
dramatic political about-face, the breaking of an election
promise that has been thought by many to have had an
enduring effect on fundamental political support for Prime
Minister Trudeau.

_____ The Collapse of the Keynesian Consensus _____

If the food and oil supply shocks of 1973 marked the end of the
remarkable postwar growth era, the turbulence caused by the
creation of the Anti-Inflation Board may be thought of as
the watershed around which the economic, political and
intellectual streams that had nurtured the Keynesian consensus began formally to reverse course in Canada. The
breakdown of the consensus cannot be fully understood,
however, without some knowledge of the elements of which it
was composed and which lent support to structures of
economic policy in all industrialized countries including
Canada.

The consensus was based on more than a shared belief in the
value of counter-cyclical fiscal policy as a tool to sustain

demand and employment. This central belief served to reinforce two further strands of economic thought: the responsibility of governments for the redistribution of incomes and wealth and the responsibility of governments for the repair and prevention of "market failures." Buttressed by both the bitter experience of the 1930s and designs for the welfare state that were planned and committed to during and after World War II, all industrial states, to varying degrees, erected a panoply of social programs and market-intervention policies. The remarkable economic growth of the postwar period seemed to confirm the wisdom of these policies. It has already been noted that Canada's version of the welfare state matured later and less fully than most of its counterparts in the Western industrialized world, since federalism complicated and slowed the process of arriving at national programs. This federal structure also imparted an additional layer to Canada's version of the welfare state as it did develop. The Canadian notion of justice and fairness demanded the redress not only of interpersonal disadvantage but also of regional and provincial disparity. In implicit and explicit ways, both within and among nations, postwar building of the welfare state met with little opposition so long as ebullient real economic growth rates provided full employment, increasing after-tax incomes and wealth and the fiscal dividends needed to finance the growth of government activities and transfer programs.

Any one of the influences that began to be felt in the early 1970s might have disturbed this consensus. In combination, they initiated its steady erosion. The strength of the 1971–73 boom itself and its support from monetary and fiscal policy the world over seriously aggravated the inflation disease, whose origins extended well back into the 1960s. While quarrels continue to this day as to the fundmental nature of that disease and the extent to which government policies were responsible for it, its presence provided basic support for those who wished to question the increasing role of government, the inefficiencies of government intervention and the peril of Keynesian full-employment policies. The consolidation of OPEC power and the quadrupling of oil prices was more than a price shock. Since industrial advance had been built, in substantial measure, on the declining real price of energy over almost three decades, the real and relative rise in the price of crude oil called many of the structures of industrial world production and consumption into question. At the same time, Japan and a tier of newly developing countries were beginning to offer dramatic competition to many traditional Western industries. Further, new sources of mineral and raw material supplies in the Third World threatened to usurp the dominant role of many resource exporters such as Canada. Finally, it was becoming evident that the intense pace of technological change would have major effects on the relative fortunes of nations and regions. Though the microelectronic revolution was to figure more prominently in the 1980s, its early effects were evident in the seventies, in the growth of service-sector and knowledge-worker employment and in the relative decline of manufacturing as a source of employment (though not as a source of economic growth). Perhaps most troublesome of all, and still not wholly understood, was the total collapse of the productivity growth that had given governments the basic capacity to tax, spend and transfer while leaving room for private real after-tax incomes to rise. Slow growth, rising unemployment rates and the continuation of inflation at uncomfortably high rates inevitably invited a broad disappointment of economic expectations, and a popular as well as a theoretical and ideological questioning of government policies.

Several peculiarly Canadian aspects of the times and events have already been noted. While Canada had benefited substantially from rising resource prices in the early 1970s, declining resource prices following the recession of the mid-seventies and new sources of world supply contributed to the collapse of growth in the later 1970s. A swelling chorus of voices also pointed to the apparent decline of Canadian manufacturing exports and the capacity of Canada to fare well in a technological race. At the same time, Canada experienced greater inflation than its principal competitors, partly as a result of having averted the 1974–75 recession. Labour-management-government relations deteriorated steadily.

___1976–1979: Slow Growth and the Search for a
    Renewed Consensus _____

Along with the introduction of wage and price controls, the

government had committed itself to pursue fiscal and monetary restraint. It had announced its support for the Bank of Canada in its efforts to reach money-supply growth targets and had pledged to allow federal government expenditure to increase no more rapidly than gross national product. In a statement published in the fall of 1976, entitled *The Way Ahead*, it offered a fuller recognition of the end of the postwar era, of the emergence of a more competitive world and of the need to restructure government policies.[10] In this paper the government conceded that excessive, badly designed or mistimed interventions could contribute to economic inefficiencies, nurture excessive expectations of the economy's capacity and exacerbate inflationary tendencies. While rejecting both minimalist and excessively interventionist government, it sought to define a "new middle" — an updating of the Keynesian consensus more in accord with leaner times.

By this middle road the Trudeau administration sought to combine the principles of the Just Society with an economic policy based on a commitment to fiscal and monetary responsibility and less direct government intervention. It sought to consult with the labour and business communities and with the provinces in order to construct policies that would continue to encourage interregional as well as interpersonal balance — creating "a more just, tolerant Canadian society . . . with greater balance in the distribution of people and in the creation and distribution of wealth between and within regions." At the same time, the government would rely more explicitly on the market economy to provide the growth to support these ends.

Throughout the 1976-79 period, while inflation diminished, the Canadian dollar depreciated sharply and growth resumed but with little productivity advance, the government pursued these principles and elaborated on them in a series of formal and informal conferences. An uneasy truce prevailed between the federal government on the one hand and the producing provinces and industry on the other — over crude oil and natural gas pricing. The struggle over the distribution of the rents from the international price quadrupling had led to a price regime that was set below the international price but approaching it in yearly increments. As the international price remained stable and indeed fell in real terms as other prices increased, the strain on the federation diminished. In this atmosphere, a series of federal-provincial first ministers' conferences were convened, the first to contrive a regime that it was hoped would lead to better control over the rate of increase of education and health costs while ensuring adequate resourcing of each. The 1977 revision of the Federal-Provincial Fiscal Relations Act linked the federal government's support of post-secondary education and health expenditures to the growth of the economy rather than setting it at 50 percent of provincial expenditures.

Two further first ministers' conferences, held in 1978, focused on industrial policy in an effort to seek broader understanding of the forces now affecting Canadian economic welfare and to develop policies that would rekindle more rapid growth. At the same time, more informal meetings were undertaken with representatives of the business community and with labour, both to discuss the mechanisms and the conditions for the exit from wage and price controls and to seek greater agreement on appropriate structures of economic policy.

While monetary policy pursued a steadily reduced rate of growth in the money supply, fiscal policy remained expansive but not increasingly so until the budget of 1978 offered significant tax relief intended to spur expansion. In the fall of 1978, Prime Minister Trudeau ordered a $2 billion reduction in existing government programs: $1 billion to fund new social and industrial policy initiatives and $1 billion as a permanent reduction in the level of expenditures. Two significant initiatives were to emerge from this reallocation of expenditures. In the long run, the creation of the Child Tax Credit, which employed the social policy share of the savings, may have been the most significant. An important initiative in its own right at a time of faltering growth in family incomes, it was equally important as a demonstration of the possibility of integrating tax policy and social expenditures through a negative income tax. The applications and refinements of this idea have had a fundamental influence on subsequent reforms of the personal income tax system. It may ultimately be seen as the first in a series of steps leading to a guaranteed annual income in Canada.

The second initiative was the creation of the Board of Economic Development, later to become the Ministry of State for Economic Development, and later still the Ministry of State for Economic and Regional Development. The Board was established to bring together federal ministers concerned with industrial policy as they searched for the most effective and systematic ways of employing their share of the newly available funds. Much of it was to go to an intensive program of modernization in the forestry, lumber, and pulp and paper industries. Again, though the modernization program was important in its own right, the organizational initiative was one of the most important policy and expenditure control innovations of the Trudeau years and shaped the structuring of similar ministries of state in social policy and in external affairs and defence.

By 1979, the Canadian economy appeared to be slowly regaining its health. Whether because of controls or lower levels of economic activity, inflation had receded, and under the influence of a sharp depreciation of the Canadian dollar, Canadian international competitiveness appeared to be largely restored. Whatever the faults of economic policy, the Canadian economy, through the 1970s, had been induced to absorb into paid employment one of the most rapidly growing labour forces among industrial countries, and in terms of jobs created relative to the size of the labour force, the Canadian performance led all industrial countries over the decade. Despite the greatly reduced pace of growth, measured by average real income per capita, Canada's growth rate was comparable to that of the leading industrial countries through the entire Trudeau period. And yet it must be said that the efforts of Prime Minister Trudeau and his government to structure a new consensus as embracing as Keynesianism, were not notably successful. Indeed, there are those who have argued that the effort to cultivate business support for a revised menu of economic policies, through a steady stream of tax reductions, was both costly and ineffective.[11] Although wage and price controls were wound down during the fall of 1978, labour remained hostile and absent from effective consultative processes. And in the spring of 1979, the Canadian public gave little evidence that a restructuring of economic expectation had lessened its disenchantment with the government.

___1980–1984: A Renewed Mandate _____

The second OPEC price shock, along with trade embargos growing out of the beginnings of the Iran-Iraq war, were to have a profound effect on the shape of economic events in the 1980s. The early evidence was that industrial economies, and particularly the oil-import-dependent, were weathering this shock better than the first. There was less interruption of real growth, and in 1980 it appeared that the pure price shock was being absorbed without re-exciting inflationary trends. However, there was increasing acceptance of the view that the world was confronting continued real and relative oil price increases, if not absolute crude oil shortages. A steadily rising import dependency in the United States seemed to confirm this assessment.

The second OPEC shock was, however, a much less happy omen for the Clark government. The fact that Canada had become a net energy exporter meant that the shock had actually improved Canadian economic performance. However, it re-escalated the struggle between the producing provinces on the one hand and the consuming provinces and the federal government on the other over the appropriate national price and revenue-sharing responses. Finding revenue-sharing mechanisms that would permit the Canadian price to move to international levels proved no easier with a Conservative government in Ottawa than it had in 1974 with a Liberal government. While there was greater recognition that Canada might pay significant industrial and consuming adjustment costs if it did not follow the world price, the failure to make progress on a national revenue-sharing scheme again drove the federal government to ask the oil-producing provinces to consider a phased adjustment of Canadian prices to world levels, rather than a sudden leap to the higher levels. In effect, the benefit of indigenous resources would be shared by establishing a less-than-world price for all Canadians, rather than by setting up a scheme that accepted world prices and redistributed the financial benefits among all the Canadian provinces.

When the Trudeau government returned in the spring of 1980, it brought with it an election commitment to pursue negotiations with the producing provinces—especially Alberta—to find a national revenue-sharing system or to pursue a schedule of oil price increases less rapid than the one the Conservatives had proposed. It also brought with it the recognition that structural reform of the Canadian economy away from heavy dependence on oil, too long delayed and now critical in the face of world oil price predictions, must proceed whatever price policy emerged. It was then widely believed that the international price of oil would continue to increase annually through the 1980s at a rate that would be 2 percent more rapid than the average rate of increase of all other prices. It appeared certain that this would lead to dramatic energy, industrial and financial consequences around the world. Largely for this reason, the Trudeau government returned to office with a renewed determination to accelerate the process of Canadianizing the resource industries. Along with this hope of constructing an enduring energy policy, the new Trudeau government asserted a continuing general commitment to fiscal and structural economic reform.

These economic policy ambitions came together to form the structure of the budget of fall 1980. The National Energy Program was not only an energy policy narrowly defined.[12] In the proposed allocation of its revenues, it addressed significant industrial policy and conservation issues, allocated funding to economic development generally and eased pressure on the government's fiscal posture outside of energy. That posture, given the continuing revival of economic performance in 1980, was to adhere to a policy of restrained expenditure increase, to continue to support the regional dispersion of economic activity and to plan for a gradual reduction in the weight of the federal deficit.

These plans were challenged by the final and most devastating international economic shock of the Trudeau era—the determination of American monetary authorities to offer resistance to accelerating inflationary forces in the United

States by dramatic monetary tightening. Through the spring and summer of 1981, interest rates were permitted to ascend to record levels. As evidence of increasing integration (what has latterly become known as the phenomenon of "globalization"), the world economy was compelled to follow in lock step. Through the late summer and fall of 1981, the seeds of a major world recession were sown, a recession that would be particularly deep in Canada but less deep in the United States than the downturn of 1974–75. Restrictive monetary policy in the United States coincided with "supply-side" fiscal policies involving major tax reductions, which, though they resulted in a shallower U.S. recession, were responsible for the trade and fiscal deficit problems that continue to persist and trouble the world economy. Falling economic activity in the industrial world combined with high interest rates to devastate the Third World and arrest growth virtually everywhere. In particular, the collapse of economic activity combined with high interest rates to expose the enormity of the debt burdens that Third World countries had assumed over the previous decade. (These were, in part, the legacy of the recycling of petro-dollars and had been initiated and facilitated by commercial banks of the developed world.)

Negotiations with Alberta with respect to the National Energy Program reached a successful conclusion in the fall of 1981, just as these international forces were beginning to call into question the crude oil price forecasts on which agreement was based.[13] Similarly, the federal budget of 1981 pursued tax reform and reductions in the rate of growth of federal transfers to the provinces in continued pursuit of deficit control, just as the bottom was about to fall out of economic activity and the automatic stabilizers were to drive deficits up rapidly. Federal-provincial transfer reform sought primarily to put the equalization system on a sound basis, given its vulnerability to shocks to particular tax bases or tax rates. It further reflected the Trudeau government's view that the decentralizing forces of the past two decades had gone far enough. Well over 50 percent of final government expenditures in Canada and 60 percent of national tax revenues were now in the hands of provincial and municipal governments.[14]

Tax reform grew out of an increasing threat to the federal

revenue base caused by the combination of inflation and high interest rates. For those who drew a substantial share of their income from property sources and for corporations offering packages of non-monetary perks to their employees, inflation and high interest rates were offering massive incentive to mechanisms of tax avoidance. The burden of the system as a whole was shifting rapidly and inequitably to the shoulders of employed wage earners.[15] These wage earners were, in turn, seeking redress and inflation catch-up just as economic activity was beginning to decline. Once again, as in the mid-seventies, more rapid rates of inflation threatened to put the Canadian economy at a disadvantage relative to its trading partners.

With the 1981 budget, the government also published a paper on industrial policy which sought both to reduce the stridency of nationalist investment policies and to offer the prospect of widely dispersed regional industrial growth.[16] This paper paralleled major organizational reforms within the federal government which integrated regional and industrial policy and positioned representatives of the Ministry of State for Economic and Regional Development (MSERD) in the provinces in an effort to improve the co-ordination of federal and federal/provincial economic initiatives. All three initiatives—tax reform, reform of the provincial transfer system and industrial policy—encountered difficulties in the face of the oncoming recession and the disruptions caused by renewed inflationary pressures.

In the summer of 1982, the government again resorted to a form of wage and price controls—the Six-and-Five program—this time addressed formally only to the government sector. Consultations with business and labour were again sought, however, to encourage voluntary compliance outside the government and to hasten economic adjustment. As with the wage and price control period in the seventies, rapidly descending rates of price increase followed, but the extent to which public policy was responsible for this outcome remains a matter of contention.

By the fall of 1982, the signs of agonizingly slow economic recovery had begun to emerge. Inflation had been dealt a dramatic blow but so, too, had worldwide economic activity. Unemployment rates were up everywhere, particularly in

Europe. Third World growth had been completely arrested.

An upper tier of southeast Asian nations, led by Japan, were the first to achieve significant rates of recovery. With this recovery came a further stage in the world's industrial transformation. The microelectronic revolution, now in full swing, transformed industrial processes and lent credence to the notion of post-industrial information societies. Once again, the recession-induced decline in resource prices called into question Canada's heavy dependence on resource industries as an engine of income and wealth generation. As recovery slowly advanced, economic policy turned to address the appropriate responses to increasing global integration.

___Conclusion_____

In *Shifting Involvements*, Albert Hirschman examines the periodic tendency of societies to shift *en masse* left and right—from intensive periods of commitment to public causes and public purpose to equally intense periods of individualist, private preoccupation, and vice versa.[17] It seems clear that the underpinnings of what this essay has described as the Keynesian consensus and the astonishing economic growth of the postwar period that supported it, had begun to weaken as the Trudeau era began. An array of international economic forces were gathering strength to provoke reaction in all industrial countries, not just in Canada. Indeed, the degree of reaction would appear to have been less in Canada than in many other of its OECD partners, particularly the United States and Britain. The commitment of Canadians to concepts of justice and fairness and interregional notions of equity continued to support a search for policies that would shape a Just Society.

Nonetheless, the world had suffered a number of significant economic shocks and the consequences of an escalating pace of technological change. The need to pay attention to the maintenance of economic fortune in a more competitive, global village was real enough and not simply a whimsical ideological shift in public disposition. Many would, in fact, argue that Canadians and Canadian economic policy had clung too long to a view that growth could be easily restored and the

Keynesian consensus refurbished. The story of economic policy in the Trudeau era, as in other industrial countries, reflects the slow process of reconciliation to a transformed world.

PART III

A Society in Ferment

"The times they are a changing," sang Bob Dylan, and in one phrase this poet-troubadour of the sixties defined the spirit of the age. Outside our borders, empires collapsed, new nations emerged and the world economy moved relentlessly towards interdependence. Within Canada, citizens' movements appeared, old verities were questioned, new issues came to the fore and structures were transformed. As Wordsworth wrote about a similar period of ferment: "Bliss was it, in that dawn to be alive. But to be young was very heaven."

In assessing Canadian history, it is sometimes easy to forget how recent was our full emergence into twentieth-century life. We achieved legal independence from Great Britain only with the declaration of the Statute of Westminster in 1931. It took the Second World War to give us a modern industrial plant. Although immigration had begun to change the dominant French and English cast of the country, John Porter's *The Vertical Mosaic*, published in 1965, demonstrates how securely the old elites had managed to perpetuate their hold.

In the sixties, the dam broke. Quebec's "Quiet Revolution" is perhaps the best-known example of how one generation of Canadians sought to modernize their institutions, but throughout Canada, reformers were on the march. In a wide-ranging essay, Jacques Hébert describes many of the critical forces that shaped the era: the baby boom, that oversized cohort of six million Canadians which stretched Canada's ability to provide education, then jobs, then housing and which in the near future will test our systems of pensions and health care; the women's movement, which in 1982 saw its long fight for equality capped by Sections 15 and 28 of the Charter of Rights and Freedoms; Canada's native peoples, so long abused and ignored, who finally succeeded in putting an agenda for change before the country; and the "third force" of Canadians, those of neither French nor British heritage, who were explicitly recognized in our 1971 multiculturalism policy and who, in 1982, had the satisfaction of seeing Section 27 enshrined in the Charter.

In John Roberts' chapter, the focus shifts to another issue that came to the forefront of public consciousness in the sixties—the right of every Canadian, rich or poor, to a clean, safe environment. Roberts outlines the growth in Canada's environmental consciousness between 1968 and 1984 and describes the part our government played in aiding that growth. As early as 1970, the White Paper on Foreign Policy made a safe environment one of the six pre-eminent goals of the state. This commitment was followed by legislation to protect the ecology of the Arctic, to extend our system of national parks and to seek American co-operation in preserving the Great Lakes and reducing the emissions that cause acid rain.

During the 1970s we talked of a "conserver society"; today the phrase "sustainable development" is on everyone's lips. Yet, as Roberts makes painfully clear, to turn these slogans into a reality, rather than just fodder for speech writers' pens, will take an unprecedented and immense effort. The first tentative steps toward environmental health were taken between 1968 and 1984, but we still have far to go.

During our four governments, social policy was, as James Coutts outlines, a source of both frustration and satisfaction. Frustration because there were never enough resources to do all we intended. Satisfaction because, despite the scarcity, we were able to reduce poverty by concentrating our resources in a targeted way. Our first task was to fund and to consolidate the great reforms in social welfare inaugurated by the Pearson government. In 1969, defence spending was frozen for three years as we made a conscious decision to place more importance on health and welfare. Next, the social security net and the real incomes of average Canadians were protected from the ravages of inflation through indexation. In 1972 the Old Age Security (OAS) was indexed annually to increases in the consumer price index. In 1973 quarterly indexation of the OAS and of the Guaranteed Income Supplement (GIS) for seniors was initiated. In 1974, the income tax system as a whole was indexed, giving every Canadian an income tax "cut" equal to inflation, and in 1975 family allowances received full quarterly indexation. (In recent years these policies have been eroded: in 1985, the Mulroney government cut back on indexation of the tax system and family allowance. It also attempted to de-index Old Age Security but retreated when confronted by a public furor.[1] In his 1989 budget, Finance Minister Michael Wilson also announced that the federal government would no longer subsidize the Unemployment Insurance fund, thereby putting the whole cost burden of this program on individual employers and employees.)

In the 1970s, having secured the advances made by the previous Liberal government, we moved on to priorities of our own. Working Canadians, families and children were the first concerns. In 1971, Bryce Mackasey's Unemployment Insurance reforms brought a greater measure of security to millions of Canadians. In 1973, family allowances were tripled to $20 per child and then indexed. In 1978, family benefits were further improved: applying the same design of a universal plan and a special supplement for the poor that had already been successfully proven in the OAS and GIS programs for seniors, we added a Child Tax Credit (today over $600 per child) to the universal system of family allowance. Refundable, nontaxable to families with incomes below $25,000 and delivered yearly, this Child Tax Credit was the first benefit in Canada to be delivered through the tax system in the form of a credit rather than through an exemption or deduction. If we ever move to a Guaranteed Annual Income, Monique Bégin deserves plaudits for having introduced the beginning of such a system in 1978.

In the 1980s, poverty among the aged became our special target. The GIS supplement was raised in 1980 and again in 1984, thereby increasing the supplement by over $1,000 a year, and assisting over 700,000 senior citizens. Overall, the old age assistance per pensioner increased from $76 per month in 1968 to $272 in 1984, and the Guaranteed Income Supplement for individual seniors in need went up from $30 per month in 1968 to $295 per month in 1984. The combined monthly assistance to poor seniors thus increased from $106 per month in 1968 to $567 per month in 1984 for individuals, and from $214 per month in 1968 to $950 per month in 1984 for families. Thus, between 1968 and 1984, according to Statistics Canada, the number of Canadians in poverty was reduced by more than one-third: from 23 percent of Canadians in 1969 to 12.8 percent in 1984.[2] Demonstrating our commitment to the elderly, the poverty rate of families headed by a senior citizen was reduced from 41 percent in 1969 to 14 percent in 1980 and to 9.5 percent in 1986.[3] These increases in security for families, children and the aged formed an essential part of the leitmotiv of a Just Society—to help first, those who need help most.

Thomas S. Axworthy
Pierre Elliott Trudeau

CHAPTER 5

Legislating for Freedom

——— by Jacques Hébert ———
translated by Patricia Claxton

During his early career as a journalist, Jacques Hébert was founder, publisher and editor of the daily newspaper Vrai *(1954–1959), and wrote for the magazine* Cité libre. *He also founded the publishing houses Les Éditions de l'Homme and Les Éditions du Jour, and is the author of twenty books on travel, human rights and the problems of developing countries. He was founder and president of Canada World Youth and Katimavik, is an Officer of the Order of Canada and has been a member of the Senate since 1983.*

WHEN PIERRE ELLIOTT TRUDEAU appeared on the political scene, Canada, like the rest of the world, was undergoing profound upheavals of many kinds. Moreover, Quebec, that vital element of Canada's soul, was seething with separatist ferment. The "Just Society" that Trudeau proposed to Canadians was about to become much more than an electoral slogan: it was to become a response to a democratic and prosperous society's wakening aspirations for greater equality for all its people, including minorities like the native peoples, youth, the elderly and ethnic groups, not to mention that majority so often treated as a minority—women.

The new prime minister possessed a quality rare in politicians, namely firm principles underlying a determination to change society, to make it more free and more just. "The first visible effect of freedom," he declared, "is change. A free man exercises his freedom by altering himself and—inevitably—his surroundings. It follows that no liberal can be other than receptive to change and highly positive in his response to it, for change is the very expression of freedom."[1] It goes without saying that this man's acts were never dictated by public opinion polls, which would not have led a government to abolish the death penalty, for example, or enshrine a charter of rights in a repatriated constitution.

One of the things the Trudeau government did that had never been done before was give a voice to categories of Canadians who previously had little or no voice. Feminist groups were anxious to influence public opinion and could not afford to? The state would provide the wherewithal. Native peoples were having trouble defending their rights? They would get subsidies the better to tell the government off.

Throughout its mandate, the Trudeau team was responsible for bold legislative measures enabling Canadians to have wider choices and the opportunity to express opinions, act and participate in the democratic process. The intent was to allow each individual more freedom, whatever his handicap—be it poverty, isolation, lack of education or minority status. As long as a single Canadian was not able to exercise a full measure of freedom, the lawmakers seemed to be saying, the rest ought not to feel truly free either.

This chapter, which is necessarily incomplete and schematic, will discuss the principal legislation and government initiatives that opened broader horizons for all minority groups.

_____The Advancement of Women _____

Since the 1960s the situation for Canadian women has changed radically. We must look back a long way . . .

In the Senate lobby is a bronze bust of Cairine Wilson, the first woman to be appointed to the Senate—in 1930, sixty-three years after Confederation! And this was possible only after a long court action taken by five women (from Alberta, appropriately) in order to establish that women were genuinely "persons in the meaning of the law." In 1921, when it received the first woman member of Parliament, Agnes McPhail, the House of Commons had beaten the Senate to the punch. But the second female MP was not elected until 1935.

Between 1968 and 1984, 39 women came to the House of Commons as new members of Parliament, and the number of candidates leapt from 36 to 217. Prime Minister Trudeau called 12 women to the Senate. He appointed 37 female judges, including the first to be appointed to a superior court and the first to be appointed to the Supreme Court of Canada. He set a precedent by having four women assigned important posts at the deputy-ministerial level, including the presidency of the Canadian International Development Agency (CIDA). Under his leadership we also had the first woman lieutenant-governor (in Ontario), the first woman speaker of the Senate, the first woman speaker of the House of Commons and the first woman governor general. These might be called merely "symbolic" gestures which did nothing to solve the real problems, except that the government also had a dynamic policy for the advancement of women.

By 1968 women had already begun to take their place on the job market, increasingly filling positions traditionally occupied by men. They were making inroads into professions like medicine, veterinary medicine, pharmacy and law. Their presence, though still not great, was being felt in the business world and in political parties, provincial legislatures, the federal government and the civil service. It was between 1968 and 1984, however, that the movement for the liberation of women really came into its own, and it owes part of its success to the Trudeau government's receptiveness to its demands.

In 1971, following submission of the report of the Royal Commission of Inquiry on the Status of Women in 1970, a minister responsible for the Status of Women was appointed, and also a Status of Women co-ordinator. The duties of both were to develop a coherent policy for women and defend their interests inside and outside government. In addition, the Secretary of State Department established a grant program for groups working for the advancement of women on a national, provincial or local scale. This financial assistance enabled women to organize their actions better and to defend their cause with remarkable effectiveness, even against government. And in 1973 the Trudeau government created the Advisory Council on the Status of Women, which helped raise the awareness of the general public and stimulate initiatives on the part of the federal government.

Critics may contend that the appointment of a minister and the creation of an advisory council were no more than window dressing—but the Trudeau government was committed to the advancement of women in more than a superficial way.

Throughout their years in office, the Trudeau Liberals took concrete, noteworthy measures that reflected their philosophical commitment to giving women a fair place in society.

- 1969   therapeutic abortion to be permitted under the Criminal Code when recommended by a committee of doctors and performed in a hospital
- 1970   establishment of the Family Planning Division of Health and Welfare
- 1971   –maternity benefits incorporated into the revised unemployment insurance plan
          –amendment of the Canada Labour Code stipulating equal pay to men and women for equal work
          –income tax deduction of child care costs for working mothers
          –establishment of the Office of Equal Opportunities within the Public Service Commission
          –indexing of family allowances (full quarterly indexation, 1975)
- 1972   –creation of the Antidiscrimination Branch for the investigation of complaints regarding employment in the public sector
          –amendment of the Canada Assistance Plan providing for child-care aid supplements for low-income families
- 1976   amendment of the Criminal Code ensuring greater protection for victims of rape and other sexual offences. In 1983, a further amendment replaced the notion of "rape" with that of "sexual assault" and for the first time made husbands subject to the law
- 1977   adoption of the Canadian Human Rights Act, which, among other things, forbade discrimination on the basis of sex
- 1982   The Charter of Rights and Freedoms, since it applies equally to men and women, established the principle of equality between the sexes.

What government since Confederation has done more for the advancement of women, or to give a voice to that part of the

population which in 1930 was not indisputably composed of
"persons in the meaning of the law"?

In fact, according to Katie Cook, president of the Advisory
Council on the Status of Women, Canada is among the most
advanced of the world's industrialized countries in this respect.
In 1974 Mrs Cook declared that with the creation of the Royal
Commission of Inquiry on the Status of Women and the
establishment of a government department responsible for the
status of women, Canada had clearly done more to ensure
equal rights between men and women than other countries.

___ Aboriginal Rights _____

The native peoples of Canada, whose ancestors lived in this
country for thousands of years before the arrival of Europeans,
have been victims of injustice arising from discrimination,
cultural isolation, illiteracy and economic and social problems.
They are our very own Third World, created by the neglect and
misunderstanding of non-native Canadians and governments.
Under every government since Confederation, the problems of
native peoples on and off the reserve were observed to be going
from bad to worse, but other Canadians did not seem to care.
And politicians seemed in no hurry to act. Our treatment of our
native peoples will remain an indelible blot on Canada's
reputation.

The Trudeau government did not find all the solutions, any
more than its predecessors had. It did more than the rest,
however, listening to the grievances of the First Nations,
helping them defend themselves by providing grants for
pressure groups, conducting in-depth studies and in 1981
concluding an historic agreement, which was hailed by the
Indian Brotherhood and the Native Council of Canada as "a
new beginning for the Indians of Canada" and "a great step
forward."

If the native peoples succeeded in a number of their
negotiations with the Department of Indian and Northern
Affairs, it was largely because, through the Core Funding
Program initiated in 1971, the Canadian government had
provided them with the financial means to organize their
associations at all levels, promote their cause with the public,

do research and obtain the services of lawyers, economists, constitutionalists and other experts. Once again, the state was providing arms for Canadians who were fighting for their rights.

In this way, the federal government played a silent role in negotiations between the Cree and the Inuit on the one hand and the Cree and the Quebec government on the other, leading to the Agreement in Principle on James Bay and Northern Quebec in 1974 and the final agreement in 1975. Under this agreement, the Trudeau government — which has been unfairly rebuked for centralizing tendencies — ceded to the Quebec government a major portion of its responsibilities for the education, health care, registration of beneficiaries and local government of the aboriginal population of northern Quebec.

During the First Ministers' Conference of 1979, Prime Minister Trudeau proposed the addition of a new item on the agenda — "Canada's Native Peoples and the Constitution." The following year, he invited the representatives of the First Nations to take part in the discussion on the Constitution and offered them the funds they would need for drawing up their constitutional position.

As a result of these discussions and negotiations, the Constitution Act of 1982 recognized the ancestral and treaty rights of the aboriginal peoples, which opened the way for further negotiations that would result in an improved definition of these rights. Section 25 of the Act is intended to prevent interpretation of any other section in such a way as to reduce the rights of the aboriginal peoples. Article 35 of Part II of the Act includes the Inuit, Indians and Métis in the definition of aboriginal peoples and confirms their "existing" rights, meaning rights arising from treaties and ancestral rights. Finally, the new Constitution provided that the rights of aboriginal peoples and constitutional matters particularly concerning them would be included on the agenda of future first ministers' conferences and would be debated with the participation of representatives of the First Nations of Canada.

During the discussions leading up to the passage of the Constitution Act in 1982, Section 35 was amended to remove the ambiguous word "existing" as a qualifier of aboriginal rights, which native representatives understandably distrusted. From this point on, any reference to existing rights would also have to include reference to future rights acquired through the settlement of claims. It was stipulated, moreover, that the rights recognized by this section were as valid for aboriginal women as for men.

In 1984, the Cree-Naskapi (of Quebec) Act was passed by Parliament, giving these two nations responsibility for their own local administration. They were the first Indians of Canada to benefit from this measure, which had been provided for in the James Bay and Northern Quebec Agreement and the North-Eastern Quebec Agreement. In the same year, the federal government signed the final Inuvialuit Agreement with the Inuit of the Western Arctic.

These were all steps in the right direction, but the march toward a just society for all the native peoples of Canada will be long, and will require an awareness on the part of all Canadians that is developing only slowly. The Trudeau government did what was essential: it recognized the fundamental rights of the native peoples and the injustices inherent in their present situation, and through the Constitution opened all doors to future negotiations.

During the Federal-Provincial Conference of March 1984, which dealt with the constitutional affairs of the aboriginal peoples, Louis Bruyère rose to speak on behalf of the Native Council of Canada and gave this tribute to Prime Minister Trudeau, who was chairing the conference: "I want to take this opportunity, Mr Chairman, to publicly thank you for your services to us as native Canadians over the past sixteen years. The aboriginal cause has been advanced under your leadership. It now remains for the rest of us to continue the progress your actions have made possible."

_____ A Bilingual and Multicultural Society _____

From its very beginnings, Canada has been a mosaic of different cultures. Long before the arrival of the French, and of the British 150 years later, the Far North was populated by the Inuit, while 59 Amerindian nations lived in various regions of the vast land that would become Canada. Today, according to

Statistics Canada, nearly 40 percent of Canadians are of ethnic origin other than French or British. It was only in 1971, however, that the Canadian government officially recognized ethnic groups other than those of French, British or aboriginal origin. Canada would remain a bilingual country, but would try not to impose a "national" culture, or even a form of biculturalism, on its citizens. It now recognized the right of each Canadian to live and be fulfilled in his or her chosen culture and of every ethnic group (there are currently 105[2]) to preserve its own cultural and linguistic heritage while respecting the rights of others and living and working in one of the two official languages.

On October 8, 1971, in the House of Commons, Prime Minister Trudeau summarized the spirit of this new policy—a major step in Canada's evolution—in these words:

> A policy of multiculturalism within a bilingual framework commends itself to the government as the most suitable means of assuring the cultural freedom of Canadians. Such a policy would help to break down discriminatory attitudes and cultural jealousies. National unity, if it is to mean anything in the deeply personal sense, must be founded on confidence in one's own individual identity; out of this can grow respect for that of others and a willingness to share ideas, attitudes and assumptions. A vigorous policy of multiculturalism will help create this initial confidence. It can form the base of a society which is based on fair play for all.[3]

The multiculturalism policy received the unanimous support of Parliament. With its adoption, we, unlike our American neighbours, were declining to sacrifice our multicultural wealth and diversity in the name of national unity. We were renouncing the notion of a cultural monolith, of an American-style melting-pot. We were espousing the principle that a free and just society must accept pluralism and allow each citizen to make a personal choice of suitable lifestyle, customs and culture, whether or not these flowed from his or her own ethnicity.

In 1972, the government created the Multiculturalism

Branch of the Secretary of State Department, and our first minister responsible for multiculturalism was appointed to the Cabinet. The purpose of these two measures was to encourage ethnic groups to feel truly Canadian while preserving the cultural riches of their countries of origin, from which all Canadians would benefit. Their members would speak English or French, but if any group wished to preserve its mother tongue, the government would help it to do so.

Once again, the state was ready to subsidize groups of citizens, some of them minuscule, and thus enable them to defend cherished values. Moreover, it was conceiving programs on its own initiative with a view to combatting racial discrimination, encouraging demonstrations of ethnic artistry and stimulating research and the publication and translation of works reflecting Canada's cultural diversity. These programs have provided a powerful stimulant to the ethnic groups of the country. Sociologist Jean Burnet writes:

> Several of the programs of the federal government under such headings as cultural integration, intercultural communications, group development, and multicultural arts give grants to ethnic voluntary associations for various purposes; a number of provinces and municipalities also give financial or moral assistance to such associations. The fact that various levels of government recognize the contribution voluntary associations make to Canadian society has encouraged their formation and their continuance perhaps more than the grants themselves.[4]

The Canadian Consultative Council on Multiculturalism was created in 1973 to help implement the new policy. In 1983, with a broader mandate, it became the Canadian Multiculturalism Council.

The banner year for multiculturalism, however, was 1982, for Section 27 of the Canadian Charter of Rights and Freedoms, which was passed into law that year, states: "This Charter shall be interpreted in a manner consistent with the preservation and enhancement of the multicultural heritage of Canadians." In this way, Canada resolutely opted for the greatest freedom offered by a pluralist society. This was a new vision, according to which our country became a society like no other in the world, and one of the most tolerant.

___ Placing Confidence in Youth _____

Young people, our country's most valuable asset, comprise nearly one-fifth of the population of Canada. Yet the state has traditionally paid them little attention, probably because they are the least well organized of any group of Canadians and have therefore been unable to make themselves heard.

During its sixteen years in power, however, the Trudeau government broke away from that trend. Those years will remain a kind of golden age for the youth of Canada.

In 1971, the Secretary of State Department conceived a bold and innovative program: Opportunities for Youth. Prime Minister Trudeau summarized its objectives in the House of Commons on March 16, 1971:

> The government believes as well that youth is sincere in its efforts to improve society and that young people are anxious to work and to engage in activities which are intended to make Canada a better place in which to live. The government proposes therefore to encourage young persons to direct their energy, their imagination and their altruism into projects which are beneficial to the entire community. The Opportunities for Youth program will combine the resources of the government with the resources of youth. We are saying, in effect, to the youth of Canada that we are impressed by their desire to fight pollution; that we believe they are well motivated in their concern for the disadvantaged; that we have confidence in their value system. We are also saying that we intend to challenge them to see if they have the stamina and self-discipline to follow through on their criticism and advice.[5]

No Canadian head of government had ever before held out such a challenge or shown such confidence in young Canadians. He was offering them millions of dollars so that they might devise projects useful to their communities and put them into action themselves (without civil servants helping), and at the same time develop their own aptitudes, their sense of responsibility and their spirit of service to others.

From 1971 to 1974, Opportunities for Youth allowed 94,467 young people to realize 9,694 concrete, valid projects in thousands of Canadian communities throughout the ten provinces, the Northwest Territories and the Yukon.

Critics of Opportunities for Youth have made much of a few projects which failed, as if hoping to obscure the fact that on the whole the program was a resounding success. They might think of applying the same critical standards to adults, governments and civil servants, whose disastrous mistakes, the Auditor General of Canada tells us every year, cost taxpayers staggering sums of money.

Opportunities for Youth was a summer program, and it was essentially addressed to students. Its success, which showed that groups of citizens were perfectly capable of administering public funds, encouraged the government to create another program, Local Initiatives, which was designed for the unemployed, of whom a great many were young people. This program encouraged retraining and permitted the realization of community projects that would never have existed otherwise.

The Trudeau government also provided complete or partial funding for two other youth programs that were proposed by nongovernment organizations: Canada World Youth (beginning in 1971) and Katimavik (beginning in 1977). These programs were open to all young Canadians between the ages of seventeen and twenty-one, and their aim was character development, involvement in community projects (many related to environmental problems), the learning of another language, discovery of various regions of Canada, and in the case of Canada World Youth, awareness of international development problems. Above all, although this was not part of the purpose of these programs, they helped bring young Canadians of different provinces and ethnic origins closer together, making them more tolerant, more generous, more open to the world around them. And more free.

Between 1968 and 1984, the Trudeau government set up

many job and training programs, which did much to help
unemployed young people. It also increased the Canada
Student Loans budget from $9.4 million in 1968–69 to $229
million in 1984–85. The program of aid to the provinces for
post-secondary education saw its budget rise from
$107,999,940 in 1968 to $2,243,787,286 in 1984.

In 1984, the government brought in the Young Offenders
Act to replace the Juvenile Delinquents Act, which had been
passed in 1908. The new law was fairer and more humane,
taking into consideration not only the protection of the public
but also the rights and responsibilities of young offenders aged
twelve to eighteen. Before the Commons Standing Committee
on Justice and Legal Affairs, the Canadian Bar Association
described the spirit of the proposed legislation as follows:

> The Act attempts to strike a reasonable and acceptable
> balance between the needs of young offenders and the
> interest of society. The Bill has been described as having
> both the scope and flexibility required to insure public
> protection while at the same time seeking better and more
> effective measures for dealing with delinquent youth. The
> legislation proposes the blending of the following three
> principles:
>
> 1. That young people should be held more responsible
> for their behaviour, but not wholly accountable since they
> are not yet fully mature;
> 2. That society has a right to protection from illegal
> behaviour;
> 3. That young people have the same rights to due
> process of law and fair and equal treatment as adults and
> these rights must be guaranteed by special safeguards.[6]

Prime Minister Trudeau gave further evidence of his
government's genuine interest in youth by creating the post of
Minister of State for Youth in 1984, at last giving a voice in
Cabinet to almost a fifth of the Canadian population.

_____ The Elderly, the Handicapped and Refugees _____

According to a number of demographers, by the year 2031, just

over forty years from now, 20 percent of the population of
Canada will be over the age of sixty-five. This projection, which
is based on our low birth rate, longer life expectancy and the
timidity of our immigration policy, was already known in
essence in 1968. Within the limitations of federal jurisdiction,
therefore, the Trudeau government implemented several
programs intended to ensure the well-being and dignity of
senior citizens.

The original Old Age Security Act, which dates from 1927,
has improved steadily since then, but particularly beginning in
1970, when cost-of-living indexing, a lower pensionable age
and higher income supplements were introduced. In 1975 came
the addition of the Spouse Allowance for low-income surviving
spouses (widows and widowers) aged sixty to sixty-five.
Provision was also made for an income tax deduction for
persons aged sixty-five and over. These advances were
enhanced by the introduction, in 1972, of a cultural and
recreational program for the elderly, New Horizons, which was
modelled after Opportunities for Youth. Finally, the National
Advisory Council on Aging was established in 1980, and the
Seniors bureau in 1981—both attached to Health and Welfare
Canada.

The Commons Special Committee on the Disabled and
the Handicapped was created in 1980, and in 1981, the
International Year of the Handicapped, the government took
action, adding physical or mental deficiency to the list of
grounds for discrimination prohibited by the Canadian
Charter of Rights and Freedoms and the Canadian Human
Rights Act. In 1983, Parliament approved a national policy on
transportation for the handicapped. This was to ensure
effective, reliable services within federal jurisdiction for the one
million Canadians who have difficulty moving about without
help.

In 1968 the government had shown compassion toward
another category of handicapped persons: handicapped
refugees. That year, by agreement with most of the provinces,
Canada took four hundred persons who were not only refugees
but also handicapped. In 1969, Canada signed the Geneva
International Convention on the Status of Refugees, which was
the turning point in our policy regarding the growing hordes of

refugees crowded into makeshift camps in countries of first refuge—all of which were poor nations.

Over the years, the Trudeau government established ad hoc programs for priority acceptance of certain groups of refugees: from Czechoslovakia in 1968 (12,000 refugees), Tibet in 1970 (228 refugees), Uganda in 1972 (7,000 refugees), Chile in 1973 (1,200 refugees), Vietnam and Cambodia in 1975 (69,000 refugees), Lebanon (11,000 refugees) and a number from various Latin American countries in 1976. On humanitarian grounds, the government accepted these groups of refugees without insisting on the usual admission criteria, and in order to expedite the process, sent teams from the Department of Manpower and Immigration to the camps where the refugees were located.

In August 1977 the new Immigration Act was passed by Parliament, and in April of the following year, the government created the Refugee Status Advisory Committee. One of the purposes of the new law was to enable Canada to fulfil its international obligations with regard to refugees, as defined by the Geneva Convention, and to maintain its traditional role as a country open to the persecuted of the world. The law now afforded adequate legal protection to anyone claiming refugee status, including the right to appeal the decision of the Department of Manpower and Immigration. Further, no refugee who met the definition under the Geneva Convention could be deported, with the exception of criminals and persons representing a security threat to Canada.

Laws for Individuals

Involving Canadians in the social, political and economic process; protecting freedom for all against discrimination, whatever the cause; enabling the weak and defenceless to obtain justice—such were the principles behind the reform of many of our laws during the Trudeau government's sixteen years in office. The two most significant years of reform were, of course, 1977 and 1982. In 1977 the Canadian Human Rights Act was passed, guaranteeing equality of opportunity to all without discrimination, protecting personal privacy and giving individuals access to government files containing personal information about them. This law also created the Human Rights Commission, whose purpose was to offer recourse to victims of discrimination and to combat sources of discrimination through research and information programs. However, the most memorable year will always be 1982, when the Charter of Rights and Freedoms was enshrined in the Constitution Act of that year. With the Charter, Canada entered a new era, in which the prime importance of individual rights would be recognized.

I have already mentioned a number of legislative measures that have improved the lot of women, native peoples, ethnic groups, young people and other categories of the disadvantaged. However, between 1968 and 1984 there were also a great many other administrative decisions, amendments to existing laws and new laws, whose purpose was to respond to changing Canadian society in the sense of allowing for greater freedom.

As soon as it came to power, the Trudeau government brought in several amendments to the Criminal Code, which were not welcomed by all Canadians — such as the abortion law of 1969, which I mentioned earlier, and the amendment that decriminalized private homosexual practices between consenting adults. These two measures gave rise to much heated debate, although they simply proposed to allow Canadians to be guided by their consciences in these respects. "I believe," declared Pierre Trudeau, "that the Criminal Code amendments are good because they will try to instill in our legal concept that there is a difference between sin and crime, and it is not the business of the lawmaker or of the police to check sin. This is a problem for each person's conscience, or his priest, or his God, but not for the police."[7]

A great many other laws and amendments inspired by the same concern for bringing more justice to Canadian society have caused less stir or have passed almost without notice. One of these was the Criminal Code amendment that makes a crime of inciting hatred against a person by reason of his belonging to a racial or religious group (1969). Another was the creation of the Law Reform Commission, whose mandate is immensely broad because it is to revise all the laws of Canada and propose amendments to bring them up to date and make them fairer.

Between 1972 and 1982, following three reports examining conditional release,[8] the Canadian correctional system underwent rapid changes toward greater fairness. The new legislation sought to ensure the protection of society against criminal behaviour while at the same time recognizing the rights of offenders.

From 1972 on, federal-provincial agreements made it possible for the federal government to provide financial support to legal aid programs so that poorer Canadians could be properly defended before courts of justice. In 1973, the government appointed a Correctional Investigator, a kind of prisoners' ombudsman who could lay complaints about the treatment of federal prison inmates. In 1982, Parliament passed the Access to Information Act and the Privacy Act, which respectively enabled access to information in government files and ensured the confidentiality of files containing personal information.

Another controversial measure—the amendment to the Criminal Code that abolished capital punishment—must be mentioned here. From 1867 to 1962, in accordance with the law of the land, more than seven hundred Canadians had been hanged. Without a shadow of doubt, this number included a few who were innocent. Some thirty countries had renounced the death penalty, most since World War II, yet Canada kept hesitating.

In the early 1960s, the people of Canada were perhaps beginning to have doubts about this primitive and ineffectual practice. Juries were increasingly reluctant to send murderers to the gallows and the Cabinet was systematically commuting death sentences. It was enough to draw an anguished cry from a celebrated Crown prosecutor: "It's got to the point where you can't get anyone hanged anymore!" Yet not until 1976 did the federal government have the courage to abolish this remnant of a less civilized era.

This, it should be said, took political courage, particularly when opinion polls at the time showed that most Canadians were in favour of the death penalty, as they still are, which explains but does not justify the agonizing debate over reinstating the death penalty which kept the House of Commons in suspense for months in 1987.

When the Trudeau government left office in 1984, it had put in place legislation and programs that met its main goal: to make society more free, more just and more humane. The initiatives described in this chapter are only a few of the changes that helped Canada realize the vision of a Just Society.

In a speech delivered on April 2, 1968, Pierre Elliott Trudeau had unequivocally stated his intentions to bring about reform for the sake of a better society. "Lawmaking," he said, "is a way to improve the lot of flesh and blood human beings. And the better governments are attuned to the problems they are called on to solve, the better are their chances of making laws for the benefit of human beings."[9]

Sixteen years after this declaration of principle, the twenty-second prime minister of Canada left the political scene. I think history will record that by then he had accomplished essentially what he had set out to do.

CHAPTER 6

Meeting the Environmental Challenge

———————— by John Roberts ————————

John Roberts is a political scientist whose working life has been divided between active politics and university teaching and research. He has served in the Canadian government under Mr Trudeau as Secretary of State, Minister of Science and Technology, Minister of the Environment and Minister of Employment and Immigration and was a candidate for the leadership of the Liberal Party in 1984. He has been a lecturer or visiting scholar at several universities in Canada as well as in the United States, Britain and Australia.

THE TIDES OF political fortune that swept the Trudeau government to office in 1968 reflected a variety of deeper currents of change within Canada.

One of these changes was a growing consciousness by Canadians – or at least many Canadians – of the way in which the practices of the modern economy were damaging the ecological base on which our society is founded and which might, if they continued unchecked, cause that society to founder.

___The Growth of Environmental Conscience _____

By the late 1960s there was a growing worldwide perception of deterioration in the environment. Innovations in communications, transportation, and manufacturing and resource technologies – and the industrialization and urbanization that had been their consequence – had created an environmentally degraded society. Environmental problems came to be seen not simply as random occurrences or the consequences of specific mistakes but as a pattern of cumulative damage generated by a structure of abuse founded on our general approach to economic activity.

The fragility of ecosystems and their vulnerability to modern techniques of industrial production were described dramatically in Rachel Carson's *Silent Spring* (1962) and Barbara Ward's *Spaceship Earth* (1966), which argued persuasively that mankind depended for life on a fragile envelope of atmosphere and soil, which could be contaminated and destroyed by the forces of science and technology.

Environmental disasters such as the devastation of shorelines that followed the sinking of the oil tanker *Torrey Canyon* in British waters and the grounding of the *Arrow* in Chedabucto Bay off Nova Scotia provided concrete confirmation of these dangers.

Many economists, too, became skeptical of the social and ecological consequences of unreflective economic growth. The Report of the Club of Rome on the Limits of Growth (1972) forecast global trends that would be environmentally insupportable. The oil crisis of 1973 brought home an understanding that cheap energy supplies, which fuelled the abundant growth of the West's consumer society, could not be relied upon, and reinforced the predictions of such economists as Galbraith and Heilbroner, who warned that the affluent industrial world must abandon the practices of wasteful growth.

The environmental concerns that had come to the fore by the late 1960s had a double thrust: on the one hand there was a demand for solutions or responses to evident, specific ecological problems; on the other, a call for a changed perspective on social and economic development. Environmentalists advocated not simply action against the legacy of past pollution but a shift away from the spendthrift consumption society that had emerged following World War II, towards a society characterized by thrift, conservation, recycling and the husbanding of resources.

___The Rise of Environmentalism in Canada _____

No country reflected this rising environmental consciousness more intensely than Canada. Canadians had long been aware of the strong dependence of their economy on the physical environment. In the past, Canadians had viewed their land with a frontier spirit—as a vast treasure house of natural wealth to be seized and exploited. The story of Canadian economic development—from codfish, to furs, to wheat, to metals, to energy—had been the adventure of finding and bringing to market the massive resources of the northern half of North America.

But in the mid-1960s, that complacent attitude began to change in some quarters: the Canadian environmental movement had come alive. In 1964 the federal-provincial Resources for Tomorrow Conference (which established the Canadian Council of Resource Ministers [CCRM]) undertook a major review of Canada's resource situation, publishing two large volumes—*Prospects for Canada's Resources*—focusing on what would be called today "sustainable development." The CCRM in turn convoked a national conference on Pollution and Our Environment in the autumn of 1966. Neighbourhood associations, concerned citizens' committees and individuals began to work actively to combat the consequences of industrial activity, focusing their attention on such hazards as waste disposal sites, contaminated beaches, nonreturnable containers and littered camp sites and portage trails. Such organizations as the Society for Pollution and Environmental Control, the Canadian Environmental Law Association and Pollution Probe were established to better educate the public and to make governments aware of the need to respond to environmental problems. Universities became concerned. York University set up a Faculty of Environmental Studies in 1968 and the Universities of Calgary, Waterloo and British Columbia followed suit.

The initial focus of this environmentalism was local pollution—that is, visible, site-specific, single-source environmental problems that could be seen (and/or smelled)—such as the effluent from pulp and paper mills, smoke from coal-fired electricity-generating plants and open garbage dumps. The response to this kind of pollution was reactive and defensive: find out what polluters were doing and force them to stop, by using government as a policeman to bring polluting malefactors to heel through regulation and control. But it was soon seen that these responses to the legacy of past and present

polluters fell far short of preventing environmental degradation—and that a comprehensive, rather than a piecemeal,
approach was required.

This theme was developed by the Science Council of Canada
in a series of reports on the implications of economic growth
published in the late 1960s and early 1970s. The Council contended that the future should not be simply an extrapolation
of the past—that escalating growth, far from being a sure route
to prosperity, was a potential disaster. The pursuit of growth
would have to be tempered by an increasing awareness of its
consequences and by a sense that human beings were biological
creatures immersed in vital environmental relationships within
the earth's biosphere.

The Council advocated what it called, in the first use of the
term, a "conserver" society—a society of responsible steward-
ship, which conserved resources, recycled products and
respected the fragility of the biosphere.

___The Trudeau Government's Environmental
   Program: The First Decade_____

The decade of the 1960s saw heated debate over environmental
issues. The new Trudeau government could not, and did not,
avoid the questions the environmentalists had raised. It was
determined to mount an attack on environmental problems
and to establish the institutional machinery to make that attack
effective.

The Trudeau government realized that environmental
problems flowed from powerful forces at work in modern
society—especially the major forces of urbanization and
technology. Prime Minister Trudeau, speaking in the debate on
the Speech from the Throne on October 24, 1969, expressed the
government's concern:

> We intend to tackle the problems of environment, not only
> in the Northern regions but everywhere in Canada, by
> directing our efforts mainly to the two major sources of
> pollution: urbanization and the invasion of modern
> technology. . . .

The same technology that has produced real miracles in the field of communication and transport, as well as in the advance of applied sciences, remains however the most formidable enemy of a safe biosphere. . . .

[Man] . . . has too often used the resources provided by his intelligence and his instinct not so much to accept the challenges confronting him as to challenge his own survival. In so doing he threatens not only his own species but also the whole life on our planet.

The present government is firmly determined that no such acts of madness will be allowed to go on indefinitely, at least in Canada.

These concerns for the management of technology were to lead to the establishment of the Ministry of State for Science and Technology, and concern for urbanization was reflected in the creation of the Ministry of State for Urban Affairs and in a series of steps which culminated in the Habitat Conference on Human Settlement held in Vancouver in 1976. However, the constitutional limitations on the federal government's role in urban affairs prevented the federal government from being as active a presence as many would have liked.

_____ The Creation of Environment Canada _____

The most evident step taken by the Trudeau government in response to environmental concerns was the establishment of the Department of the Environment (or Environment Canada), announced on October 8, 1970, put in place by an order-in-council on November 26, 1970, and formalized through the proclamation of the Government Organization Act on June 11, 1971.

The orientation of the new department was holistic: the management of Canada's resources was to be undertaken not as a series of discrete programs dealing with individual sectors, but as shared aspects of the "environment," a concept which reflected the interrelatedness of natural resources and their multiple use.

Jack Davis—Canada's first minister of the environment—expressed this conviction of the need for a comprehensive, integrated approach in describing Environment Canada to the House of Commons on January 27, 1971:

> Our new Federal Department of the Environment will be concerned with Canada's renewable resources. It will be concerned with wild, living things, resources like trees, fish and wildlife. It will also concern itself with their life support systems, other resources like air, water and soil. Taken together these living and life related resources make up a natural whole. They are interrelated. They are mutually self-sustaining. They must be managed and they must be guarded in a comprehensive way. They must be operated on a sustained yield basis now and in the future.

By mid-1973 the basic administrative structure of the Department of the Environment had been put in place. It consisted of three main activities: the Atmospheric Environment Service (AES), which incorporated the former meteorological service; the Environmental Management Service (EMS, later renamed the Environmental Conservation Service), which included the Canadian Forestry Service, the Canadian Wildlife Service, the Inland Waters Directorate and the Lands Directorate; and the Environmental Protection Service (EPS), which was a new entity. EPS would be concerned with air pollution; water pollution; waste management, including resource and energy conservation; contaminants; environmental impact assessment and control; environmental emergencies; and liaison on environmental protection matters with industry and the provincial governments. It also became a channel of communication for the public and a clearing house on environmental protection matters with departments and agencies of the federal government.

The creation of the Canadian Environmental Advisory Council (CEAC) in March 1972, to give the minister of the environment independent counsel and advice on the problems and policies concerning the Canadian environment was another important initiative. Contrary to fears expressed at the time of its creation that CEAC was too close to the minister and department to be independent in its criticisms, it has given frank and forthright advice. It has also been an important link in bringing the views of many hundreds of nongovernmental organizations concerned with the environment to the attention of government. CEAC's comments may from time to time have embarrassed ministers (or the department) but the role of an aggressive though friendly critic has been vital both as a stimulus for action and as a source of alternative advice.

___ Federal-Provincial Environmental Co-operation ___

In the 1970s Environment Canada's mandate was to be extended by an important series of legislative initiatives that fleshed out the authority of the new department to act and to regulate. One potential obstacle to doing this was confusion about the federal government's responsibility in relation to environmental matters. The Fathers of Confederation, understandably, had been oblivious to the need to allocate jurisdiction over the environment in the British North America Act. As a result, both the federal and provincial governments hold significant jurisdictional responsibilities with implications for the environment. The federal government has authority in relation to international, boundary and coastal waters (and, according to some commentators, over interprovincial waterways). It also has authority in environmental matters through legislative jurisdiction over navigation, fisheries, agriculture, the criminal law, and trade and commerce. The provincial governments hold proprietary rights over Crown land and other natural resources within their boundaries.

In default of a specific institutional allocation of environmental jurisdiction, it was, by the 1960s, unclear whether responsibility rested in federal or provincial hands, and as a result, it was difficult to establish enforceable national environmental standards. At issue, therefore, was whether Canada was to have a piecemeal environmental approach based on provincial authority or a coherent, co-ordinated national policy of environmental regulation. This question was discussed at length at the Federal-Provincial Constitutional Conference of September 14–16, 1970, which concluded that the federal government should be responsible for the defence of the environment from international dangers and for establishing national standards. The enforcement of these standards within the boundaries of the provinces, however, would be a matter of provincial jurisdiction. It was also agreed that a variety of programs—such as water resources management—would be subject to intergovernmental agreements and receive federal financial assistance. In sum, there was a consensus that proper management of the environment would require co-ordinated action by both levels of government.

To promote this co-operative approach, Environment Canada established an Intergovernmental Affairs Directorate for communication with provincial authorities. Liaison between the two levels of government was also greatly facilitated by the Canadian Council of Resource and Environment Ministers, which provided a forum for the exchange of information and views. The Council, headed by the provincial and federal ministers of resources and the environment, met annually, assisted by a permanent secretariat, for the discussion of common problems and a continuing review of environmental programs.

___ A Legislative Base for Environmental Action _____

A steady flow of legislation from 1968 until the mid-1970s vastly enhanced the capacity of the federal government to provide environmental protection. The federal Fisheries Act, the Northern Inland Waters Act and the Canada Shipping Act were amended to bolster the government's power to designate substances "deleterious" and prohibit their discharge into the sea or interprovincial inland waters. Under these acts, nationwide standards were brought forward, regulating the use of mercury and phosphorus and the effluents from the pulp and paper industry, and a system was established for reporting and clean-up of oil and other dangerous spills.

The Pest Control Products Act was revised in 1969 to regulate the manufacture, storage, distribution and use of pesticides in Canada.

The Canada Water Act (1970) authorized research and the planning and implementation of programs for the conservation, development and use of water. This legislation put in place a comprehensive framework for a co-operative approach between the federal and provincial governments for managing Canada's water resources. Although the Act provided for joint water-quality-management agencies to design and operate sewage treatment plants and to police effluent standards for waste, these agencies were never established. The Act, however, also authorized unilateral action by the federal government in relation to boundary and interprovincial waters, if the quality of those waters was of national concern, and required those responsible for producing wastes that polluted water to bear the costs of cleaning up that pollution.

The Territorial Sea and Fishing Zones Act was amended in 1970 to extend Canadian territorial waters to twelve nautical miles and to increase the size of Canada's fishing zones in the Gulf of St Lawrence, in the Bay of Fundy and off the British Columbia coast.

The Arctic Waters Pollution Prevention Act (1970) was concerned with environmental protection and the maintenance of Canada's sovereignty over Arctic waters, which many Canadians felt was at risk as a result of the voyage of the American tanker *Manhattan* into the Northwest Passage. The effect of the legislation was to make clear that Arctic waters would be opened to shipping only under conditions that protected their delicate ecology. Under the Act, Canada extended its jurisdiction for pollution-control purposes one hundred miles from its coastline in the case of commercial shipping, and farther in the case of commercial exploitation of the continental shelf. The Act also prohibited the deposit of waste within this jurisdiction.

The Clean Air Act (1970) empowered the federal government to establish, operate and maintain a system of air pollution monitoring stations throughout Canada; undertake air pollution research; establish national air-quality objectives, air-quality emissions standards and national air-quality guidelines; formulate comprehensive plans for the control and abatement of air pollution; establish demonstration projects; and publish information for the education of the public on air pollution.

The Motor Vehicle Safety Act (1971) provided the

government with the authority to establish emissions standards for motor vehicles, and led to the reduction of lead levels in gasoline and the decision in 1983 to phase out entirely the use of lead as a gasoline additive.

The Canada Wildlife Act (1973) enabled the government to take measures to protect any species in danger of extinction and authorized the federal government to acquire and manage lands for migratory bird conservation, interpretation and research, and to enter into co-operative arrangements with the provinces or private organizations for wildlife conservation. Important steps were also taken to improve the management of migrating wildlife species, and negotiations were undertaken with the United States concerning the Porcupine Caribou Herd. This last initiative led eventually to the management treaty signed in 1987.

The Environmental Contaminants Act (1975) was designed to prevent the introduction of potentially hazardous substances into the environment. It gave the federal government the power to demand that industry provide environmental impact information about substances already in use, or proposed for use, that might be harmful to the environment or to human health. The law provided for preventive action, ranging from limitations or controls to outright ban on the use, manufacture or importation of such hazardous products.

The Ocean Dumping Control Act (1975) was designed to protect Canadian fisheries, recreational areas and coastal waters from contamination by ships plying Canadian waters. The Act requires permits to be obtained for dumping, dredging, incineration at sea, disposal of vessels and disposal on ice, and these permits are not normally granted for substances that are known to cause harm to the marine environment.

This impressive record of legislation from 1968 to the mid-1970s focused, on the whole, on the direct and obvious effects of pollution. The Trudeau government's initial response to the challenge of protecting the environment—what came to be called the first generation of environmental policy—was to establish an extensive regulatory structure to curb, control and abate environmental degradation.

____ Environmental Assessment and Review _____

These efforts led, in turn, to a second generation of environmental thinking, which saw pollution in terms of the misuse of resources. The public shift towards the values of the conserver society in the early 1970s, reinforced by the energy crisis in 1973, helped governments to see that after-the-fact pollution control was a band-aid solution. With a better understanding of the complex relationships between resources, energy, technology and population growth, emphasis began to be placed on anticipating problems stemming from the impact of human activities on the environment, and on integrating resource and environmental management with Canada's economic development.

In short, as the 1970s wore on, environment policy evolved from the initial phase of combatting pollution by cleaning up after the event to the stage of planning to prevent pollution. This meant that there was a need to collect large amounts of data about the physical environment and understand its basic processes. With this knowledge, the government would be able to incorporate environmental protection measures at the design stage into resource development projects which it undertook or assisted and, through environmental assessment, to plan projects in an acceptable manner before they were constructed.

The instrument for achieving this was institutionalized environmental assessment and review. The Cabinet established the Environmental Assessment and Review Process (EARP) in 1973 to ensure that studies were carried out for all federal projects and activities that were likely to have a significant effect on the environment and to ensure that the results of these assessments were used in planning programs and in making and implementing decisions.

Undoubtedly the establishment of EARP was a great step forward. But it was not fully adequate. While Environment Canada was committed to environmental protection, other departments—especially those with a resource-development orientation—did not necessarily subscribe wholeheartedly to the conservationist ethic. There was tension in the governmental division of responsibilities between Environment

Canada on the one hand and departments like the Department of Energy and the Department of Indian Affairs and Northern Development, which held responsibility for resource development.

Some critics argued that the EARP process was flawed because it was based on the Cabinet's administrative decision, rather than legislation. They feared that departments would opt out of the review process if they found its requirements burdensome.

In fact, almost all major environmentally significant projects were subjected to the environmental assessment process. Nevertheless, the EARP process was strengthened by order-in-council regulations in June 1984, which were interpreted by Mr Justice Cullen in 1989 as requiring mandatory participation by government departments in environmental review.

___ The Mackenzie Valley Pipeline_____

One important example of environmental review, which, because of its enormous scope, took place outside the EARP process, was the Mackenzie Valley Pipeline Inquiry conducted by Justice Thomas Berger. Next to the establishment of Environment Canada, this inquiry was the most significant environmental initiative taken by the Trudeau government. The report is a landmark in Canadian environmental history and its impact on the public was profound. It heightened sensitivity to the environmental problems of economic development in ecologically sensitive areas, enhanced understanding of the cultures of native peoples and, especially, led to the understanding that social effects, as much as ecological effects, are the proper concern of environmental policy.

The Mackenzie Valley Pipeline Inquiry was designed to ensure that a full environmental assessment—including consequences for human settlements as well as ecological impact—was undertaken before any commitment was made to construct a natural gas pipeline in the Mackenzie Valley. Justice Berger concluded that the environmental losses from the project would be severe, and that the opposition of native peoples to the pipeline would be unyielding. He recommended against the pipeline's construction, and the government took his advice.

___ Canada's International Environmental Role ___

So far, I have concentrated on describing the evolution of environmental policy in a domestic context. But the government was also active—indeed, it was a leader—in promoting environmental action internationally.

Canada was co-sponsor with Sweden of the United Nations resolution that established the United Nations Conference on the Human Environment held in Stockholm in 1972. There was widespread support for the conference within Canada. Eleven public hearings took place across the country—with over 1,200 participants and 400 written or oral briefs presented to the government—to generate public interest and provide advice and counsel on the position the government should adopt. Canada's Minister of the Environment, Jack Davis, was elected as one of the vice-chairmen of the conference, and a Canadian, Maurice Strong, acted as the conference's secretary-general. Canada successfully pressed for the inclusion of two important principles in the declaration made by the conference: first, that states have an obligation to ensure that activities within their jurisdiction or control do not cause damage to the environment beyond their borders and, second, that states would co-operate to develop international law for compensating foreign victims of damage caused by polluting activities within their jurisdiction.

The Stockholm Conference adopted a Declaration on the Human Environment, which contained principles to guide the development of international law; approved 109 resolutions as an action plan for tackling the world's environmental ills; and recommended establishing a new United Nations agency and an international fund to encourage environmental action. The conference proposals were forwarded to the United Nations General Assembly in September 1972 and led to the establishment of the UN Habitat agency, the appointment of a UN under-secretary for environmental affairs and the creation of the United Nations Environmental Program (UNEP). With justice, Maurice Strong was able to salute the Stockholm

Conference as "the first step in a new journey of hope for the future of mankind."

Another Trudeau government initiative that had international implications was the passage of the Ocean Dumping Control Act (1975), which I have already described. This legislation resulted from Canada's signing the London Convention in 1972, an international agreement under UN auspices to prevent marine pollution. The convention prohibited any deliberate disposal at sea of wastes or other matter from vessels, aircraft, platforms or other manmade structures. The convention—and Canada's legislation—were part of an international consensus that the ocean should not be a garbage dump or junkyard for the refuse of industrial societies.

____ The Law of the Sea Conferences _____

Canada was equally active in the Law of the Sea Conferences (the LOSC), which began in June 1974 and which, over the next eight years, dealt with the full range of ocean interests: the exploration and exploitation of sea-bed mineral resources; the extent and nature of coastal state jurisdiction over living resources; the extent of coastal state jurisdiction over the resources of the continental margin; navigation and over-flight rights on the high seas, territorial seas and straits; the delimitation of boundaries between opposite and adjacent states; the rights of land-locked and geographically disadvantaged states; the protection of marine environments; the freedom of marine scientific research; and the peaceful settlement of disputes. Canada's negotiating team—led by Alan Beesley, who was also chairman of the drafting committee of the conference—was instrumental in making the conference a success. It also greatly furthered Canada's maritime interests. The LOSC recognized (as Canada had advocated) the authority of countries over Exclusive Economic Zones (EEZ) with the right to manage both living and non-living resources not only out to two hundred miles offshore, but in the continental shelves beyond. Canada gained jurisdiction over an estimated 400,000 square miles through the adoption of this formula. Equally important for Canada was the recognition by the LOSC that in "ice-covered areas" within their EEZ, countries had the right to adopt and enforce nondiscriminatory laws and regulations against pollution. This gave international endorsement to the Arctic Waters Pollution Prevention Act. Also important to Canada was the convention's ban on salmon fishing outside the two-hundred-mile limit.

Even more significant, however, than these specific Canadian interests were the overall provisions of the Law of the Sea Convention signed in 1982. It established a base for developing numerous aspects of marine law, including those governing pollution-reporting requirements, contingency plans for pollution spills, the dumping of wastes and a variety of other forms of marine hazards and pollutions. Though it has not yet been ratified by a sufficient number of signatories to bring it into formal legal effect (because of a lack of consensus on the issue of sea-bed mining rights), the framework of rights and obligations set forth in the convention is in fact the framework that all countries are implicitly accepting. The LOS Convention is the most ambitious agreement affecting the oceans ever concluded, an historic achievement for which Canada deserves much credit.

Canada was also active in the Organization for Economic Co-operation and Development (OECD) environmental meetings that began in the early 1970s. Canada chaired several of the OECD committees established to develop common international standards for the testing, study and treatment of the production of chemicals. These committees developed an international system for assessing and classifying chemicals, providing them in effect with a central "passport" in order to avoid the expense and confusion of different countries using different standards, and to avoid duplication of effort. The committees also developed agreements for the international disposal of hazardous wastes.

The Trudeau government was also at the forefront of efforts to combat the depletion of the stratospheric ozone layer by industrial chemicals, especially chlorofluorocarbons (CFCs). Canada, along with the United States and the Scandinavian countries, banned most uses of CFCs as aerosol propellants in the 1970s, and played an important role in the Co-ordinating Committee on the Ozone Layer at the United Nations Environment Program. This led, in 1985, to the signing of the

Vienna Convention for the Protection of the Ozone Layer (which Canada was the first country to ratify) and the Montreal Protocol on Substances That Deplete the Ozone Layer, signed in September 1987 by twenty-four countries, which established an international framework to promote research and develop controls to combat ozone layer damage.

___ Canadian-American Environmental Relations:
Co-operation and Conflict _____

Relations with the United States were, of course, at the top of Canada's international environmental agenda. This could hardly be otherwise, given the long common border between the two countries – and the north-south flow of air, water and migrating species across it. The two countries thus shared a host of environmental problems, and the actions taken in one country could, and often did, have considerable environmental consequences for its neighbour.

Co-operation for the protection and conservation of joint water resources had long-standing roots in Canadian-American relations. The Boundary Waters Treaty of 1909 contains the basic framework for international co-operation in the management of these resources. The treaty provides that "boundary waters and waters flowing across the boundary shall not be polluted on either side to the injury of health or property on the other" and established the International Joint Commission (IJC) to resolve disputes, and to examine and report on any boundary water matter referred to it by either of the two governments. Against this legislative background, a variety of border water problems were of continuing concern to the Trudeau government – the flooding of the Skagit Valley and the proposed Garrison Diversion Plan, to name only two – but the government was most preoccupied with the water quality of the Great Lakes.

___ The Great Lakes Water Quality Agreements _____

By the mid-1960s the detection of mercury in the Great Lakes and the evident level of pollution of Lake Erie had caused widespread public concern. Reports undertaken by the Great Lakes Institute of the University of Toronto for the IJC confirmed that the waters of Lake Erie were in an advanced state of eutrophication and that there was a real danger of Lake Ontario reaching a similar state. The commission found that the major sources of this pollution were municipal and industrial wastes – in particular, the discharge of phosphorus. The main recommendations of the commission were to set water-quality objectives as a basis for the establishment of local regulatory standards and to urge governments to agree on programs and schedules to achieve these objectives. The IJC also suggested that it be given authority for the co-ordination of programs, the surveillance of water quality and the monitoring of the extent to which affected states and provinces were complying with the agreements undertaken.

The basic recommendations of the commission were accepted and included in the Great Lakes Water Quality Agreement signed by Prime Minister Trudeau and President Nixon in Ottawa on April 15, 1972.

Since the signing of the 1972 agreement, great progress has been made in cleaning up conventional pollution discharge into the lakes. The reduction of phosphate pollution and upgraded sewage treatment programs have greatly improved the condition of the lakes and helped revive commercial and sports fisheries in the Great Lakes waters.

It soon became clear, nevertheless, that phosphates and solid wastes were only the tip of the pollution iceberg in the Lakes. When the incidence of fish cancers continued to rise and more and more fish species had to be added to the "unsafe to eat" list, and especially after the revelation of toxic damage flowing from the Love Canal site, public and government concern about the contamination of the Great Lakes intensified.

This led to a revised Great Lakes Water Quality Agreement, which was signed on November 22, 1978. Provisions to eliminate almost entirely the discharge of toxic substances into the Great Lakes and to establish warning systems were added to the original agreement, and revised water-quality objectives were defined for the Great Lakes as a whole. Provisions were also made for dealing with pollution from land use activities and airborne pollutants. Monitoring and surveillance requirements were revised as well, to better assess the effectiveness of control programs.

The war against toxic substances will be a long and difficult one—with no easy victories. A good start was made to reduce their presence in the Great Lakes through the accords signed between Canada and the United States in the 1970s, but the struggle was to remain a major preoccupation of the government into the next decade.

___ The First Decade of Environmental Policy ___

Looking back at the decade of the 1970s, Don Chant, chairman of the Canadian Environmental Advisory Council, provided a list of the environmental "successes" of those ten years:

1. The banning of some particularly harmful pesticides, and generally better control of pesticides and increased emphasis on non-chemical control.
2. Rigorous controls of several classes of dangerous pollutants.
3. Greater funding of environmental research.
4. Preservation of certain parklands, wilderness areas, sensitive marshes, and the like.
5. Actions to prevent heedless and destructive development in some of our urban centres.
6. Development of some systems for recycling and conservation and for the disposal of wastes.
7. And, finally, the significant changes in attitudes and perceptions that have led to such things as some of our political parties actually developing environmental platforms and formulating environmental Bills of Rights.[1]

But even if the list of successes was a matter of some satisfaction when looking at the starting point ten years earlier, there was, as Dr Chant also emphasized, a very long way yet to go.

___ The World Conservation Strategy ___

It was my task, when I became minister of the environment in

1980, to build upon the foundation of the previous decade. We began by adopting, in 1981, the World Conservation Strategy (WCS) commissioned by the United Nations Environment Program and prepared jointly by the World Wildlife Fund and the International Union for the Conservation of Nature and Natural Resources. The WCS represented a global consensus on the role of conservation in world development, and put forward a framework of priority objectives that ought to be pursued by national governments:

1. to maintain essential ecological processes and life support systems;
2. to preserve genetic diversity;
3. to ensure the sustainable utilization of species and ecosystems.

Canada committed itself to implement the principles of the World Conservation Strategy. The government of Canada took this obligation seriously.

The National Park system was a key part of this effort. When Jean Chrétien was minister of Indian and northern affairs in the early 1970s, the Trudeau government had embarked on a vigorous expansion of the national parks, especially in the creation of three new northern national parks. This initiative, along with the program for historic sites, the preservation of canal systems, the establishment of recreation corridors and the launching of Heritage Canada on April 1, 1973, went a long way to ensure that representative areas in Canada were preserved.

To help maintain essential ecological processes and preserve genetic diversity, the government participated in the International Biosphere Program (IBP). In co-operation with nongovernmental organizations, the federal and provincial governments supported a comprehensive network of designated areas, securing the habitats of threatened, unique and other important species, and protecting unique ecosystems and representative samples of ecosystem types. By the mid-1980s almost a thousand IBP sites across Canada had been identified and more than half of them were officially protected as national or provincial parks, nature reserves, natural areas, wilderness parks, ecological reserves or bird sanctuaries.

Under the Migratory Birds Convention Act and the Canada Wildlife Act, the Department of the Environment was authorized to acquire lands as natural wildlife areas. By the mid-1980s forty such areas had been established. The preservation of wetlands in Canada was accelerated with the signing in 1981 of the Ramsar Convention on Wetlands of International Importance. Canada had already signed, in 1975, the Convention on International Trade in Endangered Species (CITES), which regulated the importation of designated species, and in 1976 it signed the World Heritage Convention, which led to the designation of nine heritage sites in Canada. In 1982 the federal government and the provinces unanimously endorsed the Guidelines for Wildlife Policy, which explicitly adopted the WCS objectives for the management of wild animals and their habitat.

The government also moved to fulfil its World Conservation Strategy commitment to ensure the sustainable use of species and ecosystems. It did this largely through a series of individual strategies for natural resource activities.

In 1980 the government approved the Federal Policy on Land Use, which was designated to ensure that federal policies and programs and the management of federal lands would contribute to the wise use of land resources. Guidelines were established to maintain prime agricultural land, combat soil degradation, protect ecologically important sites and preserve important habitats for animals.

A Forest Sector Strategy for Canada was approved by the federal government in 1981 and the next year the publication of *A Framework for Forest Renewal* led to five-year shared-cost agreements with the provinces with substantial funding to promote forest renewal, help develop skilled human resources in the forestry sector and enhance research and development.

Two years later, the Task Force on Northern Conservation was established, with a wide-ranging membership from government, industries and universities. In December 1984, it brought forward a landmark report, providing a framework for creating a comprehensive conservation policy for the North and a strategy for its implementation.

In January 1984 Environment Canada initiated an Inquiry

on Federal Water Policy. This was the first comprehensive assessment of the federal government's role in managing water resources. The report recommended a national water conservation policy that would enable the federal government to initiate needed programs with the provinces through cost-sharing arrangements.

The adoption of the World Conservation Strategy and the first moves to implement its precepts represented a significant step forward, but environmentalists recognized that the battle against environmental degradation was going to be a longer and far more complicated struggle than had been originally thought. After the first generation of combatting evident sources of pollution and the next generation of undertaking preventive environmental planning, it had become clear that Canada still faced environmental problems of great technical complexity and often of international dimensions.

By 1980 two of these problems were at the top of the environmental agenda: the problem of toxic substances and the problem of acid rain.

___Combatting Toxic Pollution _____

Toxic chemical substances are the sorcerer's apprentice of the chemical revolution that has brought such great benefits to the postwar developed world. Modern chemical technology has created by-product wastes—poisons like mirex, dioxin and PCBs—which constitute widely dispersed, long-lived, long-term dangers to human health. The unanticipated damage from the chemical side effects of industrial progress is a particularly devastating example of the general environmental problem of managing the products of escalating technology.

In spite of the great progress in cleaning up waste discharges in the Great Lakes, toxic pollution had become the greatest threat to the Great Lakes ecosystem by the beginning of the eighties. Scientists in both Canada and the United States concluded that the 40 million people living in the Great Lakes region are exposed to more toxic chemicals than any other comparable population in North America. In the 1970s, the frightening seepage of wastes from the Love Canal into the Niagara River led to a public outcry to solve the toxic problem. To give the public reassurance was no easy task. Increasing technical sophistication had given us the ability to detect smaller and smaller amounts of toxic substances in the air, water and land without providing us with the knowledge of how to remove them, or even, in many cases, the knowledge of what, if any, harm might come from them.

Science does not enable us to pronounce anything absolutely safe, since we are necessarily ignorant of what new information future research might provide. Toxic chemicals had to be managed, then, on the basis of a balance of imperfect evidence, and their use had to be controlled according to concepts of "acceptable levels of risk." Of course, it is difficult to convince the public that *any* risk is acceptable; yet, in honesty, the assurance that all risk has been eliminated can never be given.

The Trudeau government's response to toxic hazards was threefold. First, as I have mentioned, the Great Lakes Water Quality Agreement was amended in 1978 to focus on toxic chemicals. Second, the government established, along with the United States, the Niagara River Toxic Committee to devise an action plan for cleaning up the Niagara River, which led to greatly improved control of industrial discharges. Third, Environment Canada established the Toxic Chemicals Management Program in 1980. Its keystone was a new Toxic Chemicals Management Centre, which served as a "command post" for all toxic chemical control activities, including cleaning up existing toxic sites, developing control strategies based on improved assessment of the risks chemicals entail and designing a "cradle-to-the-grave" management approach for the handling of toxic chemicals to prevent newly produced dangerous toxic compounds from entering the environment.

This last control was instituted through the Transportation of Dangerous Goods Act (1980), which established uniform requirements across Canada for handling and transporting dangerous goods and for regulating hazardous wastes entering or leaving Canada. The transportation of hazardous wastes came to be governed by the requirements of a federal manifest system, which recorded the movement of hazardous wastes from generation to disposal, and required that storage, treatment and disposal of wastes occurred only at provincially approved facilities.

We have not "solved" the problem of toxic chemicals—

especially the problem of coping with the accumulated wastes of the past. But in the early 1980s we did put into place the structure for managing those problems.

___ Acid Rain ___

The second major environmental fight of the Trudeau government in the 1980s was the battle against acid rain.

Acid rain is caused by the emission into the atmosphere of sulphur dioxide and nitrous oxide. These substances, often transported hundreds of miles, fall to the earth as dry depositions or as rain or snow, to an intensity that can reach the acidic level of vinegar. The cumulative effect of this fallout or of the sudden shock of its entry into lakes and streams in the spring run-off, can damage water systems in sensitive areas to such a degree that they can no longer sustain fish life.

Acid rain also affects human health (especially for those who suffer from respiratory diseases), it affects the quality of drinking water through the acidic leaching of toxic substances into water supplies and it accelerates the erosion and decay of buildings to an annual repair cost of hundreds of millions of dollars in North America. Acid rain damages the sports fisheries in Canada and the salmon fishery in the Atlantic provinces. The Canadian forestry industry, which directly or indirectly employs one in every ten Canadians, is also at risk, since acid rain retards the regeneration of forests. The slow accumulation of acidity in the Canadian water system and its impact on the land thus threatens both human health and major Canadian economic interests.

By 1977 the build-up of air-borne acidity had reached a level that made acid rain, as Roméo LeBlanc, then minister of the environment, described it, "an environmental time bomb waiting to go off."

However, acid rain was and is a problem that cannot be controlled by Canada alone. One-half of the acid rain fallout in Canada comes from industrial sources in the northeastern United States. This acid rain falls on geologically sensitive areas, which have little capacity to buffer the terrain from damage, and it causes about two-thirds to three-quarters of Canada's acid rain damage. Acid rain is therefore inescapably a joint problem for Canada and the United States, because of territorial proximity and the prevailing path of weather systems. Since the late 1970s, Canada has treated the acid rain battle as a common cause and has sought agreement with the United States to fight the problem on that basis.

At first, when President Carter held office, these efforts met with some success. In August 1980 a Memorandum of Intent was signed between Canada and the United States, which committed both countries

1. to negotiate an agreement to regulate the quality of the air that crosses the Canada-United States border;
2. to enforce vigorously existing laws and regulations against the sulphur and nitrogen emissions which cause acidic deposition;
3. to establish Working Groups to prepare the scientific and technical information necessary to draw up the provisions of the projected air quality agreement.

The Working Groups began almost immediately to provide information on the impact of acid rain and to develop the technology and control strategies required to combat it. The Canadian government hoped that the continuing work of these groups would enable boundary air pollution problems to be dealt with by the same step-by-step process that had led to progress in cleaning up the Great Lakes—that is, by a series of agreements, whereby increasingly precise objectives could be established as research and experience provided improved methods of control. Sufficient information was already available to establish a clear need for action on air-borne pollution and to design initial standards for emission controls; improvements could follow as increased knowledge warranted.

The new Reagan administration, however, took a very different view from that of the preceding government. It regarded environmental regulation as a drag on the productivity of the economy. When the Canadian government asked, as the Memorandum of Intent had promised, for the vigorous application of existing regulations, it was told that, since the regulations included exemption clauses, "vigorous application" did not exclude the increasing use of exemptions. When pressed to conclude the promised treaty on transboundary air pollution, the Reagan administration replied that much more research was needed before it would give approval for expensive measures to respond to a need that the administration considered "unproven."

It is sometimes alleged that while pressing the United States for action, Canadian governments were slow to commit themselves to the kind of cutbacks in emissions they were seeking from the United States. But that is simply not true. With the assistance of research done by Environment Canada, the government of Ontario laid down requirements for substantial reductions in acid-causing emissions from Sudbury's Inco smelter and from Ontario Hydro's thermal power plants. And in February 1982 the government of Canada and the provinces agreed to lower air pollutant emissions to a level that would result in depositions of less than 20 kg per hectare by the year 1990 — that is, to a level sufficiently low, according to scientific modelling, to diminish, rather than intensify, acidic fallout. In 1984 this federal-provincial commitment was extended to ensure a 50 percent reduction of emissions causing acid rain by 1994.

Canada also worked hard to develop an international consensus on the need for emission controls in industrialized countries. This led ultimately — in June 1984 — to the "Ottawa Declaration," in which twenty-one countries committed themselves to cutting sulphur dioxide emissions (using 1980 as a base) by 30 percent by 1993.

The Trudeau government's attack on acid rain had three primary components:

- *scientific research* to determine regional levels of sulphur and nitrogen compounds in the air and in precipitation, to guide the operation of the Canada-wide precipitation sampling network and to develop and apply scientific models to understand the acid rain process;
- *development of control strategies* to measure and control sources of pollution that contribute to acid rain;
- *information campaigns* to make the public aware of the significance of acid rain and thus bring the pressure of

opinion to bear both on provincial governments in Canada to support emission regulation and, internationally, to persuade the United States to undertake measures against acid rain.

As it became clear that the Reagan administration was obdurately opposed to concrete control action, the Trudeau government attached more and more importance to information programs to bring home to Americans how much their own health and economic interests were threatened by the blight of acid rain.

In 1981 the Canadian government launched a major information and communications blitz in the United States—an unprecedented break from the traditions of "quiet diplomacy" that had generally guided relations between Canada and its neighbour. Every conceivable device was used, short of television commercials and billboards (which Environment Canada feared might be counterproductive) to inform Americans of the causes and consequences of acid rain.

Congressmen were lobbied in Washington and provided with background data and invited to visit devastated acid rain sites; a committee of Canadian parliamentarians on acid rain was established to discuss the issue with their American counterparts; American journalists were persuaded to come and see the acid rain story in Canada firsthand; governors and state legislatures—especially in those states affected by acid rain—were asked to speak out on the issue; the government encouraged an interest group of Canadian citizens—the Coalition on Acid Rain—to establish an information office in Washington; the government also worked in concert with a variety of American environmental groups to publicize acid rain problems; the Canadian minister of the environment undertook extensive speaking tours throughout the United States; American visitors to national parks were given brochures on the acid rain problem; the National Film Board produced two effective documentaries on acid rain—*Acid Rain, Requiem or Recovery* and *Acid from Heaven*—which drew even more attention from the public after the United States Department of Justice insisted that they be labelled "foreign government propaganda."

This massive public opinion campaign had positive results despite the inevitable annoyance it caused the United States government. Instead of talking of ways to emasculate the American Clean Air Act—which seemed to be the Reagan government's purpose when it came to office—Congress began to talk about ways of strengthening the Act to respond to acid rain problems. Though we had good success in raising the profile of the acid rain issue, progress in the United States was still grudging and slow.

___The Trudeau Environmental Record ___

By the time the Liberal government left office in 1984, much good work had been done. Its approach to environmental problems had moved from the first-generation stage of combatting existing, site-specific polluting problems, through the second-generation stage of establishing structures for pollution prevention and was poised to enter on a new, third-generation stage. By the mid-1980s Environment Canada had recognized that effective environmental action must be rooted in a long-term approach, which meant husbanding our resources, managing them in a way that would sustain and renew them and guiding economic development within recognized ecological limits.

At Environment Canada, this thinking prompted scientific research on ecological systems, support for the Man and the Biosphere program of the United Nations and support for "futures" research. In a series of conserver society projects, the department explored the social, environmental, technological and economic implications of doing more with less. The culmination of this approach was the publication in 1984 of two studies sponsored by Environment Canada—*Global 2000: Implications for Canada* and *Global 2000: Canadian Economic Development Prospects, Resources and the Environment*—which outlined clearly both the environmental limits to the exploitation of Canadian resources and the need for environmental renewal.

Although the precepts of the conserver society directed Environment Canada's efforts, these values were not always shared by other departments. Effective environmental action requires a *governmental* will, not only a departmental one—and Environment Canada did not always succeed in impressing environmental values on the whole government. By 1984 there was a clear need to place stronger powers in the hands of the Department of the Environment, to work out a more effective relationship with the provincial governments and to increase awareness of the benefits of conserver principles in the government as a whole, among both ministers and senior civil servants.

The election of the Mulroney government transformed the environmental perspective. Imbued with an ideological belief in a market-driven society, its initial view seemed to be that environmental action was at best a marginal frill, at worst a brake on productive economic forces. The result, in a series of backward steps, was near-disaster.

The first Mulroney budget slashed $46 million from the funding for Environment Canada. The government closed the Marine Ecology Laboratory in Bedford, Nova Scotia; cancelled the establishment of the Guelph-Toronto Toxicological Research Centre and the Water Resources Research Program; reduced the staff of the Canadian Wildlife Service by a quarter and its budget by 20 percent; cut research on renewable energy sources, PCBs and recycling; and reduced Canada's financial commitment to UNEP by 10 percent. In the face of public anger, some of the programs were reinstated—but without funding commitments or personnel allocation, so that they could only be carried on to the detriment of other projects. If one takes into account the impact of inflation on government programs, Environment Canada lost over three hundred jobs (mainly in the scientific, technical and research areas) and $80 million in funding during the four years of the first Mulroney government.

After the Quebec summit meeting with President Reagan, Prime Minister Mulroney pulled the rug out from underneath our acid rain efforts (and those of our American Congressional allies) by abandoning our efforts to have the American government meet its agreed commitments under the 1980 Memorandum of Understanding, in favour of doing more research into acid rain.

The Canadian Environmental Protection Act (proclaimed

on June 30, 1988), which was expected to strengthen the federal government's environmental responsibility, basically delegated existing powers of environmental regulatory enforcement to provincial governments, and thus undermined national environmental standards.

The Free Trade Agreement negotiated by the Mulroney government—which includes not only the United States but also the Maquiladora area of Mexico—may well undermine environmental standards as companies seek out the least-regulated regions available (and the lowest wages) as locations for industrial activity. Moreover, a free trade area, where our natural resources are equally available to United States consumers, removes the foundation for sustaining *national* resource-based conservation policies.

While the Mulroney government has now (in 1989) come to preach the slogan "sustainable development," it seems to interpret that slogan as endorsing environmental policies that will sustain economic development rather than as a principle for limiting and guiding economic growth in order to promote a healthy environment. For the Mulroney Conservatives, "sustainable growth" reflects a much greater sensitivity to the private-sector commercial agenda than an insistence on the priority of public needs. Fortunately, there is some evidence that growing public concern will push the Conservatives back towards environmentally protective policies.

Despite this Conservative attack, the legacy of the Trudeau government remains—the creation of Environment Canada, the expanded legislative base for environmental action, the establishment of environmental assessment and review processes, the landmark Mackenzie Valley Pipeline Inquiry, international leadership at Stockholm and at the Law of the Sea Conferences, the Great Lakes Water Quality Agreements, the adoption of the World Conservation Strategy, the Toxic Chemicals Management Program and the fight against acid rain. The struggle to build an environmentally sane society is far from over—and we have still a long road to travel in adopting the principles of the conserver society and environmentally guided sustainable development—but the Trudeau governments can be proud of the work they did to take Canada giant steps in that direction.

CHAPTER 7

Expansion, Retrenchment and Protecting the Future: Social Policy in the Trudeau Years

———— by Jim Coutts ————

Jim Coutts is the Chairman of Canadian Investment Capital, a financial holding company investing in manufacturing firms in Canada and the United States. He was raised in southern Alberta and practised law in Calgary in the early 1960s. He has been in and out of politics and government throughout his career as Private Secretary to Prime Minister Lester B. Pearson and Principal Secretary to Prime Minister Pierre Trudeau. Coutts lives in Toronto and Nanton, Alberta, writes on public policy issues for national newspapers and is a trustee of the Toronto Hospital for Sick Children, The Ontario College of Art, The Canada-China Trade Council and the Advisory Council of The Centre for Canadian Studies at Johns Hopkins University.

To CALL CANADIAN social policy in the Trudeau years nothing more than a noble effort would be to downgrade the accomplishments and ignore the new ground that was broken. To call the policy an epochal period in Canada's social evolution would be to exaggerate those accomplishments and ignore history. The truth, as usual, lies somewhere in between.

There were major accomplishments in the field of social security, including the broadening of the Unemployment Insurance Act and the introduction of the Child Tax Credit. And there was more adequate funding of programs like the Guaranteed Income Supplement for seniors. But perhaps more important, the sixteen years were a period of innovation, in which social policy was defined more broadly. A great deal of thinking was done on "quality-of-life" issues in an effort to link

221

social and economic initiative, allow citizens to participate more fully in the creation of programs and bring more jobs and better incomes to all regions in Canada. Notably, in the areas of regional development, youth, women, natives and the disabled, some good ideas were put forth and implemented. Some sound thinking also went into the development of incomes policy, including a series of strategies on guaranteed income, shelter allowance, child care and pension reform.

There are always opposing forces when any government attempts to introduce social programs that seek to improve the quality of life of the less fortunate. The voices of conservatism are always raised in shrill protest against any move that threatens to disturb the status quo. In Canada, particularly during the latter part of the Trudeau administration, the attack on established social policy was heightened to levels not seen since the early part of the century. The battle became jurisdictional as well as ideological. The business and professional community heated up their attack on the cost and so-called waste of social programs. Some provinces fought long and hard against the introduction of new national programs, while others did their best to undermine the programs that were already in place.

Given the political climate during this period, what was accomplished was a great achievement. It was a constructive period in Canada's social history, one that was far more active than a superficial look at the record would indicate. It needs to be documented within the context of what was happening in other countries, what the political climate was in Canada during the period and what had gone before.

The Foundations

Social policy has been an important part of the Liberal party's agenda since the early years of Mackenzie King, who was the pioneer of modern Canadian thinking on social policy. As deputy minister of labour and later minister of labour between 1908 and 1911, he was one of the first in Canada to demonstrate the link between economic initiatives and social problems. He maintained that they went hand in hand and promoted these views to win the leadership of his party. The result was the following significant resolution passed by the Liberal party convention in 1919: "[Canada needs] an adequate system of insurance against unemployment, sickness, dependence in old age, and other disability, which would include old age pensions, widows' pensions, and maternity benefits. The system should be instituted by the Federal Government in conjunction with the Governments of the several provinces."[1]

Thus were the first strands of Canada's social security thinking woven into place. It took decades before the 1919 plans became reality, but all were passed eventually. The cumulative record is most impressive. In the decades following 1919, federal governments enacted:

- 1927 the Pension Act, Canada's first
- 1940 the Unemployment Insurance Act
- 1944 the Family Allowance Act
- 1951 a system of financial aid to universities
- 1952 universal Old Age Security for all Canadians over 70 and all those in need over 65
- 1958 a national hospital plan
- 1965 the Canada Pension Plan
- 1966 the Guaranteed Income Supplement
- 1966-67 the Canada Assistance Plan, the Occupational Training Act and the Medical Care Act

By the mid-1940s, Canada had a modest pension scheme and an unemployment insurance program. This was progress, but far from enough to meet the needs. In the years following World War II, Canadians were determined never to see again the hardship inflicted on families by the Depression of the thirties. There was also a fear that without major peacetime initiatives following the war effort, there could be another massive economic slowdown. Social and economic initiatives had to be taken to create jobs as well as care for those who would fall between the cracks of new economic growth.

In the Throne Speeches of 1943 and 1944, the government held out the bold promise of a "charter of social security for the whole of Canada." This promise was fulfilled in 1945. Two blueprint documents – the *White Paper on Income and Employment* and the *Green Book on Reconstruction* – set out the goals that became the action plan for the next forty years. So began a long and laborious cultivation period that would bear fruit in the 1950s and 1960s.

Two issues presented major stumbling blocks. As social security was, according to the Constitution, largely under provincial jurisdiction, there would have to be widespread provincial agreement to any reforms and innovations introduced by the federal government. This would not be easy, for the Unemployment Insurance Act had been held up for more than ten years by the provinces. The issue of contributory social insurance versus universality also caused wide-ranging debate.

The universality issue was ultimately resolved in 1950 when Prime Minister Louis St Laurent appointed a parliamentary committee on social security chaired by Jean Lesage and spearheaded by David Croll (now Senator Croll). This committee had great influence on public opinion. Their rejection of any hint of a means test skewed the debate in favour of universality.

As for federal-provincial relations, the squabbling of the 1920s and 1930s simply continued and escalated. World War II had fostered strong centralism, and wartime taxation and distribution structures had put more money and power into the hands of the federal government. This had the effect of turning provincial governments into parochially active bodies with short-sighted goals. The provinces were losing more battles than they won, and social security and education became two fronts on which they were determined to hold the line.

Higher postwar incomes, population growth and technological advancements, combined with Canada's regionalism and obvious central domination, made the provinces even more ambitious. Federal-provincial battles were the order of the day, but there was some progress. Ottawa introduced the "Baby Bonus" (with the Family Allowance Act of 1944) and universal Old Age Security in 1952. After a ten-year battle with the provinces, and overcoming the more reactionary elements in its own ranks, the federal government created the hospital insurance scheme.

Social reform was central to Mike Pearson's rebuilding of the Liberal party and achieving power. He and the progressives he recruited from across Canada were in tune with public opinion in setting the social policy agenda. But they perhaps miscalculated how far the pendulum was swinging toward provincialism. They were not the only political force with a reform plan.

Pearson's four main social security measures, enacted and implemented in the 1965-67 period, were the Canada Pension Plan (CPP), the Canada Assistance Plan (CAP), the Guaranteed Income Supplement (GIS) and medical care insurance (commonly known as "medicare"), through the Medical Care Act (1966). Pearson charted his political manœuvring through the federal-provincial land mines, using something he called "co-operative federalism" as his primary direction finder. He introduced this concept in his opening statement to the November 1963 Federal-Provincial Conference in Ottawa:

> [Co-operative federalism] means, first, a mutual respect for the jurisdictions and the responsibilities of Canada and of the Provinces. It means, secondly, timely and reliable two-way consultation as the basis for co-ordinating the parallel action which Canada and the Provinces must take on matters of common and overlapping interest. Thirdly, it means that if and when certain tax fields are shared, this should be done in a manner appropriate to the respective responsibilities of federal and provincial authorities. And it means, fourthly, assurance that this sharing not only is equitable between the federal government and the Provinces generally, but also is equitable among the Provinces themselves, so that each separately can discharge its own responsibilities.[2]

It was a cautious and diplomatic step forward, and seemed to be well received by the premiers. However, the Quiet Revolution in Quebec led by Jean Lesage had another agenda. While sharing the zeal for the reforms Ottawa was proposing, the Quebec administration wanted to go it alone on pensions, medicare and the Canada Assistance Plan. Indeed, Quebec's pension plan proposal, revealed during debate on the Canada Pension Plan, was better than Ottawa's. And the rest of the premiers could see it.

The constitutional crisis of 1964 was simply a new version of the battle that had gone on for forty years—much of it over social security. At stake was the question of whether there would be programs that brought a decent life within the reach of all Canadians, or whether social security would be the gift of wealthier regions to their own residents—in other words, to hell with those in poorer areas.

The result, as usual, was a compromise, and the master of compromise in this case was Pearson's chief policy advisor, Tom Kent. His task was to resolve differences between the two plans without putting co-operative federalism in jeopardy. His committee included Joe Willard, Don Thorson, Claude Morin, Claude Castonguay and Maurice Sauvé. Together they hammered out a plan that eventually became both the Quebec Pension Plan and the Canada Pension Plan.

It was typical of Pearson, when in trouble, to double the stakes. So, with the battle continuing over pensions, he called the 1965 general election and made national medical care a central theme. But the results were inconclusive: the minority government was returned, almost unchanged. The election did, however, give the government the clout it required to add medicare to the agenda. That legislation was worked out and enacted in the 1966–67 period, although its implementation was delayed until early 1968.

As the Pearson years came to a close, it seemed that the war on poverty could be won. And there was progress enough on the federal-provincial front to obtain the constitutional amendments that allowed the Pearson government to bring in medicare, CAP and GIS. So the social security net had grown from a few strands to a full-blown catch-all. It was piecemeal of necessity—a hoped-for guaranteed income was a future dream—but a basic system had been put in place that would allow future policy makers to mend the tears, fill in the gaps and expand the coverage.

The advances in creating new social security measures that took place during the Trudeau years could not match the dramatic developments that took place under the St Laurent and Pearson governments. But there was progress. In the sections that follow, four aspects of social policy and the actions taken in each are examined: expanding the social security system, using the pieces already in place, finding new directions in social policy and holding the line.

____The Troubled Seventies and Eighties _____

At the end of Canada's tenth decade, one large hole remained in the social security system. It was the need for an income supplement plan for those below retirement age. True, there were federal and provincial welfare schemes for those who had completely fallen between the cracks and were totally without income. But there was no adequate plan for Canadians such as single parents who had no work or only part-time work during the year, or for those who could only find work that didn't provide enough to raise themselves and their families out of poverty. Whatever the name of the initiative (and it changed several times—guaranteed income, negative tax, income supplement), it had been envisaged as early as the 1920s and was considered throughout the Trudeau period.

Only in 1978 was the Child Tax Credit introduced as a genuine step toward an income supplement using the tax system. It put a tax credit into the hands of parents with middle and low incomes and, for those with no income, it supplied a full payment of $200 per child per year. The system was income-tested so that lower-income families with three children received $600, whereas middle-income parents with $22,000 income and one child received nothing.

But what happened to the idea of a guaranteed income between 1968 and 1978? Why, though meeting after meeting of the Liberal party endorsed it and many Cabinet ministers and caucus members supported the program, did the guaranteed income idea constantly drop to the bottom of the agenda?

First, a great many Canadians felt the social security bus had been overloaded in the 1960s. Second, as the early years of the first Trudeau administration passed, the window of continued economic prosperity that would have allowed for the establishment of another major program began to close. Third, too much time was spent in 1972 rethinking the system instead of creating the missing piece. And finally, in the process of waiting for a new approach, the more important reformers in Cabinet adapted existing programs, rather than developing a whole new system that would have included a guaranteed income.

The Pearson administration had catapulted the country to a level of social democracy unprecedented in Canada, and a lot of people were worried about paying the bills. What is the test as to whether the programs of the 1950s and 1960s had overloaded the economic system? One indication has to be the level of national debt caused partly by the new programs compared to the size and growth of the economy (national debt as a percentage of GNP). The irony is that during the period of the greatest worry—the late 1960s and early 1970s—the national debt as a percentage of GNP shrank to its lowest level of the century. It had grown dramatically through the Great Depression and World War II—to the point where the public debt was more than 100 percent of GNP. By the middle of the Trudeau years, however, the national debt was only 25 percent of GNP—the lowest since World War I. There is always much to worry about in the Canadian economy, but the overload caused by social programs was clearly the wrong worry. The early Trudeau administration should have jumped for an income-support program while the chance existed. By 1972 it would be too late. The government was in an economic box and couldn't get out.

Al Johnson spoke of "the troubled 1970s and 1980s" in his 1986 paper, "Social Policy in Canada." These were decades that saw "the emergence of new forces which were to materially affect society's views concerning social policy."[3] The world changed. For the first time, Third World countries were becoming forces to be reckoned with. They were getting their first taste of wealth and the power that went with it. Trading patterns began to shift. Demand was down in the markets on which the economies of Canada and the other industrialized nations largely depended. The squeeze was on for every country that was in the export business. Protectionist noises began to be heard around the world, from rich and poor nations alike. The beginning of the end was in sight for the easy touch so long enjoyed by the powerful Western nations in their foreign trade practices. Once-captive markets were threatening to disappear, and Canada was among the nations that were likely to be hit the hardest.

For the first time in years, Canada's growth rate slowed, and by the mid-1970s it was at a virtual standstill. Unemployment soared. So did inflation. The term *stagflation* was coined and immediately came into common usage.

Canada experienced a particularly rapid growth in its labour force during this period. Baby boomers were entering the job market for the first time, in the hundreds of thousands. The ranks of those seeking employment were further swelled as more and more women went to work outside the home. And while the country did produce new jobs in record numbers, the increase could not keep pace with the growth in the number of people looking for work. For the first time since the 1930s, unemployment rose to more than 10 percent of the labour force.

There were other problems. In 1976 the Parti québécois came to power. The federal government had already been preoccupied for some time with the spectre of Quebec trying to opt out of federal programs, but with the 1976 Quebec election, total secession became a real possibility. The enormity of it—indeed, the absolute unacceptability of it—was enough to divert the attention of the federal government's principal decision makers away from matters of social security. It wasn't until 1980, when Quebec's referendum on sovereignty-association was finally defeated, that Ottawa was able to breath a sigh of relief on the question of Quebec's independence.

Other distractions had also arisen. Even by 1976, the government was deeply embroiled in the fight against inflation, partly triggered by the OPEC crisis. Price and wage controls were introduced on Thanksgiving Day, 1976, and two years later, the prime minister announced major cutbacks in government spending. The country was fighting for its economic life. All this came at a time when Ottawa was trying to place limits on the growth of federal fiscal transfers to the provinces for the financing of health and secondary education programs.

Despite the growing economic and political turbulence in Canada in the 1970s, there were two attempts to expand the social security net. The first resulted in a wide-ranging review, the second in the Child Tax Credit. The circumstances of the two initiatives could not have been more different.

_____ A Blueprint for the Future _____

Following the 1972 election, the government called for a
comprehensive review of the country's social security system.
This was not just another study. It was a focused attempt to
achieve change. The prime minister had appointed one of his
strongest associates, Marc Lalonde, to the health and welfare
portfolio, and he had given Lalonde first-rate assistance by
appointing Al Johnson, one of Ottawa's most able civil
servants, to the post of deputy-minister of national health and
welfare. Lalonde and Johnson became the chief architects of
what was later dubbed the Orange Paper, the most ambitious
endeavour in the social policy field since the Green Book of
1945 and Tom Kent's work in the early 1960s.

The 1973 Orange Paper was a sweeping review, tantamount
to a blueprint for the future. It was based on the advancement
of five major strategies:

> ... an "*employment strategy*" whose goal would be
> "near-universal income from employment" – which
> meant jobs; a "*social insurance strategy*" which would
> make contributory social insurance the first line of
> defence against the contingencies of life; an "*income
> supplementation strategy*" through which income from
> employment or from social insurance would be supple-
> mented to meet family needs using a mix of universal and
> income-tested supplements; an "*income support plan*"
> twinned with income supplementation to meet the basic
> needs of people who could not work, or could not find
> work, or could not be expected to work; and, finally, an
> "*employment and social services strategy*" through which
> social services would be provided with the object (along
> with the incentives built into the income supplementation
> plans) of contributing to the optimum personal function,
> and self-reliance, of the beneficiaries.[4]

Johnson went on to say that "implicit in these strategies were
two simple propositions. The first was that a good and
successful social security system depends upon good and
successful economic policy – one which leads to the full
employment of resources. The second was that a good and

successful social security system turns upon an effective system of income support and supplementation – one which provides financial incentives for beneficiaries to return to work as soon as possible, and social services to make the 'possible' an earlier reality for the beneficiaries."[5]

What "small-*l*" liberal could argue with the kind of thinking that went into that paper? It was all the more remarkable for the fact that the initial review was completed and the working paper published within three months. Not only that, but it was underpinned by a sound approach to the jurisdictional issues: in effect, the provinces would be able to design their own income-security systems and to vary the federal income supplements according to their particular requirements. That flexibility was the whole premise of the review, according to Johnson. The provinces found the new approach highly acceptable, Quebec in particular.

Yet the Orange Paper's major value was as a blueprint rather than an action plan, for two obstacles appeared even before the review was completed: the economy was getting into trouble, and the provinces once again dug in their heels. Even though the federal government had offered to pay most of the plan's incremental costs, the provinces questioned whether those contributions would really be adequate. The provinces put the brakes on, although some later picked up on the principles and translated them into provincial legislation. Quebec's Work Income Supplement Program (1979) and Manitoba's child-related Income Support Program (1980) are two examples.

If three months seemed a short time to produce the Orange Paper, it was long compared to the three days required to announce the Child Tax Credit. But as often happens in government, political crisis can produce good results.

The economic troubles of the mid-1970s had led the government to initiate a massive three-billion-dollar cut in expenditures in the summer of 1978. The cutting effort was led by the secretary of the Treasury Board, Bob Andras, and his officials. Some of us who were less keen about the cuts argued with key ministers and officials for a scheme in which one-third of the proceeds from the cuts would be put back and redistributed to Canadians with the lowest incomes. I remember Bruce Rawson, then deputy-minister of national health and welfare, speaking to me at the end of one of these meetings. He talked about a plan in his department for the Child Tax Credit that included an important redistribution feature. It was, in fact, a negative income tax with all the features of credit and grant, based on the size of family and family income. In a period of three days we were able to convince the finance department and other key agencies that the scheme could work. It was announced by the minister of finance as part of the details of the cuts and redistribution package. It was a major step toward income supplement.

Building on the Past

The Trudeau governments had some success in expanding the social security system by adding comprehensive programs to supplement income; they were, however, very successful in adapting and expanding already existing programs to arrive at similar results. Of major significance were the changes made in the Unemployment Insurance Act in 1971, the work done in housing at the Central Mortgage and Housing Corporation* in the mid-1970s and the enhancement of the Guaranteed Income Supplement from 1979 to 1984.

The boldest move of this kind, and the one that has remained the most controversial, was made during the first Trudeau term. It was the attempt to introduce greater income security in the guise of unemployment insurance measures – the Unemployment Insurance reform of 1971, a maverick piece of legislation championed by a maverick politician, Bryce Mackasey.

Mackasey had pitted himself against his more conservative Cabinet colleagues in seeking reform. He had little patience with the cautious, slow-grinding wheels of change that existed at the time within the Department of National Health and Welfare, but he had too little clout to make them move any faster. As minister of employment and immigration his only advantage lay in his strong relationship with the prime minister and a number of progressive Cabinet colleagues who had long shared his desire for a stronger income-support system. His

---

*The name of the agency was changed to Canada Mortgage and Housing Corporation in 1979.

"ace" was the Unemployment Insurance Act, which was under his control.

UI reform had its critics and still has, but without question, it accomplished sweeping changes that, for all their lack of conformity to the governmental proprieties, had a far-reaching effect not just on unemployment practices but also on the broader social security system.

For the first time, UI benefits were raised substantially—from about 40 percent of insured earnings to two-thirds. For the first time, Canadians on unemployment insurance found themselves taking home something approaching a living wage—and the increased benefits applied to all the newly created categories of beneficiary as well as the traditional long-term labour force members who had "earned" their UI paycheques.

The qualifying period was reduced to as little as eight weeks; the benefits period was increased to as long as fifty-one weeks. This was hardly an unemployment insurance program. It was the nucleus of an income-support system, and Mackasey made no bones about it. Although the new plan took the insured labour force from 90 to more than 95 percent and increased the individual worker's contributions, it also called for substantial government financing. In particular, the government would make heavy contributions to UI costs in areas of high unemployment.

The plan had faults. It was seen to open up increased potential for abuses and to discriminate against unemployed people in high-employment areas. Moreover, some people who had contributed for years without making a claim considered the new plan unfair. And it proved to be a lot more expensive, as Canada experienced levels of unemployment over the next few years that were higher than had been anticipated. Nevertheless, it was an effective reform in the sense that it addressed the problems of low income and seasonal unemployment. One can argue that they should not have been addressed through the instrument of unemployment insurance. But as Mackasey saw it, in the circumstances that prevailed at the time, it was the only instrument at hand.

It can be argued that long-time workers are contributing unfairly to a wage supplement for others. It can be argued that some seasonal workers make more than those who work all year at low wages. Why should a seasonal fisherman earning $30,000 annually have UI benefits? And it is true that, because the benefits are tied to unemployment, the plan does nothing for the working poor who work full-time but require income supplement or single parents who do not work at all because their family costs are simply not covered by low-wage jobs. It was also argued that the serious flaws in its income aspect provided an opening for a general attack on the program by those who disliked UI itself. This last argument has proved to be tragically true in the late 1980s.

In defence of the changes, however, it must be made clear that as long as the government tops up UI monies with general revenues, there is little difference between this and any other income-support system. It must also be clearly stated that, haphazard as this program is, at least we have a program.

Providing affordable housing was another way in which the Trudeau administration tackled the incomes question through machinery already in place. One can either provide more income or lower the family cost for shelter—the effect is the same. So, following the election of 1974, the Trudeau administration made a commitment to increase the housing stock by one million new starts in four years. In fact, it exceeded that goal.

Simply increasing the number of available housing units does not automatically ensure that homes will be available for lower-income groups. Thus, a good part of the work that was undertaken under the direction of housing minister Ron Basford and Central Mortgage and Housing Corporation president Bill Teron concentrated on shelter for low-income Canadians. Some of the brightest and most innovative talents were attracted to CMHC, including Walter Rudnicki, Mike McCabe, Bob Adamson, David Crenna and Lorenz Schmidt. Together with ministers, they produced inventive changes to and applications of the CMHC Act that resulted in greatly increased urban public housing, native housing, rural housing, housing for the disabled and housing for seniors and students. In addition, a massive program of co-op housing was undertaken that brought reasonable shelter within the reach of thousands of Canadians who would otherwise have been without.

A third area of expansion and adaptation for the Trudeau administration involved the Guaranteed Income Supplement, the pension that is provided in addition to Old Age Security to those with no other income. It was clear in the mid-1970s that the largest group within the ranks of those living in poverty were the elderly poor. They were mostly single women. No new program was needed to deal with this situation – the GIS could provide all the income support required.

With the support of the more progressive ministers in Cabinet, the GIS was raised three times between 1979 and 1984. By 1984, the combined payment of OAS/GIS was $7,200 per year per pensioner – a level finally above the poverty line. Over 700,000 pensioners benefited from this income and the percentage of individual Canadians living in poverty decreased from 23 percent of the total population in 1969 to 12.8 percent in 1984. There was significant progress in reducing poverty in the Trudeau years and the GIS made a superb contribution to this success.

___Quality of Life_____

One of the important features of the Trudeau years was the way in which both politicians and bureaucrats began to call into question the traditional ways of thinking about governing. At its best, this kind of questioning in the administration resulted in innovative action. Where it failed, it simply produced a reworking of old policies after much delay. Social policy was an area where new thinking produced some good results.

From the start of the Trudeau period, people began to think of social policy as more than a network of social security programs that maintained and redistributed income. It was argued that the focus of social policy should be on "quality-of-life" issues. Programs should be more readily available and those who needed government action should participate in the design and implementation of programs. As a result of this kind of thinking, the barriers between economic policy and social policy began to be knocked down as leaders saw that without a fair language policy there would be unfair access to work in Canada and that without a regional economic focus

(DREE), citizens in many less prosperous parts of Canada would not share in the better life that was being achieved.

Language and regional initiatives had their impact, but it was in the realm of youth and employment that we saw, within the definitions of social policy development, the true visionary nature of the Trudeau administration. We saw the administration at its pragmatic best, in the most positive sense of the term. The government acted with imagination, yet with a clear sense of both the immediate practicalities and the even more critical needs of the future.

In the mid-1970s, unemployed youth had become a fact of life in Canada. Their numbers included those with both high and low levels of skills, from high school dropouts right up to those with post-graduate degrees. The lucky ones worked as waiters and waitresses, for the minimum wage. The rest didn't work at all. Unemployment had risen well beyond the "norm" upon which Bryce Mackasey's unemployment insurance reforms had been predicated back in 1970–71. And the outlook for the future was increasingly bleak, particularly for the young and the unskilled. Some young people, discouraged by repeated fruitless attempts to find jobs, gave up. They became drifters, UI abusers, alcoholics, drug addicts and dropouts from society, in numbers that the country could ill afford. A substantial chunk of our most important resource for the future was going down the drain. Something had to be done.

The government acted on a number of fronts, each of which fed into the others to create a dramatic change in the job outlook for young people. One was Opportunities for Youth (OFY), the most extensive program of its kind ever undertaken in the world, and certainly the most successful. (It was a job-creation program for youth, in which the young people invented the jobs.) The youth initiative was led by Secretary of State Gérard Pelletier and Minister of State Robert Stanbury, with much of the creativity being generated by Bernard Ostry, the assistant deputy-minister within the department. We grew accustomed in Ottawa over the next few years to playing host to numerous delegations from Europe, Australia and the United States, all of them drawn by the success of the OFY program. The problem of unemployed youth was fast approaching global proportions at the time.

Even the grants initiated by the government under the Local Initiatives Program (LIP) contributed substantially to youth employment. The projects to be financed by LIP grants, and the manner in which the work would be done, were essentially the choice of municipal governments. If there was a great need for a library or a convention centre or even a new landfill site, the LIP grants would accommodate it. And when it came to addressing the specific problems of local unemployment, the LIP system was infinitely adaptable. Local councils could opt for all part-time employees, job sharing, paid work for hard-up pensioners or, as many of them did, giving jobs to people on social assistance to relieve the strain on welfare costs. The City of Toronto's director of social assistance at the time told a magazine interviewer that the LIP system more than paid for itself, along with giving thousands of defeated people a new lease on life: it put them to work, and the costs to the city were less than it would have had to pay them in social assistance allowances.

LIP grants, of course, helped a great many disadvantaged Canadians besides unemployed youth and urban welfare recipients. Native groups, for instance, benefited significantly. For the first time, the government set out to give native Canadians more clout by providing them with funding.

Native groups were poised to launch campaigns on two major fronts at the time—land claims, and the battle to stop the building of the Mackenzie Valley pipeline. In both cases, the Government of Canada was seen as one of the major opponents, yet the government not only financed those campaigns in large part but also provided research and expertise to help the native community make their case. Since that time, Canadian native groups have become highly skilled and sophisticated lobbyists, well equipped to deal with complex legal actions, political issues and even media events. The LIP grants were the launching pad for that build-up of experience and expertise.

There were other gains made for minority groups during the Trudeau administration. Women's issues, in general, were taken more seriously and found champions at higher levels. For the first time, the prime minister appointed a senior Cabinet minister responsible for the interests of women.

Disabled Canadians benefited enormously, as well. The government implemented nearly all of the eighty-odd recommendations contained in a report called *Obstacles,* prepared by a House of Commons task force on the handicapped chaired by David Smith in 1980. Most had to do with changes in government services. One of these changes, symbolic of the government's concern, was the provision of wheelchair access to the Peace Tower for the first time.

The industrial pension story is a mixed tale of triumph and lost opportunity. On at least two occasions, the administration laid out a plan for major reform of private pensions systems, but the plans were never fully implemented. In Canada, as in the United States, industry was slow to create pension programs for its workers. Indeed, most of the load of caring for the work force in Canada is carried by the public through government, not by the private sector. It is government that educates children, provides day care, subsidizes housing, underwrites training, pays the largest share of unemployment benefits and carries the pension load through OAS, GIS and CPP.

On more than one occasion in the mid-1970s when plants were closed, the stark reality of private pensions was revealed. Often no plan existed. Where one did exist, benefits could be as low as twenty-five dollars per month for workers who had spent a lifetime with one company. Even worse, there were four clear flaws in most private plans. They were not fully funded, not indexed to deal with inflation, not portable (they could not be carried from job to job) and benefits for surviving spouses were small or nonexistent.

The administration pledged action in 1980. It was to follow constitutional reform and the National Energy Program as a third wave of bold initiatives in the closing years of the administration. Much work had gone into the plan. And there was good thinking on alternative incentive schemes. One plan would have given financial incentives to firms that made their employees shareholders in the company as part of their pension arrangements. (This method had been tried by a few private firms, including Dofasco, and had been very successful.) Regrettably, there was more promise and planning than action, and federal legislation was not passed. However, the Ottawa initiative resulted in several provinces introducing their own pension reform legislation.

___ Protecting the Future_____

It is only in hindsight that we see clearly what should have been. Although the Trudeau government lived up to its promise to create a just society by introducing social policy reforms like the ones just described, it did not always ensure that those programs would be safeguarded for the future. The OFY and LIP programs were two of the most noticeable initiatives to fall victim to cutbacks. Other programs had a happier fate, however, and many of these were protected by indexation. By indexing OAS and GIS in 1974, Family Allowance in 1975 and the Child Tax Credit at its inception in 1978, the administration prevented their being killed by constant-level funding over years of inflation. The importance of such protection was made evident during the years since 1984 as blatant attempts have been made to tear down the achievements in social policy of preceding years. There have been major efforts to turn back the clock on pension indexation, UI benefits, child care, women's issues, regional expansion programs—and even on the guarantees of universality in Old Age Security.

It was in medicare, however, that the most important battle to hold the line in social security was fought and won. The creation of medicare was a triumph of the Pearson years. The architects did a better job of it than even they realized, and it was to stand the Trudeau government in good stead almost twenty years later, when the plan was assailed from within. What in fact was built into Canada's medical care system was a set of national standards, which gave later federal health ministers the leverage required to save the system.

The first set of problems arose in the late 1970s, in the area of hospital services. A few hospitals began to charge user fees—a fraction of the actual cost, but enough to impose a serious financial penalty on lower-income Canadians and even those in the middle-income category, if they were unlucky enough to get sick and end up in hospital. If their stay in hospital was a lengthy one, the cost with user fees added could be crippling. Hospital user fees became fairly widespread across the country as one province after another found this a convenient way of dealing with the rising costs of medical care. For some time, there was no apparent solution to the problem.

Encouraged, perhaps, by the apparent success of the hospitals in finding the vulnerabilities of the system, medical doctors increased their "extra-billing"—charging patients an add-on fee for a visit to the doctor's office, to cover services the doctor deemed not to be covered under medicare. The practice became a serious threat to the concept of universality, which was the very foundation of medicare in Canada. The medical profession supported extra-billing, and in fact defended it to the point of threatening province-wide doctors' strikes.

By the early 1980s, a two-tiered medical care system was developing in this country: one level of care for the rich and another for the poor. It was an alarming trend, to say the least. The Canadian medical care system—one of the best in the world—was in danger of ceasing to exist. At the centre of the battle for its survival was a remarkably determined woman, Monique Bégin, then minister of national health and welfare.

Bégin found the ammunition she needed in the legislation itself. Firmly embedded in it were the four essential principles of medicare: universality, comprehensiveness, portability and public administration. These were national standards that had to be upheld; it was the law. Accordingly, Bégin introduced legislation that would enable the government to impose a dollar-for-dollar reduction in federal payments to the provinces whenever and wherever patients were charged for medical services beyond their coverage under medicare. The legislation was passed in April 1984.

If Ottawa had allowed the forces of conservatism, coupled with provincial jurisdictional squabbling, to erode Canada's medical care system, it would have been sacrificing the basic social principles on which this country is founded. The Canadian way has always been to strike a healthy balance between pulling our own weight and ensuring that our neighbours' basic needs are met. Health care is one of the most basic needs, and it took decades to establish a national health care system. Had Bégin and the administration been less determined, it could have been lost.

Fortunately, the Trudeau government preserved Canada's

excellent system of health care—one that is founded on all the right principles and administered through an effective if sometimes complex system of co-operation among governments, hospitals, medical practitioners and others. It works. It is not surprising that American politicians are constantly comparing the U.S. health care system with ours, which they consider vastly superior. And it is not a costly system, in relative terms. In 1983, just before the battle to entrench medicare was finally won, the program was costing us only 8.2 percent of our gross national product. At that time in the United States, the largely privately run health care system, with all its inherent inequities, was costing Americans 10.5 percent of their GNP.

The Canadian system is not perfect. One obvious weakness is that it is made up of ten different systems, with resulting inequality of access. The quality of medical care available to Canadians who live within forty miles of a major teaching hospital is also quite different from that which is available to residents of Red Lake or Fort Nelson. And there are some important pieces missing in the system—dental care, prescription drugs, glasses, hearing devices—all remedies for the things that tend to go wrong with people as they get older. It's an odd system that, in effect, says it's okay to break a leg—that's covered—but whatever you do, don't break a tooth or develop a thyroid condition that will entail going on prescription drugs for the rest of your life.

Medicare does a good job of caring for the sick, but the Trudeau administration thought too about how to keep us well. This is an area, however, where a great deal more could have been done. There should be built-in incentives for health care professionals and institutions to devote a much greater share of time, effort and money to preventive medicine, including research, wellness clinics, public education programs on specific health problems, the provision of aids such as wheelchairs and hearing aids and standardized levels of community care for the recently hospitalized and the chronically ill or disabled. The irony in many parts of Canada is that home care is provided only to the point where the patient is beginning to get better. Then it stops, with the all-too-frequent result that the patient falters in a recovery program and ends up back in hospital. Considering that a stay in hospital can cost the system as much as $1,000 a day, this doesn't make economic sense, quite apart from what it says about our treatment of people who are sick and need help.

It might have made more sense to shift resources to preventive care than to squabble over total health costs. But what was built was a good system. Those who participated in its development and defence can be proud that here, most of all, the line was held.

A More Just Society

I remain convinced that most Canadians would like to see their country provide a fair chance, access to jobs, a decent retirement and a minimum income for everybody. I believe they are willing to pay tax dollars in order to make that happen.

Most of us are well aware that our fortunes can change. Many of us have had experience with a sudden, devastating alteration of circumstances, sometimes in our own families. Things can happen. People get too old to work, or too sick. Sometimes the answer they get from employers is that they're too young to work. They don't have the skills that are currently in demand in the marketplace, nor do they have the means to acquire them. They have to stay home to care for a chronically ill child or one that is severely disabled. Any number of unlucky circumstances can strike us at any time, and I believe that most Canadians look at such people and say to themselves: There, but for the grace of God, go I. Above all, they do not want to see people homeless or starving, and forced to beg for charity.

There are other Canadians – some of whom find their way into government – who speak loudly and wield a lot of power in Canadian society, who don't trust a system that hands out taxpayers' money to people, no questions asked. They trust even less their fellow man who is the beneficiary of such a system. They believe it makes bums and cheaters out of people who would otherwise go to work and earn a living.

Slowly, over the last seventy years, those who believe in providing the basics have won the day. It was one of the chief social policy goals of the Trudeau administration to achieve a system in which there were more jobs and income for Canadians, but also where the access to those jobs was available nationwide and the quality of life on the job and at home was vastly improved. Not all of that was achieved. But the government took major initiatives in that direction during the sixteen years it was in power. Among the most significant were these:

1. The unemployment insurance reforms of the early seventies were an attempt to bring about income support, albeit through the back door. It is not the system Canada should have, but the reforms did produce better income redistribution.

2. Through programs such as OFY and LIP, thousands of citizens were involved in the evolution of social policy and local programs. This was a major breakthrough in social policy. Citizens were not on the dole; they were helping to change society.

3. The Orange Paper of 1973 was a bold blueprint for sweeping reforms to the social security system. The provinces scuttled it. More experienced political hands might well have bypassed the niceties of federal-provincial negotiations and found the federal tools to force a national solution. Regardless, it remains a model for future action.

4. The National Housing Act was amended dramatically to facilitate the creation of a wide variety of assisted and co-operative housing.

5. Canada's core social programs—Family Allowance and Old Age Security—were indexed.

6. The Child Tax Credit was introduced as an important income redistribution tool designed to benefit lower-income families with children. Coupled with the somewhat haphazard UI benefits, the CTC went a long way towards establishing an income-support framework for the country.

7. The Guaranteed Income Supplement was raised, not once but three times, by amounts sufficient to bring more than a million Canadians—everybody over the age of sixty-five—out of poverty.

8. Perhaps most important of all, the Trudeau government insisted on social policy that worked for all of Canada. It

designed programs that forced fair and adequate standards
in all provinces and regions, held the line against provinces
that wanted to escape those commitments and created a
constitution that made future national programs possible.

How did the Trudeau period score in the final analysis? To
answer that question we have to look at how Canada's social
security system compared to those of other nations during the
period and in relation to its own past programs. And we have to
measure the achievements against the standard of the promised
Just Society.

Compared to the United States during the same period, the
Trudeau administration did well. By 1984 we had wider
medical coverage and a better medicare plan for 2 percent less
of the Gross Domestic Product. Canada also had better
pension plans. We did a better job of building and entrenching
an effective social security system than a lot of other
industrialized nations, including Japan. But compared to much
of Western Europe we did not do as well, particularly in the
areas of training, health, pensions and retirement age.

Compared to other periods in Canadian history, the Trudeau
administration has to be credited with some major triumphs.
There were significant increases in federally funded medical
research, some of which was beginning to pay off in areas like
cancer treatment. Life expectancy was up; disabled benefits
up; low-income housing activity up; training and apprentice-
ship opportunities up; federal contributions to hospitals,
universities and other social-security-related agencies up.
Levels of poverty were down and infant mortality was down.
Fewer Canadians were poor, more were protected against
hardship and illness, and a fair and decent life was easier to
achieve.

How far along did the Trudeau government get with its
vision of the Just Society? Not as far as Canadians would have
liked perhaps. Too many good ideas stalled in the planning
stage; too many, soon after implementation, were sacrificed at
the altar of fiscal restraint. In some respects, the Trudeau years
were a time of consolidation, rather than creation. But the
Trudeau administration held the line against growing conservative elements that wanted to tear down the systems that had

been built by previous governments. It went a long way in establishing the framework of a Just Society, given the climate of the times and the rallying strength of the opposition forces during those sobering, often nerve-wracking, sometimes anxious years.

They were also exhilarating years. New ways of thinking were brought to bear on social policy and the machinery of government that implemented that policy. There was a sense among Canadians that things were possible. That kind of self-confidence, once stirred to life in a country's consciousness, never leaves it.

PART IV

The Challenge of Federalism

Two visions of Canadian federalism have traditionally competed for the affections of Canadians. Tracing its lineage back to Honoré Mercier and Oliver Mowat, one tradition sees the provinces as the essential building blocks of Confederation. In the constitutional discussion of 1980–81, for example, the provinces' suggested preamble to the Constitution declared that "the provinces of Canada choose to remain freely united," not the people. As Premier Brian Peckford told the nation, Ottawa was "the agent of the provinces . . . and not the other way around."[1] The provincial vision saw a Canada in which authority—best expressed through the supremacy of provincial legislatures—was the organizing core of society: minority rights such as those relating to language were to be decided by the legislative majority in each province; the benefits of local diversity were extolled at the expense of a national perspective; and sovereignty rested on a provincial compact, not on the will of the Canadian people. This provincial perspective, of course, forms the essence of the proposed Meech Lake Accord.

Competing with this view is a vision of Canada that builds on the heritage of Sir John A. Macdonald, Sir George-Etienne Cartier, Sir Wilfrid Laurier, Henri Bourassa and William Lyon Mackenzie King. It is this tradition of nation building that animated our efforts between 1968 and 1984. Personal rights form the core of this belief, according to which individual Canadians, possessed of inalienable rights, including linguistic rights, make up a national community in which the people are ultimately sovereign. It is essential that provinces possess the necessary resources to carry out the large tasks that the Constitution assigns to them, but no province can be allowed to rank local interests above the common good of the Canadian people, since the basis of the state must be the equality of *all* citizens. In the preamble to the Constitution proposed by our government in June 1980, we wrote that it is "the people of Canada" who "have chosen to live together," and thus "Parliament and provincial legislatures, our various governments and their agencies, shall have no other purpose than to strive for the happiness and fulfilment of each and all of us."[2]

Expanding on this liberal commitment, Gérard Pelletier persuasively argues the thesis that Canada can survive only if it provides linguistic equality for all its citizens, including French Canadians who must feel that they can live in their language anywhere in Canada, not just in Quebec. Pelletier makes it clear that the Official Languages Act was no panacea – unilingualism, as he says, is alive and well – but through it we did achieve a transformation in the public service, and more importantly, there was an outpouring of goodwill and changed behaviour across Canada as hundreds of thousands of Canadians endorsed the ethic of bilingualism. In 1965, for example, francophones comprised 22 percent of the federal public service; by 1984 that percentage had increased to 28 percent, well above the percentage of francophones in the population as a whole (24 percent). Indeed, by 1988 francophones held 30.5 percent of officer positions in the national capital region of Ottawa-Hull.

Even more impressively, across Canada, individual Canadians have recognized the value of bilingualism: in 1977, for example, 237 schools had 37,835 students enrolled in French-language immersion programs. By 1988 this figure had increased sevenfold, with 1,512 schools and 241,140 students enrolled in French immersion. Quebec nationalists may repeat the old refrain that English Canadians have no appreciation of the French language, but how do they explain away the 27,000 students in British Columbia, the 26,000 students in Alberta, the 18,000 students in Manitoba, and the 115,000 students in Ontario who were daily *studying in French* in 1988?

An oft-repeated criticism of our government is that we were "centralizers," intent on increasing the power of the federal government at the expense of the provinces. In fact, we believed in a classic system of federalism, in which each level of government has the necessary powers and resources to carry out its functions. We sought not to aggrandize federal power but instead to prevent aggressive provinces from totally usurping the power of the national government. Where conflict with the provinces was most intense—over the Charter of Rights and Freedoms, for example—we sought to reduce the powers of *all* levels of government, including the federal, in favour of increasing the rights of individuals.

Tommy Shoyama's chapter demonstrates how sensitive our government was to the increasing fiscal pressures on the provinces. As a result of the baby boom and all the other social forces discussed in the previous section, demands on provincial resources for health and education spending were intense. We responded by increasing equalization grants tenfold between 1968 and 1984 and by delivering transfers in block grants and tax points through the Established Programs Financing Act of 1977 (which gave the provinces wide discretion over the use of funds). In 1958, for example, the federal government took in 61 percent of total government revenues and at the beginning of our government in 1969, the federal government had 50 percent of total revenues. By 1983 this had been reduced to 43 percent, a 7 percent decline.[3] Our government resisted provincial efforts to transfer powers from the Government of Canada to the provinces, but we did transfer enormous fiscal resources. As William Riker, a noted American student of federalism, wrote in 1975: "Among all the . . . federations of the world most writers would agree that Canada is about as decentralized as it can get."[4] These facts should be kept in mind when critics propound the myth of Liberal "centralization."

Regional economic equality was as central to our concept of federalism as language rights—to the extent that fiscal equality between the provinces was enshrined in the Constitution Act of 1982. Beyond the transfer of grants and tax points, as Lloyd Axworthy demonstrates in his case study of the West, we believed in using the power of government in an active way to shape the flow of market forces. Canadians in the Gaspé, Cape Breton or northern Saskatchewan have as much right to economic security as Canadians living in Toronto or Montreal. To that end, we made the Department of Regional Economic Expansion (DREE) into a major economic player. Economists have often emphasized that we promoted regional equity as much as economic efficiency. To these charges, we happily plead guilty. Unemployment and regional disparity obviously remained too high, but progress was made. Average family income in the Atlantic provinces, for example, improved from 73.7 percent of the national average in 1967 to 83.5 percent of the national average in 1984.[5] In the 1961–66 period, prior to the creation of DREE, the Maritimes suffered a net outward migration of 70,986; by 1971–76, 30,005 more Canadians were moving to Atlantic Canada than were leaving.[6] Whatever the impact of DREE on provincial economies, what can be stated with certainty is that the disparity in public services between have and have-not provinces was reduced considerably. With federal transfer payments making up over 50 percent of the provincial revenues of the four Atlantic provinces, inequalities decreased. In health expenditure, for example, Newfoundland moved from 46 percent of the national average in 1962 to 81 percent by 1979. There are no easy solutions to regional disparity, but economic equality is as critical to a Just Society as personal liberty.

Thomas S. Axworthy
Pierre Elliott Trudeau

CHAPTER 8

1968: Language Policy and the Mood in Quebec

————————by Gérard Pelletier ————————
translated by Patricia Claxton

Gérard Pelletier is a professional journalist. He was a staff reporter for Le Devoir, *publisher and editor of the union weekly* Le Travail *and editor-in-chief of the Montreal daily* La Presse. *Elected to the House of Commons in 1965, he served as Secretary of State of Canada and then as Minister of Communications. In 1975 he became Canadian ambassador to France, and in 1981, ambassador to the United Nations in New York. He is currently president of the Canadian Centre for International Research and Cooperation.*

"HISTORY TAKES NO time out," said P. L. Landsberg. Every political act takes its place in an evolving historical context.

My purpose here is to recall the circumstances in which Canada found itself in 1968 and the related social pressures of the time. Without knowing these fundamental facts, it would be difficult to understand the Trudeau team's behaviour, the options before it, the goals it set for itself and the thrust of the action it took – particularly its language policy, which I shall discuss in the latter part of this chapter.

First, we must remember that the Canadian federation was experiencing the most serious crisis in its history. At least this was the opinion of the Laurendeau-Dunton Royal Commission[1] in its preliminary report of February 1, 1965. The Commission, whose members included some of the best political minds of the day, had just completed a thorough sounding of the nation's pulse, one that would have made the most meticulous opinion polls of today look like child's play. For months, the commissioners had travelled the length and breadth of the country, hearing hundreds of Canadians expound their vision of Canada, its unity and its future.

When they had finished, the commissioners declared themselves flabbergasted by their discoveries. Why such consternation?

The commissioners recalled a number of "spectacular" junctures such as the conscription crises of 1917 and 1942, then drew the following conclusion:

> The previous conflicts did not seriously threaten the fundamentals of the state. The crisis today is of a different order. There has never been the feeling, except perhaps among a few individuals and groups, that the fundamental conditions for the existence of the Canadian people were in jeopardy.
>
> This time, as we have noted on many occasions throughout these pages, the themes of the situation are complex and difficult to define because they are global. It is not only one aspect of Canadian life that is at issue; the vital centre is in danger: we mean the will to live together, at least under present conditions.
>
> What is at stake is the very fact of Canada: what kind of country will it be? Will it continue to exist? These questions are not matters for theoreticians only, they are posed by human beings. And other groups by refusing to ask themselves the same questions actually increase the seriousness of the situation.[2]

It is recognized that federations like Canada are generally more fragile than centralized countries, at least in appearance. Their unity depends indispensably on an equilibrium among the various orders of power vested in their component parts. The components that join to form a coherent whole when a federation is created no doubt take the step without too many reservations. Yet not one of them can forget its history, and in each collective psyche the memory of the days of living apart will fade very slowly.

Countries like France and the United Kingdom forged their unity over more than a thousand years. In 1968, barely a century had passed since the signing of the federative pact that gave birth to Canada. We should therefore not be surprised that at this point cracks should have appeared in the traditional *bonne entente* which had hitherto been the cement holding the federal edifice together. Particularly since the founding provinces and the several later adherents had all begun to realize that the federation was benefiting everyone . . . but not equally. From the beginning, various provinces and sectors of the population had been expressing serious worries about this.

We all know that the union of former colonies in 1867 had aroused determined opposition, in Quebec for instance, where the dissidents were not all nationalist extremists: the ranks of the Dorion brothers' *Parti rouge* included the likes of Wilfrid Laurier, future prime minister of Canada, and Antoine-Aimé Dorion himself, who ended his days as chief justice of the province of Quebec.

We all know as well that some of the Atlantic provinces had serious reservations about joining the federation. In Nova Scotia, the anti-confederate Repeal Movement, which favoured repeal of the British North America Act, was the most popular political group in the province until 1869. Prince Edward Island joined only in 1873, when it was forced to do so by crippling railway construction debts. And Newfoundland waited another seventy-five years to follow suit.

As for the western provinces of Canada, in 1867 none of them existed yet. Their objections to Canadian federalism began to be voiced only in the twentieth century, but then with increasing rancour. Between 1968 and 1984 there were journalists, some naïve and others with an axe to grind, who believed, and spread the belief, that westerners harboured a grudge against Pierre Trudeau in particular. But since Louis St-Laurent's first election in 1949, the Liberals had never won a majority in the West. It has become clear, particularly since 1984 when a Conservative government came to power, that western provincial politicians bear a fundamental grudge against Ottawa, whichever party or prime minister is in power.

But let's return to Quebec, where anti-federalist sentiment was very strong in the late 1960s. In order to realize the depth of the discontent in Quebec, we must first understand the *nature* of the troubles at its root.

Having joined Canada, British Columbia might well have

been impatient: to persuade it to join, Ottawa had promised it a railway, which was a long time in coming. After central Canada had begun to prosper, the Atlantic provinces suffered a relative decline economically. The governments of the Prairie provinces could hardly blame themselves for the slowness of industrialization on the Prairies. The federal government (plus Ontario, plus Quebec) were convenient whipping boys. Yet all these reasons for resentment against Ottawa were really only surface blemishes. Financial sores are not fatal, as the French proverb goes.

However, the reasons for discontent on the part of French-speaking Quebeckers were very different and much more serious. After 1939, Quebec's economy began to develop, spurred by one of the most rapid industrial revolutions ever seen in the Western world.[3] But it was the anglophones, the overseers of the industrial revolution and development, who were the prime beneficiaries. In Quebec, if you spoke French, on average you earned far less than your English-speaking companions in the workplace.

Added to this was an even deeper malaise, to which the term "cultural anxiety" applies rather well because it was the product of many years of linguistic bullying and acts of intolerance toward the cultural characteristics of the French-Canadian community. While the economic inferiority of French Canadians had many causes, of which a number had nothing to do with the political structure of the country, this cultural anxiety can be blamed above all on the attitudes of the federal government and the provincial governments of English-speaking provinces.

In 1967, the Rassemblement pour l'indépendance nationale dreamed up the idea of celebrating the centenary of Confederation by having all Quebeckers affix stickers to their car licence plates proclaiming "*Cent ans d'injustice* [A Hundred Years of Injustice]." This was making light indeed of the benefits derived by Quebec from the federal framework. Even so, it was also a reflection of a widespread feeling among French Canadians, a result of a long history of episodes, each more insulting and unbearable than the last.

They remembered the shameful dispossession of the French-speaking Métis and the hanging of Louis Riel; they remembered the Manitoba School Question and the New Brunswick Common Schools Act of 1871, the latter creating free schools from which Catholics (meaning all francophones) were virtually excluded; they remembered the article of the Saskatchewan school law of 1931 which declared, "The sole language of instruction shall be English"; they remembered the proclamation of Regulation 17 in Ontario. The entire French-speaking community of Canada felt rejected by English Canada. And not merely rejected but savaged, the victims of a plan whose purpose was their disappearance through forced assimilation. This was no financial sore but something very different: a matter of cultural life or death.

The autonomy of the federated states meant that the francophones of Quebec, who had control of the government of their province, were shielded from attempts at deculturation through the schools. However, at the time there was strong solidarity among all French-speaking groups in the country, and wherever intolerance of French was displayed by the English-speaking majority, in the press, among the intelligentsia or in the federal government, Quebec francophones felt just as despised, just as threatened, as francophones elsewhere in the country.

Referring to the 1930s, the American sociologist Everett C. Hughes wrote in 1953, "I might add in all frankness that those of my colleagues at McGill University who were in the least interested in contemporary French Canada were unconsciously inclined to think of it as an entity in the process of assimilation. The postulate of their thinking was that French Canadians as an ethnic group would sooner or later be absorbed in the great English-speaking Canadian whole."[4]

Another example comes to mind, which is telling by virtue of its very insignificance. In 1919 the magazine *Saturday Night*, which at the time "with dedicated snobbishness [. . .] sought readers among Toronto's high society," according to the *Canadian Encyclopedia*, raised a cry of indignation. Imagine! French Canadians wanted railway tickets and pertinent information printed *also* in French. Had they at least calculated the cost of such an extravagance? What irresponsibility to be making such exorbitant requests!

It never for a second occurred to the editors of the

publication that tens of thousands of French-speaking taxpayers, 85 percent of them unilingual, took the train every year. Did these people have rights? One would not believe so from reading Toronto publications, either the respectable daily newspapers or Orange extremist rags, of which there was no dearth in this period.

The same tendencies were of course demonstrated by the federal government, which was mostly English-speaking. Ottawa was then a provincial small town in the Ontario hinterland, with all the narrowness of mind that this might lead one to expect, and the Parliament of Canada was no more disposed to reflect the French fact than to give expression to the culture of Islam. French was tolerated; it had to be, because every government owed its stability, if not its very existence, to the support of the French-speaking members of Parliament. But this was where the majority's sense of "fair play" stopped.

Until the 1930s (a half-century after Confederation), almost everything that emanated from the federal capital was drafted in English only, from postage stamps and coins to the countless official publications and government cheques. In 1958, geographical maps prepared by the Department of Mines were supplied free of charge to any citizen who asked for them, but even maps of areas in Quebec were provided in English only. If you wanted to have a copy of a royal commission report or a work published by some museum or federal government department, either you resigned yourself to having the English version or you waited months, sometimes years, before being able to obtain the work in French. I recall that this lopsided linguistic morality kept us French-speaking journalists in an almost permanent state of controlled rage.

French-speaking members of Parliament were in the same boat, for the representatives of the people were no better served. Here's one small detail among a thousand: when we arrived in Ottawa in 1965, the commissionaires guarding the doors to the Parliament buildings were almost all unilingual anglophones. Not only were they unable to understand what the visitors from my riding of Hochelaga might be trying to say to them, but they would bluntly and rudely refuse to make the least effort to understand.

These types were to be found outside of Canada as well. One day in 1956, when I was in London on a reporting assignment for the National Film Board, a Canadian guard at Canada House, when I insisted on speaking French, finally (in all seriousness) showed me the address to which I should direct my steps . . . the French embassy.

I have been at pains to describe this deplorable situation because the reader will not understand Quebec's discontent without being aware of these things. Indeed, in the early sixties, with the very question "What does Quebec want?", English-speaking Canadians were demonstrating a lack of awareness verging on contempt.

Some will say that at least the question was evidence of a certain belated curiosity concerning a part of the country that had hitherto been the object of supreme ignorance in most anglophones. This is true. An awakening did occur, but not spontaneously.

Since 1950, a growing number of Toronto and Montreal English-speaking intellectuals—university teachers, journalists and writers—had been taking an interest in developments in Quebec. I am thinking of Blair Fraser, Ramsay Cook, Eugene Forsey, Frank Scott and ten or so others I could name. They organized conferences with their French-speaking counterparts, opening a dialogue whose effect soon began to register in the English-speaking press. But only limited interest was aroused.

What really wakened English-speaking Canada to developments in Quebec was the Quiet Revolution of 1960, which is to say, the awakening of Quebec itself. With the end of Duplessis's reign, and with it the end of clericalism and morbid traditionalism, it was getting hard not to notice that something was going on in Quebec. An entire society was now marching toward a modernization that it had shunned, to its detriment, for over a century.

Now, instead of simply defending its institutions, this society was bent on reforming them, developing them, adapting them to the twentieth century. French-speaking Quebeckers were finally opening their eyes to their real condition and their real weaknesses. They were taking note of the democratic methods available for redressing those weaknesses. The meek majority which for so long had tolerated corruption in its politicians, mediocrity in its teachers, passivity in its businessmen and inertia in its authorities, this very same majority was now making demands. It wanted up-to-date laws, reform of education and initiatives on the part of governments and private enterprise to stimulate the economy and bring about the advance of francophones in all spheres of activity. In short, a drowsy community was waking up.

However, conservatism in politicians and the clergy, together with the attitudes of the Canadian majority, had kept the lid clamped on the pot for too long. When the Quiet Revolution came in the early sixties, it was already very late in the game. Too late for *all* of the energy suddenly released to be channelled into productive outlets.

A small but rowdy part of this energy was vented in the senseless terrorism of the F.L.Q. (Front de libération du Québec). Another, much larger part embraced all-out nationalism, preaching independence. This element was beginning a long detour which, in twenty years, was to take it from the R.I.N. (Rassemblement pour l'indépendance nationale) to the P.Q. (Parti québécois) and on to the defeat of 1980, which is to say, the rejection, by a solid majority of Quebeckers, of any idea of secession, even the watered-down concept of sovereignty-association developed by René Lévesque. Later, in the autumn of 1984, Lévesque himself was heard to allow that federalism was "a risk, but a good risk." The detour was complete.

This same majority of 1980 had steadfastly supported the Trudeau team in federal politics, and continued to do so. Even in 1979, when English Canada withdrew its confidence for a few months, Quebec remained steadfast.

The reason was that the Trudeau team was offering Quebeckers, as it was offering all Canadians, a somewhat different Canada than the one they had always known. The team's policies from 1968 on are discussed by other contributors to this book. I shall merely describe the linguistic revolution that soon had the West accusing us of shoving French down the throats of farmers who did not want or need it.

What was it really all about? And why did otherwise

mild-mannered Canadians react with such ferocity to a few French words on cereal boxes, a few signs in airports and national parks and a French television channel which they were perfectly free not to switch to?

The answer can be found without reading the whole Official Languages Act. It is contained in the first section, which proclaims equality for English and French in all operations of Canadian federal institutions. The French language, which many had been trying for a century to wipe off the landscape, was now on an equal footing with English. This was quite enough to offend some segments of the population. There was even one minister in the Trudeau Cabinet who finally resigned, declaring that there could be no great political entity that recognized the use of more than one language. He was forgetting only the Roman Empire, the British Empire and, in our own time, the European Economic Community. A mere detail!

But how was Quebec to be kept in the federation if francophones were going to be treated as second-class citizens by the central government? Inequalities there were, and the most flagrant and most visible was certainly linguistic inequality. When the Laurendeau-Dunton Commission had completed its inquiry, it observed that "apart from the language aspect, few French-speaking Canadians claimed to be victims of flagrant discrimination."[5]

We had often discussed this problem before we entered active politics. We had applauded the isolated corrective steps taken by the Diefenbaker and Pearson governments (simultaneous translation in the House of Commons under Diefenbaker and the creation of the Laurendeau-Dunton Commission under Pearson). However, to us it appeared that total reform was needed and it would have to be carried much further than anything that had been done up to that point.

There are inequalities which no law can redress. Appropriate measures can improve the lot of the poor, protect the weak from the powerful, help the development of this or that type of business to counterbalance some other type, assist this or that region of the country to catch up economically. In short, you can encourage but not legislate equality between men, to borrow a familiar American expression.

You can, however, legislate "equal" government treatment with respect to two languages, and this is what the Trudeau government did in 1968.[6] In August, having won the general election in June, a number of Cabinet ministers sat down with a team of lawyers to draft the Official Languages Act.

Of all the legislation passed under the Trudeau government, this has without a doubt aroused more asinine commentary than all the rest put together. The most destructive of these interpretations came to light at the same time as the legislation. It saw the government wanting to make the whole population of Canada bilingual. Once this goal was ascribed to the government, once this totally fictitious spectre was raised, opponents found it easy to demonstrate the idiocy of such an ambition.

And when Pierre Trudeau explained that, on the contrary, the intention was to enable all Canadians to communicate with the government and its agencies in the official language of their choice, therefore enabling them in fact to stay unilingual if they wanted, his critics accused him of being dishonest.

A typical example of this kind of criticism is contained in Richard Gwyn's *Northern Magus*. Published in 1980, it reviewed the bilingualism debate retrospectively. On page 222, Gwyn writes, "The puzzle of Trudeau's bilingualism policy is, how could something so necessary and so reasonable have caused such trouble?" From this, one would think that Gwyn himself was in favour of the Official Languages Act, as with most of the English-speaking intelligensia of Canada.

Continuing, as written on the very next page, though, Mr. Gwyn served up the classic argument favoured by the most subtle opponents:

Yet even before 1969 was out, Trudeau was driven to say, "Our policy on bilingualism has been widely misunderstood . . . It does not mean that every English Canadian must learn French."

Part of the problem was that bilingualism, in the end, had to mean, well, *two equal languages*; being a little bit bilingual being as impossible to achieve as being a little bit pregnant. On the day after the Official Languages Act was passed, the *Calgary Herald* came right to the point: "For the more rewarding jobs, bilingualism is being made a practical necessity." Initially, these "rewarding" jobs meant just the top ones at Ottawa; inevitably, though, it would soon mean all the middle-rank jobs that fed the top; then jobs in the "para-government," all the way from the Canadian Manufacturers' Association to the Canadian Labour Congress, on down the line to jobs in all companies which had dealings with francophones, and to some provincial government positions. Eventually, unilingualism could mean a life sentence to job immobility.

Trudeau knew this all along. He fibbed about it as a necessary means to an end. As late as April 1977, for instance, he said in Winnipeg that bilingualism did not mean "that a lot more Canadians will have to be bilingual", nor even "most civil servants"; indeed, "this policy will make it possible for the vast majority of Canadians not to have to speak a second language."

White lies like these are the acceptable tools of every politician's trade.... In 1979, Dalton Camp put it shrewdly in *Points of Departure*: "The persistence and growing pervasiveness of bilingualism had alienated English Canadians from their federal government, turning them inwards to more familiar, compatible and nearer political jurisdictions in the provinces.... The government of Canada had lost its constituency."[7]

In fact, Mr Camp was so shrewd that events proved his predictions wrong even before anyone had time to read his book. The Liberal government's "lost constituency" hurried back to the fold in the spring of 1980, though the official languages policy had not changed one iota.

But I return to Mr Gwyn. According to him, the prime minister of the day had lied when he said that the Official Languages Act would not force many Canadians, even most civil servants, to become bilingual. Far from disproving this, the statistics twenty years down the road have confirmed it beyond a shadow of doubt.

Except in Quebec, where anglophones have had to learn French for reasons having nothing to do with this federal law, the number of new bilinguals is hardly impressive. The modest figures are confined almost entirely to the very young, who, at the free choice of their parents, have been enrolled in immersion classes. As for the federal public service, barely a third is "officially" bilingual. And Heaven knows that the language courses lavished on English-speaking civil servants have often resulted in extremely theoretical certificates of bilingualism!

Had bilingualism become a practical necessity for the "more rewarding" civil service jobs, as the *Calgary Herald* claimed? Yes, but in practice, only for the francophones. In twenty years, I never met a single deputy-minister who did not speak English. And even in External Affairs, where I myself had become a civil servant, I worked under a deputy-minister who understood perhaps eight or ten words of French and could not articulate a single one. Unfortunately, he was far from being alone. And today, the upper echelons of whole departments are still filled with totally unilingual anglophone senior civil servants, who are in no way serving "a life sentence to job immobility." The civil service has made a lot of progress in French, even great strides in some sectors. But English unilingualism is still doing very well, thank you.

As for the notion that our official languages policy would "inevitably" affect "jobs in the 'para-government,' all the way from the Canadian Manufacturers' Association to the Canadian Labour Congress, on down the line to jobs in all companies which had dealings with francophones," this was simply a product of fantasy, or fatuousness, or panic.

If Bob White, vice-president of the Canadian Labour Congress, is eloquent in French, he has been careful to hide it; he has never been heard to pronounce a single word of the language in public. Yet this did not stop him from being elected to his post, twenty years after the Official Languages Act came into effect. As for companies doing business with franco-phones, their use of French is notably parsimonious, just enough so as not to lose their francophone customers. I know, for example, a major Canadian trust company whose Ottawa office is headed by a man who speaks not a word of French, yet his ambition is some day to preside over the destinies of the company that employs him. And Mr Gwyn would be hard put to find bank presidents outside of Quebec who speak any language but English—which by no means prevents them from having dealings with thousands of francophones. . . . As for the bosses of other big companies with head offices in Toronto, only by the wildest fantasy could anyone pretend that for them unilingualism has meant life sentences to job immobility.

Let's be serious.

There is a very simple reason why anglophones subjected the language policy of 1969 to the most idiotic and unfair criticism: "their governing linguistic principles, when forced even to consider languages other than their own, were smugness, stubbornness, and not to dodge the word, blind stupidity." These are not my words. They are Richard Gwyn's.[8]

I agree with his diagnosis. Having been a victim of these attitudes, I know them well. But I would restrict the reach of his judgment somewhat. Stubbornness, smugness and blind stupidity have never been characteristic of all English-speaking Canadians or even the great majority. Still, such inclinations have been visible in politicians at every level of all parties (even in the Trudeau government itself) and in a surprising number of intellectuals, teachers and business and professional people, not to mention old-fashioned fanatics of all stripes. Also, alas, in journalists, those of my own profession. I remember one of the first tours I took to the West to explain the official languages policy. The very day of my arrival in one city, before I had even had a chance to open my mouth, an article appeared in the local daily, written in Ottawa by the parliamentary correspondent of the newspaper chain, painting me as a francophone fanatic who should be regarded with suspicion.

But when I met with parent groups, young people in the schools, worker associations and groups of recent immigrants, there were no such obstacles to communication. The most avid opponents were members of the middle class and the intelligentsia.

And it was the same story in Quebec. Language equality in the federal government, which Quebec francophones had been demanding for generations, was no longer of any interest to our sovereigntist intellectuals. From the minute the first measure of our language policy came into effect, this element was continually trying to persuade people that our efforts were doomed to failure. Some pretended to be anxious about this, but you had the impression that deep down, consciously or not, they were fervently hoping we would fall on our faces.

They would never say so, of course. For an all-out nationalist, opposing any expansion of French whatever would have been close to absurd. Fighting aid for official language minority groups, when 90 percent of their members were francophones, would have been unthinkable and, more important, indefensible in the eyes of the public. The Quebec nationalists had not yet developed their latest argument, namely that any institutional bilingualism is a mortal threat to French. Nevertheless, the last thing they wanted was for our policy to succeed.

I observed earlier that it was language discrimination that was most resented by the country's francophones, including those of Quebec. This had been established by the Laurendeau-Dunton Commission, after an inquiry whose credibility was questioned by no one, to my knowledge. If the central government succeeded, even in merely reducing the bitterness of this grievance, French-speaking Quebeckers would begin to see federalism as more acceptable and hospitable – which was hardly a pleasing prospect for the nationalists bent on promoting independence.

And the nationalists were increasing in number. When the Official Languages Act came into force, Pierre Bourgault's Rassemblement pour l'indépendance nationale and Gilles Grégoire's Ralliement national had just amalgamated with the Souveraineté-Association movement to form the Parti québécois under the leadership of René Lévesque. More and more nationalists were rallying to the cause of sovereignty. Any action likely to give pause to any who had not yet taken the plunge, any visible progress in the federal sphere that favoured causes dear to the hearts of Quebeckers, was now considered highly undesirable by the Parti québécois.

The *péquistes* moved to the attack, but gently at first. Our intentions were perhaps good, they said, but our policy would lead nowhere. In the first place, the anglophones would not agree to our fundamental objective, which was not realistic anyway: how could we ever hope to make an entire population bilingual? On this, the Quebec sovereigntists were in total agreement with the anti-French extremists: they, too, were pretending to see the spectre. Members of the Quebec delegation in Paris even persuaded *Le Monde* that our goal was to make everyone bilingual, and in August 1979 the prestigious daily gave this piece of rubbish front-page exposure. And then, the argument went, Quebeckers could hardly care less about an expansion of French in the eastern and western regions of Canada. What about the French minorities outside Quebec? They were already "dead ducks," said René Lévesque in an interview in Winnipeg.

According to secessionist logic, Quebec was the only place where it was worthwhile making an effort. And since independence would bring an end to all relations between the people of Quebec and the federal government, why worry about what language was spoken in Ottawa? If I had the space, I could give a great number of quotations to illustrate each of these points. Yet I must express my amazement at something that I have never been able to understand: the almost automatic adherence of many francophones outside Quebec to the arguments of the Quebec sovereigntists, who were coldly condemning them to isolation, the worst that could befall groups as fragile as theirs. They must have changed their minds since, judging by their opposition to the Meech Lake Accord.

So from the very beginning, the official languages policy was given the squeeze by simultaneous opposition from two quarters: anglophone reactionaries on the one side and Quebec sovereigntists on the other. Yet for all this hostility, it made a respectable impact. With the support of the majority of Canadians on both sides of the linguistic border, it reached most of the objectives that had inspired it.

Taking stock today, twenty years after the Act was passed, we see that despite the resistance, some mistakes and endless obstacles (including foot dragging by most English-speaking Cabinet ministers, who supported it only for the sake of solidarity), the official languages policy launched in 1969 has brought major changes throughout all of Canada and a real transformation in Ottawa.

The first and most telling of these effects has occurred in public opinion—that is to say, in attitudes. I shall never forget the Newfoundland Cabinet minister who phoned me one day to ask for help for his French community.

"A French community?" I said in astonishment. "I didn't even know there was one in Newfoundland; you never said a word about it before."

"No," he replied, "I never mentioned it to you in the past, but since French has become respectable, ..."

In a remarkably short time, French had indeed become "respectable" in English Canada. Except for the incurable fanatics, no one talked about the Quebec *"patois"* anymore. And then, since the vast majority of our English-speaking compatriots have a profound respect for the rule of law, there was never any question of not complying.

In the most open-minded circles, tens of thousands of English-speaking parents demanded (and obtained) French immersion courses for their children. And to everyone's surprise, from the minute Radio-Canada opened its French radio and television stations in Vancouver, large numbers of francophile anglophones were among their listeners and viewers.

While many provincial politicians kept grimly fighting the federal initiatives, refusing their French communities the minimum of the fair play that they were calling for, thousands of their constituents showed the opposite attitude. In Ontario, for example, the Toronto press almost unanimously advocated institutional bilingualism in provincial government bodies. But the Ontario government, to paraphrase the nineteenth-century French humourist Alphonse Allais, "listened only to its courage, which said nothing," and nothing was what it did, insisting that any initiative in favour of bilingualism would be too "offensive" to the people of the province. New Brunswick, on the other hand, passed a law establishing a system similar to the ones that existed in Quebec and at the federal level.

Naturally enough, the most dramatic changes were seen in

the workings of the federal government. They did not happen overnight. When it introduced its language policy, the government had given itself ten years for the application of most of its provisions. This turned out to be too optimistic, but here also, reversals in attitude could be detected from the beginning.

I'll cite just one example. A certain English-speaking senior civil servant spoke French fluently but had always refused to speak it at work, even forbidding his French-speaking subordinates to speak to him or write him memos in their mother tongue. Suddenly, getting wind of the benefits that his own bilingualism could now bring him, he became an apostle of the new policy in his department.

Hundreds of other civil servants set to work to learn the official language of Canada with which they were not yet familiar, some kicking and screaming but many enthusiastically. One colleague of mine who was over forty at the time became perfectly at home in "the other language," as the saying went then, in less than a year.

The goal of the policy, of course, was not only to generalize the use of both languages in the government's relations with the public. It was also intended to attract more francophones to federal employment and make it possible for them to use their mother tongue as a language of work. To this end, French-speaking units were created in both the civil service and the armed forces. Whereas not a word of French had ever been spoken in the Canadian navy, certain ships were to function entirely in French; so also were whole squadrons of the air force. Gradually, French was also introduced at Canada's NATO base at Lahr, West Germany.

There were setbacks, as might be expected. For instance, when the 1972 general election returned a minority Trudeau government, many English-speaking civil servants took for granted that the official languages policy had been just an aberration and its time was now past. Certain deputy-ministers even rushed to reinstate the unilingualism of the previous time, convinced that the government would let the policy drop. Much to their disappointment, in June 1973, a few months following the election, the minority government tabled a resolution in the House confirming pursuit of the language objectives previously defined. This motion fixed 1978 as the deadline for an acceptable level of bilingualism to be achieved in the civil service. Only sixteen Conservative members of Parliament voted against it.[9]

After the government was defeated in the spring of 1979, it was clear that the lesson had been learned. There were no attempts this time to turn back the clock. The new prime minister, Joe Clark, I hasten to note, had made clear his intention to maintain the language objectives laid down by the Liberal government eleven years earlier.

When Jules Léger was under-secretary of state, he used to wonder aloud how effective our language policy would be. Were we like Sisyphus, he asked, rolling our huge stone up the mountain, and would it roll back on top of us before we reached the summit?

While the political will was still present at this time, there was no shortage of practical problems. The apparatus that had to be built for language teaching proved to be very complex and very expensive. The results obtained did not always match the expectations. Jules Léger was worrying especially about the fact that, following second language instruction, too many civil servants were not retaining what they had learned, because they lacked frequent opportunities to use it. This problem was unique to the anglophone side, it must be said. All of us wondered with some anxiety when the point of no return, or critical mass, would be reached.

Soon the Commissioner of Official Languages, Keith Spicer, was echoing these worries. In his 1976 report, he let it be clearly understood that in his opinion the government was barking up the wrong tree and should instead be encouraging the teaching of second languages in the schools.

To an extraterrestrial observer, this would no doubt look like the ideal solution. But when francophones had already been waiting for a century to be served in French, we could hardly ask them to wait another whole generation. Besides, in Canada education is a provincial domain, and the provinces had never shown much enthusiasm, to say the least, for teaching a second language. Bill Davis, when he was Ontario's minister of education, confided to me one day, "I have six thousand French teachers in my schools. Of these, I don't know if there are a thousand who really speak your language."

The revolution begun in 1968 continues. After twenty years of effort, many of the objectives set for it then have yet to be reached.

Fortunately, the determination that launched the revolution remains too.

Chapter 9

Fiscal Federalism in Evolution

———————by Thomas K. Shoyama———————

Thomas K. Shoyama is a Visiting Professor in Public Administration and Pacific Studies at the University of Victoria. He served as Economic Advisor to the Premier of Saskatchewan and held several senior posts in the federal public service. He was also a member of the Macdonald Royal Commission on the Economic Union and Development Prospects for Canada.

THE EVOLUTION OF Canadian federalism from the late sixties to the early eighties has been portrayed as a search to give meaning and substance to the concept of "strong provinces in a strong Canada." Much of this search took place in the constitutional forum—through the struggle for changes in the distribution of powers and in the patriation and amending formula of the Constitution itself, and through the adoption of the Charter of Rights and Freedoms. But no less significant developments of a broadly parallel nature also emerged at the more mundane level of federal-provincial fiscal and financial relationships. In this context, the Trudeau government's constant objective was to seek a balance in the distribution of tax and financial resources that would be consistent with the country's constitutional framework but still responsive to the changing realities of the Canadian economy, its underlying structure and its regional dimensions.

In many ways the political pressures at work in the public revenue and expenditure system were familiar constants, reflecting the recurring push and pull of the centralizing and decentralizing forces inherent in Canadian federalism. During the period of the Trudeau administration, however, the tension between these forces was exacerbated by the expanding roles of governments at all levels in domestic social and economic development and by the increasing economic and financial interdependence of countries around the world. Another important if unfortunate dimension was the growing complexity and technocratic nature of the revenue systems and federal-provincial fiscal arrangements themselves. It was no longer possible, as it had been at the beginning of the 1950s, for a Quebec premier to sum up a protracted debate on revenue sharing with the simple, blunt demand, "Where's the cash!"[1]

No doubt that straightforward demand has continued to lie at the nub of federal-provincial financial relationships in Canada. However, the pursuit of fiscal balance between the national government and the provinces in this regionally diverse federal state has become a more and more complicated exercise. It has required elaborate arrangements, covering several distinct though interrelated areas, which are usually described as "fiscal federalism." These arrangements were greatly extended and revised during the Trudeau years. In part, this was done in response to the demands from the provinces for increased revenues, and greater flexibility and autonomy in taxing and spending. Under the Trudeau administration, however, equally compelling influences were the federal objectives which demanded that, as far as possible within the resources available to it, each government should be responsible for its own revenue and expenditure decisions, and that both levels of government, acting jointly within a constitutional framework, should be able to provide public services that met a nationwide standard.

This essay takes a retrospective view of the developments in the fiscal arrangements intended to further these objectives. It begins with the basic issue of joint occupancy of the income-tax field, the implied constraints that this placed on the provinces and the transfer to the provinces of greater room in these revenue sources. During this period the equalization system also matured and expanded. It emerged as a finely tuned and flexible instrument, crucial to the financial stability of the poorer provinces and capable of responding to the shocks that stemmed from the huge increase in resource revenues that took place during the seventies—most notably in Alberta. A sea change occurred in the financing of public health insurance programs and post-secondary education as well, when 1977 legislation governing the financing of established programs transformed earlier conditional grants into functional block grants. Special-purpose conditional grants continued to play a significant role and important new ventures were launched in support of bilingualism and regional economic development. Finally, renewed and innovative efforts were made to achieve co-ordination in fiscal policy, in macroeconomic stabilization and in sectoral economic planning. All these issues were approached with a consistency that derived from the Trudeau government's view of Canadian federalism and the ways in which the fiscal arrangements might best be adapted to serve the needs of Canadians in all regions of the country.

____ Revenue Sharing and Tax Occupancy____

In the late sixties, federal-provincial joint occupancy of particular tax fields was clearly a more complicated affair than it had been a century earlier. This reflected both the greatly expanded role of government and the parallel development of new sources and methods of taxation. In particular, through two world wars and alternating periods of prosperity and depression, personal and corporate income taxes had replaced customs duties and indirect sales taxes as the most important sources of public revenue, especially for the federal government. At the provincial level, the years following the Second World War witnessed a comparable development of various forms of so-called direct sales taxes (retail sales taxes) on consumption. But from the time of the Rowell-Sirois report of 1940, and particularly throughout the two postwar decades, the competitive and frequently acrimonious wrangle over shares of income tax revenues had had the greatest influence on federal-provincial fiscal relations. Although new issues arose, particularly in the context of the tax reforms of the early 1970s, the redrawing of certain features of the tax-sharing and collection arrangements under the Trudeau government did much to improve the flexibility and equilibrium of a uniquely harmonized system.

The foundations of that system had been laid in the wartime tax-rental agreements, under which the provinces received rental payments from the federal government in return for withdrawing from the income and estate tax fields. The arrangements that evolved out of successive negotiations undertaken up to 1967 preserved a unified personal income tax system in all provinces except Quebec, and a significantly harmonized corporate income tax regime across the country. In the increasingly vital personal tax field, the federal government continued to be in control, defining the tax base and rate structure, maintaining an agreed-upon allocation of taxable income among the provinces and administering the great bulk of the collection system.

Beginning in 1957, however, the provinces had been enabled and encouraged to exercise their constitutional rights and to re-enter the fields of both personal and corporate income tax through two important federal measures. The first was the reduction, or abatement, of nominal federal taxes—which left room for the provinces to impose their own taxes without increasing the burden on taxpayers. The second was the establishment of a collection system under which the federal government continued to collect provincial taxes as long as these levies conformed to the same tax base and rate structure as those defined for federal taxes. This collection service was provided at no cost to the provinces and at the same time minimized the costs to taxpayers of complying with the tax laws.

In the early 1970s three important revenue-sharing innovations were introduced into the federal-provincial fiscal system, partly by legislative enactment and partly by administrative agreement. The first of these attracted little public or professional attention except among the administrative officials involved. This was the abolition of the abatement system and its substitution with the explicit technique of fixing provincial personal tax rates as percentages of basic federal taxes, which is still used today. Although usually dismissed as a minor technical adjustment, the change was actually of major symbolic and psychological importance. The earlier abatement system had carried with it the implicit notion that the nominal level of federal taxes before abatement for the provinces represented a necessary or appropriate ceiling on the taxation of personal income (even though two provinces had in fact imposed levies above the amount of the abatement, as they were free to do). In the early 1970s the changed approach went far to shift the debate away from the narrow ground of how far the federal government could or should go in reducing its own levies in order to provide more tax room for the provinces. Tax sharing was no longer a zero-sum game, inciting a continuous wrangle between the provinces and Ottawa, and this, in turn, gave the provinces the clear indication that the exercise of fiscal power carried with it the responsibility of deliberate decision making. At the same time it helped to bring home the concepts of fiscal responsibility to taxpayers themselves by clarifying the role that the provinces played in establishing the total income tax burden.

In its second important measure, the federal government responded to provincial requests to administer a range of credits and adjustments to provincial taxes payable under the collection system. This made it possible for the provinces to introduce significant selective changes to the structure of their tax systems without disrupting the overall federal-provincial system—a particularly important development in that it enabled provinces to make changes in their social policies through the tax system by such devices as tax credits for sales or real property tax levies scaled to the income levels of taxpayers. Reductions of the tax payable for low-income recipients and surcharges (increases) on tax payable for high-income earners were also administered on behalf of provinces. The overall result was that the provinces acquired a great deal of flexibility in changing the structure, degree or progressivity of their income taxes to their special needs or wishes, but all within the framework of the harmonized national tax system.

The third major initiative in the area of revenue sharing was taken as part of the 1970–72 tax reform that followed the major report of the Carter commission on taxation. In addition to making changes in federal income tax, the national government made a deliberate policy decision to obtain provincial participation in the development of the reform package, in order to maintain the essential unity of the federal and provincial income tax systems. The provinces were given a special guarantee that they would not experience any loss of revenue by joining in the reform rather than continuing with the pre-reform system.

In the event, all nine participating provinces accepted the federal proposals, but the implementation of the special revenue guarantee proved to be a difficult technical exercise. Although the tax reforms were intended to be revenue-neutral, the federal government accepted calculations that required it to make substantial payments to all the provinces. Indeed, although the federal offer was to provide the guarantee for a period of only three years, during which the revenue yields of the changed system could be tested, the payments had grown to such a level by the end of the period that provinces were reluctant to increase their own rates to make up for the guarantee payments they were receiving from the federal government. The federal government consequently acceded to urgent pleas to extend the guarantee payments for a further two years. This, in turn, kept the issue alive until the regular quinquennial fiscal negotiations of 1977. In that year the issue was put to rest through the financing arrangements made for established programs.

In all of this it can be said that federal policy throughout the period was clear and consistent. First, it was based on a full recognition of the provinces' constitutional right to have access to the income tax fields and on the expectation that the provinces would exercise their responsibilities as senior governments to raise their own revenues in order to finance their own expenditures. Second, it emphasized the value of the harmonized federal-provincial tax system, not only in minimizing collection and taxpayer compliance costs but also in promoting national economic efficiency. Third, it acknowledged fully the revenue needs of the provinces and revised the system for sharing so that the provincial share of total income tax revenues was substantially increased—not at a cost to the federal treasury but rather through the deliberate exercise of the provinces' own taxing powers.

Fiscal Equalization

While this increase in provincial tax shares was of major benefit to the larger and wealthier provinces, it was of less real value to provinces that had limited income tax potential. This increased the importance of the federal equalization grants that had been progressively developed over the previous three decades. The conceptual basis of the fiscal equalization program can be traced back to the recommendations on national adjustment grants for poorer provinces advanced by the Rowell-Sirois commission in 1940. The actual groundwork, however, was laid in the wartime and postwar tax rental agreements, since the rental payments by the federal government to all provinces were determined largely on an equal per-capita basis and only minimally by the actual yield of the rented tax fields in each province. In 1957, when an explicit equalization system was adopted and equalization payments began to be calculated separately from tax-rental payments, two main issues pertaining to the new system were addressed. These were (1) the particular revenue sources to be equalized and (2) the level of per-capita revenue to which the provinces with lower tax yields should be raised. It was fairly simple to determine which revenue sources should be equalized, since only the income and succession-duty tax fields were covered under the rental agreements. As for the level of per-capita revenue, it was fixed at the average level of the two provinces with the highest yields—Ontario and British Columbia. However, the emergence of large natural resource revenues in one or two provinces, particularly in Alberta, soon raised questions of interprovincial equity in the program and successive adjustments had to be made during the first decade of experience with the system. More important, it became clear that there was a need to consider the full revenue-raising potential of each province. This brought forward again the question of the level or standard of equalization that would be appropriate under a broader system. It also emphasized the need to develop a practical technology for measuring objectively the relative revenue-raising capacity of each province.

All these elements were brought together when the system was substantially extended in 1967. All provincial revenues were taken into account and the standard of equalization was fixed as the national average for all ten provinces. The explicit purpose of the expanded federal program was to provide unconditional federal payments sufficient "to enable each province to provide an adequate level of public services without resort to rates of taxation substantially higher than those of other provinces."[2]

This basic objective was largely maintained throughout the decades that followed, although changing economic and fiscal circumstances made adjustments necessary from time to time. Many of these adjustments were of a technical nature and were aimed at more precise measurement of fiscal capacity, which would help ensure interprovincial equity in equalization payments. A significant broadening of the actual scope of the system occurred in the early 1970s with the inclusion of local government taxes levied for school purposes, and subsequently the addition of all local government revenues. Major conceptual and methodological problems were encountered as massive and concentrated provincial revenues from petroleum resources in Alberta had to be integrated into the system. Retention of the original formula of 1967 would have resulted in equalization payments to Ontario in the early 1980s, and it was necessary to devise some important technical adjustments in both the total provincial revenues to be included in the calculations and the determination of the per-capita level of equalization. In the end, however, by 1984-85 the equalization system took into account a total of thirty-three separate sources of provincial revenues, as collected in all provinces except Alberta and the four Atlantic provinces, and the equalization level to which all provinces were raised was the average per-capita revenue yield of the other five middle-income provinces. This transferred unconditional cash payments to six recipient provinces amounting to $5,394 million, which represented more than a tenfold increase over the total provided in 1967-68. On a per-capita basis, equalization payments ranged from about $460 in Quebec and Manitoba up to over $1,000 in Prince Edward Island and Newfoundland. They provided about 10 percent of total revenues for the first two provinces and up to 30 percent for the latter two, and greatly reduced the disparities in the ten provinces' fiscal capacity and ability to provide public services.

Moreover, by 1982 the fiscal equalization system, once strongly resisted by the wealthier provinces, had matured not only as a finely tuned and flexible mechanism for the regional redistribution of national financial resources under the aegis of the federal government, but also as a fundamental tenet of Canada's political and financial culture. As is well known, the acceptance of the concept culminated in its adoption as a constitutional principle in the Constitution Act of 1982. Significantly, the language adopted in Section 36 (2) of the Constitution itself closely reflected that enunciated by the federal government fifteen years earlier: "Parliament and the government of Canada are committed to the principle of making equalization payments to ensure that provincial governments have sufficient revenues to provide reasonably comparable levels of public services at reasonably comparable levels of taxation."

___ Established-Programs Financing___

In the mid-1970s, radical changes were initiated by the federal government in the method by which it helped the provinces finance established social programs—public hospital insurance and medical care insurance—and post-secondary education. Originally introduced one by one as shared-cost programs in the decade from the late 1950s, these programs constituted major elements in the overall growth of the Canadian welfare state. Both provincial and federal initiatives had fostered this development, but federal conditional grants played a vital role in ensuring that these public services were provided across the nation.

The essence of the change introduced in 1977 was to transform narrowly defined federal grants into general-purpose block grants. It thus represented a significant effort to recognize primary provincial jurisdiction in health and education while retaining the federal interest in preserving high-quality programs accessible to all Canadians.

A considerable amount of contentious debate surrounded the introduction of each of these programs. Much of the controversy arose because a majority of the provinces saw federal conditional grants in these areas as trespassing on their constitutional jurisdiction. Consequently, in the early and mid-sixties the federal government had responded in part to these concerns, voiced especially by Quebec, through the Established Programs (Interim Arrangements) Act, which allowed provinces to "opt out" or "contract out." Under this federal legislation, provinces could take the federal financial aid partly in the form of additional tax room, instead of a cash grant. Nevertheless, continuing jurisdictional complaints from the provinces focused on the argument that the grants tended to distort provincial expenditure allocations because of their conditional nature and because they were tied to defined shared-cost services. This applied not only within the particular program areas themselves, but also across the whole range of provincial spending. The allure of so-called fifty-cent dollars was widely regarded as a distorting influence in provincial decision making.

The transformation of federal conditional grants into functional block grants thus provided several advantages. First, it helped the provinces develop these program areas according to their own priorities and perceived needs. Second, the separation of the amount of federal funding from actual expenditures by provinces and the substitution of an alternative, statistically determined calculation of the amount of federal aid to be provided promoted improved stability, predictability and even discipline in spending decisions at both levels of government. Third, by placing federal payments on an equal per-capita basis for all provinces, rather than calculating them as a 50 percent share (more or less) of spending by each province, an important element of program equalization support was provided for the lower-income provinces.

The new arrangements also provided that the federal financial contribution would take the form of a transfer of additional tax room to all provinces, with the remaining part to be paid in cash as previously. It thus bolstered the autonomous taxing power and unconditional revenue shares of the provinces. Moreover, the equalization system discussed above meant that this additional tax room was of approximately equal value to all the provinces. However, the fact that a significant part of the federal aid was still to be paid by a cash grant helped to maintain a residual federal influence in the continued provision and design of the services themselves. In particular, the widespread support for the 1984 Canada Health Act, which helped preserve the basic elements of the original health insurance schemes as first designed in Saskatchewan (comprehensiveness, universality, accessibility, portability and non-profit public administration) showed that federal funding could still influence the nature of one public service.

On the other hand, because of constitutional sensitivities, the federal government was unable to have direct influence on the continuing provision and growth of post-secondary education services. This serves as a useful lesson and especially underlines the need to obtain clear and explicit undertakings, or even contractual commitments, from the provinces, to ensure that national objectives and standards are maintained even as provincial flexibility and autonomy are broadened.

___ A Continued Role for Conditional Grants ___

The apparent advantages of the block-funding approach, especially in the health insurance field, raised the question of its possible application in other areas of shared-cost programs. The most likely candidate for such application was the Canada Assistance Plan, under which the federal government paid half the actual cost of provincial spending for social assistance and a defined range of social services. First enacted in 1966, this federal legislation expanded and consolidated a number of specific grants-in-aid for social welfare and thus provided the basis of the wide-ranging cost-sharing program as it is now formulated.

Although the amount of federal funding under the plan remained tied on a shared-cost basis to actual provincial expenditure, the broad compass of the legislation, the mechanics of its operation and its method of administration resulted to a significant degree in a federal transfer that was much like a block grant. These features had been developed through continuing administrative consultations after the plan was first legislated. But social policy analysts have noted that the gains in the extent and quality of social assistance across the country as a whole rested in no small measure not only on the wide scope and variety of eligible services but also on the conditions imposed for cost-sharing in the federal legislation. The ban on requiring a period of residence within the province to qualify for assistance was one particularly important condition.

The Breau parliamentary task force inquiry into the 1982

review of the Federal-Provincial Fiscal Arrangements Act reported that a large number of citizen associations and interest groups urged the retention of the conditional-grant form of federal assistance in the areas of social assistance and social services. Conditional grants were considered to be of continuing importance in a program area where perceptions, values and standards were still in the process of development. Moreover, it was not immediately obvious what alternative to cost sharing would be fair and equitable for all the provinces, given the wide disparities in numbers of welfare recipients and the differing cost conditions across the country.

Much the same analysis applies in the distinctly different field of regional economic development grants. In 1974 the federal Department of Regional Economic Expansion (DREE) set up the framework of a block-type umbrella agreement, called a general development agreement, which extended over a ten-year period. But specific subsidiary or program agreements covering either particular projects or economic sectors still had to be negotiated, with the particulars of cost sharing having to be worked out in some detail in each case. Some modifications in approach were introduced through a new series of agreements put in place in 1984, with the result that more emphasis was placed on the separate inputs from each level of government. Nevertheless, the objective was still to devise a system that was conducive to provincial independence and flexibility but fully consistent with the broad federal objective of facilitating country-wide regional development.

More traditional, specific-purpose conditional grants were also used in many special situations where federal assistance in provincial areas of expenditure could be justified. An outstanding case was the introduction in 1970 of federal grants to further bilingualism in Canada through the official languages in education programs. In this case, as is typically true of conditional grant programs, substantial federal financing was provided, but it was restricted to specific categories of programs that were judged to be particularly relevant to the federal objective. The descriptive inventory of federal-provincial programs and activities now published annually by the Federal-Provincial Relations Office in Ottawa provides evidence of the myriad ways in which conditional grants remain a useful part of the overall framework of fiscal federalism. In 1984–85 these grants and the aggregate of transfers in the form of cash payments and the yield of tax potential ceded to the provinces amounted to over $26 billion, or approximately one-quarter of the federal government's total spending in that year.

___ Fiscal Policy Co-ordination _____

This review of developments in fiscal federalism in Canada during the 1970s would not be complete without taking note of the federal effort to engage the provinces in an economic dialogue transcending the transfer of tax room or cash. The severe economic disturbances of the period – the energy shock, spiralling price inflation, the large upward shift in unemployment and the unfortunate slowdown in productivity gains – all combined to create unprecedented challenges for governments throughout most of the industrially advanced world. The formation of an effective policy response was made even more difficult by the apparent breakdown of previously accepted economic theory and analysis.

This complex of problems was intensified in Canada, not only by the constitutional fragmentation of jurisdiction, but also by the transfer of federal fiscal power to the provinces and the increase in interregional conflict. In the fiscal realm, efforts at intergovernmental analysis and documentation were improved at the bureaucratic level, but ministerial consultations and conferences aimed at policy co-ordination achieved only minor results. On the other hand, when Ottawa resorted to an emergency régime of price and wage controls – as an alternative to harshly restrictive fiscal and monetary policy – it was assisted to a great extent by co-operative provincial effort. This occurred, even though the federal initiative was also resisted by some provinces on constitutional and substantive grounds.

However, less progress was made at the economic conferences which were held later in the decade in an effort to reach agreement on measures and programs to deal with the more difficult issues of improved sectoral economic performance. In fact, these discussions proved largely abortive, providing little more than a further forum for special pleading and renewed provincial complaint. Ideology, parochial self-interest, turf-guarding and lack of understanding all threw up formidable obstacles to effective and concerted action on sectoral economic policy making. The lesson from this experience seems to parallel that observed in other areas of fiscal federalism. The arts of gentle persuasion and intelligent understanding are helpful and useful tools in intergovernmental relations in Canada, but both fiscal and jurisdictional clout are almost always needed to achieve major national objectives.

As a brief concluding note, it may be observed that most commentators on the federal-provincial scene from the late sixties to the early eighties tend to recall it as a period of intense struggle and conflict, and no doubt the continuous debate over the appropriate balance between federal and provincial powers and interests rose at times to high levels of stridency. This may be traced in part to a series of special factors which aggravated the conflict engendered by the underlying trend of decentralization, as the trauma of the Great Depression and the exigencies of wartime finance faded into history. Prominent among these factors were the election of an avowedly separatist government in Quebec, the rapid increase in new wealth in the resource-rich western region and macroeconomic destabilization of major proportions throughout the country. Important underlying social and cultural factors such as the increased emphasis on citizens' rights and the decline in the prestige of institutions were also at work. So, too, was the increased flow of powerful economic forces across international boundaries.

Canada, of course, was not alone in this experience. The entire Western world faced similar destabilizing social, economic and political pressures. But in our case, a crucial energizing element was the presence of a federal administration that was sensitive to the longer-term implications of unchecked decentralization and a seriously weakened federal state. In the event, the federal government was not making a simple attempt to retain or reinforce power at the centre. Rather, it consistently undertook to find and maintain an appropriate balance between the needs of an effective national state and the legitimate aspirations of provinces for appropriate autonomy, flexibility and resources. Throughout the period, the evolutionary development of fiscal federalism in all its ramifications—a workable system of revenue sharing, a finely tuned system of fiscal equalization, the introduction of block transfers, the continued use of special-purpose conditional grants, and innovative approaches to economic policy making—clearly showed that Canada, as a functional whole, could be more than the sum of its parts.

Regional Development: Innovations in the West

———————————by Lloyd Axworthy ———————————

Lloyd Axworthy has been an elected Liberal for western Canada for over sixteen years, serving as both a provincial MLA and a federal MP. In the Trudeau government he was Minister of Employment and Immigration, Minister of Transport and Chairman of the Cabinet Committee on Western Affairs. Lately he has served as the Trade Critic for the Official Opposition and was Chairman of the Western Liberal Caucus for five years. He is married with one child and holds a B.A. degree from the University of Winnipeg and an M.A. and Ph.D. from Princeton University.

THROUGHOUT THE YEARS of Canadian nationhood, beginning with the national policy of Sir John A. Macdonald, a wide variety of regional policy initiatives have been pursued, some with enthusiasm and creativity, others grudgingly, as concessions to regional political pressures. But in the long history of Canadian regional policy, the successive Liberal administrations under Pierre Elliott Trudeau stand out for their dedication and ingenuity in addressing regional economic disparities.

Regional development formed a core element of Pierre Trudeau's quest for national unity. In reply to the Speech from the Throne in 1968, he stressed that ". . . the reduction of regional disparities must be one of the objectives of a healthy confederation for the future. This government fully shares this view. . . ."[1]

From the outset of the Trudeau régime, major policy and program initiatives were launched to implement the concept. Beginning in 1969, the Department of Regional Economic Expansion (DREE) was established, with Jean Marchand, a close friend and advisor of Trudeau, as its first minister. The new department had broad powers to issue grants and loans to develop infrastructure and attract industry to low-income regions. At the same time, the government moved in other sectors of programming. There was the enrichment of Unemployment Insurance benefits in high-unemployment areas, job creation allocations tied to the unemployment rate and regional tax incentives. After the 1972 election, a review of the regional development program was launched by Don Jamieson, another powerful minister of DREE, leading to the inauguration of General Development Agreements (GDAs) with the provinces. Under this program, key sectors of investment such as roads, fisheries and forestry were identified in disadvantaged regions, and a cost-sharing formula was developed between the two levels of government. This approach was later modified by Pierre De Bané, the minister responsible for DREE in the early eighties, who began to develop a capacity for direct delivery of regional programs while retaining the GDA planning framework.

In 1982, the principle of regional equalization was entrenched in the new Constitution, giving it the status of a basic economic right. This was followed by another reorganization of the economic departments in the federal system in a further attempt to instill regional sensitivity as a paramount goal in all national programming. In short, regional equity was a consistent and continuing preoccupation of the Trudeau Liberals.

It was a daunting task. The natural flow of market forces in Canada led to the increased concentration of economic growth in the urban areas, especially in the Ontario heartland. At the same time, in the 1970s, the resource and commodity industries that are the economic backbone of the Canadian hinterland were subject to price volatility as a result of technological change and international market developments. In short, economic disparity and inequities in economic opportunity continued to plague the nation.

In the face of such strong underlying economic trends, the government was hard pressed to close the gaps in spite of federal regional development efforts. There was also criticism that Ottawa-directed programs were often too rigid or overcentralized and could not contend with powerful market forces.

Nevertheless, both caucus and party members believed strongly in regional development, and their dedication to the concept served as a bulwark of Liberal support in the Atlantic provinces and Quebec. It was a practical response to the experience of many caucus members—especially in Atlantic Canada and in parts of Quebec, northern Ontario and western Canada—who felt that in Canada the federal government should help bring jobs to people, rather than forcing people to go to the jobs. As Prime Minister Trudeau emphasized in his reply to the 1968 Throne Speech, it was part and parcel of a fundamental belief in regional, linguistic and economic balance—a dialectic of creative tensions at work within the federal state.

The last Trudeau period, beginning in 1980, was beset with a particularly vexing test of this belief. The election of 1980 had resulted in a virtual wipe-out of elected government members west of Ontario. Only two Liberal MPs were elected in the West—myself and Bob Bockstael—both from the city of Winnipeg. This representational gap occurred at a time when the Trudeau government was faced with extremely difficult choices about western energy and resource policy and a phalanx of hostile provincial governments. So, in addition to the ongoing task of combatting the severe disparities existing in regions like the Maritimes, northern Quebec, northern Ontario and the Territories, a special effort at regional reconciliation and development was required in western Canada to fill the political void and to offset the strengthening drumbeat of western alienation.

The rest of this chapter will focus on the way in which the Trudeau government dealt with this political conundrum in the West through a series of innovative political and economic development initiatives—that little-understood portion of the Trudeau record. But this is not simply an exercise in historical fence mending. The innovations of the Trudeau period can provide useful models to guide future efforts by federal governments committed to an activist role in rebalancing the predominance of the central provinces.

___ The Cabinet Committee on Western Affairs and the Western Development Fund ___

Necessity is the mother of invention. Thus the period from 1980 to 1984 saw an interesting array of federal activities in the West. Major efforts were undertaken to promote the development of new coal fields in northeastern British Columbia, and Senator Jack Austin was successful in developing an active role for the federal government in the Expo '86 celebrations in Vancouver. Senator Hazen Argue was an ardent promoter of the co-op movement, resulting in an agreement by the federal government to fund a co-op energy project in Saskatchewan. And there were significant transportation, industrial and urban development initiatives, as described in more detail in the following pages.

At the heart of these efforts was a fundamental change in the nature of Cabinet decision making as it affected the western region. Perhaps one of the most keenly observed criteria for selecting a federal Cabinet is regional representation. The regional press, provincial and municipal governments and provincially based business, labour and cultural organizations all take great interest in appointments from their region. Not surprisingly, with only two elected members west of the Manitoba-Ontario border, the first priority for the government after 1980 was to decide how to provide some form of effective, credible western representation in the government. Immediately following the election, Prime Minister Trudeau asked the two Manitoba MPs to undertake consultations in the western provinces and return with recommendations.

This process yielded two results. First, from the provinces where there were no elected members, Liberal Senators were asked to take on a Cabinet role. Second, the prime minister formed a special Cabinet Committee on Western Affairs, designed as a clearing house/co-ordinating agency for western concerns, issues and problems. This committee reported, through its chairman, to the Planning and Priorities Committee of Cabinet, had its own secretariat in the Privy Council Office and drew its membership not only from western ministers, but also from ministries such as Transport, Agriculture, DREE and

Indian Affairs and Northern Development, which had strong impact on western Canada.

The basic concept in political terms was that the Cabinet committee would be a surrogate western caucus. As it developed, the committee took on a substantive policy role, rather than a purely political one. Western views on national policies were offered and western solutions to economic and regional problems were developed, while the more political decisions of Cabinet, involving order-in-council appointments, for example, were left to the conventional machinery of Cabinet.

Interestingly enough, this newly devised regional Cabinet committee quickly became the focal point both for one of the most contentious policy decisions taken during the 1980–84 mandate and for one of the most significant efforts made by a national government in regional economic development.

The committee played an active role in debating the proposals for the establishment of the National Energy Program — one of the most controversial of all decisions taken between 1980 and 1984. The NEP was the fulfilment of Liberal campaign promises to deal with the burgeoning problem of increasing fuel prices and apparently dwindling oil resources.

The NEP inevitably led to outcries from western provincial governments, the oil industry, the U.S. government and a host of economic commentators who recoiled from this major federal intervention into a strategic resource sector. The western provincial reaction can only be understood in its historical and political context going back to the creation of the western provinces, which were denied the power to manage natural resources, unlike their eastern counterparts. This inequity in resource rights was redressed in 1928 by the Resources Transfer Act, but there remained an historical scar that was easily reopened. Despite the broad front of opposition, the Trudeau government, led by a resolute Marc Lalonde, pursued the policy and became embroiled in a bitter conflict with western provincial governments.

Members of the Cabinet Committee on Western Affairs felt the political impact of the NEP. Most agreed with the essential correctness of the claim that the regional balance of benefits associated with energy development was being tilted toward eastern Canada at a time when at least some western provinces were experiencing an unusual burst of resource-based wealth and economic development. The committee therefore recommended that a significant portion of the funds flowing to the federal government because of the NEP be earmarked specifically for western economic development. This accommodation was accepted, and in the budget of 1981 $4.6 billion was set aside as part of a newly established Western Development Fund. The intent of the fund was to recycle western petro-revenues in a focused way, in order to reduce some of the major obstacles to western economic development.

As chairman of the Western Cabinet Committee, I was charged with the task of developing this "Western Development Strategy." Various government departments were invited to submit proposals, and a process of consultation was continued with western-based interest groups. With such a large sum of unallocated dollars on the table, the bidding was fierce. A new water/environment policy, a native economic development proposal and an ambitious agri-food strategy were among the major initiatives considered.

Eventually, the focus of the Cabinet committee centred on a proposal for modernization of the western rail system, through revisions to western grain freight rates.[2] In 1897, an Act known as the Crow Statute had frozen shipment rates for grain going through west coast ports and Thunder Bay at prevailing levels as a way of meeting western farm demand for a fair economic deal and to offset gouging by the railroads.[3] Inevitably, by the 1970s, the railways were losing a significant amount of money on every bushel of grain they carried. The result was a seriously deteriorating rail system, bottlenecks restricting grain exports in a hungry world and, generally, a choking off of economic diversification and investment potential. Most economists pointed out that the structure of the rates worked against the development of the value-added agricultural processing industry in the West. Coal, sulphur and forestry shippers, among others, similarly suffered from bottlenecks and lost opportunity.

However, changing the Crow Rate was a major headache—

as it had been perennially for successive federal governments. In the seventies, there were two main obstacles. The first was the entrenched opposition from some powerful western grain groups. The second was the lack of public funds that could be used to make up the difference between the real costs of moving grain and what the farmer could afford to pay even on an increasing graduated scale.

Jean-Luc Pepin, then the minister of transport, was prepared to take on the tough political task of working through a new freight-rate program. The Western Development Fund offered the possibility of finally locating sufficient funds to underwrite the new arrangements.

After an extensive task force and consultative exercise and a protracted debate in the Western Cabinet Committee, the Crow proposal became the number one priority for Fund resources. The argument that eventually convinced western ministers and the entire Cabinet to support this proposal was the incentive the new structure offered for economic growth and diversification in the West. By making the rate applying to transportation realistic, there would be a stronger incentive to process materials in the region, especially if a way could be found to pay the Crow benefit directly to the farmers, rather than directly to the railroads, thus giving the farmers a choice in how they would ship their products and in what form. To further stimulate the western industrial base, the Western Cabinet Committee secured both a statutory requirement that the railroads would source their capital expenditures in the West and a special industrial grant program enabling western firms to upgrade their capacity to bid on railway work. It was estimated that $12 billion would be injected into the economy as a result of construction and procurement expenditures.

Unfortunately, when the final decision on the program was taken, a coalition of western grain groups, led by the powerful Saskatchewan Wheat Pool, mounted a strong lobby in favour of direct payment to the railways as a means of preserving their grain elevator system. They were supported by the Quebec government, the Quebec Liberal caucus in Ottawa and Quebec farm organizations, and succeeded in having a key component changed. The pay-the-producer option was rejected in favour of direct payment to the railroads, thereby weakening the incentive to do more value-added processing in western Canada.

Nevertheless, the change to the Crow Rate represented one of the most significant public-private infrastructure investment programs undertaken on behalf of a single Canadian region in modern times. The vital rail transportation of western Canada was substantially improved as the railroads immediately began major capital improvements such as the Rogers Pass tunnel reconstruction, grade modifications and new communications systems, which greatly added to the efficiency of moving the valuable commodities from the West.

The Crow Rate change also demonstrated the continuing importance of the national government as an agent of substantial investment in essential regional infrastructures. The railway program, which cut across the boundaries of four western provinces, was truly regional in scope and magnitude, addressing a serious structural flaw in the regional economy. It was not likely to have been implemented if the job had depended solely on provincial agreement or collaboration or if the resource revenues had been retained by individual provinces. Only a determined national government drawing upon a consolidated fiscal pool could make it happen.

The program also proved the value of having within the Cabinet system a regional forum in which the specific concerns of a region could be raised and where the activities and interests of various departments influential in that region could be integrated. Having the chairman of the Cabinet Committee on Western Affairs report directly to the Planning and Priorities Committee, then the most powerful Cabinet committee, gave the regional committee clout in the decision-making system.

This stands in sharp contrast with the approach recently adopted by the Mulroney government of setting up a series of separate development agencies (headed by a variety of ministers often not represented on the Planning and Priorities Committee). These agencies, located in the regions, are limited to giving discrete individual offers of financial support. Because they lack central leverage, they are effectively precluded from developing regional investment blueprints or investing in regional infrastructure. Under the Mulroney system, the regions have lost political leverage in Ottawa and are reduced to a responsive, rather than a pro-active, role.

___The Economic and Regional Development
Agreements _____

Beginning in the early 1980s, a new acronym entered Ottawa's
vocabulary—ERDA. It stood for Economic and Regional
Development Agreements, another innovative attempt of the
last Trudeau administration to revise federal government
approaches to regional development. The establishment of
ERDA represented a change in philosophy by the Trudeau
Liberals from an earlier view, according to which regional
assistance was targeted primarily at areas of poverty and
disadvantage.

Throughout the 1970s and early 1980s, regional development had been the preserve of DREE, which had the budget to
run a regional industrial incentives program and a program of
federal-provincial initiatives. Both were carried out under
General Development Agreements signed with each province.
This approach, however, presented three problems.

First, regional spending was inevitably pushed by political
pressures into projects that did not necessarily merit the
financial support. Second, regional development spending in
fact represented a relatively modest portion of total federal
spending and it was becoming increasingly obvious that it was
not sufficient to make a real impact on disparities. Third, with
DREE handling regional development in the federal system,
other federal departments with economic mandates tended to
take less responsibility for the regional dimensions of their
programs.

To correct these deficiencies, the prime minister introduced
in 1982 a fundamental government reorganization based on an
idea developed by Michael Pitfield, then clerk of the Privy
Council. The thrust of the reorganization was to assign regional
development responsibility to *all* federal departments involved
in the economic field. DREE was wound up, and many of its
industrial programs transferred into the Department of
Regional and Industrial Expansion (DRIE). To ensure that
regional development criteria guided program and policy
development in all the "economic" departments, a central
agency called the Ministry of State for Economic and Regional
Development (MSERD) was heavily involved in scrutinizing
Cabinet memoranda. The chairman of the Economic and

Regional Development Committee of Cabinet received briefings on regional implications of department activities. Regional ministers, who played an important and often determining role in making decisions on regional initiatives, were also active in this Cabinet committee. With the ERDA agreements, Canada came as close as it ever had to developing a national industrial strategy.

In Manitoba the ERDA system worked well. After extensive negotiations involving myself as the federal regional minister for the province; the chairman of the Economic and Regional Development Committee of the federal Cabinet; the Manitoba federal economic development co-ordinator, who was a central agency representative; and provincial ministers and officials, a package of ERDA agreements was signed in 1983 allowing for over $550 million dollars' worth of investment in five key economic sectors over five years.

It was not just the amount that was important, because in fact the agreement co-ordinated programming activity far beyond the incremental spending profiled in the document. The significance of the ERDA was that it represented a serious effort to combine federal-provincial funding across numerous departments on a series of agreed priorities designed to strengthen regional economic activity. In Manitoba, it was determined that transportation was a crucial sector of the provincial economy. Thus, a combination of initiatives were planned with a view to consolidating the role of Manitoba as a transportation hub for the West. These initiatives included upgrading the port of Churchill, capital investments in the Winnipeg airport, establishment of the University of Manitoba Transport Institute (integrated with the University of Manitoba's business school), development of a new grain-hopper car production at the CN shops in Winnipeg and a new VIA car maintenance facility, among others.

The ERDA system was also used in Manitoba as a way of promoting the potential of new service industries. Building on the strong local arts community and multicultural community, a subsidiary agreement provided resources for development of the culture and communications industry. In addition, a subsidiary agreement covering the production of urban transit buses was signed as a way of expanding the potential of local bus-manufacturing companies. Subsidiary agreements were also signed to encourage the agriculture and mining sectors to undertake research and development in the areas of new product technology and market expansion. In all cases, the purpose of the public funding was to provide facilities, resources and training opportunities that would open up opportunities for local private enterprise.

With this approach, the conventional "grants for plants" method was largely avoided and the focus was shifted to developing a regional infrastructure and reducing obstacles to economic growth. Efforts were made to target regional strengths and build on them through a combination of complementary federal and provincial support programs.

Regional development, therefore, was not just a function of specified regional grants, but became a responsibility of all federal departments, working in conjunction with provincial counterparts to develop long-term public investment strategies.

___ Core Area Initiative _____

The early eighties saw the beginning of a re-evaluation of traditional regional development programming. The centralized grant-in-aid program directed from Ottawa and the various forms of federal-provincial agreements were considered too bureaucratic, and direct assistance for industrial location had not resulted in the hoped-for development results. Increasingly, the focus of interest was turning towards the notion of stimulating economic growth by concentrating on improving the economic climate of the local community. Good schools, training, transportation and environmental upgrading were seen as the basis for attracting private investment.

The 1980–84 Trudeau government had begun some early experiments in this regard. As minister of employment and immigration, I had initiated the Local Economic Development Agreements (LEDA) program, a federally supported pilot program of local economic development corporations. We also introduced the Industrial Labour Adjustment Program (ILAP), jointly operated by the ministries of Employment and Immigration, and Industry and Labour, and designed to help key industries in a number of communities that were facing major adjustment problems caused by corporate restructuring, plant closure and so on. An innovative dimension of ILAP was its focus on combining labour, employment and economic incentive programs at the local community level.

Perhaps the most interesting of the Trudeau government innovations, however, was the Winnipeg Core Area Initiative (CAI) begun in 1981. Among other things, the CAI demonstrated that the national government could be a major partner at the local-community level of development.

The Core Area Initiative was launched at a meeting of inner-city residents of Winnipeg, where $30 million in federal funds was offered to support a comprehensive inner-city renewal program if that funding was matched by the other levels of government. This was not traditional urban renewal. The main rationale accepted by our Cabinet for underwriting this activity was that economic development could occur in Winnipeg only after it began tackling the deteriorating conditions of the inner city in a comprehensive way and began providing jobs for the in-migrating native population. It was felt that economic development of the city could proceed only with an integrated, combined effort by all levels of government to improve the environmental infrastructure, promote new enterprise, upgrade the level of skill of individuals and encourage a true sense of participation by local residents.

After some tough bargaining, the provincial and city governments agreed to an eight-point plan of attack, including training, education, housing, support of community organizations, a small business incentive program, a neighbourhood renewal program and provisions for major capital investment in removing railway yards at the historic Forks and rebuilding on the north side of Portage—an area so deteriorated that it cast a pall over the entire downtown.

Unlike the case in most regional development efforts, the federal government was not a silent partner, providing only funds. Nor was the program administered by officials. Central to the Core Area Initiative was a policy-making committee composed of myself as the regional federal minister, a designated provincial minister and the mayor, who met on a monthly basis to make joint decisions on the implementation of the program.

This unique arrangement brought political accountability and initiative to the program and resulted in a number of complementary benefits. Because of the direct involvement of a federal Cabinet minister, additional federal contributions were made to supplement the agreement. A new Air Canada computer centre, the National Research Council Industrial Technology Lab, funding for the North Portage Development Center and additional training and employment programs were added to the mix. Having a clear development blueprint made these additional initiatives possible. Federal investments could now be targeted and co-ordinated, and all federal departments and agencies could be recruited to help create a critical mass of activity.

The CAI also relied on the active involvement of inner-city residents and local agencies. Public hearings were held initially to help define the program. The result was a program that supported the creation of local, community-based organizations that could go on to apply for capital or operating funds to build health clinics or self-help employment centres, turn old garages into community theatre sites or initiate in-fill housing. This spawned a network of community-based organizations and gave rise to new leadership in the inner city. After initial growing pains, the CAI became a striking success and highly popular. The physical face of the downtown was dramatically changed, hundreds of new small business were started, over 3,000 disadvantaged Core Area residents received job training, more than 7,000 housing units were rehabilitated and 30 heritage buildings were renovated in the warehouse area, creating a new site for business activity.

Private funds were invested on a large scale, and a new climate of confidence and optimism emerged within Winnipeg's political, cultural and business communities. The CAI was such a success that, following a very positive series of public hearings, the Mulroney government felt compelled to renew it for a second term.

As a demonstration project, the CAI's principal achievements were sixfold:

1. The initiative served to rationalize and maximize effectiveness of the efforts of a number of previously unconnected federal departments and focus them on a common objective of improving the overall economic and social environment of a targeted area.
2. It provided a framework and plan of sufficient scope and comprehensiveness to justify reinforcing the CAI with complementary federal expenditures on projects such as the National Research Council Industrial Technology Lab and supplying additional training funds in order to build a critical mass for development.
3. It provided a sufficiently large, focused and durable demonstration of governmental will that it then became possible to attract private-sector spending on a large scale (over $300 million).
4. It was sufficiently broad in outline that the issue of inner-city development was attacked in its full economic, physical and social dimensions, instead of in piecemeal fashion.
5. It provided tangible and unprecedented evidence of intergovernmental collaboration, at both the political and the official levels. At the CAI's regular meetings, representatives of the three levels of government discuss a set of common objectives—creating a forum that remains without precedent in Canadian federalism.
6. The degree of decentralization and delegation to community organizations that occurred is also unprecedented. The CAI has explicitly relied on the notion of community renewal-development from the bottom up, not from the top down.

As important as the Core Area Initiative has been for Winnipeg, it also has considerable significance as a general *model* for federally supported regional development—what might be labelled community entrepreneurship. In fact, the CAI has already gained the recognition and approval of the Organization for Economic Co-operation and Development, the European Economic Community, the United Nations and the World Bank as a model for comprehensive community-level economic and social development.

The success of the CAI suggests that the federal government can and should play an ongoing direct role as facilitator and innovator. The federal government must get back into the renewal of our towns and cities for both economic and environmental reasons. By bringing together the activities of various departments and agencies, by enlisting the efforts of different levels of government, by working to facilitate private activity—both profit and nonprofit, real growth can be generated. The federal government can be a major player in developing such an integrated, rationalized but decentralized approach to development. This doesn't mean supplying more money. It does mean a major shift in the way we conceive of regional economic environmental development in this country—towards a view that encourages diversity, flexibility and co-operation at the city, town and local community level.

For the four and a half years of its last mandate, the Trudeau government operated with virtually no elected representation from western Canada. Yet it not only managed to maintain an active presence in the West, but also succeeded in introducing several important and innovative regional development initiatives which responded to western conditions as well as regional economic challenges across the country. These accomplishments were overshadowed by the strong reaction against the National Energy Program and by continuous political assaults from the provincial premiers and Opposition parties. Thus, the immediate political result was a continuation of the electoral blackout in the West during the 1984 election. In Manitoba, however, a base was maintained in the 1984 election—partly as a result of the active efforts at regional development undertaken by the Trudeau government. The respect of the populace that was thus secured contributed substantially to the Liberal resurgence in that province seen in the 1987 provincial election and the 1988 federal election.

In spite of the swing away from Liberal support that occurred in other western regions, the achievements of the 1980–84 Trudeau administration were substantial. The railway infrastructure program, the ERDA agreements, the Core Area Initiative all produced tangible results in strengthening the economic fabric of the West. Modernizing the railway system was crucial in helping western commodities reach export markets, the ERDA programs focused on basic infrastructure constraints and provided major support for the newly burgeoning service industries of the West and the Core Area Initiative was the catalyst for major renewal on many fronts in the city of Winnipeg.

In the longer term, the regional initiatives of the last Trudeau administration began laying a major part of the groundwork for a revised Liberal approach to regional development. What are the major lessons to be drawn? First, public investment in infrastructure is of central importance to maintaining regional vitality and responsiveness to economic opportunity. In this formulation, infrastructure is broadly defined. It does not just consist of bricks and mortar, it involves institutions to educate and train people, the organization of technical research, the quality of community, environmental and cultural facilities and the quality of economic leadership in the private as well as public spheres. This is an area that has been largely abandoned by the Mulroney Conservatives in the operation of regional agencies. Investment in transportation, training, communication, research and development and cultural infrastructure is not easily undertaken by the private sector. Nor are provincial and municipal governments often able to address the challenge freely. The federal government has the reach and the resources to act if political will can be marshalled to the task.

Second, the conventional "grants for plants" approach has severe limitations. This approach fails in so many ways that it is surprising that it has continued to exist in one form or another in an era when hard choices have to be made about allocating federal resources. The problems are manifold: grants wasted on investments that would have proceeded without public-sector support, distortion and inequities within industry sectors, inappropriate roles for public servants, trade policy difficulties. All of these objections suggest that the role for grants to industry must be much more limited in the future.

A third lesson is that the system for federal regional economic decision making is of vital importance. There must be a place in the government's central decision-making apparatus for regional policy considerations to be forcefully injected. Regional Cabinet committees consisting of major line departments and regional ministers should play an active role in the design and implementation of policies and programs. These committees should be issue- and task-driven and should report to the central committee of Cabinet responsible for policy and resource allocation. The responsibilities of these committees should be reflected in the federal budgeting system. Policy and financial leverage must be exerted to ensure that all federal economic departments share responsibility for regional development.

A corollary of this point is the need for a system of strong regional ministers. In the old model of Cabinet, regional ministers played a role that was primarily political. To this must be added a more active policy role. Regional ministers can work with the key economic decision makers in their region to develop appropriate strategies. They can also play an integrative role in their regions, drawing together the resources of federal departments to determine key development priorities. One might even extend the regional minister system to provide for accountability to House of Commons and Senate committees.

A fourth lesson is that federally driven procurement and the location of federal departments and Crown agencies have great regional economic importance. The experience with railway procurement and the location of Air Canada's computer reservations system in Winnipeg's core demonstrates the feasibility of making these decisions. In an era when communication and transportation costs are falling on a per-unit basis, it is fully possible to disperse some of the federal overhead operations more widely. Fewer staff are required in headquarters and more are needed out in the field serving the consumer.

Finally, there is the lesson of the efficiency of community entrepreneurship models. Many such models exist, but all of them share the basic notion of enhancing the capacity of local institutions, individuals and groups to undertake their own development. The community-based model seeks to create an environment where small business, individual entrepreneurs and community groups can flourish. Training and investment in people is a critical element of the model. So, too, is the nurturing of local organizations and of the people who provide vision in the local economy. In this model, the federal government need not be a distant monolith. As the Core Area Initiative demonstrated, the community-based approach provides for a creative federal role in strengthening local resources and permits leverage over a wide array of federal capabilities.

These are lessons from which governments can develop principles for effective federal contribution toward regional economic development. Federal intervention need not be rigidly bureaucratic or overly centralized, but there must be a national commitment and a national plan. There will always be an imperative for regional economic policy, and the challenge is to develop good policy that uses resources effectively and efficiently. As Jack Pickersgill once said, "Canadians are not against public enterprise. They are for enterprise." What is clear is that federal decision makers must recognize the policy failures of the past and build on the successful experiences.

The end result should be to involve the federal government with people and their communities to promote the development of our regions in a way that stimulates their contribution to a strong national economy while still maintaining their diversity and essential character. As the Trudeau years have shown, the federal government can constructively use the power of the state to modify the impact of market forces and seek a more equitable and effective distribution of opportunities for Canadians.

————————— Part V —————————
The Institutional Framework

In any democracy, leaders must build a reciprocal relationship of trust and support with their fellow citizens. Pericles understood well the nature of democracy when he told the inhabitants of Athens: "We say that a man who takes no interest in politics and does not participate in the affairs of his city has no business here at all."[1]

Participation is the essential requirement of self-government. That is why we changed the Cabinet system so ministers could better participate; that is why we altered the rules of Parliament so members of Parliament could play a more effective role; that is why we introduced reforms into the system of election financing so that representatives of every party would be on a more even footing; and that is why we fought for a referendum provision in the Constitution so that every citizen would have the opportunity to participate in shaping the fundamental law of the land.

Lorna Marsden's chapter on Parliament and the Party outlines how we attempted to improve these basic institutions. Research funds, adequate Parliamentary offices, decent travel allowances and sensible working hours, all made Parliament a more efficient and humane place in which to work under the Trudeau Liberals. Yet, of all the reforms mentioned by Marsden, perhaps the most important was public financing of political parties in 1974. Prior to our changes in election financing, third parties were systematically disadvantaged because they could not count on support from the corporate sector. By limiting the amounts that could be spent on elections, by allowing all parties a portion of public funding and through the incentive of political tax credits, we made the electoral process much cleaner and fairer.

Jean Chrétien's survey of the great constitutional debate of 1980–82 illustrates well our belief in the transcendent importance of the individual, without regard to ethnic, geographic or religious accidents. Liberals believe that every individual has a special dimension, a uniqueness that cries out to be realized, and that the purpose of life is to realize that potential. The role of the state is to create the conditions under which individuals have the broadest possible choice in pursuing the goal of self-fulfilment. In his chapter, Chrétien rightly emphasizes the importance of the Charter of Rights and Freedoms; the Charter not only protects every Canadian from arbitrary misuse of power, but also defines the values that Canadians hold in common. It is a particularly active instrument, used by Canadians to defend their rights or improve their lot.

The Charter was a new beginning for Canada, where everyone would be on an equal footing and where citizenship would ultimately be founded on a set of shared values. With the Charter we had begun to achieve the dream of Edward Blake, who said some dozen years after the beginning of Confederation: "The future of Canada depends very largely upon the cultivation of a national spirit. We must find some common ground on which to unite, some common aspiration to be shared."[2] Provincialists, who fear the cultivation of a national spirit, were opposed to the Charter in 1981 and are seeking to weaken it still, either through the use of the "notwithstanding clause" or by the introduction of "distinct society" provisions.

Whether the provincialists will succeed in their campaign to destroy the Charter we do not yet know. What we do know is that Canadians everywhere have found the Charter to be a powerful ally in the quest for justice. Sir Wilfrid Laurier once defined a liberal state as a "regime of tolerance." Through the Charter, we have made that vision part of the basic law of the land.

Thomas S. Axworthy
Pierre Elliott Trudeau

---CHAPTER 11---

The Party and Parliament:
Participatory Democracy in
the Trudeau Years

---by Lorna Marsden---

*Lorna Marsden served on the National Executive of the Liberal
Party of Canada from 1973 to 1984. She has a Ph.D. from
Princeton University, and until called to the Senate in 1984, was
a professor of Sociology at the University of Toronto, where she
continues on a part-time basis.*

WHEN HE WAS chosen leader of the Canadian Liberals at the
April 1968 Convention, Pierre Trudeau brought major changes
to the spirit and operations of the Liberal federation. Equally
important were the changes he brought to the working
conditions of parliamentarians in his capacity as prime
minister. Though different in form, these changes were
introduced for the same purpose. Working from his own
political philosophy and the mood of the country – which he
had captured so well in the 1968 leadership campaign and
election – the purpose of the changes was to create "participatory democracy," a mandatory feature of any "just society."

The idea of participatory democracy was scarcely a new one.
After the 1957 defeat of Louis St Laurent, a group of young
Liberal party activists (an Ontario-based group known as "Cell
13" and their colleagues across the country) had cleaned up and
reorganized the Party for Lester B. Pearson using this idea. But
Pierre Trudeau was a new man, a new image, and so the idea of
participatory democracy took on a new meaning. Part of the
excitement Trudeau generated among Liberals came from his
work in Quebec, where by his pen and actions, he challenged
that closed society and the closed politics that characterized its

postwar period. It was not only the patronage and authoritarianism of the Duplessis régime that had been overturned, but also the practice of keeping political parties closed to all but a few influential citizens. The Liberals expected no less for the rest of Canada and for the federal Party. To a much greater extent than many realize, significant changes in the Liberal Party stemmed directly from the ideas of Pierre Trudeau, a leader not widely regarded as a "Party man."

Participatory democracy is a broad concept. In organizational terms, it suggests including not only a wider group of people but also different kinds of people in the decision-making process. In the 1960s, many kinds of people were asking to participate in the decision making that would shape our society. Students were placed on the governing councils of universities, workers were occasionally put in decision-making positions at plants and offices, consumer preferences were being studied rather than assumed, and the legitimacy of closed decision making was routinely called into question by reform movements of many kinds—and reported in the press.

Based on his experiences with Parliament both in the Privy Council Office from 1949 to 1951 and as an MP and Cabinet minister in the mid-1960s, Trudeau knew that reforms in Parliament were urgently required. The national Liberal Party was less familiar turf for him, but many of his supporters in 1968 were the Party reformers who urged him on. His determination to enact reform in these key areas gives us an indication of Pierre Trudeau's strong personal commitment to participatory democracy.

Reforms of Parliament

Mr Trudeau's ideas for participatory democracy were reflected in a series of changes to House rules and procedures, in the important Election Expenses Act and in the working conditions of parliamentarians. Despite many reforms to parliamentary procedure over the years—such as the 1906 restrictions on the right to move adjournment; the establishment of a closure procedure in 1913; and time rules on the length of speeches in 1927 and on major debates in 1955—there were serious inefficiencies in the way in which the House and Parliament addressed the Government agenda.

By the late 1960s, after difficult and stormy years in Parliament because of the frequent procedural delay of Government business, Prime Minister Lester B. Pearson enacted several reforms as sessional orders. They were designed to allow the Government to get on with its work, while respecting the rights of the Opposition and of individual members. Committees were restructured and the process of supply was revamped.[1] These reforms "disappeared" when the House was dissolved for the 1968 election.

In his first session, Mr Trudeau not only reintroduced the Pearson rules but entrenched them. This task was entrusted to president of the Privy Council Donald Macdonald, who established a House committee (the Special Committee on Procedure, 1968) to modernize procedures of the House specifically in areas that had been in contention in the previous Parliaments.[2] In the short term, the reforms proposed and accepted dealt with time allocation, deadlines for voting supply and changes to the committee system to give specialized standing committees more importance in the legislative process. Bills would now be routinely forwarded to the appropriate standing committee, with the exception of those concerning taxation.

With these moves, Mr Trudeau fulfilled one part of his commitment to participatory democracy by increasing the effectiveness of the House of Commons. His desire to do so was based on many years of experience with both the House of Commons and other branches of Parliament, first as an economic advisor to the Privy Council from 1949 to 1951; then as a member of Parliament from 1965 on and, during that time, as parliamentary secretary to Prime Minister Pearson. As minister of justice, he had first come to public attention when he introduced an omnibus reform bill that changed many outmoded and unpopular criminal laws. Based on this experience and his sound knowledge of political theory, he believed that participatory democracy should apply not only to extra-parliamentary politics, but also to Parliament. Not only should ministers be able to enact the Government agenda, but members of Parliament should be able to influence the

Government through work in the House and more effectively represent their constituents in legislation and services.[3]

Through reforms to committees and procedure, Opposition members and, indeed, backbenchers of the Government party were able to bring their views on most legislation to committees very quickly. This gave those members some countervailing powers against the government agenda that were substantive, as opposed to merely procedural. At the same time, the government agenda was not held up unduly by procedural disputes.[4]

But the early phase of reforms did not solve all the problems of Parliament. In 1974 the Standing Committee on Procedure came back to life (now called the Standing Committee on Procedure and Organization) and a series of further changes was enacted in 1975. These included a rescheduling of the oral question period; the right of the Opposition to have days allotted to it to bring before the Whole House items from the estimates; and the establishment of a new Standing Committee on Management and Members' Services. While the effectiveness of standing committees was discussed, no changes were enacted at this stage. In 1982, further reforms, for which responsibility was given to president of the Privy Council Yvan Pinard, included the fixing of the parliamentary calendar into three terms, which allowed members to plan the time they would spend with their families and in their constituencies. Evening sittings gave way to additional sitting hours in the mornings, except Wednesdays. Divisions on debatable motions called on Fridays were now to be called the next sitting day, allowing members to get to their ridings across the country by Friday night. The length of speeches at certain points was reduced. And as the years went on, the committees of the House and their business were changed to make the business of Parliament more orderly and efficient.[5]

The first Trudeau government also introduced many reforms to increase the ability of members to effectively represent their constituents. Taking into account the differences between the working conditions for MPs in their previous workplaces, the conditions of other Parliaments and those which Canadian MPs faced in the House of Commons, the first Trudeau government made many changes. In terms of physical facilities,

MPs went from sharing offices, telephones and secretaries to separate office suites, improved telephone access to their constituents and across the country and a more adequate staff both on Parliament Hill and in their constituencies. Furthermore, each MP was allotted a sum of money to cover these office expenses, subject to certain guidelines. Printing facilities were made available to parliamentarians, enabling them to send out constituency newsletters—also according to suitable guidelines. The Standing Committee on Management and Members' Services that was created in this period introduced a large number of improvements. These improvements, and others initiated by its successors, have made MPs much more effective in providing services to their constituents and have made the work of an MP more attractive to those citizens who may wish to run for office. In particular, the position of leader of the Opposition was greatly enhanced by reforms in services, allowances and physical facilities.

By 1984, the working conditions of all MPs, leaders of the Opposition parties, Cabinet ministers, staff and all those on Parliament Hill had been dramatically changed. All these changes were based on Pierre Trudeau's fundamental belief that participation in democracy is not possible without adequate material and economic support.

Equally important changes were made in the access that MPs, caucuses and Cabinet ministers had to research. In 1968, when research services to Government or Opposition caucuses were not funded by public monies, the parties differed in their capacity to fund such services themselves. MPs could use the research services of the Library of Parliament, which, though a valuable resource, undertakes no research of a partisan nature. In addition, the staff of the library was small, with only 9 research officers for 18 House committees and 264 MPs. In late 1968, the Parliamentary Centre for Foreign Affairs and Foreign Trade was established to provide research services for committees that dealt with foreign relations and trade, funded jointly by Parliament and the private sector. This supplemented the work of the Library of Parliament in staffing and serving the committees of both the House and the Senate.

By 1984, all research and information services had been improved and expanded. The improvements included on-line bibliographic and data-base services in the Library, and caucus research divisions for each party (funded by Parliament under a formula based on number of MPs) to provide partisan research to the members and caucuses.

These changes were put in place gradually through the work of many members and staff, but all had a common purpose—they were designed to open up the process. The results are self-evident. The most recent election shows a decline in the number of lawyers sitting in Parliament and an increase in other less well-paid occupational groups. In the House there is a dynamic balance between Government and Opposition and the third party. Members provide many more services for their constituents both in Ottawa and in their ridings. MPs are much better and more equitably informed and this shows in their questions and speeches. Although the public seldom see their MPs speaking in committees or in the House—because only Question Period is televised—those MPs who are willing and equipped to use the resources provided are among the best parliamentarians in the world.

In addition to these reforms of Parliament, Pierre Trudeau was also committed to electoral reform. Distressed as he had been by the Duplessis politics which established a particularly offensive patronage relationship in the culture, he determined to make appointments on merit and to change the means by which the parties raised money. There are differing views both about the evolution of the patronage system and the qualities of particular appointees during his years in power.[6] However, the Canada Election Expenses Act of 1974 did radically change the manner in which parties in Canada raise, spend and account for monies used in elections and at other times.

The Election Expenses Act

The Election Expenses Act exemplifies at many levels the type of participatory democracy that Trudeau was committed to enact. From the beginning, fund raising for Canadian political parties had always depended on the generosity of private donors. Since only a few Canadians were rich enough to make large political donations, a small group held considerable power in the parties and over individual candidates. Ordinary

Canadians could not think of standing for Parliament without substantial financial backing and the political parties could not run their operations or their campaigns without similar support. In effect, the system was a closed one—closed to those without sources of funding. This had deeply troubled several previous Liberal leaders. Louis St Laurent and Lester B. Pearson had both favoured change. In 1964, after extensive discussions, Mr Pearson established the Barbeau Commission to develop an analysis and plan for reforms.[7] But dealing with the sensitivities of the other parties and developing a practical plan for reform took many years. Mr Trudeau took up the cause and through the work of Cabinet minister John Reid and others won the agreement of all parties to the legislation and steered it through Parliament in 1974.

This opened up party politics in many ways. Donations over a minimal amount were now made public. Because of a tax credit given to donors, a way was opened to a huge pool of potential donors and the influence of the few larger ones was reduced.[8] Also, it was now easier—because of this and other reforms—for an entirely new group of Canadians to stand for Parliament. Women, those on small incomes and many others who had been unable to secure the required financial backing of the wealthy or generous were given the opportunity to take part in greater numbers. The more Canadians who participated in politics, the more complete democracy would be.

Clearly, not all reforms of Parliament sought by Pierre Trudeau—such as reform of the Senate—were realized, but those he achieved all moved towards his goal of participatory democracy for Canada's Parliament.

___ The Party* _____

The Liberal Party of Canada is almost as complex and fractious in its functioning as the Canadian confederation. It is

_____

*This account is based on experiences as a member of the LPC National Executive and its subcommittees, as well as discussions with many party activists and readings acknowledged in the endnotes. Many were kind enough to help with this work, including the Rt. Hon. Pierre Trudeau, Audrey Gill, Dr Tom Axworthy, Gordon Dryden, Senator Keith Davey and Professor Stephen Clarkson.

organized as a federation, the Party in each province[9] being an independent member. Within the Party, united by a progressive and pragmatic philosophy of government and a strong sense of the values held by Canadians, there can be found four estates.[10] These estates must be welded together in a workable way by each Party leader. The leader knows, or soon becomes aware, that in order to have a strong and winning Party, each of these demanding, competitive fractions must be kept happy. It was Pierre Trudeau's solutions to the problems posed by these competing interests that really constituted the participatory democracy of his era.

The first and most important estate consists of the people who join the Party as adherents and work in the ridings, uphold the Party positions in daily conversations and do volunteer work in elections.[11] When Pierre Trudeau came to the leadership, this estate was strengthened by Canadians of all walks of life who were impelled by his ideas and charisma to identify themselves as Liberals.

Capturing and holding these people is the work of the second estate. This consists of the elected Party officers at the national level or elsewhere in the federation, all of whom are volunteers; the paid workers or Party staff at national and provincial headquarters who work under the direction of a national director; and other paid advisors such as pollsters. It is a sense of identification with the leader and his purposes that holds many of these volunteers and others to the long hours on weekends and evenings and the endless frustrations of loyal Party work.

The parliamentary wing of the Party, its third estate, has its own complexity. Since it is the part of the Party that is most visible to the public, it tends to consider itself the most powerful. The national caucus brings this wing together: ministers (or ex-ministers when in Opposition), other members of Parliament and senators make up the caucus and set the policy directions of the Party. The second estate has the job of trying to influence and modify the actions of the parliamentary wing on behalf of the first estate in a situation where the power is shared quite unevenly.

The fourth estate consists of the staff of the leader's office and some of the key political staff in the ministers' offices. The political staff play the major role in mediating the relationship between the Party president and executive, the national director of the Party, the caucus and, both independently and through all those networks, the Party membership. In Trudeau's years as leader there were five principal secretaries: Marc Lalonde, Martin O'Connell, Jack Austin, Jim Coutts and Tom Axworthy. The role of principal secretary is the pivotal point in these relationships.

There were also five presidents of the Liberal Party during the Trudeau years: Richard Stanbury (1968–73), Gildas Molgat (1973–75), Alisdair Graham (1975–80), Norman MacLeod (1980–82) and Iona Campagnolo (1982–84).[12] Finally, the seven national directors of the LPC who served during this period were Al O'Brien and Torrance Wylie, who served with president Dick Stanbury; Blair Williams, who served with Gil Molgat; Gerry Robinson with Al Graham; Gordon Gibson and Gordon Ashworth with Norm MacLeod; and Gordon Ashworth and Danielle Dansereau with Iona Campagnolo. The competition of all these players for time, attention and resources from the leader and each estate of the Party sets up checks and balances to power within the Party. But these had to be mobilized. To understand the dynamics of the Party in the Trudeau years it is important to understand how many of the lines among the estates operated through, or were routed through, the office of the principal secretary to the leader.

By the time Pierre Trudeau took over as leader and Richard Stanbury as president at the 1968 convention, the reforms of the Pearson years had revised many of the operations of the Party[13] and whetted the appetite of Liberals for more change. One new experience for Liberals had been a national policy conference held in October 1966 when the Party was in Government, at which a complete legislative agenda was created. Until then, parties held policy conferences only when in Opposition, as in the case of the 1960 Kingston Liberal Conference. These two types of conferences pioneered a role for ordinary Party members in policy formation.

But the Pearson reforms had been only partly completed, and the main challenge was to institutionalize participatory democracy in the Liberal Party. In 1968, the champions of reform in the Party addressed that challenge. Three periods can be identified: 1968 to the start of the minority government that resulted from the election of 1972; 1972 to December 13, 1979, when the Clark government was defeated; and the period that ran from that time to the June 1984 leadership convention.

_____ The Charisma Years _____

The first period is described by Joseph Wearing as the "charisma years," in which the Party attempted to use the personality of Trudeau to entrench in the members and organization of the Party the ideas of openness between all estates, wider participation and greater democracy. This routinization of charisma was not entirely successful.

In the first phase, the movement for participation was led by Senator Richard Stanbury, who became Party president at the 1968 Convention after serving as chair of policy. Stanbury was a vigorous advocate of change who, as his memoranda show,[14] spared no effort to keep the competing estates in the Party in a balance of power by implementing reformist ideas and using the charismatic authority of the leader. He established advisory groups in each province and territory to do the political work on behalf of the Liberal Party. The deliberations of the group were passed on to the meetings of "political Cabinet." Political Cabinet, not an entirely new idea, was a method by which Cabinet decisions could be reviewed for their political impact after the deputy-ministers and other public servants had withdrawn from Cabinet meetings. With a vibrant new membership, vigorous leadership from their president and a willing leader, Party members were certain that the membership as a whole would have significant influence on the Government agenda as it was put into place, based on the ideological direction given by the Party and expressed by the new leader. A great deal of progress was made.

On the policy side, the Harrison Hot Springs Policy Conference in 1969 brought together key "thinkers" in the country with Party members from all estates to develop ideas for the Government. The ideas became policy resolutions at the 1970 National Convention. The convention of November 1970 was only the eighth national convention in the history of the

Liberal Party. Its style followed the pattern that had been set at the 1966 policy convention under Mr Pearson, but this convention was carried out on an even more ambitious scale. Delegates from every riding participated in the election of Party officers (and as the years went on more and more elected officers were added to the roster), changing the constitution of the Party, and debating and voting on policy.

Between conventions, there was a process of continuing interaction within the Party on policy through the "Consultative Council." This Council was based on the idea that the Party was in continuing convention and that the second estate had an obligation to gather Party members' views to influence the third estate on an ongoing basis. In effect, this meant that one of the vice-presidents of the Party was charged with surveying the Party membership annually to discover their views on key policy matters. To help in this process, a report evolved, and was issued annually or at least before each convention. This report showed what action had been taken on each of the resolutions passed by the previous convention and indicated whether the caucus or Cabinet had considered the ideas, acted on them, brought them into legislation or done nothing.

In 1966, Mr Pearson was asked to account to the Party for his leadership in the previous two years. This process was continued under Mr Trudeau and eventually written into the constitution of the Party. Mr Trudeau's addresses to the delegates were the main inspiring event of each convention, reinforcing commitment to the policies of the Party and the Government, explaining the context of recent events and, above all, providing proof of the leader's continuing charismatic power in the Party and in the country.[15]

On the communications side, vital to any participation by the first estate in the Party's activities, the Liberal newsletters were transformed. Although the Party had always published some sort of newsletter, in 1969 it was decided to publish a combined federal-provincial tabloid to serve the Liberals at both levels across the country. Called *The Canadian Liberal*,[16] this publication continued until the 1972 electoral disappointments and the second phase of Party fortunes began.

But resources posed a problem. The elected officers of the

Party had always been volunteers, most of whom lived far away from Ottawa, where the headquarters staff, the caucus and the leader conducted the day-to-day Party work. This had always restricted their ability to take advantage of all the opportunities of participatory democracy, especially since they had to pay their own expenses, including travel to most Party meetings. The Party welcomed new groups to its conventions and national executive with enthusiasm. Now, groups in society with few resources were elected as officers–youth, women, people from all provinces and parts of the country. But then the problem arose of how to bring these new groups together. No longer was a national executive meeting a small gathering of those able to find their own way to Ottawa. Financing their travel became a heavy burden to the Party, diverting funds to Party operations from other electoral and organizational activities.

Because of the reforms in the working conditions of MPs, the third and fourth estates were now better placed in terms of time, staff and other resources. In the prime minister's office (PMO) the staff resources had doubled during these early years and regional desks had been established to attend to political matters in the provinces and territories. These regional desks were sometimes in competition with the Party officers and were certainly alternative sources of information–and therefore power–for the leader and his staff.[17]

To keep all the new groups in the Party active, executive meetings had to be held frequently and the leader's attendance was desired at all of them. This led to another problem. When the leader could not be present, the executive demanded a surrogate to transmit messages from the Party back to the leader. The desirable surrogates were Senator Keith Davey or the Honourable Marc Lalonde and the principal secretary of the day. When the messages sent by the Party militants were not acted upon, the messenger was blamed. The surrogates for the leader became the object of much frustration and criticism by those who were not prepared to believe that Mr Trudeau would not act on their advice if he received it. This was especially so in the case of Jim Coutts, who had a long and difficult tenure as principal secretary, and in the case of Senator Davey, a much-loved personality in the Liberal Party, who later became the object of a youth-led "purge" movement, which lasted long after Pierre Trudeau had left the leadership.

The expectations of the Party adherents—the first estate—were disappointed when they found that influencing Party policy and especially Government policy was much more difficult than they had expected. Party members did not want or expect to be only a vehicle for electing the leader or members of Parliament who would then act without reference to their ideas or objectives. They were frustrated and disappointed to find that influence did not run through the Party, but through the principal secretary, senior officials and ministers. Those struggling to maintain the proper purpose of a political party, which is the public discussion of political ideas that may be put into effect if the Party achieves power of government, found themselves in serious competition for the time and attention of the leader and his ministers and, indeed, of the leader's political staff. Most of the notorious fights among the Party estates arose out of this situation of scarce resources and competing power interests. By the time of the 1972 election, disillusionment had set in, which was reflected in the 1972 campaign and its result—minority government.

The Years of Discontent

The second period, after the 1972 election, was one in which the inside forces (the third and fourth estates) asserted themselves to gain control of the Party apparatus, caucus and the leader's agenda. The immediate rationale for this was the need to achieve a majority in the next election. Party activists, disappointed with the election campaign and anxious to ensure that the ideals of 1968 were implemented by the Government, conceded the need for a new strategy. At the same time, increased staff permitted the prime minister's office to gain control of all elements of the Party. The factor that most powerfully mediated the shift of power from the Party operation to the leader's office was the entry of pollsters as the major means of testing public opinion. Not only does public opinion polling provide relatively quick and comprehensive pictures of the issues in the minds of the voters and their evaluations of the political leaders but the results are presented discreetly to the client without passing through the hands of the factional interests, which happens when the Party is used as the means of gathering opinion. Partly because of disillusionment about being bypassed like this, the Party developed a deep antipathy to the PMO. The manipulation of the Party's influence and agenda, and the separation of the caucus from the activists, were not a deliberate strategy but a side-effect of the need to control the agenda and focus on the goal of winning a majority government in the next election. This was recognized by all estates as a fact of political life. But when a majority was won in 1974, the expectation was raised that the progress toward participatory democracy could be resumed. And there was some further reform.

At the national policy conventions of 1973, 1975 and 1978, changes were made to the constitution of the party, increasing the elected positions on the national executive and formalizing debate on policy. As the pollsters' reports became more frequent and reliable, however, the Party gatherings were used more as an opportunity to deliver the message from the leader and the caucus and less as a method of sampling Party opinion. They became the means of recruiting new workers, rather than the means by which a collective view of the Party's position was arrived at. As the difficult period of 1974–79 wore on and the Government struggled with the oil shock, wage and price controls, inflation and the effects of the election of the Parti québécois government in Quebec, the Party's desire to influence the policy agenda increased.

To satisfy this, a "thinkers' conference" was held at the Constellation Hotel[18] in Toronto in March 1977. This led up to the national policy convention the following February in Ottawa, where over 3,500 delegates debated 1,100 resolutions, listened to the leader and his ministers give an account of their actions in government and chose new Party officers.

At the 1978 convention, Céline Hervieux-Payette was elected chair of the Standing Committee on Policy. In an attempt to avoid a repeat of the problems that stemmed from having to deal with the mass of policy resolutions at the 1978 convention, she tried a different process for the next convention, held in 1980, based on the model of European parties, in which an overarching manifesto of Party policy is developed. Work on this project was carried out by a small team of selected experts which offended many who believed in participatory democracy. The paper they produced, called "A Discussion Paper," was meant to be accepted by the convention as a whole as a guide to the Liberal electoral campaigns and the governing of the country. When the paper was presented to the Party Convention, delegates were confused by it because they were unfamiliar with this process. However, resolutions were once more given the central role in policy formation at the 1982 convention.

Communications inside the Party in this period included the bimonthly newsletter *Contact*, and a new publication called *Dialogue*, edited by Audrey Gill. In 1980, the *Liberal Policy Newsletter* was launched.

Throughout these years, the PMO staff, and ministers and their staff, were working their telephone networks, conveying messages, hearing complaints and trying out ideas. Whenever the national executive held a meeting, and at all national, provincial and regional Party conventions, the leader or his representatives, the caucus members and staff were in attendance. Until 1979, Pierre Trudeau always had the support of a majority of all estates of the Party. His speeches at Party meetings were personal triumphs for him and ritual acts of solidarity for the membership. The television coverage of these events conveyed to those Liberals not present the importance and excitement of Party membership.

Nevertheless, in these years collective unhappiness rose to a crescendo until, by 1979, open grumblings and revolt emerged in the Party ranks not only against the usual victims—the principal secretary and the regional staff of the ministers—but also against the leader himself. The election, earlier that year, had been lost to the Conservatives, who formed a minority government led by Joe Clark, and the Party was very unhappy. It had been a difficult election but the leader and his staff had tried to show their appreciation of the Party activists—the first estate—for their work during that election. The Grindstone Group[19] organized a challenge conference in Winnipeg, tripartite committees were struck with caucus and Party as well as some nongovernmental organizations to establish policy and priorities for a future Liberal government, and after years on the outside, Herb Gray was taken back into the shadow Cabinet as finance critic, which proved a popular move with the Party. At the annual meeting of the Liberal Party of Canada (Ontario), the leader spoke about Party reform and circulated a proposal outlining the initiatives he supported to reknit a frayed relationship. His reforms included modernizing the Party by expanding staff and communications; democratizing the Party by, among other changes, the creation of a platform committee; restructuring the Party by a Party Reform Commission; and paying special attention to rebuilding in the West and opening the Party to the views of the community.[20] But like the country, the Party could not be reconciled to the Liberal leader. Recognizing the symptoms and the difficulties of satisfying the Party, Pierre Trudeau gave notice of his intention to resign as leader in November 1979.

Then came the Clark government's defeat in the House on December 13. Only the national executive of the Party had the constitutional power to decide who should be leader of the Party in these circumstances. A meeting of the national executive was promptly called for the weekend. But the caucus met the day before and pre-empted the powers of the executive by publicly calling on Pierre Trudeau to resume leadership. Members of the national executive were enraged by this high-handedness. Pierre Trudeau, in a move much appreciated by the executive, declared that he could only return if he had the support of both the caucus and the Party. Would the national executive – already in a feisty mood – accept the view of the caucus?

The powerful minister and deputy prime minister, Allan J. MacEachen, and the principal secretary, Jim Coutts, were both dispatched to the meeting of the national executive to try to avoid a serious split between the second and third estates. Powerful interests advocating other leadership candidates were already at work, but, taken aback by the speed of events, they were unable to mobilize their forces to convince the members of the national executive to reject this resurrection. The members of the national executive, however, especially the leaders of the youth wing, were not going to act with the sentimentality that the caucus had shown. Some of them felt that they had suffered too much at the hands of the caucus and the PMO.

Their terms included the creation of a platform committee to determine the content of the election campaign.[21] They wanted considerably more accountability to the Party on the part of the PMO and the leader. One result was that the 1980 Biennial Convention was held outside Ottawa—in Winnipeg—as a symbol of the distribution of Party work and interests.[22]

That weekend brought to a head the discontent of the Party activists and shows clearly how Pierre Trudeau dealt with it—by inviting response. While the constant criticisms of the Party leader in the late 1970s bothered some Liberals, it had always been Mr Trudeau's view that the people should speak freely and fully and should be, in a sense, colleagues in the enterprise of governing—colleagues in the sense that they should voice their views. While many Canadians found it disconcerting to have their prime minister treat them as colleagues and dispute their opinions and their desires, those inside the Liberal Party who shared the vision of politics as a set of ideas to be debated, a set of opportunities for debate to be seized and exploited, a set of competing visions of the country, found nothing more stimulating than an exchange of views with Pierre Trudeau, who framed the questions in the most searching and provocative manner possible. While Canadians were tut-tutting about conflict with the premiers, many Liberals (and probably many other Canadians) felt that a rigorous challenge was the best antidote to the lazy assumption of barony on the part of the premiers; and at a later stage, when the press and perhaps many Canadians felt that the prime minister engaged in undignified behaviour, others felt that our country had never had so nonimperial a leader—one who so profoundly believed that all human beings are equal in reason and passions and should be allowed to explore those possibilities both in symbols and in personal and institutional debate.

___ The "Restoration" Years _____

With the defeat of the Clark government, the restoration of Pierre Trudeau to the Party leadership and the election of 1980 which brought a majority Liberal government, we enter the third and final phase of the Party under the leadership of Pierre

Trudeau. In many ways, these last four years restored the movement toward institutionalizing participatory democracy that had prevailed in the first years. The Party once again had its resolutions attached to Cabinet documents; once again the Party executive had a direct influence on political decision making and on the Government's agenda.

In preparation for the 1982 Convention and as a follow-up to the Hervieux-Payette discussion paper, a policy conference of one hundred Liberals, representing the provinces and territories, women, youth and native peoples, was held at Carleton University in June 1981. Following the Carleton conference, the policy resolutions process was reformed to ensure that each provincial and territorial wing, as well as the commissions, had fair opportunity to get their "priority" concerns into debate at national conventions.[23]

This spurred other changes. When Lorna Marsden was elected chair of the Standing Committee on Policy of the LPC at the Biennial Convention in Winnipeg in 1980, all provinces and territories except British Columbia appointed their representatives to the committee. By 1984 a majority of members of that committee had been elected in, and so were accountable to, their provincial conventions.

Pierre Trudeau demonstrated his commitment to participatory democracy in the Party in many ways during these years. For one thing, Party members were better informed. From 1980 to 1984, the *Liberal Policy Newsletter* let them know what policy issues were current in Ottawa and let those in Ottawa know the policy ideas, criticisms and reactions of the Party. Furthermore, when the second session of Parliament was being prepared early in 1983, the Speech from the Throne was delayed, despite considerable political inconvenience for the Government, so that the Party resolutions process, national policy convention and platform committee could complete their work.

Meanwhile, the platform committee, proposed by Mr Trudeau in 1979 and developed in response to the crisis of 1979, was at work. Chaired jointly by members of the second and third estates (Allan J. MacEachen with Céline Hervieux-Payette and Lorna Marsden in 1979, and with Lorna Marsden in 1980, 1981, 1982 and 1983), the platform committee was a remarkably effective vehicle for participatory democracy. It brought the various estates of the Party into a working relationship not mediated by the PMO, the caucus or the Party office. On the issues of the National Energy Program, the Western Development Fund, the Crow Rate changes and others, the balance of power among the four estates was more equal in these years than it had ever been.[24]

What were the results of participatory democracy in the Liberal Party? In 1974, the Election Expenses Act was passed, recognizing that the more Canadians who participated in the funding of their party, the more democratic action there would be. In the Trudeau years, the composition of the Party decision makers changed and the checks and balances within the four estates were increased. In general, the LPC evolved from being a group consisting mainly of white males to one of great diversity in terms of gender, ethnicity and age. This diversity was institutionalized through the constitutionally established commissions on women and youth and new standing committees. The commissions and standing committees reflected different sex, age, regional and language groups.

The Liberal Party became a Party in which both official languages were the working languages. This was institutionalized, after some glaring problems, by a rule requiring all duly called meetings of the Party to operate with simultaneous translation and all documents to be produced in both French and English.

It became a Party more interested in the national unity question and the building of strong relationships among individuals, groups and constituencies throughout the country than in maintaining a series of provincial fiefdoms. Finally, although this work is still not fully realized, the Party moved to centralize fund raising and communications operations within the Party's various estates and segments.

These changes came about in spite of serious setbacks in the process of institutionalizing participatory democracy. While the first period was characterized by idealism and the second by a painful coming to terms with the constraints of power, the third period accomplished for the Party what was in many ways the most effective institutionalization of those aspects of participatory democracy that had not been achieved before. The changes which saw the Charter of Rights and

Freedoms entrenched in a patriated Constitution in some ways symbolized the entire period of opening up of the Liberal Party.

And yet, of course, this period ended with the calls for reform that led to the public denunciation of Senator Keith Davey and of Jim Coutts, two of the chief architects of the opening up of the Party. Why should this be? It was largely because the conundrum of Party democracy had not been solved. The tools of power — resources of information, time, staff, money, ideas and position — were so unevenly distributed. How could it be otherwise? The vision that Pierre Trudeau had of a truly participatory democracy depended on an equality of resources that was beyond realization. Those without these resources were resentful of those with them. The leader could not act as mediator for all problems and, indeed, given his experiences with the Party of his early years in Quebec, had little reason to believe in the benign motives and interests of most Party activists. With their increased reliance on the sophisticated information available from pollsters, communication experts and the public service, Party members must often have appeared as self-interested, self-serving and narrow petitioners for favours. Unquestionably some were. But most were not. Most believed in the importance of the underlying ideology, the need for a national debate on the issues in the context of Liberal values, and the necessity of a vehicle for their development, maintenance and propagation.

The people of the country were also subject to the same barrage of polling, information and ideas from their television sets and were more inclined to believe that source than the Party member with a pamphlet at their door or the MP with the riding newsletter or the Cabinet minister on a public platform. The Party felt pressured by both the media and the caucus. The messengers, such as Davey and Coutts, were blamed, perhaps in confusion. But the movement for "reform" that arose in the period from 1982 to 1984 and which was taken up by most of the candidates for the leadership in 1984, was for the most part a movement of the "outs" against the "ins," for the reforms resulted in reduced accountability. They restricted the role of the Party and marked the end of participation by Party members at least in the ways that had been dreamt of by Richard Stanbury and others in 1968.

CHAPTER 12

Bringing the Constitution Home

———————— by Jean Chrétien ————————

Jean Chrétien served as a senior minister in a variety of portfolios from 1968 to 1984. From 1980 to 1982, he was Minister of Justice. In this capacity he was responsible for the federal government's referendum campaign and was the senior federal representative during the constitutional negotiations which resulted in the patriation of the Constitution and the enshrining of the Charter of Rights and Freedoms.

Changing the Constitution confronts a society with the most important choices, for in the Constitution will be found the philosophical principles and rules which largely determine the relations of the individual and of cultural groups to one another and to the State. If human rights and harmonious relations between cultures are forms of the beautiful, then the State is a work of art that is never finished. Law thus takes its place, in its theory and its practice, among man's highest and most creative activities.

—F.R. Scott, *Essays on the Constitution: Aspects of Canadian Law and Politics* (Toronto, 1977)

THE PROCESS OF constitutional reform which culminated in the patriation of the Constitution in 1982 began not with the Trudeau government, but with the British government's Balfour Declaration in 1927. It was then that the Imperial

---

I would like to thank my colleague Edward Goldenberg for his assistance in the preparation of this chapter.

government agreed to give full political autonomy to the self-governing dominions of its empire and that Prime Minister Mackenzie King began the process of looking for a mechanism that would allow Canada to amend its own Constitution. At that time no one would have expected that Canada would be the last part of what was then the British Empire to achieve complete legal independence. Indeed, it was not because Canadians wanted to maintain a last colonial link with London that their country was unable to achieve that independence for so long. The problem was that the federal and provincial governments could not agree on a constitutional amendment formula.

After the 1931 proclamation of the Statute of Westminster, enshrining in law the independence of the dominions, Prime Minister Bennett promised the British government that he would meet with the premiers of the provinces within a few months and that he would then ask the British Parliament to turn over to the federal Parliament the power to amend the Canadian Constitution. This was the beginning of the long saga of the patriation of our Constitution.

Bennett soon discovered, however, that it was still not possible to find an amending formula acceptable to both the federal government and the provincial premiers. Therefore, while the other former British colonies all gained control over their constitutions, the power to amend the Canadian Constitution was left with the Parliament of Westminster. Over the next thirty years unsuccessful attempts were made by Prime Ministers King, St Laurent and Diefenbaker to establish an acceptable constitutional amendment formula.

By the end of the Diefenbaker régime and the beginning of the Pearson government, political debate in Canada had altered to some extent. The issue of constitutional change, at least from Quebec's perspective, no longer centred on trying to find an acceptable amending formula; it was viewed more as a means of reopening the whole question of the division of powers between the federal and provincial governments. Until 1960, the provincial autonomy propounded by successive Quebec governments and particularly by Maurice Duplessis was characterized by a *laissez-faire* approach to government. Provincial governments in Quebec had tried to restrict various actions of the federal government but did little in a positive sense to exercise powers themselves.

With the Lesage government and the Quiet Revolution came a considerable change in the context of the constitutional discussion. Influential elements in Quebec's Cabinet, public service and intelligentsia began agitating for more powers for the government of Quebec. Some spoke of "special status" for the province, others of "particular status" or "associate statehood." As far as they were concerned, discussions of constitutional reform would no longer be limited merely to finding an acceptable amending formula.

This new approach was revealed most dramatically by the failure of what had been, up to then, the most promising attempt at patriating the Constitution with an amending formula. In 1964, the Fulton-Favreau amending formula, named for its authors, Conservative Justice Minister Davie Fulton and Liberal Justice Minister Guy Favreau, had been agreed upon by all ten premiers and by the prime minister of Canada. By 1966, before it had been ratified, Premier Lesage withdrew his support for the formula. The reason for that decision can almost certainly be found in the pressures for constitutional change then beginning to be made by intellectuals and the media. Jacques Yvan Morin, who later joined the Parti québécois and eventually became deputy-premier, was the leader of the opposition to Fulton-Favreau, arguing that if it was adopted, Quebec would be blocked in its search for greater powers by the veto of other governments.

Premier Lesage's veto of the Fulton-Favreau formula came in the context of a revival of the old separatist movement in Quebec. In the 1960s, it developed new strength under the leadership of young intellectuals such as Pierre Bourgault. More radical elements decided to use violence to achieve their ends. Canada, as peaceful a country as any, was traumatized each time there was news of the explosion of another separatist bomb in Quebec.

In June 1966, Daniel Johnson, who had written a book entitled *Equality or Independence*, became premier of Quebec. That September, Premier Johnson set out a series of demands saying that his government was committed to a new constitution to give Quebec all the powers needed to safeguard

its own identity. Within a few weeks, Premier Robarts of
Ontario indicated a willingness to contemplate the reshaping of
the Canadian federation, and in November 1967, Premier
Robarts held a conference of provincial premiers in Toronto
called "The Confederation of Tomorrow Conference." The
debate at that conference dealt with social, cultural and
linguistic matters as well as matters of regional disparity. The
provinces had very mixed views on whether constitutional
change was needed at all.

In late 1967, René Lévesque left the Liberal party and began
the formation of a new separatist party, which became the Parti
québécois. It was in the context of ferment in Quebec that
Pierre Trudeau became minister of justice in April 1967 and
prime minister of Canada in April 1968.

___ 1968–1971: The First Trudeau Government___

The Trudeau government took office with strong views on the
nature of Canada and the role of the federal government. At the
same time, the whole constitutional debate took a new turn as a
result of the ferment in Quebec. The issue was no longer only
the amending formula but the very nature of Canada. It was
time for people to take a stand. Was Canada to be an extremely
decentralized country of two nations or a strong country with
two official languages and room for minority linguistic groups
to prosper everywhere in the country? Was the role of the
federal government to foster a Canada with two official
languages and access for all Canadians to federal services in
both languages? Was its role to be strong enough to achieve
redistribution of wealth or was the federal government merely
to run what Joe Clark later called a community of
communities? It was this basic philosophical question that
characterized the constitutional debate from 1968 through to
the spring of 1982.

A series of intensive federal-provincial constitutional
conferences began in February 1968, culminating in the
Victoria Conference in 1971. During that time, seven first
ministers' meetings were held. They dealt with many subjects,
ranging from what was required to implement recommendations that had recently been made by the Royal Commission on

Bilingualism and Biculturalism to taxing and spending jurisdictions, jurisdiction over income security and social services, the regulation of capital markets and financial institutions and environmental management. In all of this, it became evident that there was no consensus in favour of changing the constitutional division of powers.

By February 1971, discussion was concentrated on patriation and an amending formula, language rights and social policy. In Victoria in June 1971, the federal government agreed upon administrative arrangements with Quebec relating to social policy matters, and full agreement was reached on patriation, an amending formula and limited entrenchement of language and fundamental human rights. The amending formula agreed upon by the prime minister and all ten provinces in Victoria provided that constitutional amendments would require the approval of two Atlantic provinces, Quebec, Ontario and two western provinces with the majority of the population of western Canada.

Despite the unanimity that was achieved at the conference in Victoria, the agreement was never implemented because Quebec soon withdrew its consent. Claude Castonguay, then Quebec's minister of social affairs, was engaged in a review and reform of social policy. He was persuaded by Claude Morin, then deputy-minister of intergovernmental affairs in Quebec, of the need for change in the constitutional division of powers as they affected family allowances. The two succeeded in shaking Premier Bourassa's willingness to proceed with the Victoria accord. It is interesting to note that Claude Morin later joined the Parti québécois and became its constitutional spokesman as minister of intergovernmental affairs; he played an important role in the patriation debate of the early 1980s.

So despite his role in crafting the Victoria formula and his success in convincing all the other premiers to agree to an amending formula that provided a veto for the province of Quebec on all constitutional change, Premier Bourassa was unable to convince some members of his Cabinet and some of his advisors to accept the accord. Within ten days, he withdrew his consent.

Like the Fulton-Favreau formula, the Victoria formula died

because one province withdrew its support after the first ministers had reached unanimous agreement. Premier Bourassa and Premier Lesage before him taught Canadians that agreement among first ministers is not a guarantee that constitutional change will proceed. Public debate and public opinion have a role to play in the period after a first ministers' conference and before ratification by legislatures.

___ 1971–1979: The Parti québécois and Western Concerns ___

In the period after Victoria and leading up to the next constitutional effort in 1975–76, two new and major developments took place which served to alter provincial priorities for constitutional change. One of these developments was the finding of an acceptable administrative solution to the social policy question, to the point where constitutional change in this sector became a much lower priority for Quebec—which then switched its attention to the need for constitutional protection on the cultural front.

The other development was the oil crisis of 1973 and the subsequent active role of the federal government in influencing crude oil prices and developing energy policy for Canada as a whole. This new federal role produced a hostile reaction in the oil- and gas-producing provinces of western Canada and gave rise to a whole new provincial concern that the Constitution did not give sufficient protection to their control over natural resources.

The constitutional effort of 1975–76 began at a first ministers' conference in April 1975. At that conference, the prime minister proposed to move forward with patriation alone, but he also hoped to adopt the essence of the Victoria amending formula and possibly make some provision to satisfy Mr Bourassa's only other demand—that "constitutional guarantees" be included to protect the French language and culture. Apart from Quebec's interest in guarantees for language and culture, however, no premier raised the question of powers. Discussions continued behind the scenes, particularly with Quebec.

In January 1976, information regarding the patriation

exercise became public and it soon became clear that Mr Bourassa's conception of "cultural guarantees" was vast in scope. It seemed to be in clear contradiction to the prime minister's proposal, which was designed to prevent action by Parliament or the government of Canada that would be harmful to the French language and culture. Unanimous agreement to a "package" began to look doubtful. In the event, on March 31, 1976, the prime minister wrote to the premiers with definite proposals that he hoped would address the concerns of all the premiers.

The letter was worded to leave the impression that if the premiers were not ready to agree unanimously on one of the alternatives, the federal government would have to decide whether to go ahead on its own. The government of Quebec was upset by this federal line and sought allies among the other provinces. Given the new tensions over resources, Quebec was able to persuade the others, over the course the summer of 1976, that changes in a number of items relating to powers should be demanded as the price of provincial agreement to patriation. This collective decision was set out in Premier Lougheed's letter to the prime minister of October 14, 1976, written on behalf of all the premiers.

The provincial decision reported in the Lougheed letter represents the first time in Canadian history that the provinces, collectively, asked that the division of powers be changed in their favour. Their demands included powers in the fields of culture, communications, resource taxation, spending power and declaratory power. None of these, apart from spending power, had been discussed at Victoria.

In November 1976, the Bourassa government was defeated by the Parti québécois, a party dedicated to the separation of Quebec from the rest of Canada. Canada had arrived at an historic crossroads. While Canadians were traumatized by the possibility of the break-up of the country, provincial governments soon saw in the victory of the Parti québécois and in the perceived desire of the prime minister of Canada for constitutional patriation and a charter of rights an opportunity to seek extensive transfer of powers from the federal jurisdiction to the provinces.

By midsummer 1978, a conference of provincial premiers

chaired by Premier Blakeney of Saskatchewan agreed to a lengthy list of federal powers which should be restricted in some cases and transferred to the provinces in others. The list included immigration, language rights, resource taxation, federal declaratory power, culture, communications, federal spending power, power of reservation or disallowance, treaty-making power, fisheries, natural resources, appointments to superior district and county courts, appointments to the Supreme Court of Canada and consideration of emergency power, federal residual power, indirect taxation and the delegation of legislative powers between governments.

In late 1978 and early 1979, the federal government expressed a willingness to compromise on resources and declaratory power, but any federal offer was not enough to achieve provincial agreement. It later became evident that nothing less than total federal surrender to the provinces' demands would have been required to reach "agreement."

The defeat of the Trudeau government in the spring of 1979 permitted the Parti québécois to keep its promise of a referendum on the independence of Quebec before the end of its first mandate. The timing of a referendum while a federal government with effectively no representation from Quebec held power in Ottawa appeared favourable to the separatist option, and a great number of federalists believed that the end of Canada might very well be at hand.

Unexpectedly, in December 1979 the government of Prime Minister Joe Clark was defeated and by the end of February 1980, Pierre Trudeau was once again holding the reigns of power in Ottawa.

1980–1982: The Referendum and Constitutional Reform

The spring of 1980 saw the political confrontation of the century in Canada. Federalists and separatists fought a great battle. While the population saw the supreme confrontation between Trudeau and Lévesque, the daily fight for the federalist forces was led by the Quebec Liberal leader, Claude Ryan, whom I assisted as the federal lieutenant delegated by Mr Trudeau. A campaign of almost two months touched all the extremes from the initial despair and disorganization to the almost joyous collaboration of the last weeks, from initial lack of interest to the great enthusiasm of the larger rallies, from mistakes caused by the inexperience of volunteers unused to such strong emotions, to the unexpected successes of the federalist women who called themselves "Yvettes." The result was an unequivocal expression by Quebeckers of their will to belong to Canada.

During the referendum campaign Prime Minister Trudeau and his Quebec members and ministers formally promised constitutional reform in the event of a victory for the federalist forces. The Trudeau position was clear—patriation of the Constitution, a constitutional charter of rights and freedoms which would protect the two official languages across the country, a federal government strong enough to redistribute income and to equalize opportunity among the regions of Canada and a willingness to negotiate on the distribution of powers on a functional basis while ensuring that the federal government's role of serving all Canadians was not threatened.

The prime minister set out his constitutional philosophy clearly in the House of Commons on April 15, 1980, during the referendum campaign. He stated:

> The feeling of being a Canadian, that individual feeling which we must cultivate, the feeling of being loyal to something which is bigger than the province or the city in which we happen to live, must be based on a protection of the basic rights of the citizen, of an access by that citizen to a fair share of the abundance of wealth in this country and to the richness and diversity of its laws. In that sense, the national interest must prevail over the regional interest, difficult as it is for some of us sometimes to set aside our feelings as citizens of this town or inhabitants of that province, because the provincial governments and other groups are there to speak for their interests. That is their duty and that is what they are elected for. But we are elected to speak for all of Canada, and if a person cannot feel that in any part of the country he or she will get a fair share, then they will transfer their loyalty from the whole to the particular part of the country in which they choose

to live. . . . That concept of sharing can only be guaranteed, I repeat, if there is a national government which is prepared to state that the national interest must prevail in any situation of conflict over regional differences.[1]

On May 21, the morning after the referendum, the prime minister asked me to visit all provincial premiers over the next seventy-two hours to begin the process of constitutional reform. With a small group of officials I travelled across the country and met each premier except the premier of Quebec, who for obvious reasons was not then open to consultation. The reception in all provincial capitals was excellent; all were prepared to proceed immediately with constitutional reform and I stressed the need for the charter of rights, for patriation, for finding an acceptable amending formula and for entrenching minority language education rights in all provinces. There was also discussion about the need to examine the division of powers and to examine reform of federal institutions such as the Supreme Court and the Senate. The charter of rights remained controversial: Premier Sterling Lyon of Manitoba, for example, was convinced that the British principle of parliamentary sovereignty was better than the American supremacy of the Bill of Rights.

The result of my trip across the country was agreement on an early federal-provincial meeting of first ministers to set an agenda for what became a summer of intensive federal-provincial constitutional negotiations. Three consecutive weeks of negotiations were scheduled for July—the first in Montreal, the second in Toronto and the third in Vancouver. They were to be followed by a break of several weeks and were to resume in mid-August in Ottawa in preparation for a final first ministers' conference at the beginning of September 1980.

In preparing for the negotiations, the federal government took to heart the lessons of constitutional negotiations learned over the previous fifteen years as well as the realities of decentralization in Canada. A decision was made that rights of individuals and the juridical independence of the country would not be traded for powers claimed by the provincial governments. The federal position from which we never wavered was that the questions of patriation, an amending formula, a preamble to the Constitution, a charter of rights and freedoms and the reform of institutions such as the Supreme Court of Canada and the Senate would be discussed at one negotiating table and that the issues dealing with division of powers, such as communications, offshore resources, family law and the Canadian economic union, international trade in natural resources and indirect taxation of natural resources, and other similar powers, would be discussed at another negotiating table.

The federal government was determined to look at rights as a package on its own—apart from negotiations over the federal-provincial power split. We were prepared to discuss what should or should not be in a charter of rights based on international covenants, provincial and federal bills of rights, the changing nature of society, the conflict between parliamentary supremacy and the supremacy of the courts, and so on. We were prepared to look at an amending formula based on how rigid a constitution should be, whether all provinces should be equal, or whether certain provinces as a function of size or linguistic composition should have vetoes and so on. In essence, the federal government was prepared to take a functional and pragmatic approach to constitutional reform and refused to be drawn into a bargaining session that would have involved giving up federal jurisdiction over powers to the provinces in return for unrelated protection of fundamental human rights.

The federal government also made a basic decision that all the demands should not come from the provinces and all the concessions from the federal government. If constitutional reform was to be meaningful, it had to reflect a society that was more than a community of communities and indeed was one where the bonds of citizenship were strong. We realized the long-term dangers to Canada if we did not lay to rest the myth that Canada is a highly centralized federation. The evidence was clear that despite all the speeches to the contrary, Canada was becoming too decentralized.

In 1959, the federal government had collected 58 percent of total government revenues. Because of some transfer payments to the provinces, federal spending represented 52 percent of all government spending. The provinces, on the other hand, collected 42 percent of all government revenues in 1959 and were responsible for 48 percent of all government spending.

In the twenty years after 1959, the provinces had assumed a much greater role in social programs and a corresponding role in raising revenues to pay for those programs. The federal government had also substantially increased its payments to the provinces so as to ensure some degree of equality of opportunity across the country. The result of this transfer of revenues to the provinces meant that in 1979, instead of collecting 58 percent of total revenues, the federal level of government was collecting only 46 percent and the provinces were collecting 54 percent instead of 42 percent. After transfer payments, the federal government was responsible for only one-third of total government spending instead of more than one-half, and the provinces were responsible for two-thirds of total spending in Canada, rather than less than one-half.

The effect of this was that as the federal government levied a smaller proportion of the taxes, the rich provinces got richer and the poor got poorer. Over the previous two decades, contrary to the myth of ever-increasing centralization, we had seen a weakening of the fiscal and economic muscle of the federal government and a corresponding increase in the fiscal and economic muscle of the provinces, or at least of the richer provinces. The result of the OPEC pricing increase threatened to throw the whole fiscal equation of federalism out of kilter as the wealth of the oil-producing provinces increased.

We also had more and more evidence of new barriers being created within Canada. Provincial governments had blocked the sale of provincial companies to Canadians from other provinces. There had been cases of discriminatory treatment by provincial governments against products manufactured in another province; preferential hiring laws in some provinces gave rise to retaliation by other provinces. It was the view of the federal government that this type of balkanization could not be allowed to continue. Otherwise we could end up with ten countries instead of one.

In light of increasing fiscal decentralization, the growth of internal economic barriers and the development of serious centrifugal political forces, the federal government set constitutional objectives. We did not seek a highly centralized or a quasi-unitary state as some have suggested. We did not seek broad new powers for the federal government. But we did seek to take steps to rebalance the federation to ensure that there could be such a thing as a meaningful Canadian citizenship that provides some degree of equality of opportunity everywhere in Canada.

The summer started well. The first week of meetings in Montreal was characterized by an initial staking out of positions. As federal representative, I spoke of patriation, the charter of rights and an amending formula based on the one that had been approved in Victoria some nine years earlier, and I made the first allusions to the need to strengthen the Canadian economic union. The provinces directed their opening salvos to changes in the division of powers, especially with respect to indirect taxation of resources and international trade in resources, communications and fisheries.

There was some agreement that both the Senate and the Supreme Court needed reform, but there was anything but unanimity on what powers the Senate should have or on how representation should be accorded by province in the Senate. To illustrate the diversity of opinions, while Premier Bennett of British Columbia was strongly in favour of Senate reform, Premier Lougheed of Alberta was strongly against it, on the grounds that a more important Senate might result in weakening the role of provincial governments.

By the second week of meetings, held in Toronto, the federal government made clear its position on the economic union. The provincial governments discovered to their surprise that these negotiations were qualitatively different from anything that had taken place in the past. The agenda was no longer made up merely of provincial shopping lists; and while the federal government was prepared to discuss provincial demands for changes in distribution of powers on functional grounds, it was not prepared to sacrifice a Canada that is greater than the sum of its parts.

The federal position on economic union had three elements:

1. inclusion of mobility rights in the charter of rights;

2. strengthening constitutional provisions to prohibit discrimination in law or practice based on province of residence of
persons and province of origin or destination of goods,
services and capital; and
3. making explicit federal jurisdiction to regulate trade and
commerce to include trade and commerce in services and
capital as well as goods; to make explicit federal jurisdiction
to regulate competition, and to set product standards.

The provinces were first put off balance because they did not
expect the federal proposals to be so direct. They were then
shocked when they realized the federal government was serious
about its proposals and had no intention of backing away. In
his book *Lendemains piégés*, Claude Morin says that the federal
position was characterized as an "aggression against the
provinces unprecedented in the history of federal-provincial
relations."[2] He does not comment on the effects that the
provincial demands for decentralization had on federalism.

   The debate over the strengthening of the Canadian economic
union demonstrated a basic difference of principle between
the federal government and the provinces as to whether the
national economy transcends or is simply an aggregation of the
regional economies. The western provinces that wanted to
regulate the external trade in their major resources—for
example, potash in Saskatchewan and oil and gas in
Alberta—seemed to argue, at least implicitly, that the national
economy consists of a series of regional economies that the
provinces themselves should control. This was a fundamentally
different view of Canada than that held by all federal
governments since 1867.

   In hindsight, it was in Toronto during the second week of
negotiations that the divergences in the concept of Canada first
became apparent. During those meetings, two other aspects
of the negotiations also appeared, which would come to
be significant later. The first was this: officials from all
governments were meeting on a nearly continuous basis to
discuss and debate technical wording of potential constitutional amendments subject to political agreement on their
substance. The second matter of importance was that personal

relationships were forming among the ministers who were negotiating on behalf of their respective governments and this personal chemistry could have been important in producing agreement.

During the third week, in Vancouver, I began to feel that unanimous agreement was less and less likely. Little progress was made in discussions of the linguistic rights of minorities. The amending formula desired by the provinces was very different from the one preferred by the federal government. There was no agreement on economic union, and without agreement on economic union, the federal government would not make any concessions on resources.

In addition, I was concerned about a discussion I had with Claude Charron, then a minister in the Quebec government. In trying to determine Quebec's minimum position, I understood from him that despite the appearance that Quebec was participating in the negotiations in good faith, his party's commitment to independence for Quebec would make it almost impossible for his government ever to sign a new Canadian constitution. Despite the loss of the referendum battle, the Parti québécois did not consider the war of independence over and they remained faithful to their principles and to Article 1 of their program, the independence of Quebec.

In spite of our belief that unanimous agreement was most unlikely, we continued our reflections, discussions and debates on the content of a charter of rights, on the amending formula, on Senate reform, on Supreme Court reform, on the role of the provinces in international trade in natural resources, on communications and on the Canadian economic union. Officials continued to produce what are called "best efforts drafts" on each item. The wording of potential constitutional amendments was carefully considered.

During the last week of negotiations in August there was a sudden flash of optimism. The chemistry that had developed between ministers in Montreal, Toronto, Vancouver and Ottawa over the summer seemed to have produced results. We as ministers began to believe that the work we had done and the work the officials had done may have opened the way to an agreement that could be reached among the premiers and the prime minister. Some even held the view that if ministers themselves had the authority to negotiate and decide a final agreement, the personal rapport between the ministers might have been sufficient to avoid the débâcle that occurred later at the first ministers' conference. I, however, believe that this was simply wishful thinking. While the good work of ministers and officials had produced the possibility of agreement on a variety of individual items, the gulf between the two visions of Canada had not in any way been bridged. The proof was in the federal-provincial first ministers' conference, which began on September 8, 1980.

The evening before the official opening of the conference featured a dinner hosted by the governor general. It was certainly the most unpleasant official reception I have ever had occasion to attend. Many of the premiers who had received me with such warmth and goodwill the day after the referendum were now prepared to destroy the authority of both the prime minister of the country and the federal Parliament so as to make the provinces into powerful principalities. There was even an attempt to remove the prime minister of Canada from his role as chairman of the federal-provincial conferences. The atmosphere became so tense and disagreeable that the governor general had to adjourn the dinner before the end of the meal.

The conference began the next day, and it was not long before the premiers presented Mr Trudeau with a catalogue of demands that would have left the federal Parliament with jurisdiction over little more than Parliament Hill itself. The result of the provincial demands, combined with provincial reaction to a leaked federal strategy paper, was that the goodwill that had developed over the summer had completely evaporated. The conference adjourned with the incredible declaration by Premier Peckford of Newfoundland that he preferred the Canada of René Lévesque to the Canada of Pierre Trudeau.

It became evident that some premiers were merely power hungry; others were political opponents of the federal government and were prepared to operate on the basis of the principle that the enemy of my enemy is my friend; still others genuinely disagreed with the federal vision of Canada. They had all come to the conclusion that the prime minister was so committed to patriation, an amending formula and a charter of rights that in the end he would give up important federal powers to achieve his objectives. They were wrong.

When the demands of the provinces became so extravagant, it became clear to the federal government that the only alternative was to proceed rapidly to request the British Parliament to patriate the Constitution with an amending formula and a charter of rights. On October 6, 1980, a constitutional resolution was introduced in the House of Commons. The resolution provided for patriation of the Constitution, a charter of rights with guarantees of minority language education rights and mobility rights, and two years to reach agreement on an amending formula, failing which, effect would be given to the Victoria amending formula with a provision for a national referendum to break deadlocks. Later, the resolution was amended to clarify and increase provincial jurisdiction over trade and taxation of natural resources.

The federal government's decision to proceed with unilateral patriation eventually received the support of the New Democratic Party in Parliament and of the governments of Ontario and New Brunswick. The Progressive Conservative Party led by Mr Clark and the other eight provinces took strong exception to the federal action; Newfoundland, Quebec and Manitoba decided to refer the question of the constitutionality of unilateral patriation to their courts of appeal.

While the legal issue was referred to the courts of appeal of those three provinces, the substance of the constitutional resolution was referred to a joint committee of the Senate and the House of Commons for study and recommendations. The story of the joint committee is an extraordinary example of the political process working as it should. In 56 days and 267 hours of hearings, the committee received representations by 914 individuals and 294 groups. Its proceedings were televised nationally.

These are the bald figures. But the real story is the successful nature of the lobbies of the normally unpowerful and unorganized — natives, women's groups, representatives of the handicapped, multicultural groups. Canadians spoke clearly to the committee of their desire for a charter of rights and freedoms that would provide equality of rights and treatment to all people and equal justice for minority groups and the disadvantaged.

As a result of the committee hearings, the government proposed numerous amendments to strengthen the draft of the Charter of Rights and Freedoms that had been presented to Parliament in October 1980. While the Progressive Conservative Opposition remained opposed to the process of constitutional change, the substance of the constitutional resolution was considerably improved by all members of the joint parliamentary committee. As minister of justice, I – along with senior officials in the Department of Justice – spent many hours scrutinizing and giving testimony about the wording and intent of constitutional amendments. By the end of February 1981, a new constitutional resolution was ready for study by Parliament.

While the parliamentary committee had been deliberating, so had the three provincial courts of appeal. The courts of Manitoba and Quebec held that the federal government was legally entitled to seek British approval of unilateral patriation. However, the court of appeal of Newfoundland held to the contrary, and the whole issue was referred to the Supreme Court of Canada before final parliamentary approval of the constitutional resolution. The case was heard in late April and early May of 1981.

At the same time, the eight dissident provinces were meeting to formulate proposals of their own. The Group of Eight agreed in April upon an amending formula whereby there would be no veto for any province and all provinces would be considered equal. The most surprising element was the signature of René Lévesque on a document in which he effectively renounced the right of veto claimed by all previous Quebec premiers and endorsed by all the provinces of Canada in Victoria in 1971. The amending formula agreed upon by the eight provinces provided for constitutional amendments with the consent of seven provinces representing more than 50 percent of the population. Where the rights of any particular province were affected and that province disagreed with the amendment, such a province would be allowed to opt out with full fiscal compensation. The Group of Eight also opposed the entrenchment of any charter of rights and freedoms.

In September 1981, the Supreme Court held that unilateral patriation was technically legal but was in violation of constitutional convention. The court held that constitutional convention required consent of more than two provinces but not necessarily of all the provinces. The court did not state how many and which provinces had to give consent; in fact, the court was implicitly telling the federal government and the provinces to get back to the negotiating table. This the federal government was prepared to do, although the British government had already indicated to the prime minister of Canada that it would accede at any time to any request from the Parliament of Canada.

It was agreed that a last effort would be made to find a broader consensus so as to satisfy the judgment of the Supreme Court with respect to constitutional conventions. This final effort started on November 2, 1981, in Ottawa. The atmosphere was better than at previous conferences because the eight dissenting provinces saw the convening of the conference as a victory in itself. The Group of Eight believed that while the Supreme Court had recognized a narrow legal right of the federal government, in fact it had given a moral victory to the opponents of unilateral patriation by finding the federal action to be unconventional. Despite the better atmosphere, however, the fundamentals had not changed.

For the federal government, the position of the Group of Eight on the amending formula and the Charter of Rights was completely unacceptable. The result of constitutional reform as propounded by the Group of Eight would do nothing to strengthen a sense of Canadian nationhood and would do nothing to confirm the value of our citizenship. Instead, it would produce a country where opting out would be rewarded with fiscal compensation. In hindsight it is evident that for most of the dissenting provinces, their April 1981 position was a negotiating one, but for Quebec there was no room for negotiation.

The prime minister could not accept what was effectively a vision of Canada as a country founded by the provinces, with the federal government existing through their will. Mr Trudeau argued that the whole is greater than the sum of its parts and that the repository of real power in Canada is the people of the nation as a whole. Therefore he argued that an amending formula should contain a referendum provision as a deadlock-breaking mechanism. The prime minister insisted on enshrining in the Constitution a recognition of values and ideals shared by Canadians wherever they live.

In addition to the two different philosophies of Canada, another apparently insurmountable difficulty was the determination of Premier Sterling Lyon of Manitoba to oppose any charter of rights on the grounds that parliamentary supremacy is preferable to the supremacy of the courts, a position he had maintained from the very start of negotiations.

For the first two and a half days of the November 1981 conference, there appeared to be complete deadlock. However, some of the eight dissenting provinces had already been talking among themselves about trying to find some compromise. Quebec's response was that it would not make any concessions. It is no wonder that Quebec was not part of a compromise at the end of the day, when it had categorically refused from the beginning of the conference to compromise on anything in formal or informal meetings with the other provinces.

At noon of the third day, to break the apparent deadlock, the prime minister suggested a national referendum with a requirement that the Charter of Rights and the amending formula be approved by a majority of the electors in each of the Atlantic region, Quebec, Ontario and the West.

Premier Lévesque immediately agreed to the idea of a referendum. He saw in it the occasion to fight Trudeau again in Quebec and perhaps to avenge the referendum defeat of May 1980. It is my view that Premier Lévesque thought he could win the referendum on the charter by campaigning in favour of protecting the rights of the National Assembly against any form of limitation. Whether by accident or design, the Trudeau proposal broke the public unanimity of the Group of Eight and led to the final compromise.

While Prime Minister Trudeau had a deep philosophical commitment to the referendum as a deadlock-breaking mechanism to express the will of the people, others opposed it on more pragmatic grounds. Premier Peter Lougheed of Alberta and Premier Allan Blakeney of Saskatchewan were particularly furious at Premier Lévesque for accepting the Trudeau proposal because they did not see how Prairie politicians could campaign against a charter of rights which in a sense was the legacy of the great Prairie populists like John Diefenbaker and Tommy Douglas. It would have been even more difficult for Premier Lougheed himself because a Bill of Rights was the first piece of legislation he had introduced in the Alberta legislature after he became premier.

Premiers William Davis of Ontario and Richard Hatfield of New Brunswick only accepted the proposal as a means to break the unanimity of the Group of Eight so as to achieve some compromise in further negotiations. They themselves did not want to see federal-provincial conflicts become the subject of frequent referenda.

As minister of justice, I too was opposed from the beginning to the idea of national referenda as institutionalized instruments of policy formulation. As the principal federal spokesman during the Quebec referendum of May 1980, I saw the way in which families, towns and cities were divided by the emotion that a referendum can produce. I feared further national division between East and West, and between English- and French-speaking Canadians. Whatever our views on the merits of a referendum, the proposal by the prime minister produced the desired effect. Seven dissident provinces recognized that a Parti québécois government dedicated to the independence of Quebec was not a trustworthy ally. The national referendum issue was the straw that broke the camel's back.

The chemistry that had brought ministers together over the summer of 1980 and that had formed friendships among us served very well on the afternoon of that third day, and the evening and night of November 4, 1981. A number of informal meetings took place while the conference was in adjournment until the following morning, and there was general recognition that the only way to avoid a divisive referendum was to arrive at a compromise constitutional solution.

So it was that Roy Romanow, then attorney general of Saskatchewan, Roy McMurtry, then attorney general of Ontario and myself, as minister of justice of Canada, found ourselves late that afternoon in a small kitchen on the fifth floor of the National Conference Centre. I told Mr Romanow that I thought I could persuade the prime minister to accept constitutional reform that would be based on patriation, a different amending formula and a charter of rights with certain restrictions, as long as the basic guarantees of minority language education rights and mobility rights were preserved. Mr Romanow and Mr McMurtry thought that such a compromise would be acceptable to most provinces but that Quebec would refuse and Manitoba would not be able to accept a charter of rights in any form.

That evening, several senior federal ministers met at 24 Sussex Drive. The prime minister was at first reluctant to accept any compromise. Many ministers supported him and seemed to welcome a referendum campaign. My own view was that in the event of a referendum, on the one hand the West could reject an amending formula that allowed a veto for Quebec and Ontario, which would leave no amending formula; and on the other hand, Quebec could reject a charter of rights limiting the powers of the National Assembly, which would mean no charter of rights.

Prime Minister Trudeau then took a telephone call from Premier Davis, who informed him that Ontario would support the compromise developed by Romanow, McMurtry and myself. This seemed to soften the prime minister's opposition to a compromise, although he was particularly concerned about any modification to the Charter of Rights and about giving up the referendum mechanism in an amending formula to break deadlocks. Because of his deep belief that Canada exists through the will of the people and not through a compact of provinces, the prime minister wanted such a concept clearly inscribed in the Constitution. However, the political disadvantages of going to London completely alone were such that he agreed to accept the compromise that I had negotiated with Romanow and McMurtry if it were to receive the approval of a majority of provinces with a majority of the population.

There were no further negotiations that night between federal ministers and the provinces. But various provincial ministers and officals met with each other and they agreed on a compromise proposal. First thing in the morning of November 5, the eight dissenting provinces held a meeting, as they had done each day of the conference. The compromise was put on the table and rejected by the province of Quebec. The other provinces had seen Quebec go its own way on the referendum proposal the day before, and they came to the conclusion that no constitutional deal was possible with Premier Lévesque. They therefore decided to make a proposal to the federal government which met the criterion of substantial provincial support that had been set by the Supreme Court of Canada.

There was never any night of the long knives. A compromise was reached by those who had come in good faith to a conference that was called to find compromise. The Supreme Court had made it clear that both sides should move from their original positions. All parties were prepared to do so except the separatist government of Quebec. The testimony of Claude Morin leaves nothing to the imagination:

> The accord of April 16 represented the maximum concessions which Quebec would accept. Quebec agreed for the sole purpose of blocking the federal project. . . . There was no question for Quebec to accept any other concessions. All concessions had been made. Quebec had gone as far as it could on the amendment formula. As for the Charter of Rights, Quebec would never tolerate any dispositions reducing its powers especially in linguistic matters. The other members of the common front knew that from the beginning. Nothing would make us change our minds.[3]

There was no conspiracy between the federal government and the other provinces; there was the simple reality confirmed by the author of the Quebec strategy that Quebec came to the conference of November 1981 intent only on blocking the federal project and not on finding compromise. So much for the myth of Quebec having been stabbed in the back.

The constitutional deal itself was the product of compromise and negotiation. The federal government agreed to a formula which required in most cases that seven provinces with 50 percent of the population approve constitutional amendments. Where provinces wished to opt out of constitutional change affecting their powers, except for those pertaining to education and culture, there would be no fiscal compensation and therefore no reward for opting out. As far as a charter of rights was concerned, the provinces accepted the charter that had been studied and amended by the joint parliamentary committee. There was also a provision for enshrining the principle of equalization in the constitution and for increasing provincial powers with respect to indirect taxation of resources and international trade in resources.

The major and controversial change to the Charter was the inclusion of a notwithstanding clause which would apply to fundamental freedoms, legal rights and equality rights. However, there could be no opting out or derogation from the obligation of governments to provide education for French language minorities outside of Quebec and the English language minority in Quebec, nor could there be opting out of the guarantees protecting mobility rights.

The notwithstanding clause requires some explanation. First, it was a compromise required by western premiers to provide the flexibility necessary to ensure that legislatures rather than judges would theoretically have the final say on important matters of public policy. The clause requires that a law state specifically that part or all of it applies notwithstanding a particular section of the Charter. Such a law automatically expires after five years unless specifically renewed by a legislature. These requirements were intended to discourage use of the provision by making it politically very difficult for a government to introduce a measure which applies notwithstanding the Charter of Rights. The "sunset provision" of review every five years was intended to discourage ill-considered use of the notwithstanding clause by requiring periodic public debate on the desirability of continuing the derogation further.

It is important to understand the type of reasoning used by proponents of the notwithstanding clause. Premier Blakeney favoured an override clause to protect against possible court decisions that might use the guarantee of freedom of association to render certain protections for trade unions unconstitutional, for example, or that might use other constitutional protections to upset social security legislation, as happened in the United States in the 1930s. Others gave as an example the need for an override clause to ensure that freedom of speech not render unconstitutional legislation banning child pornography.

It should also be noted that the concept of an override clause was not new in Canada. The Canadian Bill of Rights enacted in 1960 by Mr Diefenbaker's government contained an override provision. The Alberta Bill of Rights enacted in 1972 included an override clause. So did the Saskatchewan Human Rights Code of 1979. The Quebec Charter of Rights and Freedoms contained an override clause, which had been used in a noncontroversial way, to ensure that strict application of the Charter would not lead to otherwise absurd results. For example, the Quebec Highway Safety Act requires a doctor to inform the licence bureau of the name of a patient who is medically incapable of driving a motor vehicle despite protection in the Quebec Charter for the privileged doctor-patient relationship.

Because of the history of the use of the override clause and more particularly because of its lack of use, because of the argument for a safety valve to correct absurd situations without going through the difficulty of obtaining constitutional amendments, the override clause was considered to be an acceptable compromise. Allan Borovoy, general counsel of the Canadian Civil Liberties Association, stated,

> our reaction is one of great relief. They did not emasculate the Charter. The process is a rather ingenious marriage of a Bill of Rights notion and a parliamentary democracy. The result is a strong charter with an escape valve for the legislatures. The notwithstanding clause will be a red flag for opposition parties and the press. That will make it politically difficult for a government to override the Charter. Political difficulty is a reasonable safeguard for the Charter.[4]

The notwithstanding clause is to a charter of rights and freedoms what a federal disallowance power is to a federal constitution – an instrument to be used, not merely because it is there, but only in the most extreme and compelling circumstances. To do otherwise is to invite long-term damage to political reputation in a society where respect of fundamental liberties represents a supreme value.

The immediate result of the compromise of November 5 was less protection for equality rights and for native rights than had been found in previous federal drafts. Lobby groups pressured for reinstatement of that constitutional protection. Women's groups, representatives of native peoples and even the media discovered that compromises had been made because of the provinces. After months of controversy over process and after an unprecedented amount of what can be called "fed-bashing," these groups discovered somewhat to their surprise and perhaps even to their embarrassment that "Trudeau's Obsession" was indeed a reflection of what the people of Canada wanted, and rather than "fed-bashing," these groups put pressure on the provinces. In the days following November 5, as minister of justice, I was able to convince Premier Blakeney to drop his opposition to full entrenchment of equality rights for women and to convince Premier Lougheed to drop his opposition to entrenchment of aboriginal rights. The result was that the Charter was substantially improved.

Shared Values, Equal Rights

We sought to achieve constitutional recognition of values and ideals shared by Canadians wherever they lived. We sought to enshrine in the Constitution a concept of Canadian citizenship that not only guarantees fundamental liberties and democratic and legal rights, but also guarantees that no one shall suffer discrimination anywhere in Canada because of any law—federal or provincial—on grounds such as race, colour, religion, national or ethnic origin, sex, age, or physical or mental handicap. We sought to ensure that Canadians would be able to seek work anywhere in Canada, regardless of province of origin, and that Canadians would be able to educate their children anywhere in Canada in their own official language, be it English or French. We sought to enshrine the constitutional guarantee that Canadians could communicate with or receive services from their federal government in both English and French; and beyond the Charter of Rights, we wanted to enshrine in the Constitution the principle of sharing, or equalization, which is a cornerstone of our federalism.

We have a Charter of Rights that in a few short years has come to be looked upon as one of the most profound and progressive social and legal reforms in Canadian history. The Supreme Court of Canada has taken the view, according to Chief Justice Dickson, that "the interpretation shall be a generous rather than a legalistic one, aimed at fulfilling the purpose of the guarantee and procuring for individuals the full benefit of the Charter's protection." Furthermore, none of this was achieved at the expense of powers that the federal government must exercise in the national interest. The price of further decentralization was not paid to enshrine common values in the Constitution.

There are important lessons to be learned from the process that led to the most fundamental reform of the Canadian Constitution in history. The first lesson is that constitutional reform is very difficult to achieve and takes a long time. It requires compromise, negotiating ability, enormous political will and tenacity, and most of all, a substantial national consensus, which can come only after much debate and public discussion.

The second lesson is that the difficulty of obtaining constitutional change means that when made, it should be right or as right as possible. Changes—even improvements—cannot be made easily and flaws cannot be easily corrected. Flaws that are recognized while discussions are still going on should be corrected before they become entrenched in the Constitution as part of the basic law of the land, when they can be changed only by amendments to the Constitution.

The third lesson is that negotiations which are effectively structured on the basis of ten provinces against the federal government risk leading to a reduction of federal authority unless those representing the federal government have a strength of purpose and a commitment to principle that can overcome the tendency to be worn down by incessant "fed-bashing" by the provinces.

The final lesson, which comes from the testimony before the joint parliamentary committee and from the controversy that arose over the treatment of equality rights and native rights in the accord of November 5, 1981, is that the people of Canada want a citizenship that means holding shared values and not merely a shared passport.

PART VI

Quebec and Confederation: Views from the Outside

We have organized this book as a "participants' seminar," in the belief that there is value in asking former decision makers to record their hopes, fears and frustrations. But in such accounts perfect objectivity is not always assured. Dean Acheson, a former American secretary of state and no mean chronicler himself, once cautioned that he had never read a report of a conversation in which the author came out second best in the exchange.

To provide some balance, therefore, we asked two of Canada's most distinguished historians to join the discussion. Each chose as his theme the changing role of Quebec within Confederation. This obviously reflects the central place that Quebec occupied in Canadian history during the Trudeau years, a place which it still occupies. Fernand Ouellet demonstrates convincingly that, contrary to the nostrums of Quebec nationalists, who blame everyone but themselves for the ills of Quebec society, Quebec's backwardness prior to 1960 was largely of its own making. It is impossible to comprehend the tidal wave of change that swept over Quebec in the 1960s unless one appreciates how great was the need. Ouellet sets the stage for both the policy innovations of our government and the reaction our policies provoked within Quebec. Ramsay

Cook begins where Fernand Ouellet leaves off, focusing on the debate between the federalist and separatist camps, a debate that began in earnest in 1967–68 with the founding of the Parti québécois and the ascension to power of the Trudeau government. We sought to build a Just Society for all of Canada, but since for us justice meant a Canada where French and English would be treated equally across the land, inevitably the struggle with Quebec nationalism took much of our time and effort. The two essays in this section describe and analyze that debate from a historical perspective.

Thomas S. Axworthy
Pierre Elliott Trudeau

CHAPTER 13

The Quiet Revolution:
A Turning Point

—————— by Fernand Ouellet ——————
translated by Patricia Claxton

The historian Fernand Ouellet has taught at Laval University in the faculty of Commerce and at Carleton University and the University of Ottawa. He is currently titular Professor of History at York University in Toronto. He is a member of the Royal Society of Canada and an Officer of the Order of Canada. He has received the Grand Prix littéraire *of the City of Montreal, the prize of the* Concours littéraires *of the province of Quebec, the Prix David, the Sir John A. Macdonald Prize, the Tyrrell Medal of the Royal Society of Canada and the Governor General's Award. He has published many books on the economic and social history of Quebec.*

Although social change was the keynote of the Quiet Revolution, from the moment it began, the relationships between social and national preoccupations have been argued constantly and with a shrillness almost unequalled in the history of Quebec. The multiplicity and complexity of these relationships can be seen not only in the struggles waged between federalists and independentists after 1960, but also within the two camps, where conservatives, liberals, socialists, social-democrats and even democratic humanists have often been in vehement disagreement with each other. All this was new to Quebec in the sixties. Yet for all this apparent anarchy in the realm of beliefs, there were polarizations durable enough to reflect the true nature of the Quiet Revolution, which, seen through this tangle, does appear to have been a major turning point in the social development of Quebec. Begun in 1960 under the auspices of the Lesage government, it eventually touched all elements of Quebec society, signalling Quebec's unmistakable entry into the modern age.

___ Recent Nationalist Historiography _____

This image naturally does not correspond to that advanced by the great majority of nationalist historians since 1980, who underestimate the reach of the upheaval it represents.

Indeed, in reaction to the notion of backwardness that was popular among liberal intellectuals of the 1950s, the latest Quebec nationalist historiography has tended to depict the Quiet Revolution as a rather superficial phenomenon of a few years' duration that was dictated purely by the need to remedy a few major but temporary instances of backwardness accumulated during the Duplessis years. This version of events stresses the idea that the modernization of Quebec society, far from beginning only in the twentieth century, was the result of a long evolutionary process begun in about 1850.[1]

According to this view, there was nothing particularly significant about the emergence of an urban and industrial society in Quebec because it occurred at more or less the same time and in the same way as elsewhere in the Western world. If we are to believe the champions of this reconstruction of the past, neither the French-speaking nor other inhabitants of the province had been waiting for the thinkers of the fifties before embarking upon a development that had been held back for a time by the Duplessis régime but was set vigorously in motion by a new generation after 1960. This historiography has won a considerable following in the post-referendum era; it is largely a product of the Quiet Revolution's successful drive toward modernization, together with the current popularity of theories of modernization in the social sciences.

This interpretation, though it rightly discounts certain excesses in analyses of the 1950s inspired by the Folk Society model,[2] does not really adequately consider the ethnic dimension in the complex workings of the urban and industrial process in a heterogeneous society. By ignoring certain aspects of this development, it attempts to justify the credo that the long road to modernization will necessarily lead to independence for Quebec. But if the urban and industrial society was really built in the way that this view insists, how is it that the power of the clergy grew phenomenally in this society from 1830 until 1960, ultimately imposing its priorities in almost all sectors necessary to the development of the French-speaking community? It might be suggested that, all things considered, this nationalist, ultramontanist clergy had in effect guided Quebeckers in their march toward modernization despite its reactionary words and deeds. This version might be acceptable if French-speaking Quebeckers had continued to urbanize as rapidly and in the same manner as other Quebeckers after 1850, but this was obviously not the case. Since they were always underrepresented in the cities and particularly in Montreal, the hub of the province's manufacturing industry, they were bound to industrialize differently.[3]

_____ The Quiet Revolution: A Major Turning Point _____

In fact, all this goes to show that, seen in a long-term context focused on a conception of urbanization that considers the diversity of ethnic groups, the Quiet Revolution was incontestably the pivotal point at which French-speaking Quebeckers entered the modern age. In the thirty years since 1960, nowhere has their break with the past been more apparent than among a certain element that began to question existing structures as early as 1950. Before 1950, whenever groups turned to an examination of the problems facing their society, they had always looked to external causes for the collectivity's misfortunes—namely the French, British or Americans. In painting the dark deeds of these outsiders to explain the backwardness of Quebec society, such groups would always evoke the Conquest and blame conditions that they could trace back to this dire event, such as urbanization and industrialization. And in the 1950s, the neo-nationalists were still at it, attributing all of French-Canadian society's weaknesses to the Conquest and looking to an eventual political independence for their rectification. In their eyes, modernization and independence were synonymous.

And so, around 1950, a French-speaking urban intelligentsia appeared for the first time, turning a critical eye on clerical nationalism and the internal structures of their society and maintaining that, although Quebec was now indeed an urban and industrial habitat, what was urgently needed in order to remedy the long-accumulated backwardness was a thorough overhaul of existing socio-political ideology and institutions. To this end, these intellectuals advocated both declericalization of Quebec society and a redefined role for the state as the instigator of a revolution in education and a major participant in economic, social and cultural development.[4] It was a program that was to bring about a substantial closing of the long-standing gap between Quebec and Ontario and, internally, between the French-speaking and English-speaking populations.

___ Quebec and Ontario_____

On the disparities between the two provinces, which no one denied but for which everyone had a different explanation, Albert Faucher and Maurice Lamontagne propounded a thesis in 1953 in their book *Essais sur le Québec contemporain* that absolves French-speaking Quebeckers of almost all blame for their weaknesses;[5] this was echoed eight years later by André Raynauld in *Croissances et structures économiques de la Province de Québec.*[6] Leaning on the theory of continentalism, Faucher and Lamontagne more or less deny Quebec's backwardness, since, according to them, 1911 was a major turning point in industrial development for both the province and the neighbouring American states. However, they qualify this by observing the slowness of industrialization over the next three decades. Between the beginning of manufacturing in New England and comparable expansion in Quebec, it should be noted as well, there was a lag of over half a century. By drawing parallels between Ontario's fortunes and those of wealthier American states, all more advantageously situated in the economic space, Faucher and Lamontagne depict the Quebec-Ontario disparities as more or less normal. However, from their statement that French-Canadian entrepreneurs were not the artisans of industrialization in Quebec, we can infer an admission that the industrial revolution did not affect all ethnic groups equally.

André Raynauld raises even stronger doubts that industrialization in Quebec was late in coming. Backed by an extensive

statistical study, he concludes that Quebec entered a period of
rapid industrialization between 1896 and 1913 and that,
furthermore, its economy grew at a rate comparable to
Ontario's after 1870. However, he recognizes major disparities
between the two economies, particularly in the manufacturing
sector and in earnings and wage levels, and in this and
subsequent texts, he emphasizes the minor role played by
French-Canadian entrepreneurs.

The arguments of these economists aroused considerable
interest at the time of their publication, but did not dispel the
existing and largely justifiable conviction that the backwardness in question did exist.

For an understanding of these imbalances between Quebec
and Ontario, it should be remembered that their relations go
back to the pre-industrial era, not merely the last quarter of the
nineteenth century. Disparities between the two were much
discussed from the moment Quebec was divided into two
provinces. Upper Canada was created as a separate political
entity with its own relationship to Great Britain, true enough,
but in many respects the new territory was little more than
a colony of Lower Canada. The Lower Canadians were
empowered to levy taxes to which their neighbours were
subject, and the opening of Upper Canada to agricultural
colonization further strengthened Montreal's dominance over
a commercial and, later, industrial space extending infinitely
toward the west. Beyond doubt, the Upper Canadians knew
how important Montreal was to their development, which
explains why they demanded its annexation to Upper Canada
after 1825.

Upper Canada's expansion lagged for a time, while in Lower
Canada, agriculture based on wheat production remained
prosperous. The decline in Lower Canada's wheat production,
a decade before the construction of the Erie Canal, gave rise to
strong agitation from English-speaking merchants for canal-
ling of the St Lawrence. The opening of the Lachine Canal in
1825 was the first step in the realization of the canal system,
which was completed in 1848 and which stimulated the
development of Montreal and its hinterland all the way to the
far end of Lake Ontario. By 1850, Upper Canada was already
outstripping Lower Canada, not only in population but also in

agricultural production, number of industrial establishments and even equipment and steam engines (around 400 compared to 40). In 1861, while the population of Quebec was 79.5% of that of Canada West, its agricultural production was worth only 57% of the value of its neighbour's.[7]

Thus, Upper Canada, which had been in a position of disadvantage in relation to Lower Canada at first, steadily gained ground to the point of becoming Canada's principal centre of industrial development, thanks to the canals and railways and a diversified and prosperous agriculture that stimulated industrialization and the growth of cities. It must be said that this progress was partly attributable to its geographical situation and the establishment of a relatively flexible system of institutions, which enabled more rapid development in several strategic sectors, particularly all levels of education.

Toronto developed similarly, growing steadily from a small regional city totally dependent on Montreal in 1871 into Ontario's metropolis, and more recently Canada's. In this development, the years from 1940 to 1960 were critical. Table 1 illustrates the progress of Ontario and its capital and, on analysis, strongly suggests long-term trends underlying Quebec's backwardness in relation to Ontario.

Table 1
Population Comparison: Quebec/Ontario, Quebec City/Montreal,
and Montreal/Toronto, 1832–1986
(percentages)

| | | Cities | |
	Quebec/Ontario (population)	Quebec/Montreal (population)	Montreal/Toronto (population)
1832	217.8	87.6	—
1842	143.1	—	—
1851	93.5	79.2	191.2
1871	73.5	55.4	192.0
1911	79.4	30.2	131.6
1951	88.2	18.8	116.4
1971	78.2	17.5	104.7
1981	74.6	20.4	94.2
1986	71.7	20.6	85.2

Source: Canada Census.

Seen in the context of this long-term polarization of demographic and economic forces toward Ontario and Toronto, the decline in the population of British origin in Quebec and Montreal, as shown in Table 2, appears to be an almost natural development. In absolute figures, the decline began in 1941 for Montreal and twenty years later for the province.

Table 2
Evolution of the Population of French and British Origin, 1831-1981
(percentages)

| | Province of Quebec | | Montreal | |
	Fr.-speaking	Br. Origin	Fr.-speaking	Br. Origin
1831	–	–	47.2	52.8
1851	75.2	22.8	45.3	52.4
1871	78.0	20.4	52.8	44.8
1911	80.1	15.8	54.8	29.6
1951	82.0	12.1	67.6	17.7
1971	78.9	10.6	64.2	10.9
1981	80.2	7.6	62.3	8.9

Sources: F. Ouellet, *Lower Canada 1791-1840: Social Change and Nationalism* (Toronto, 1980); G. Bernier and R. Boily, eds., *Le Québec en chiffres de 1850 à nos jours* (Montreal, 1986).

On the strength of these few long-term indicators alone, the worries of the architects of the Quiet Revolution over the future of Quebec look far from unfounded. For those Quebeckers who, in the 1950s, perceived and were alarmed by the proportional changes, the imperative was not only to reduce the existing differential but to prevent it from expanding to catastrophic proportions. Indeed, the urgent need for change was clear without looking back a century; the immediately preceding decades alone were amply revealing. From 1931 to 1951, urbanization in Quebec had slowed (see Table 3) and Ontario had handily recovered the lead it had taken in 1871 and lost shortly after 1921. In these twenty years, the urbanization rate grew only 3% in Quebec, compared to 9.7% in Ontario, where Toronto and smaller cities were now growing vigorously.

Table 3
Metropolitan Populations of 100,000 and Over: Quebec and Ontario,
1931-1986
(percentage of total population)

	Quebec	Ontario	Difference
1931	41.6	36.7	4.9
1941	40.2	37.7	2.5
1951	45.1	52.4	−7.3
1961	51.8	60.5	−8.7
1971	55.7	66.3	−10.6
1981	58.7	65.8	−7.1
1986	60.4	70.2	−9.8

Source: *Canada Year Book.*

This does not take into account the fact that, since 1871,
despite rapid growth in sectors like forestry and services, the
Quebec economy had showed sluggish growth relative to total
population and active population in certain essential sectors
like manufacturing and agriculture (see Table 4).

Table 4
Quebec-Ontario Comparison: (1) Population; (2) Active Population;
(3) Manufacturing Production Value; (4) Gross Agricultural
Production Value, 1871-1981
(percentage)

	(1)	(2)	(1 − 2)	(3)	(2 − 3)	(4)	(2 − 4)
1871	73.5	68.9	−4.6	67.3	−1.6	47.9	−21.0
1891	70.4	62.2	−8.2	61.7	−0.5	39.9	−22.3
1901	75.5	65.8	−9.7	65.5	−0.3	42.7	−23.1
1921	80.5	70.2	−10.3	56.5	−13.7	70.9	0.7
1931	83.7	76.3	−7.4	59.7	−16.6	50.4	−25.9
1941	87.9	81.7	−6.2	59.0	−22.7	57.4	−24.3
1951	88.2	76.7	−11.5	60.7	−16.0	53.8	−22.9
1961	84.3	73.3	−11.0	61.7	−11.6	47.8	−25.5
1971	78.2	63.6	−14.6	53.7	−9.9	48.4	−15.2
1981	74.6	69.0	−5.6	53.3	−15.7	53.9	−15.1

Sources: A. Raynauld, *Structure et croissance économique de la province de Québec* (Quebec, 1961),
pp. 570, 590ff.; G. Bernier and R. Boily, eds., *Le Québec en chiffres de 1850 à nos jours*, pp. 181,
197ff.

___ The Urbanization of French-speaking
and Other Quebeckers _____

The constant urge to draw comparisons between Quebec and
Ontario in the fifties and sixties was prompted by a feeling
among many French-speaking Quebeckers that their society's
development was more or less stymied, that society was
incapable of assuming a full and proper role in the
development of the province and the country. This feeling was
the more acute for the fact that control of institutions
established under the French régime was more than ever in the
hands of the clergy and the petite bourgeoisie, who had ruled
their society for over a century and were held responsible for
the slowness with which French-speaking Quebeckers were
urbanizing and industrializing, relative to other Quebeckers.

The truth is that the clergy, although hostile to urbanization
and industrialization, had been powerless to stop French-
Canadian emigration to New England, or the exodus from
rural areas to the cities, or the decline in the birth rate. They
could only resign themselves to making the best of it and,
judging by the results, with the help of the leading lay classes,
concentrate on slowing, rather than stopping, the flow of their
French-speaking flocks to urban and industrial society.
Whichever way the flow was going, there were internal and
external political and socio-economic forces at work which
were beyond the control of the clergy and the leading
French-speaking laity in any event.

Before 1850, Quebec, unlike Ontario, experienced a long
period of ruralization.[8] For almost two centuries, rural areas
developed more rapidly than the cities, the ruralization rate
rising from 74% in 1700 to 85% in 1850 (not including villages).
This resulted, above all, from the relationship between
agriculture and the other sectors of the economy—namely, furs,
fisheries and lumbering; labour for the development of these
sectors was mostly recruited on a seasonal basis from farming
areas. In spite of major economic and demographic changes
after 1800, the trend continued until mid-century. During this

period, French-speaking and other inhabitants of the colony alike were becoming more rural, but not equally: in 1851, 88.8% of francophones and 74.2% of others were in rural areas (see Table 5).

Table 5
Urbanization in Quebec, 1851–1981
(percentage of total population of the same group)

	French-speaking	Others	Difference	Total
1851	11.2	25.8	−14.6	14.8
1871	17.2	29.9	−12.8	19.9
1911	42.4	78.4	−36.0	48.2
1941	58.9	82.0	−23.1	63.3
1971	78.1	90.6	−12.5	80.8
1981	74.8	87.9	−13.1	80.2

Source: Canada Census. The urban population consists of the combined populations of the cities, towns and villages of the province.

In 1850, then, francophones were overrepresented in the rural areas, while anglophones, after the massive immigration that began in 1815, were proportionately more numerous in the cities, towns and villages; between 1831 and 1851, they comprised nearly 50% of the combined populations of the colony's three cities, Quebec, Trois-Rivières and Montreal. Moreover, this overrepresentation involved more than the leading classes; tradesmen and labourers in Quebec City and Montreal were an important factor, and English-speaking labourers were even in the majority in Montreal.[9]

There was thus a sharp contrast between the two groups from the beginning of the process of urbanization. Table 5 shows this clearly.

In fact, all ethnic groups were involved in the trend to urbanization, which began slowly and continued uninterrupted until 1971. However, among the French-speaking, the movement was less rapid than among the English-speaking. Here the notion of backwardness, freed from the outdated baggage of the Folk Society model, usefully illuminates the profile of French-speaking Quebeckers, for instead of going more or less directly to the cities and particularly Montreal, they tended to be concentrated in the smaller urban centres (see Table 6). This does much to explain the nature of their migration and highlights their underrepresentation in the manufacturing sector, both as employers and as workers, for in 1891, manufacturing was concentrated in Montreal: it had 32.7% of the manufacturing establishments, 51.3% of the manpower and 66.5% of the production value. In 1982, the proportions were, respectively, 67.2%, 65.0% and 66.1%.

Table 6
Quebeckers Living in Montreal, 1851–1981
(percentage of the total of the same group in the province)

	French-speaking	Others	All Quebeckers
1851	3.9	14.3	6.5
1871	6.1	19.2	9.0
1901	8.6	27.2	12.3
1921	20.6	48.4	26.2
1941	22.2	49.3	27.1
1961	18.7	39.0	22.6
1981	11.8	28.8	15.2

Source: Canada Census.

And so, around 1920, when half of the French-speaking population was urbanized, urban French Canadians were typically small-town dwellers. It was not until 1981 that as many as 50% of them were living in cities with populations of 100,000 or more, indicating that their gravitation to the major cities can be said to have taken place only after 1950 (see Table 7). They were therefore half a century behind other Quebeckers, nearly 80% of whom were already urban in 1911.

Table 7
French-speaking and Other Quebeckers in Quebec Cities with
Populations of 100,000 and Over
(percentage)

	Fr.-speaking	Others	Difference	Total Population
1931	28.3	50.8	−22.5	33.0
1941	27.4	49.6	−22.2	31.6
1951	25.5	46.7	−21.2	29.2
1971	46.2	78.1	−31.9	52.9
1981	50.8	79.5	−28.7	56.9

Source: G. Bernier and R. Boily, eds. *Le Québec en chiffres de 1850 à nos jours* (Montreal, 1986), pp. 43–45. These figures are for cities, not greater metropolitan areas.

___ Clericalization and Declericalization of the Society ___

If there had not already been examples elsewhere in the world
of a certain dechristianization associated with the emergence of
urban and industrial societies, this slow but steady movement
of francophones to the city would not have seemed so
revolutionary. True, the exodus of French Canadians to the
industrial towns of New England around 1850 had provoked
alarm over the outlook for Catholicism in Lower Canada, but
this was twenty years before the signs of urbanization or
industrialization began to manifest themselves. Monseigneur
Lartigue, first bishop of Montreal and the leading proponent of
ultramontanist notions regarding the supremacy of the church
over the state and of the clergy in society, was already
convinced that local Catholicism was in dire peril. To him, the
colonial government's intervention in primary education in
1801 and 1829, following the confiscation of the Jesuit estates
in 1800, was proof positive of the danger facing the Catholic
Church. His fear was also fed by massive immigration from the
British Isles and the diffusion of liberal and republican ideas by
the *Patriote* party. All this led him to conclude that it was of the
utmost urgency to thwart the machinations of the Protestants
and the secularizing plans of the liberals.[10]

Lartigue was sure that there were powerful groups in this
pre-rebellion Lower Canada, both French-speaking and
Protestant, who would like nothing better than to end the
Catholic clergy's monopolies in education, the hospitals, aid to
the poor and the keeping of the civil register. And since, in this
period, there were more and more liberal movements in the
world advocating the separation of church and state, he further
suspected that the fate of the vast ecclesiastical landholdings
was also in question.

To counter these threats, Lartigue devised a strategy which
was continued with the utmost vigour by his successor,
Monseigneur Bourget. In the mind of the ultramontanist
Lartigue, the clergy must not only to be close to the people and
proliferate institutions serving the diffusion of the faith, but it
must also regain full control of all domains that had been the
clergy's prerogative since time immemorial. On March 28,

1836, he suggested to the bishop of Quebec that he avoid openly expressing a "desire to snatch the education of the people as by right."[11] Indeed, Lartigue was aiming even higher than his predecessors, for he was determined that the clergy, besides extending their power over all social and cultural institutions, should make up the entire personnel of these institutions.

It is clear that at this date the clergy was not sufficiently numerous to fulfill the Bishop of Montreal's theocratic dream. The shortage of secular clergy was real, but the situation was worst among the priests, brothers and nuns of the regular clergy. Indeed, the number of faithful per priest had risen from around a hundred in 1663 to 350 in 1760 and 1,834 in 1830.[12] During the French régime, even after the number of Catholics per priest had begun to increase, the clergy had never considered its numbers inadequate. Still, together with the aristocracy, it was one of the two dominant classes of the colony. During this period it was operating in a Gallican world, in which the church-state alliance worked to the advantage of state power, in a society that was increasingly rural and in a context where the notion of an elementary education for all was yet to appear. Increasingly, the secular clergy was being recruited in the colony, most often in the towns and cities, from the ranks of the aristocracy, the bourgeoisie and the upper strata of tradesmen. The regular clergy, which was even more élitist in social background, was mostly recruited abroad.[13]

The British forbade the immigration of French priests after the Conquest, accelerating the numerical decline of the male religious communities. The aristocracy had entered a long phase of decline, which complicated things. To counter the shortage, church leaders were obliged to seek recruits in rural areas, where they built many classical colleges. Here, Lartigue had no great cause for concern, since the clerics had total control over these institutions and the desired results could be obtained simply by adding more colleges associated with the *grands séminaires*. The promotion of religious vocations was, of course, also extended to women's religious orders. Once the British government ceased to object, efforts were also made to encourage French and Belgian orders of priests, brothers and nuns to establish themselves in Quebec.

By 1850, more than a decade after inviting French Canadians to join in the building of a Catholic and clerical society on ultramontanist principles, the clergy knew they were on the right track. It must be said that the program would never have succeeded so remarkably if the clerics themselves had not been imbued with the ultramontanist message and if there had not been considerable support from the faithful of both the lower and dominant lay classes. This is clear from the proliferation of religious orders of various specialties and the extraordinary growth in their membership. From 1851 to 1960, the number of priests multiplied 42 times, male regular clergy 35 times, and nuns 70 times, while the population increased only sixfold. In the same period, the number of men's orders increased from 6 to 63 and the number of women's orders went from 15 to 128 (see Table 8). The number of Catholics per cleric thus became the lowest in the Western world.

Table 8
Number of Catholics per Cleric in Quebec, 1810–1961

| | | Catholics per Member of Religious Order | | |
	Catholics per Priest	per male	per female	per total
1810	1,375	9,418	1,009	912
1851	1,080	2,068	1,100	722
1911	652	457	120	96
1931	567	355	90	71
1951	504	309	88	68
1961	509	367	98	78

Sources: L.-E. Hamelin, "Evolution numérique séculaire du clergé catholique dans le Québec," *Recherches sociographiques* 2 (1961): 189-241; B. Denaut and B. Lévesque, *Eléments pour une sociologie des communautés religieuses au Québec* (Montreal/Sherbrooke, 1975).

This extraordinary growth was to have profound effects on the evolution of the state and the advancement of the laity in Quebec society. This was because the state, under the leadership of middle-class laymen, far from becoming the guardian of individual freedoms, kept giving way to pressure from the clerics. Even the powers the state had assumed over primary education before 1840 were gradually eroded, particularly after the creation of a provincial state in 1867. That year a ministry of education had been established. In this sector, which Lartigue considered paramount for the integration of the young, the clergy not only obtained the suppression of the ministry in 1875 but succeeded in having the supremacy of the bishops recognized throughout the school system, including normal schools, domestic arts schools and family institutes. Only technical and professional training escaped.

There is no doubt that the low educational standards among French-speaking Quebeckers compared to other Quebeckers and Ontarians could be attributed not only to a higher proportion of rural population but also to active discouragement of education by manipulators of the educational system (in 1950, 51.3% of the active population in Ontario had at least nine years' schooling, compared to only 36.9% in Quebec);[14] today, the spread between the two provinces has been reduced to 9.0. The fact that the population of Quebec, along with those of Newfoundland and New Brunswick, was one of the least educated of all provincial populations in 1961 is certainly connected with the bishops' traditional opposition to compulsory schooling. This cramped vision is also seen in the late introduction and slow development of classical colleges for women, and in clerical attitudes to university teaching.

The foundation of Laval University in 1852 as a pontifical institution attached to the Seminary of Quebec was the first step toward the clergy's total hold over the network of French-speaking universities, which was to include the Universities of Montreal and Sherbrooke—a development that was no more benign than other clerical interventions. The state might have subsidized the system, but when it left teaching so overwhelmingly in the hands of a powerful group hostile to the notion of a lay and liberal state, there was little chance of keeping enough authority to tailor priorities to the needs of an increasingly urban and industrialized society. This is clear in the extraordinary popularity of theological studies among students at French-speaking universities at the beginning of the twentieth century. It appears to be no coincidence that 34% of students at these institutions were studying theology at this time, while only 4% were studying applied sciences; in English-speaking universities, 0.6% were studying theology and 28.1% applied sciences.

Seen against this background, it is hardly surprising that the

1961 Parent Commission noted many inadequacies in the French-language universities (in research, libraries, teaching personnel and budgets). In the period 1936–45, non-French-speaking Quebeckers made up 20% of the population, yet 42% of all university graduates and 66.6% of those with doctorate degrees were graduates of English universities.

The burgeoning of clerical power is no less evident in the health sector, where religious orders and communities created many general hospitals and others for the mentally ill and unwed mothers, and also extended their control to a number of existing lay institutions. Clerical supremacy was similarly apparent in welfare institutions, where in due course laymen and the state were hardly present at all. While the creation of the Ministry of Social Welfare and Youth in 1946 began the process of declericalization, little headway was made until the eve of 1960.[15]

The motivation behind the clerical strategy also led to intervention in the press, public libraries and associations of every description; anywhere, in fact, where some good might come of it, or some ill might be averted. About 1850, when the clergy took charge of colonization in order to counter emigration to the United States, the state made no objection, but gradually the clerical presence intensified until one day a cleric had to be appointed deputy-minister of colonization. In short, the state, by giving way time after time to clerical pressure, far from liberalizing, as recent nationalist historiography would have us believe, gradually allowed itself to be sapped of substance in essential matters, including the economy.

The fact is that, long before the days of the church's social doctrine and Christian feminism, which were developed to win highly industrialized and dechristianized societies back to religion, the clergy had been treating the whole of the slowly industrializing French-speaking Quebec as mission territory, although the church was already united with the state and the population solidly Catholic. Yet the clergy did have to make some compromises, such as accepting, not always with good grace, a degree of industrialization and urbanization in order to keep colonists in their regions of colonization. And in order to promote their own solutions to the problems of an industrial society, they were obliged to concentrate their numbers in the cities, where the working class was beginning to form and where the problems were the worst. In 1901, when only 8.6% of the French-speaking population was in Montreal, 31.5% of the clergy at large and 66.7% of the regular clergy were there.[16] The church's social doctrine and Christian feminism may have changed the minds of a few regarding the modern world, but for the majority, these ideas simply confirmed the conviction that the church must have supremacy over the state and total control over social institutions, including labour organizations.

The first labour organizations were openly condemned by the clergy, and even after the formal censure was lifted, clerical hostility to the Knights of Labour and the international unions never wavered. However, realizing perforce that the working class was there to stay, the clergy turned to encouraging the right kind of unions. Where the labour force was massively French-speaking, Catholic unions were no doubt relatively easy to establish. However, in Montreal, where most manufacturing and union activity was concentrated (61% to 66% of the labour force between 1901 and 1951, and 57% to 70% of the unionized workers in the province between 1921 and 1941), the working class was ethnically and religiously heterogeneous and the French-speaking were underrepresented in the class. Not surprisingly, the Catholic unions were not very successful, even after the confessional nature of these unions disappeared in the early 1960s. They accounted for only 6.7% of unionized workers in Montreal in 1921, 20.1% in 1941 and 14.8% in 1971.[17]

Outside of Montreal, where clerical influence was strongest, the Catholic unions did help to spread unionism. So much so that, until the Duplessis era, Quebec was more heavily unionized than Ontario. But the growth was accompanied by substantially less militancy, judging by the number of strikes that took place in Quebec compared to the number that took place in Ontario. (Between 1901 and 1910, Quebec had only 47.8% of the strikes that Ontario had; between 1931 and 1941 that percentage was 38.7%; and between 1941 and 1951, it was 67.8%.) This suggests that the preoccupations and activities of the Catholic unions had complied with the clergy's expectations at least until 1940. However, there were more workers involved and more hours lost per strike than in Ontario, which should indicate that the strikes occurred in larger establishments, most of which were in Montreal, where the working class was too heterogeneous to be attracted to the Catholic unions.

And so it appears that French-speaking workers in Montreal, because they were employed in a pluralist milieu, were those who most readily escaped the control sought by the clergy through Catholic unionism. Montreal's early French-speaking feminists, who were middle-class women, might also have escaped clerical control, for, around 1893, they aligned themselves with a movement that was liberal, reformist and deliberately neutral in religion and ethnicity—the Montreal Local of the National Council of Women—and thus effectively distanced themselves from the priests, nuns and people of their own milieu. However, inspired by Christian feminism, they finally decided to return to the fold, founding a women's section of the Saint-Jean-Baptiste Society, whose activities adhered strictly to Catholic teachings. This was the beginning of a series of compromises, which escalated in 1907 when these women created La Fedération nationale Saint-Jean Baptiste, uniting a large number of women's associations, half of them run by nuns. So they could hardly use this association in the fight for compulsory schooling, women's suffrage and reform of the civil law, since, one way or another, any initiative had to meet with the approval of the clergy. Tutelage was inevitable, given the large number of charitable and educational institutions owned by the nuns. All went smoothly as long as the feminists engaged in activities approved by the nuns. But the fight for legal and political rights for women would have to find other forums.

Even when women workers' and teachers' associations and unions were formed by these women, they tended to propound clerical and employer views far more than they defended their members' interests.[18] One of the favourite solutions for the middle-class feminists of the time was to create women's sections of the Catholic unions, which meant that in practice the women attended only to fringe activities, leaving true labour matters to the men.

The development of this vast institutional network, then,

meant that almost absolute authority over sectors essential to the advancement of the French-speaking laity had been given to a class of celibate men and women fired with spiritual fatherhood and motherhood and dominated by fear of liberalism and secularism. Since the prime purpose of these institutions was to recruit personnel for the clergy, those seeking careers in certain fields were made to understand that they had more chance of success if they became priests, monks, brothers or nuns. The longest-established institutions had accumulated vast amounts of land, and a complicated financial system involving gifts, subsidies and salaries enabled members of the clergy to offer their services at rates that defied competition from lay people. Generally, the clerical élites not only owned and operated the institutions, but fully expected to staff them as well.

The progression of clerical power is most striking in primary education, where the clergy operated their own schools and were also solidly ensconced in the public schools. In 1832, three years after the creation of the Legislative Assembly schools so vehemently denounced by Monseigneur Lartigue, the 1,062 teachers were 57.7% French-speaking, 96% male, and 97.9% lay; surprisingly, there was pay parity for all teachers after this reform.[19] However, with new legislation after 1840, the balance was altered radically, apparently in favour of female lay teachers but actually favouring the religious, for the pay structure, in application, entrenched discrepancies between men and women, lay and religious teachers, and Protestants and Catholics. Brothers and nuns received the lowest pay, followed by women, then Catholics. The discrepancies were advantageous to frugal school administrators and remained until the Quiet Revolution, when the lay teachers' associations, realizing to whose advantage they were working, began demanding parity for religious and lay teachers.[20]

These discrepancies, particularly those between Protestants and Catholics, reflected only in part the more rural character of the French-speaking population and did much to keep Catholic lay teachers in a condition near poverty. The result was that there were fewer and fewer male lay Catholic teachers. Even at a salary more than twice that of a brother, a man inclined to marry and raise a family could not afford a teaching career in any event. Their female counterparts, facing similar competition and earning a miserable stipend, nevertheless maintained a strong presence, tending to regard their teaching as temporary employment pending marriage. Their number and percentage continued to increase for a time, and then dropped, giving place to the nuns. This relative decline for lay Catholic teachers continued until the 1930s, when the clerics were no longer numerous enough to fill the demand.[21]

This salary structure was especially detrimental to male and female lay teachers because it included a fourth level of salary differentiation – that which existed between cities and rural areas. This, along with the other differentiations, marginalized male and female lay teachers to an extraordinary degree (see Table 9).

It will be noted that the clerics offered their services at the lowest rates in the cities. The great variation in pay rates between urban and rural areas strongly indicates a connection linking clerical strategy, the pay structure for teachers and the high percentage of rural lay teachers (88.8%).

Clerical strategy had therefore produced an urban clerical teaching aristocracy and a kind of lay teaching proletariat more rural than the population, in which female lay teachers were the lowest of the low. Even the male lay teachers were considered to be of a lower order than the teaching brothers. These facts go to show that the clerics did not need to be in the majority in order to dominate the system. Most of the administrative posts were also in clerical hands: 48.5% in those of nuns and 20% in those of brothers in the primary and secondary schools in 1960-61, according to Micheline Dumont and Nadia Fahmy-Eid. The rest were shared unequally (21.3% and 10%) between male and female lay personnel. At this time, brothers and nuns comprised only 30.9% of the teaching profession (7% brothers and 23.9% nuns); the percentage of female lay teachers was 55.9%, eight times that of male lay teachers.[22]

Things were even worse for lay teachers in the classical colleges. These institutions provided the transition from secondary to university education, but their main purpose was

Table 9
Pay Scales and Geographical Distribution of Teachers, 1882-1883

	Urban	Rural	Total
Lay (nmbr 4,431)			
(a) Male (nmbr 590)			
percentage	28.8	71.2	100
average pay	737	271	405
(b) Female (nmbr 3,781)			
percentage	8.2	91.8	100
average pay	217	101	110
(c) Total			
percentage	11.2	88.8	100
average pay	397	119	149
Religious (nmbr 1,553)			
(a) Male (nmbr 556)			
percentage	72.8	27.2	100
average pay	165	154	162
(b) Female (nmbr 997)			
percentage	57.5	42.5	100
average pay	95	95	95
(c) Total			
percentage	62.9	37.1	100
average pay	124	110	119
Grand total			
percentage	23.6	76.4	100
average pay	230	118	144

Source: A. Labarrère-Paulé, *Les instituteurs laïcs au Canada français. 1836-1900.* (Quebec: Presses de l'Université Laval, 1965).

to recruit clerics, and consequently, none were initially envisaged for girls. The first for girls was founded two and a half centuries after the Jesuit College in Quebec. Twenty years later, there were still no more than 100 female classical college students. Not surprisingly, in 1961, when 31% of English-speaking university students were women, only 15% of French-speaking students were women. In these classical colleges, there were no lay directors and hardly any lay teachers before the period 1940-50, and during this period the lay personnel still formed an underpaid, powerless proletariat.

The universities, which were also considered to be works of the church[23] and which were run by the clergy, were obliged quite early and increasingly to resort to a largely lay teaching personnel, even Protestant teachers in certain cases. But while lay Catholics made steady inroads at the faculty level, access by the laity to managerial positions was very slow in coming. Given the clerical control and the overwhelming importance of theology, law and medicine in the traditional curriculum, it is not surprising that the disciplines most in demand in an industrial society were developed with great difficulty. The reason was that the universities reflected the nature of French-speaking urbanization as well as the effectiveness of the ecclesiastical roadblocks to initiatives liable to give the faithful ideas about progress.

The structure that worked to the disadvantage of laymen, and even more to laywomen, worked equally well in the health sector, where the nuns remained in place as long as the religious orders that owned or operated the hospitals could provide sufficient personnel from their own ranks. When they were eventually obliged to accept laywomen, it was first in menial positions, but by 1930 roughly half the nurses were laywomen. One wonders how many of them shared any authority with the nuns.

In social services, the evolution was even slower; social work as a lay profession took form only after 1940, with the introduction of programs in the universities.

And so, between 1850 and 1960, the French-speaking Quebecker became urbanized and in a number of ways played a part in the industrialization of the province. By 1960 he had fewer children than his forebear, was less vulnerable to illness, lived longer and was better educated. It must be said that, directly or indirectly, both the clergy and the state had contributed to these changes. Yet certain critical functions that might have been used by the state to change the profile of the French-speaking population had been left almost entirely to clerical and capitalist private interests. The clergy, whose institutions were an undeniably powerful economic force, were consumed by fear and had erected a system so negative to laymen and the state that, while it supported them in certain ways, it did much to hold them back. In 1960, the French-speaking society as a whole (men and women, religious and laity) was lagging behind other Quebeckers.

To be sure, there were a few clerics who attempted to distance themselves from those in power before 1940, and Premier Godbout (1939-44) came close to launching a kind of social revolution, which failed for lack of support. But then Duplessis came forth and, lo, the danger perceived by the leading classes receded. No doubt he made some compromises that he later found awkward, but, drawing attention to encroachments by the federalists and vigorously fighting the perils of unionism, nonconformist clerics and "leftist" tendencies, he effectively put everything back in order for another two decades.

So the Quiet Revolution that declericalized Quebec and updated its intellectual and material resources after 1960 did not happen all at once. However, its full and irreversible momentum would have taken another two decades to surface if the solidarity of the clergy had not already been eroded from within to some extent. The number of clerics was at its peak in 1960, after all, and per capita, was higher than anywhere else in the Catholic world: one priest for every 509 Catholics and one member of a religious order for every 78 Catholics.[24] Who would have guessed that twenty years later this density would have declined faster and further than anywhere else? As a result of massive resignations and a radical reduction in recruitment, the number of nuns, for instance, fell from 46,933 in 1961 to 26,786 in 1979.[25] The same thing happened among secular priests and male regular clergy, whose numbers declined 50 percent and 75 percent, respectively.

The fall-off in clerical numbers, occurring as the majority of francophones was beginning to be concentrated in large cities, did much to undermine clerical power and accelerate the secularization of Quebec society and the separation of church and state. At this point, to the benefit of all and to the outrage of convinced ultramontanists, the state assumed responsibilities that had hitherto been the exclusive domain of the clergy. In 1968 it took charge of the civil registry of births and began to offer the option of civil marriage and burial. In a society that had always recognized the pre-eminence of the religious or "national" collectivity, this recognition of individual rights was a revolutionary event in itself.

The state's intervention in education, the crucial sector nurtured so long and jealously by the clergy, through which the clerics had controlled access by laymen to certain professions, was not accomplished without battles and trade-offs. The ministry of education, the junior colleges known as CEGEPs and the Université du Québec were all created for the purpose of bringing French-speaking Quebeckers up to par with the rest of North America. Besides creating pressure for the deconfessionalization of the existing universities and the primary schools, this initiative enabled laymen and the state to define their own priorities for society in technical and professional training and in literary, artistic and scientific development. In 1941, education and culture absorbed only 8.2% of the provincial budget; by 1983-84, this had risen to 31.8%, with total budgetary expenditures having multiplied 240 times.

A similar reorientation was imposed in health care and social services, the two other sectors that were previously clerical monopolies. The budgetary share of these services combined also rose dramatically, from 19.5% in 1941 to 38.7% in 1983-84, with corresponding increases in the proportion of lay personnel.

____ The State _____

One of the fundamental objectives of the Quiet Revolution had been to modernize and expand the state apparatus and make it an effective agent in the economic and social development of the province, for the benefit of all Quebeckers and of French-speaking Quebeckers in particular. For in 1950, the traditional underrepresentation of both male and female French-speaking Quebeckers in commerce, finance and industry was not only at the ownership and management level but also in the labour force in manufacturing, construction and the service industries. This underrepresentation was particularly great in Montreal.

Table 10
French-speaking Quebeckers in (I) the population,
(II) the active population aged 15 and over, (III) professions,
administration and commerce, (IV) services, (V) manufacturing,
(VI) construction, (VII) the primary sector (1931-1981)
(percentage)

	1931	1941	1951	1961	1971	1981
I.	78.4	80.9	82.0	80.6	78.9	80.2
II.	75.1	78.5	79.4	77.8	75.5	79.4
III.	69.8	74.1	70.8	69.9	71.3	76.9
IV.	69.5	75.4	74.1	75.0	74.7	79.7
V.	69.4	72.9	81.3	79.8	76.3	78.7
VI.	74.2	82.1	86.2	82.9	81.7	84.2
VII.	87.4	88.8	90.6	91.1	88.9	88.4

Source: G. Bernier and R. Boily, eds., *Le Québec en chiffres de 1850 à nos jours* (Montreal: ACFAS, 1986), pp. 208-13.

In 1931, the only field in which the French-speaking population was overrepresented was the primary sector (agriculture, forestry and mining), joined by construction in 1941 (see Table 10). The presence of francophones in manufacturing surpassed the active population first in 1951. In the service sector, where education is more important and where there are large numbers of women, this did not occur until 1981. At this date, francophones were still slightly underrepresented in relation to the total population in manufacturing and services and particularly in the professions, administration and commerce. The steady transformation of the French-speaking working class, which had engaged in rare but violent militancy before 1960, as in the Asbestos strike,[26] was so deep that after 1970, it became more militant and radical than its Ontario counterpart.

Women, and French-speaking women in particular, benefited from the lifting of institutional barriers to secondary and university education. Between 1975 and 1983, the percentage of women among university students rose from 39.3% to 46.6%. In doctoral studies, their presence was weaker but still increased from 20.9% to 25.6%. The effect of these changes on French-speaking women in paid employment would be more measurable if the available statistics took ethnic origins into account (see Table 11).

Table 11
Working Women by Category of Occupation, 1951-1981
(percentage)

	1951	1961	1971	1981
Total work force	25.7	30.4	33.0	39.4
Professions, commerce	22.2	23.7	24.4	31.4
Services	55.2	56.5	45.5	47.1
Primary sector	1.8	2.6	1.3	1.2
Secondary sector	20.8	14.4	13.6	11.7
Other	—	2.7	14.3	8.5
Total	100	99.9	99.1	99.9

Sources: G. Bernier and R. Boily, eds., *Le Québec en chiffres de 1850 à nos jours* (Montreal: ACFAS, 1986), pp. 203-13.

After the minor successes of the feminists early in the century, the women's movement was revived in the cities in the thirties when the issue of women's suffrage in provincial elections came up. Federally, all women had had the right to vote since 1919 and Quebec women had used their right (71%) with as much enthusiasm as men. Yet the clergy and the more conservative elements of the leading classes, supported by certain powerful women's groups, had always opposed the vote for women. The reform was finally introduced in 1940 under the Godbout government.

In Quebec, true feminism based on egalitarian and liberationist thinking dates from the mid-1960s, when the Quiet Revolution had begun to affect the advancement of women in paid employment and in the society in general. During the next fifteen years there was rapid development, with a radicalism reflecting the rise of nationalism and socialism in Quebec. Since 1980, although the latter tendencies seem to have abated, the movement has not slackened its vigilance in the pursuit of its fundamental goals.

The strategists of the Quiet Revolution had also judged that the role of the state would have to be broadened if the disparities between francophones and others in big business ownership and management were ever to disappear. Consequently, after 1960, there appeared a great many state-owned companies whose purpose was both to make the economy of Quebec more competitive and to increase the presence of francophones in organizations whose contacts with the private sector were many and ongoing. With this new economic power, the "national state of Quebec," as it came to be known, could be seen either as a training ground for French-speaking entrepreneurs or, pending the unshackling of the French-speaking businessman through independence, as the only French-speaking capitalist enterprise powerful enough to thwart English-speaking economic power. Another line of thought, looking to the emergence of an independent state that was also socialist, was that the rise of a great national business class was not a condition essential to the full liberation of the French-speaking people of Quebec.

The fact is that the Quiet Revolution, with its theme of secularization and modernization, had taken place in such vital segments of the society that, with time, it was bound to affect all aspects of the lives of men and women in all walks of life. Each phase led to another, and the upheavals in social structures and attitudes were so radical that Quebec society has eventually come to be much like any other. Contrary to independentist dogma, given the increasing fascination with economic development on the part of the people and the new training opportunities available to young people, independence has not been a necessary precondition for the emergence of a strong French-speaking capitalist business class. In 1961, recalls André Raynauld, French-speaking Quebeckers controlled only 15.4% of the manufacturing sector and 47.1% of the overall economy of Quebec; by 1978, those proportions had risen to 22.3% and 54.8%, respectively.[27] Since 1980, francophone business ownership has progressed to a point where French-speaking businessmen are more confident in relation to their competitors inside and outside Quebec, and they are more independent of the state.[28] As a result, they tend today to promote a much less interventionist conception of the role of government in the economy.

The statistical data that I have presented here show that a transformation of this magnitude in a society that, in many respects, had been marking time for a couple of centuries, could not occur in a mere few decades – particularly considering that the primary sector, which in 1931 was the only one in which French-speaking workers were overrepresented, was relatively more important in Quebec than in Ontario, where heavy industry predominated. Since then, there has been a more vigorous increase in the tertiary sector and government bureaucracy than in Ontario, where the manufacturing sector remains relatively more important. Undoubtedly, these structural differences, together with the slow rate of social change in French-speaking Quebec before 1960, are responsible for the persisting disparities between Quebec and Ontario and between francophones and non-francophones within Quebec. However, it must be noted that the extraordinary changes in the economy and in scientific and cultural activity have in fact occurred during a period in which all Western societies have been undergoing rapid change.

Although the French-speaking Quebecker is now comfortable in the modern world and is more culturally active than he has ever been, since he is no longer shy about asserting his presence in most fields of human activity, he still has a strong feeling of vulnerability. The decline in the birthrate, whose economic, linguistic, cultural and political implications are studied with anxious intensity, has been far more pronounced among French-speaking Quebeckers than among Ontarians—since 1951 there has been a drop of 55 percent in Quebec, as compared to 41 percent in Ontario. Around 1970, this appeared so alarming that the Quebec government felt obliged to adopt measures not only to encourage a higher birthrate and improve the economic and social environment for the French language but also to force immigrants to integrate into the French-speaking milieu. The policy has not changed the birth rate, which today is the lowest among all Western countries, but has been so effective with immigrants that those demographers who, twenty years ago, were predicting that the integration of immigrants into the English milieu would soon relegate francophones to minority status in Quebec are now predicting the disappearance of the *pure laine* or old stock Québécois in a sea of a new kind of francophone of multiple traditions and cultural backgrounds.

So the Quiet Revolution has not only contributed to an acceleration of developments begun in the more or less distant past, but has caused profound breaks with the past. Although the process begun around 1960 is far from complete, present-day French-speaking Quebec society is so different from what it was thirty years ago that it is hard to believe it could all have happened so quickly. It helps us understand the strong urge in French-speaking Quebeckers to reconstruct their past, as if Montreal had always been the wellspring of progress for Quebec society and, as such, the economic grail to be sought and brought home.

Seen in this light, the Quiet Revolution appears to have been primarily a major social reform that has been going on under all governments since 1960. But in the late sixties, by appealing to the pride of French-speaking Quebeckers and brandishing the red flag of cultural decline, independentist leaders tried to capitalize on the strong nationalist overtones of the social reform and convert it into an independence movement. However, in their efforts to mobilize the population in that direction, they kept diluting the independence message, which amounted to recognizing that for most French-speaking Quebeckers, nationalist though they might be and however much they may have been tempted, the social question had become paramount.

The success of the Quiet Revolution and the failure of the independentist movement show that independence was not an indispensable step in the modernization and democratization of French-speaking society in Quebec. The neo-nationalists of the 1950s had proclaimed that it was indispensable, but, according to them, the business class was the only one capable of bringing independence about, and since, in their view, that class was incurably decadent, the dream was unrealizable. During the sixties, nationalist intellectuals, historians and social scientists reworked Quebec's past in the light of theories of the development of underdevelopment and predicted the imminent emergence of a modern, independent Quebec state, enriched with a home-grown socialism and spearheaded by the French-speaking, foreign-exploited working class. The failure of the referendum destroyed this reasoning and paved the way for the credo according to which independence would be the natural outgrowth of modernity.

CHAPTER 14

"I never thought I could be as proud ... ": The Trudeau-Lévesque Debate

—————— by Ramsay Cook ——————

Ramsay Cook, Professor of History at York University, Toronto, is also General Editor of the Dictionary of Canadian Biography/Dictionnaire Biographique du Canada. *His recent books include* Canada, Quebec and the Uses of Nationalism *and* The Regenerators, *which was awarded the Governor General's Literary Award for Non-Fiction.*

It is not the idea of *nation* that is retrograde; it is the idea that the nation must necessarily be sovereign.

> — Pierre Elliott Trudeau,
> "New Treason of the Intellectuals,"
> *Federalism and the French Canadians* (Toronto, 1968)

What does this French Quebec want? Sometime during the next few years, the question will be answered. And there are growing possibilities that the answer could very well be—independence.

> — René Lévesque, "For an Independent Quebec,"
> *Foreign Affairs* (October 1976)

... only two positions seem logical to me: that of Mr Trudeau, who won the referendum of 1980, and that which

preaches the independence of Quebec. The rest look like a
kind of constitutional embroidery.

—Marcel Rioux, *Une Saison à la Renardière*
(Montreal, 1988) [translation]

MANY CANADIANS, AND doubtless foreigners too, found the
Canadian constitutional debate of the 1970s something of a
puzzle. Quite apart from the confusion created by arcane
constitutional details best left to lawyers and other addicts,
there was the dominant role played by two francophone
Quebeckers: Pierre Elliott Trudeau and René Lévesque. If this
was a Canadian drama, surely central casting had been
mischievous in failing to assign one starring role to an English
Canadian thespian. And the theatre analogy could be carried
further: the particularly obtuse premier of Newfoundland,
Brian Peckford, once described the debate as "The René and
Pierre Show." That suggested it was just a soap opera in which
two middle-aged matinée idols made increasingly melodramat-
ic gestures in a personal competition for the hearts of their
sentimental viewers. Sunset Boulevard North. Or, if another
simplifying analogy were needed, there was always sport. Now
Lévesque and Trudeau could become aspiring champions
lurching round after round from corners marked "Quebec" and
"Canada," urged on by their seconds to deliver the final
knock-out blow. Muhammad Alis in the federal-provincial
ring. In the age of television, personality simplifies, ideas
confuse. Or so we are told.

But reducing the debates of the 1970s to mere personality
clashes, however dramatic, banishes confusion at the risk of
introducing obfuscation. Trudeau and Lévesque *were* powerful
personalities and ambitious men. One had been a television
star, the other an accomplished athlete. Each, doubtless,
wanted to finish first in his chosen sport: politics. But each was
also a politician with fixed conclusions on an issue that went to
the very essence of the history and existence of the community
in which they were both deeply rooted. Neither Trudeau nor
Lévesque created an issue that divided them: it existed before
they came on the scene and lives after them. It can be simply
stated: "All we need to know is this: is it in the interests of

French-speaking Canadians to be a majority in a pluralist
Quebec state, or a minority in a pluralist Canadian state? That
is what the whole debate is about."[1]

Those are Trudeau's words, but Lévesque could easily have
uttered them. They agreed on the question; they disputed the
answer. Yet both were champions of the community Trudeau
called *francophones canadiens*, though Lévesque would have
used the term "French Quebeckers." The debate turned on that
nuance. It measured the gap between the federalist and the
nationalist and made it appropriate, though not necessary, that
both gladiators should be francophone Quebeckers. But the
nuance also created confusion for those who would have
preferred a simpler dichotomy: French against English,
Quebec against Canada. That Trudeau and Lévesque were
both francophone Quebeckers made that simplification
impossible. The confusion can be dispelled only by examining
the ideas they expounded.

As Canada's Centennial celebrations drew to a close in 1967,
two Quebec politicians published books setting out proposed
courses for the future of Canada, French Canada and Quebec.
Le Fédéralisme et la Société canadienne-française appeared just
as Expo '67 was closing its doors on the Ile Ste-Hélène in
Montreal. Its author, Pierre Elliott Trudeau, was the federal
minister of justice, a post which included responsibility for
tending Canada's Constitution. A politician of only two years'
experience, he was just beginning to develop a public profile.
Long known among Quebec intellectuals—and by a few in
English Canada—as a brilliant lawyer, political writer and one
of the founders of the little magazine *Cité libre*, he seemed
always out of step with the dominant views of his province's
leaders and, by 1967, increasingly so. In English Canada he was
hardly known at all except as something of a nonconformist
bachelor who had coined the aphorism that the state had no
place in the bedrooms of the nation.

Trudeau's book, a series of essays and documented polemics,
had been written over a period stretching from 1957 to 1964.
The essays were devoted to analyzing Canadian federalism and
the place of French Canadians in that system. The focus was on
Quebec. The earliest articles were critical of the centralizing
tendencies of Ottawa and of those French Canadians—usually

on the left—who supported that tendency. The later essays were sharp, even shrill, assaults on those French Quebeckers who, by the early 1960s, had taken up various versions of the slogan, *Québec d'abord*. A book of this sort with chapter headings like "De libro, tributo ... et quibusdam aliis" and "Federalism, Nationalism and Reason," was hardly, at least in normal times, expected to hit the bestseller list. But in fact the book, and the English version which appeared early in 1968, was soon on that list (though not all buyers were readers), and Trudeau was launched on a trajectory that would make him prime minister of Canada for over a decade and a half.

The author of the second book, this one entitled *Option Québec*, whose sales in French and English were also brisk, was much better known both inside and outside Quebec. René Lévesque, former journalist and television *vedette*, had joined Jean Lesage's *équipe du tonnerre* in 1960 and played a leading part in launching the Quiet Revolution. As minister of natural resources, he had led a successful campaign in 1962 to bring the last eleven privately owned power companies into the publicly owned Hydro-Québec. Later, as minister of family and social affairs, he had continued the building of the Quebec *État-providence*. But he also acquired the reputation of being a loose cannon on the deck of the Quebec ship of state. And as that ship heaved through the sometimes heavy waves aroused by fundamental reforms in education, the economy, labour laws, the civil service and social policy, Lévesque became increasingly, if unsystematically, critical of the federal system. He also became more openly nationalist in his outlook and discovered that nationalist rhetoric was effective in mobilizing popular support for government measures. In 1963 he defined "nation" as "a group of men of the same cultural family with a place on the map," and went on to say that "nationalism" had to be used to overcome the "economic sickness" of Quebec. "The question," he said, "is to use it as much as possible, because no one is ever sure of controlling it, no one can actually control this force."[2] Hydro nationalization, in Lévesque's hands, was not merely an economic measure, rather it was a step toward French Quebeckers becoming masters in their own house.[3]

While Lévesque's frequent jabs at Ottawa and at the "Rhodesians of Westmount" (the English Canadian establishment in Quebec) made him something of a hero among French Canadians, especially with the student population where nationalism had witnessed a new birth,[4] they also jarred English Canadian complacency. In 1963 he bluntly told an English Canadian television audience that "I am a Quebecker first, a French Canadian second . . . and I really have . . . well, no sense at all of being a Canadian."[5] His use of terms revealed a lot—being a "French Canadian" apparently meant being a French-speaking Quebecker, not a French-speaking Canadian. But those implications, and others, were only gradually becoming clear.

Lévesque's remarks—he rarely used prepared texts—were those of a man who, in contrast to the more academic approach of Pierre Trudeau, thought as he acted, or better, talked as he thought. As a radio and television journalist by trade, Lévesque was more at home with the spoken word than the written word. (At one of their early meetings Trudeau, waiting for Lévesque to finish a promised article for *Cité libre*, had snapped, "Say, Lévesque, you talk damn well, but I'm beginning to wonder if you can write at all." "Write . . . write . . . ," Lévesque replied, "first I've got to have the time. . . ." And Trudeau shot back, "And something to say."[6]) Of course, Lévesque would prove to have lots to say, but he reacted more than he analyzed. He was always a man of action, where Trudeau, at least until 1965, was an intellectual, one whose critics claimed was nothing but a dilettante in a Mercedes. Lévesque's book, *Option Québec*, was characteristic: it was not really a book at all, but rather a compilation of newspaper articles, government documents, snippets of speeches written and spoken by a variety of people. Lévesque's *imprimatur* was on it, since he had led the group of former Liberals and bureaucrats out of Lesage's Liberal party in the fall of 1967. He made the founding of the *mouvement souveraineté-association* possible. He would be the leader of the Parti québécois when it was established in 1968.

During the 1950s Trudeau and Lévesque had become casual acquaintances. Lévesque's work and interests had concentrated on international affairs—his program *Point de mire* had brought the world's events into hundreds of thousands of Quebec living rooms. Trudeau, whose wealth made permanent employment unnecessary and whose liberal views kept him out of regular academic life, concentrated his attention on Quebec, though foreign travel and international affairs also appealed to him. But Quebec politics and the trade union movement absorbed much of his time.

The events of the 1960s drew Lévesque and Trudeau into closer touch. Trudeau was part of a small group of intellectuals who met fairly regularly with Lévesque, now a minister, who used them as a sounding board for ideas he hoped to advance in Cabinet. Obviously, the two men were fascinated by each other, but each had reservations. In his marvellous memoir, *Les Années d'impatience 1950–1960*, Gérard Pelletier provides a revealing glimpse of the two men. Trudeau, he writes, admired

> René's vitality, his lively intelligence, his aptly chosen words, his unexpected turns of thought, his imagination, the quirkiness of his learning, his extensive knowledge of history and astonishing memory for the smallest items of news — all this left Trudeau breathless.... I suspected him at the time of thinking privately that a journalist's background, combined with a star temperament, could only produce a tainted or at least dubious political philosophy.

As for Lévesque, he

> could not help having a deep respect for the other's intelligence.... Trudeau's political erudition clearly impressed him.... For Lévesque, Trudeau embodied the scholar type, whose profound, authoritative knowledge he envied, but also the ivory tower intellectual, insensitive to certain realities, whose facetious brand of humour irritated him exceedingly.[7]

These attitudes, doubtless hardened and occasionally touched with anger, remained constant after Trudeau entered federal politics in 1965 intending to defend the federal system (Lévesque, interestingly, had urged Jean Marchand not to go alone to Ottawa but to take his two "*copains*" with him)[8] — and after Lévesque moved to establish a political party whose goal

was to destroy that system. At that point in 1968, Trudeau and
Lévesque agreed on at least two fundamental propositions. The
first was that Quebec's future had to be settled democratically.
Each man believed profoundly in the sovereignty of the people.
Secondly, they agreed that the time of choice, individual and
collective, was fast arriving. What that meant was that each had
concluded that the fuzzy, rhetorical debates about Quebec's
place in Canada that had consumed so much energy for the
previous decade, were futile. The proposed panaceas—*une
province pas comme les autres*, a particular status, a special
status (today we call it "distinct society")—all missed the point.
French Canadians would either be equal partners in a federal
system that gave full guarantees to their rights throughout
Canada or they would achieve equality through the establishment of a sovereign state. Special status, Trudeau and
Lévesque agreed, was neither fish nor fowl.

By 1968 Trudeau's option had been worked out systematically and tested in numerous intellectual jousts. The essence of
his position was contained in a paragraph which formed part
of a bitingly sarcastic attack on the early proponents of
separatism. In "La Nouvelle Trahison des clercs," published in
1962, he declared:

> The die is cast in Canada: there are two main ethnic and
> linguistic groups; each is too strongly and too deeply
> rooted in the past, too firmly bound to a mother culture, to
> be able to engulf the other. But if the two will collaborate
> at the hub of a truly pluralistic state, Canada will become
> the envied seat of a form of federalism that belongs to
> tomorrow's world. Better than the American melting pot,
> Canada could offer an example to all those new Asian and
> African states . . . who must discover how to govern their
> polyethnic populations with proper regard for justice and
> liberty. What better reason for cold-shouldering the lure
> of annexation to the United States?[9]

If Trudeau's option was intellectually elegant and idealistic,
Lévesque's option carried a powerful emotional resonance. His
book began, "*Nous sommes des Québécois*," and went on to
explain:

What that means first and foremost—if need be, all that it means—is that we are attached to this one corner of the earth where we can be completely ourselves; this Quebec where we have the unmistakable feeling that here we can really be at home. . . .

At the core of this personality is the fact that we speak French. Everything else depends on this essential element and follows from it or leads infallibly back to it.[10]

Where Lévesque had once described himself as a *Quebecker* and a *French Canadian*, the second designation had now disappeared: he was a *Québécois*. Early in 1969 he told a reporter that "I've never had any feeling of being Canadian, but I've always had an incredibly strong sense of being North American. The place where I'm most at home outside Quebec is the United States."[11] Trudeau and Lévesque differed not only about Canada; they felt quite differently about the United States.

The origins of Lévesque's nationalism and his gradual transition into an *indépendantiste* are difficult to trace in detail. Nor do his published memoirs help much. But like many young French Canadians, he was introduced to nationalist sentiments at school, and living side-by-side with the English in New Carlisle may have made him a ready subject. At seventeen he wrote in the student newspaper at the Collège des Jésuites in Quebec City that "French Canada will be what French Canadians deserve,"[12] sentiments remarkably like those held by Pierre Trudeau. He learned some Canadian history, and like all Quebec nationalists came to see the Conquest of 1759 as both the source of Quebec's inferiority and the historical event that needed undoing. In later years he recalled his admiration for Abbé Groulx's novel, *L'Appel de la race*, the story of the break-up of a mixed marriage which symbolized Confederation.[13] But action, not theory, always attracted Lévesque, and he drew his general conclusions from personal experience. As a journalist who had devoted most of his attention to international events, his mind was turned to Canadian affairs by a strike of French-language Radio-Canada producers in 1959. He joined that strike as a sympathizer and soon came to share the frustration of the producers at the failure of the federal government to step in and settle the dispute in the publicly owned network. Lévesque concluded that nothing of the kind would have been allowed to happen in the English network. "Of such signal advantages," he told the Montreal *Gazette*, "is the privilege of being French made up in this country. And even at the risk of being termed 'horrid nationalists,' we feel that at least once before the conflict is over, we have to make plain our deep appreciation of such an enviable place in the great bilingual, bicultural and fraternal Canadian sun."[14] Here was an expression of that minority sensitivity that would lead to the idea of independence.

Lévesque's years in the Lesage government made him increasingly impatient with what he believed to be the intransigence of the English-speaking business elite in Quebec and the rigidity of the Canadian federal system. In these years, when French Canadian representation at Ottawa under John Diefenbaker's Conservatives and in the early Pearson years was ineffective, Lévesque became convinced that Quebeckers were ready to run their own affairs. "Now that our new generations are bringing us more and more proficiency every year," he observed in 1967, "there is no reason which can, which should prevent Quebec from realizing that thing that's been kicking around in our collective back room for the last two hundred years, which is to get our chance to make our own way as a society."[15]

The term which Lévesque preferred to use to describe the option he chose by 1967 and which he would defend so ably and determinedly until his departure from office in 1985, was not "nationalist" or "separatist." Even *indépendantiste*, though he used it, was less preferred than *souverainiste*. And that was important. Though Lévesque never felt "Canadian," he never proposed complete separation from English Canada. Instead, he favoured a continuing economic association within a structure where each "nation" would be equal, despite differences of size. He once called it "sovereignty-cum-association," and that position revealed his moderation, even conservatism. For all his rhetoric about "colonialism" and "Westmount Rhodesians," Lévesque knew that Quebec and Quebeckers were neither oppressed in the manner known in the colonial world, nor did Francophones hate Anglophones in any systematic way. As he wrote in 1976, "undoubtedly French Quebec was (and remains to this day) the least ill-treated of all colonies in the world."[16] Hardly the language of a firebrand nationalist. Moreover, it should be added that René Lévesque, for all of his suspicions of the Anglophone minority in Quebec, consistently defended that minority's right to the use of its language, though not as an equal right with French. This was not always a popular view in his party.

The Lévesque vision of Canada, if he can be said to have had one, was based on a view of what was convenient, necessary and practical. For him, that had to be a relationship between equal nations. In that vision Quebec was central, Quebec was first. In preparation for the 1980 referendum, the Parti québécois issued a program whose title summed up the objective: *D'égal à égal*.

For Trudeau, too, Quebec was central. Though perhaps the most clear-headed defender of federalism in our history, Pierre Trudeau was French Canadian from Quebec. Before he entered politics, his writings were almost exclusively about Quebec. His goal was to help rid his province of the reactionary, paternalistic, nationalist régime of Maurice Duplessis, and the road to that goal, as he saw it, was to educate Quebeckers in the values and uses of democracy. To those who cried *"Québec d'abord!*," he replied *"Démocratie d'abord!"* His brilliant essay entitled "Some Obstacles to Democracy in Quebec" and the popular articles published in *Vrai* and collected later in *Les Cheminements de la politique* (1970) were passionate pleas for democratization and attacks on the nationalism which he thought stood in its way. For him, the checks and balances of federalism provided desirable guarantees for pluralism and freedom.

. In his youth Pierre Trudeau may have been attracted to French Canadian nationalism. He campaigned in 1942 on behalf of a nationalist candidate named Jean Drapeau, who was an opponent of conscription for overseas service. And in 1944, at age twenty-four, after a long canoe trip in the Canadian North, he wrote a lyrical essay entitled "L'ascéti- cisme en canot" ("Asceticism in a Canoe"), which concluded: ". . . I know a man who had never learned 'nationalism' in school, but who contracted this virtue when he felt the immensity of his country in his bones, and saw how great his country's creators had been."[17]

This "nationalism" was not connected with ethnicity, but rather with a sense of place and pride in ancestral achievement. That perhaps explains why he altered the word to "patriotism" when it was translated into English a quarter of a century later.[18]

If René Lévesque's political baptism during the 1959 Radio-Canada producers' strike led him to a nationalist conclusion, Pierre Trudeau's first association with the Quebec working class resulted in a quite different analysis. In the spring of 1949 Trudeau travelled to Thetford Mines with his friend, the labour journalist Gérard Pelletier. There he met Jean Marchand, the secretary-general of the Confédération des travailleurs catholiques du Canada, who was leading an illegal strike in the asbestos industry. Trudeau addressed the workers, joined the pickets and concluded that the union movement represented the best hope for the future of democracy in Quebec. In that strike he witnessed an alliance between an American-owned corporation and the nationalist government of Quebec, an alliance sanctioned by many of the leaders of the Roman Catholic Church and which was devoted to crushing a French Canadian workers' organization. This reactionary provincial government promoted a narrow ideology founded on "clericalism, agriculturalism and paternalism toward the workers,"[19] an ideology utterly out of tune with the dominant industrial order of Quebec. That ideology and the institutions which promoted it, Trudeau concluded, had to be undermined.

In the years after the asbestos strike, when Trudeau worked as a legal advisor to various union movements, his conviction that nationalism was a primary obstacle to French Canadian progress hardened into an unshakable conviction, one that he would never change. In his lengthy polemical introduction to a collection of essays entitled La Grève de l'amiante, he set out to dismantle traditional social and nationalist thought and to call upon his contemporaries to replace a priori nationalist idealism with a hard-headed empirical approach to Quebec's social realities. He concluded: "An entire generation is hesitating at the brink of commitment. May this book provide elements to enlighten its choice."[20] Thus he was dubbed an "antinationalist" and, unlike some of his comrades in the fight against Duplessis who later found the "reform" nationalism of the 1960s appealing, Trudeau maintained that stance, and, if anything, intensified and clarified it in the battle against the so-called "new nationalism." In 1964 he and six other intellectuals – all younger than Trudeau – set out their answer to the "national question" which was once more consuming so much energy. In their "Manifeste pour une politique fonctionnelle," published in *Cité libre* and *The Canadian Forum*, they proclaimed:

> In the present political context, what matters is to put the emphasis back on the individual, regardless of what his ethnicity, geography or religion happens to be. The social and political order must be founded primarily on the universal attributes of man, not on what makes him different. A set of political and social priorities based on the individual is totally incompatible with an order of priorities based on race, religion or nationality.[21]

Thus by the time he chose to plunge into federal politics in 1965, he had become a fierce critic of nationalism – though he never denied the existence or value of nations. He had also become a proponent of Actonian ethnic pluralism as the soundest basis for a liberal democracy. By working to strengthen federal representation from Quebec in Ottawa, the balance could be restored to a situation in which Quebec, under Lesage's Liberals, appeared to be pulling itself, step by step, out of Confederation. Moreover, since he and his friends believed that nationalism in Quebec was the product of the failure of Canadian federalism to provide enough space for French Canadians to exercise their rights, that space would have to be made by reforming federalism, not by seceding from Canada. "The most effective way to cure nationalist alienation would probably be to put in a better kind of government," he explained to his somewhat unhappy readers of *Cité libre*. As Dorval Brunelle has put it so exactly, the goal was twofold: "against both French Canadian nationalism and passive federalism."[22]

Separation, independence, sovereignty – all these, in Trudeau's view, meant the identification of state and nation, an inward-turning by French Canadians and, at least in the worst case scenarios implied in some of the early separatist writings, a return to the reactionary society of pre-1960. This was counter-revolution, a return to what he disdainfully called "the wigwam complex."[23] Where Lévesque accepted nationalism as a positive sentiment that could energize reform, Trudeau believed that nationalism based on ethnic homogeneity was negative, bound in the end to stifle reform. Actonian pluralism, a state in which ethnic distinctions balanced each other and were accepted as positive virtues, guarantees of liberty, was Trudeau's ideal; that stood at the heart of his political ideas, and the basis of his vision of Canada. And it was the point on which he and René Lévesque differed irreconcilably.

Well before the *trois colombes* – the labour leader Jean Marchand, the journalist Gérard Pelletier and Trudeau – set off for Ottawa, Trudeau had set out explicitly the conditions that were necessary if his gamble was to succeed. There were two conditions for successful federalism:

> First, French Canadians must really want it; that is to say, they must abandon their role of oppressed nation and decide to participate boldly and intelligently in the Canadian experience. . . . The second condition is that the dice not be loaded against French Canadians in the "Confederation game." This means that if French Canadians abandon their concept of a national state, English Canadians must do the same. We must not find Toronto, or Fredericton, or above all, Ottawa exalting the *English* Canadian nation . . .[24]

Thirty months after his decision to join the Liberals – they were not sure they wanted him at first – and work in Ottawa, Pierre Trudeau was prime minister of Canada. At about that same time his old associate, René Lévesque, no longer a Cabinet minister, began to build a new political party devoted to his ideas and his leadership. His ascent to power was almost as spectacular as that of Trudeau: on November 15, 1976, his party was elected on its third attempt. ("We're not a minor people," he told his joyous supporters that night, "we're maybe something like a great people.")[25] The road to sovereignty-association had opened up. The stage was set for the final act in the great debate about Quebec's future and Canada's future. It would last six years, include the defeat and resurrection of Pierre Trudeau and then the referendum. On May 20, 1980, Quebec voters, by a sixty/forty split, rejected Lévesque's request for permission to begin negotiations on the sovereignty-association question. Trudeau now moved to patriate the Canadian constitution, complete with a new charter of rights and freedoms and an amending formula. Lévesque, on behalf of his province, rejected that constitution, demonstrating that the referendum had not ended the debate.

When Pierre Trudeau left office in 1984, he knew that while Lévesque had lost, he himself had not won—at least not unconditionally. Speaking at Laval University in the spring of 1984 he once again defended his conception of Canadian federalism. In closing, he admitted that there was still much work to be done to harmonize the several "little homelands" with "the bigger homeland." He continued:

> Our Canadian attachment will probably always be more distant, less deeply rooted in the soil than our attachments as Quebeckers, Newfoundlanders or Albertans. But, exactly for this reason, we must make sure our institutions can embody our collective will to live and instill it in the minds of all Canadians, and in the minds of foreigners wishing to do business and build a better world with us.[26]

In 1962, Hubert Aquin, who would soon be recognized as one of Quebec's finest novelists, explained to his fellow Quebec nationalists that while hostility to English Canadians was at the root of the quest for independence, the English were not the essential problem. "It's the French Canadians we have to fight," he explained.[27] That was a shrewd judgment. Indeed, it is the key to understanding the history of Quebec and of Canada between 1960 and 1980.

Pierre Trudeau and René Lévesque: two Quebeckers devoted to the survival and full flowering of a modern French-speaking society. In Lévesque's view that could be achieved only if his "minor people" became a "great people":

sovereignty for Quebec. Trudeau believed that the future of his "little homeland" would best be guaranteed through participation in the "bigger homeland," a federal system built on equality between French- and English-speaking Canadians throughout Canada. For the *francophone canadien*, Trudeau, Canada was central; for the *Québécois*, Lévesque, Canada was marginal—at best. Nevertheless, both leaders, Trudeau and Lévesque, were, in Gérard Bergeron's happy phrase, "our two-sided mirror"—both reflections of the same community.[28]

On the evening of November 15, 1976, following the Parti québécois's stunning victory in that day's election, René Lévesque, in a state of barely controlled emotion, told his supporters: "I never thought I could be as proud to be a Quebecker as I am tonight."

On the evening of May 20, 1980, following the victory of the federalist option in the Quebec referendum, Pierre Elliott Trudeau, his reason only just controlling his passion, confessed: "I never thought I could be as proud to be a Quebecker and a Canadian as I am tonight . . . "[29]

The parallel was intentional; the summary perfect.

——————— PART VII ———————

The Values of a Just Society

——————— by Pierre Elliott Trudeau ———————

translated by Patricia Claxton

Pierre Elliott Trudeau joined the staff of the office of the Privy Council in Ottawa in 1949. In 1952 he returned to Montreal, where he practised law, specializing in labour law and civil liberties, and from 1961, he taught constitutional law at the University of Montreal. During this time he co-founded the magazine Cité libre. *Elected to the Parliament of Canada for the riding of Mount Royal in 1965, he became prime minister in 1968. On his retirement from politics in 1984, he joined the firm of Heenan Blaikie in Montreal as counsel.*

The Values

I have long believed that freedom is the most important value of a just society, and the exercise of freedom its principal characteristic. Without these, a human being could not hope for true fulfilment – an individual in society could not realize his or her full potential. And deprived of its freedom, a people could not pursue its own destiny – the destiny that best suits its collective will to live.

That is why, in June 1950, my friends and I gave the name *Cité libre* to the magazine that served to express our views of the

Quebec society in which we were beginning our adult lives. A few years later, our younger counterparts founded their own magazine, which they named *Liberté*.

At that time the province of Quebec was still under the heel of a reactionary and authoritarian government, and the politically powerful Catholic clergy in Quebec was theocratic and obscurantist. Meanwhile, most of our secular leaders, those who smugly considered themselves to be "the élite," were quite content with a "people" accustomed to submission and ignorance. Gérard Pelletier gives an excellent description of this period of our history in *Years of Impatience*.[1] Impatience was also plain to see in my early articles in *Cité libre*. And in 1947 I had defined progress as "civilization's slow march toward freedom."[2]

However, shortly before my friends and I decided to enter politics, all this had changed, and Quebec had entered a period of contestation. Civil institutions were being shaken to their foundations by the Quiet Revolution. The Church was in great disarray, almost a state of rout. Universities were teaching relativism, even Marxism. The family was slowly disintegrating. And youth was challenging authority in all forms.

Elsewhere in the world, decolonization was proceeding apace, except in the case of France, which, since the Thermidorean reaction to the Revolution, has often been quicker to preach freedom for others than to accept it for its own colonies.

At a time like this, what led me to enter politics was not a desire to fight for freedom; in a way, that was already yesterday's battle. In my thinking, the value with the highest priority in the pursuit of a Just Society had become equality. Not the procrustean kind of equality where everyone is raised or lowered to a kind of middle ground. I mean equality of opportunity.

For where is the justice in a country in which an individual has the freedom to be totally fulfilled, but where inequality denies him the means? And how can we call a society just unless it is organized in such a way as to give each his due, regardless of his state of birth, his means or his health?

A child's notion of injustice relates mostly to his own experience—like the punishment he never deserved. . . . But in adolescence he becomes a social creature, more conscious of the injustice of disparities in people's conditions. This is the age when a young person's idealism may lean toward socialistic thinking and many experiment with egalitarian practices in the form of community living, shoe-string travel, volunteer work among the disadvantaged and so on.

Anatole France rightly poked fun at the law which, with majestic impartiality, denied the rich as well as the poor the right to sleep under bridges. Saint-Exupéry saw how profoundly wretched is a society in which hardship prevents a gifted child from becoming another Mozart. Throughout history, Utopians have recognized the worth of distributive justice in the ideally organized society.

But when active politics gave me a way to bring a larger measure of justice to the organization of the state, I recall that I found the most useful thinking to be that underlying the liberal philosophies of Lord Acton, T. H. Green and Jacques Maritain.[3]

Canada seemed to me to be an ideal country for a policy of greater equality of opportunity. A young country, a rich country, a country of two languages, of ethnic and religious plurality and of federative structure, Canada also possessed a political tradition that was neither entirely libertarian nor entirely socialist, but rested on an indispensable partnership between government and the private sector, and on direct action by the state to protect the weak from the strong, the disadvantaged from the well-heeled.

This was what was uppermost in my mind on the night of my election as leader of the Liberal party, when I proclaimed our intention to work for a "Just Society." But where should we begin? The choice was vast.

As I remember, the dominant theme of the election campaign in the spring of 1968—a strong and united Canada founded on a policy of equal opportunity for all—was the one I approached with the greatest conviction and the one to which others responded with the greatest enthusiasm. There were many facets to this policy, to be sure, which I would bring out in response to the occasion—or to hecklers. Yes, we would introduce a tax on capital gains; yes, we would implement medicare; yes, we would reform the penal code; yes, we would update our international policies; yes to anything that would make us more free and more equal. . . .

However, without a doubt, the two main facets of the policy lay in equality of opportunity for all Canadians regardless of the economic region in which they lived, and regardless of the language that they spoke—French or English. In Chapter 8, Gérard Pelletier discusses how, from the beginning of our mandate, the Official Languages Act attempted to rectify the inequalities with which French-speaking Canadians had been confronted ever since 1867 in their communications with the Canadian government and as its employees. And in Chapter 10, Lloyd Axworthy shows how the Department of Regional Economic Expansion, established by Jean Marchand in April 1969, tried to improve the lot of Canadians living in economically disadvantaged regions.

It is important to stress that these two goals—equality of French with English and equality of economic opportunity wherever one lived—were conducive to a conception of the country as a place in which all Canadians were working together to make it strong and united. It would even be correct to say that these goals were the spearheads of our political action at a moment in Canadian history when the centrifugal forces were more potent than the centripetal, and were threatening to break the country apart.

The Constitution Act of 1982

To explain why we were entering federal politics, Gérard Pelletier and I wrote in Cité libre[4] that, since the Quiet Revolution of 1960, "Quebeckers have turned increasingly toward the provincial sphere . . . [; they] continue to be governed by Ottawa, but they are less and less present there, intellectually, psychologically, and even physically. . . . The course of federal affairs, if it continues in the same climate as in recent years, may shortly have detrimental results for the political union of Canada."

I believed in federalism as a superior form of government; by definition, it is more pluralist than monolithic and therefore respects diversity among people and groups. In general, freedom has a firmer foundation under federalism.

Small wonder that I should choose the federal cause at this particular point in our history. In the past, I had sometimes sided with the provinces against the central government, sometimes with the central government against the provinces, whichever was the opposite of the way the political scales were tipping, creating dangerous imbalances. About this time I wrote, "My political action, or my theory–insomuch as I can be said to have one–can be expressed very simply: create counterweights."[5]

While on this subject, it is amusing to note in passing that the political thinking of the nationalist intelligentsia in Quebec–that is, the kind that thrives on slogans and clichés–has always regarded me as a hard-eyed centralizer, whereas in fact I led the only government since Confederation that has ever given the provinces legislative power that previously belonged to the federal Parliament (Section 92A as adopted in the Constitution Act of 1982), and while I was prime minister, public finances evolved steadily toward decentralization of revenues and expenditures. (See the introduction to Part IV of this book and Jean Chrétien, Chapter 12.)

I shall therefore briefly examine what I referred to above as the centrifugal forces that were threatening to break the federation apart, and then describe how the Canadian government tried to counterbalance those forces between 1968 and 1984 by implementing policies whose goal was to create a Just Society.

On the one hand, the Quiet Revolution and its effects had transformed the province of Quebec into a modern society in which francophones were at last feeling capable of handling the political, economic and cultural challenges inherent on a predominantly English-speaking continent. In Quebec, however, the political classes seemed increasingly to be bent on emphasizing the defence of French Quebec rather than the advancement of *all* Quebeckers and of francophones in other provinces. Hence the infatuation of Quebec politicians with all those turns of phrase that imply a loosening of federal ties: special status, distinct society, equality or independence, sovereignty-association.

On the other hand, the provinces as a whole had progressed enormously since the end of the Second World War. Once freed of the tutelage made necessary by a wartime economy, they had moved massively into those economic and social spheres of jurisdiction to which they had previously attached little importance. The result was that, between 1954 and 1964, while at the federal level final expenditures rose from $4.2 billion to $6.6 billion (a 57 percent increase), expenditures by provincial and municipal governments rose from $2.6 billion to $8.1 billion (an increase of 211 percent).[6]

Furthermore, these rapid budgetary changes had been facilitated by successive federal governments through transfers of income tax points. It gave the provinces a painless way of tapping financial sources previously reserved for the federal government (see Tommy Shoyama, Chapter 9).

But the feast had only made the provinces hungrier. Having outstripped the federal government in budgetary resources, they began looking for ways to outstrip it in constitutional jurisdictions as well.

At the urging of Daniel Johnson's Quebec government, Premier John Roberts of Ontario called a constitutional conference in November 1967; the Quebec government's express purpose in calling for the meeting was to discuss a broadening of provincial powers. The federal government, which the provinces condescended to invite, chose simply to send observers. But now that the constitutional ball was beginning, we would have to join in the dance.

The momentum was such that from 1967 to 1971, then from 1975 until the repatriation of the Constitution in 1982, the federal and provincial governments discussed the constitution interminably. Jean Chrétien leads us through this labyrinth in Chapter 12. All I intend to do here is highlight some facts that are central to my subject.

The Constitution Act of 1982 was proclaimed on April 17. Essentially, it enshrined the values which, back in 1968, I had defined as those that should be respected in the constitution of a Just Society.

First, the principle of equal economic opportunity was stated in Section 36(1), under which "the government of Canada and the provincial governments undertake to promote equal opportunities for the well-being of all Canadians," and in

Section 36(2), which guarantees the principle of equalization
payments for the redistribution of revenues from wealthy
provinces to the less wealthy ones. Further, Section 6 gives all
Canadians the right to take up residence and earn their living
anywhere in the country. And, of course, the federal government
did not give up the powers it possessed under the old constitution
concerning redistribution of wealth through subsidies and fiscal
measures as well as through its general spending powers.
(Jacques Hébert and Jim Coutts, in chapters 5 and 7, recall the
many ways in which these powers were exercised for the
promotion of equal economic opportunities.)

Secondly, the principle of equality of French and English in
all domains of federal jurisdiction and in New Brunswick was
guaranteed by Sections 16 to 20, while Section 23 guaranteed
francophones and anglophones the right to education in their
own language anywhere in Canada.

But the Canadian Charter of Rights and Freedoms went
much further, of course. In the grand tradition of the 1789
Declaration of the Rights of Man and the Citizen and the 1791
Bill of Rights of the United States of America, it implicitly
established the primacy of the individual over the state and all
government institutions, and in so doing, recognized that all
sovereignty resides in the people. (Provincial charters of rights
cannot have this effect because they are simply laws and can be
abrogated at any time merely through further legislation.) In
this respect, the Canadian Charter was a new beginning for the
Canadian nation: it sought to strengthen the country's unity by
basing the sovereignty of the Canadian people on a set of values
common to all, and in particular on the notion of equality
among all Canadians.

Clearly, the very adoption of a constitutional charter is in
keeping with the purest liberalism, according to which all
members of a civil society enjoy certain fundamental,
inalienable rights[7] and cannot be deprived of them by any
collectivity (state or government) or on behalf of any
collectivity (nation, ethnic group, religious group or other). To
use Maritain's phrase, they are "human personalities," they are
beings of a moral order—that is, free and equal among
themselves, each having absolute dignity and infinite value. As

such, they transcend the accidents of place and time, and partake in the essence of universal Humanity. They are therefore not coercible by any ancestral tradition, being vassals neither to their race, nor to their religion, nor to their condition of birth, nor to their collective history.

It follows that only the individual is the possessor of rights. A collectivity can exercise only those rights it has received by delegation from its members; it holds them in trust, so to speak, and on certain conditions.[8] Thus, the state, which is the supreme collectivity for a given territory, and the organs of the state, which are the governments, legislatures and courts, are limited in the exercise of their functions by the Charter and the Constitution in which the Charter is enshrined.

Indeed, the Charter specifies that the governments must meet Parliament or the legislatures at least once a year (Section 5); that Parliament and the legislatures must hold elections at least every five years (Section 4); and that the courts may act only "in accordance with the principles of fundamental justice" (Sections 7 to 14).

___ The Role of the Charter _____

Thus, the individual is protected from the arbitrary authority of the state. But within a federal or provincial state, individuals may gather together in ethnic, linguistic, religious, professional, political or other collectivities, and delegate to this or that collectivity the task of promoting their collective interests. And since, in a democracy, governments receive their powers from the people by majority vote at elections, what is to prevent a majority from riding roughshod over the rights of a minority?

The answer, of course, is the Charter of Rights and Freedoms and the Constitution. They do this generally, by enshrining the rights of the individual members within minorities; but in certain instances, where the rights of individuals may be indistinct and difficult to define, they also enshrine some collective rights of minorities.

For example, the Canadian Constitution of 1867 provided that in educational matters, Section 93(1) would protect any "*Class* of Persons ... with respect to Denominational

Schools," and Section 93(3) would apply to the "Protestant or Roman Catholic Minority."

Similarly, the Charter has clauses to protect certain minority collectivities whose interests could be overlooked in the conduct of the business of the state; this is what Sections 25 and 35 do for "the aboriginal peoples of Canada," and Section 27 for "the preservation and enhancement of the multicultural heritage of Canadians."

Section 93(2) of the 1867 Constitution, on the other hand, addresses individuals as such, in order to protect them: "Protestant and Roman Catholic *Subjects*." Likewise, Section 133 (language before the legislatures and courts) protects "*any Person*."

Except in the two cases I mentioned in the next-to-last paragraph, the Charter always seeks to define rights exclusively as belonging to a person rather than a collectivity: "everyone" (Sections 2, 7, 8, 9, 10, 12, 13), "every citizen of Canada" (Sections 3, 6), "any person charged with an offence" (Section 11), "any party or witness" (Section 14), "every individual" (Section 15), "anyone" (Section 24). It should be noted that this preference holds good even where the official languages are concerned; individuals, not linguistic groups, are ensured of their right to use either language: "everyone" (Section 17), "any person" (Section 19), "any member of the public" (Section 20), "citizens of Canada" (Section 23).

It is clear, then, that the spirit and substance of the Charter is to protect the individual against tyranny—not only that of the state but also any other to which the individual may be subjected by virtue of his belonging to a minority group. Section 15 of the Charter leaves no doubt: all are equal before the law and are entitled to the same protection "without discrimination based on race, national or ethnic origin, colour, religion, sex, age or mental or physical disability."

The reason for this approach is evident. Canada is by nature pluralist—"a mosaic" as Laurier put it—not an American-style melting pot. The Canadian nation is composed of citizens who belong to minorities of many kinds: linguistic, ethnic, racial, religious, regional and so on. Throughout the negotiations leading to the Charter in 1982, our government kept in mind that Canadian history has consisted of a difficult advance toward a national unity that is still fragile and is often threatened by intolerance—the intolerance of the English-speaking majority toward francophones, the intolerance of whites toward the indigenous populations and non-white immigrants, intolerance toward political and religious dissidents such as Communists and Jehovah's Witnesses.

If we had tried to identify each of the minorities in Canada in order to protect all the characteristics that made them different, not only would we have been faced with an impossible task, but we would shortly have been presiding over the balkanization of Canada. The danger inherent in this would have been particularly acute in the case of minorities that are in a position to be identified with a given territory, like the Celts in Nova Scotia, the Acadians in New Brunswick, the French Canadians in Quebec and the Indians and Inuit in the Far North.

This is why Sections 25 and 37 on the aboriginal peoples and Section 27 on multiculturalism avoid any identification of these collectivities with a particular government. Thus, throughout our negotiations with the aboriginal peoples, we refused to talk about "self-determination," and only envisaged the possibility of "self-government" on condition that a heterogeneous population might still live in a given territory.

The case of the collectivity referred to as French Canadians demanded particularly close attention, since the tensions between anglophones and francophones have always been the major source of disunity in Canada. And we were very aware that Quebec nationalist thinking tends both to identify the interests of the French-Canadian collectivity with the province of Quebec and to confuse language with ethnicity, which gives rise to expressions like "the two founding nations of Canada" and "Quebec, the national state of French Canadians." Thus, on May 22, 1963, the Legislative Assembly of Quebec voted unanimously to give itself a mandate to determine "the objectives to be pursued by *French Canada* in the revision of the constitution of Canada, and the best means of obtaining these objectives."

At the time, I was opposed to this approach for several reasons, the most important being that "a state that defined its function essentially in terms of ethnic attributes would inevitably become chauvinistic and intolerant. The state, whether provincial, federal or perhaps later supra-national, must seek the general welfare of all its citizens regardless of sex, colour, race, religious beliefs, or ethnic origin."⁹

Shortly after I wrote this, my friends and I entered federal politics for the precise purpose of proving that French Canadians could be at home in Canada outside Quebec and could exercise their rights in the federal capital and throughout the country. This was also the purpose of the Official Languages Act and of the emergence of what the English-speaking press was soon calling "French power."

The separatists of both Quebec and the West well understood what was happening. Conscious that their ultimate goal presupposed an exclusively English-speaking Canada and an exclusively French-speaking Quebec, they abandoned their minorities in other provinces—French-speaking and English-speaking—and fought tooth and nail against the policy of bilingualism, which in their terms was the work of traitors and double-dealers.

As for the Quebec nationalists, the Quiet Revolution had given them the means to be full-fledged Canadians but also a desire to be not exactly Canadian. Now they were dancing a hesitation waltz, flitting from "special status" to "equality or independence"; from "cultural sovereignty" to "profitable federalism" (profitable or else . . .).

In answer to our federal law proclaiming English and French to be the official languages everywhere in Canada, Mr Bourassa saw fit to reply with a provincial law declaring that French alone would be the official language in Quebec—and he observed later that Quebec's self-determination was still an option in his party's platform.

Taking a stand in opposition to the federal policy of bilingualism meant shifting the political debate in Quebec to the only ground on which the separatist party had an advantage over Mr Bourassa. So, in 1976, a Péquiste government was elected and in due course held a referendum, in which that government asked for a mandate to make Quebec a sovereign country.

Two months after the federalist victory in the referendum, we presented the provinces with a draft charter that would embody a set of values common to all Canadians. Language rights were assigned directly to individuals rather than collectivities. And the reader will understand why, in the lengthy negotiations that followed, we rejected any proposal whose effect would have been to identify a linguistic collectivity (French Canadians) with the government of a province (Quebec).

What we were seeking was for the individual himself to have the *right* to demand his choice of French or English in his relationships with the federal government, and the *right* to demand a French or English education for his children from a provincial government. And the individual himself would have access to the courts to enforce these rights.

This is not to say that we were denying the importance of a linguistic community in the defence and advancement of the language spoken by its members. However, it seemed clear to us that these matters would never be settled unless the *individual* language rights of each person were enshrined in the constitution of the country, since the English-speaking community would always outnumber the French-speaking in Canada.

Our approach was indisputably more effective and more respectful of the dignity of Canadians. However, it made things awkward for Quebec nationalist politicians because it made them largely redundant; the moment the survival of "the race" no longer depended on them, their racist preachings became superfluous. So they fought the Charter with much sound and fury and racked their brains for some ploy that would allow Quebec to elude its authority. Years were to pass before they hit upon the "distinct society" formula for interpreting the Charter — and a Canadian prime minister ready to accept it.

But that is another story ...

___ The Charter: Strengths and Weaknesses ___

I have been talking about the Charter as the culmination of a political endeavour whose purpose was to strengthen Canadian unity through the pursuit of a Just Society based on freedom and equality, a pursuit which continued for sixteen long years.

It is not my intention to assess that endeavour here. Were I to try, I would often have to echo Saint Thomas Aquinas: "What comes first in intention comes last in execution." But a reader who has read all the chapters of this book and considered the facts should be able to make his own assessment. However, even he—"two-faced reader, so like me, my brother"[10]—is bound to encounter the insoluble problem: how would history have unfolded *if* another government had been in power during those years?

History cannot be judged by comparison with what might have been. All we can do is wonder if the players who made history found correct answers to the challenges presented by the unfolding of events.

So let us look at the record . . . In the preceding chapters the reader will have perceived a government fired by the will to bring about justice through equal opportunities; and having studied the various assessments, he may be able to weigh degrees of success and failure. But to a large extent all this happened *before* the Charter and without it; why, then, is a charter so important in a Just Society? And how can it guarantee both freedom and equality, since the unimpeded exercise of freedom by some will invariably lead to inequality for others? And then, is the Charter not nullified by its derogatory clause, the notorious "notwithstanding" clause? Most of all, how can the Charter strengthen Canadian unity when its pursuit has caused such discord?

The paradox is real: freedom for some is detrimental to the equality of others. And it has been the subject of many philosophical dissertations. In the present case, the problem is this: Section 2 of the Charter guarantees that "everyone has . . . [certain] fundamental freedoms"; how, then, can we prevent strong individuals from using their superior strength to create economic, social and institutional conditions in which the weak cannot find equal opportunities?

The reply is given partly by Section 36(1), according to which "the government of Canada and the provincial governments are committed to . . . promoting equal opportunities for the well-being of Canadians . . . [and] furthering economic development to reduce disparity in opportunities." Laws and policies devised to realize these objectives must apply equally

to all (Sections 15(1) and 28). And specifically to prevent the
wealthier or more numerous or more intelligent from abusing
their freedom, Section 15(2) is there to ensure that the principle
of equality before the law "does not preclude any law, program
or activity that has as its object the amelioration of conditions
of disadvantaged individuals or groups."

Here is where we come to the heart of the problem. Our
Charter exists to prevent abuses of power by governments or
people in positions of authority, so that individuals may find
fulfilment in freedom within the civil society. But its purpose is
not to make governments more intelligent or wiser, nor to
instill in them any particular ideology. That is left to the
representatives of the people and to those who elect them.

Our Charter, along with the Constitution, presupposes and
guarantees the exercise of democratic choice by the electors. It
is for them to elect governments that will bring in laws,
programs and activities whose object is "the amelioration of
conditions of disadvantaged individuals and groups" and the
furtherance of "economic development to reduce disparity in
opportunities" (Sections 15(2) and 36(1)(b)).

This is where Section 1 of the Charter proves important: it
enables governments to restrain freedoms "to such reasonable
limits prescribed by law as can be demonstrably justified in a
free and democratic society." Far from debasing the Charter,
as some have claimed, this clause resolves the dilemma I
mentioned above—namely, how can freedoms be restricted if
they are fundamental and inalienable? The answer is that they
can be restricted by recourse to Section 1 of the Charter,
precisely because, being fundamental, these freedoms must be
available to everyone. So the state may restrain the exercise of a
freedom by some if this exercise negates a freedom for others.
In other words, the state may limit one individual's freedom if
this is necessary (economically, socially, linguistically . . .) to
enable others to enjoy theirs. In this way, the concepts of
society and of the common good have a place in the application
of a Charter that is intrinsically centred on the freedom and
equality of individuals.

In other countries that have charters of rights, the courts
have had to assume the role played by Section 1 of our Charter,
taking the initiative to moderate by common sense the

interpretation of freedoms whose too literal application could have a ridiculous or even harmful effect. Oliver Wendell Holmes of the United States Supreme Court observed long ago that the freedom of speech guaranteed by Article 1 of the Bill of Rights does not entitle a person to shout "Fire!" in a crowded theatre.

Our Section 1 is better, in that it does not leave it entirely to the wisdom of judges to validate a law restricting freedom; it places the onus on whoever invokes such a law to show that the restraint is reasonable and justified in a free and democratic society. In other words, the lawmaker who wishes to restrain a freedom guaranteed by the Charter must be able to invoke the wisdom of nations, so to speak. The rule is not unlike that underlying the dogmas of Christianity: *quod semper, quod ubique, quod ab omnibus* . . .[11]

It is therefore wrong to pretend that the existence of a Charter is in contradiction with the supremacy of Parliament, and that it replaces the people's representatives with judges who are appointed for life. For Section 1 speaks of a "free and democratic society," which is to say, a society in which sovereignty belongs to the people. Also, the Charter itself is the work of parliamentarians; they have imposed restrictions on themselves (Sections 4 and 5) and on judges as well (Sections 7 to 14). There is nothing strange, therefore, about these same parliamentarians wanting to place limits on their power of derogation from fundamental freedoms and about recognizing that they themselves may be reminded of these limits when they attempt to restrain a fundamental freedom.

This leads me to talk about Section 33, which allows a lawmaker to pass a law limiting certain freedoms guaranteed by the Charter by simply declaring that the law will take effect notwithstanding Section 2 and Sections 7 to 15.

I must make it clear immediately that in my opinion this clause is in flagrant contradiction with the very essence and existence of the Charter. I know that many respectable jurists are perfectly comfortable with this "derogatory" clause, and justify it by the necessity of re-establishing the authority of laws made by the people's representatives over laws "made" by judges.

This is not the place to settle this debate. I shall add only that what I said a few paragraphs back about Sections 1 and 15(2) of the Charter explains clearly the extent to which I recognize that the authority of the lawmaker should prevail over those of the Charter and of judges. What I cannot accept is that such authority be made to prevail in a purely arbitrary way, in the manner of a dictate, as Section 33 allows.

All the malignancy of this clause came glaringly to light late in December 1988, when Premier Bourassa invoked it to validate Bill 178 forbidding the use of one of Canada's two official languages, and, to make matters worse, bragged about having trampled one of the country's fundamental freedoms.

It is useful to recall that the courts have used Section 1 many times to uphold measures limiting fundamental freedoms (even in Bill 101, which was introduced by the Péquiste government of Quebec to promote the French language). The judges have asked simply whether the law in question has been proven reasonable and justifiable. The fact is that the government of Mr Bourassa, not being able or willing to prove Bill 178 reasonable or justifiable, allowed itself to resort to a purely arbitrary act.

The government I led fought from 1968 to 1982 to incorporate the elements of a charter of rights and freedoms into the Canadian constitution without ever envisioning the possibility of including a derogatory clause. And Mr Chrétien, as minister of justice, fought to have our Charter accepted by provincial governments that were ferociously opposed to it. However, some of these governments (particularly the government of Saskatchewan under Mr Blakeney) declared themselves ready to accept a charter if it contained a derogatory clause. Also, the Château Consensus, drawn up by Quebec and presented by the group of ten provinces, had already raised the possibility of such a clause.

And so, in November 1981, I agreed to let the Charter be saddled with a derogatory clause rather than give up the idea of a charter altogether—on condition, however, that this clause not be usable to effect derogations from the principle of language equality (Sections 16 to 23)[12] or from the principle of equal economic opportunity (Sections 6 and 36), principles which were central to my political commitment in 1968.

It seemed clear to me that it would be infinitely more difficult to repatriate a constitution without a charter and then, some time in the future, amend it in order to incorporate a charter, than to repatriate a constitution complete with a charter containing a derogatory clause and then amend it some time in the future to set aside the derogatory clause.

So I agreed to accept the clause with a heavy heart, exhorting anyone willing to listen to put pressure on the provinces so that we might dispense with it in future negotiations. (In my opinion the abrogation of this clause would not need unanimous consent on the part of the provinces, although, of course, the matter is for the courts to decide.)

Alas, when the time came for those future negotiations, at Meech Lake in 1987, the shame was that enormous concessions were made to the provinces, but no demands were made for the abolition of the derogatory clause in return. And with consummate irresponsibility, the prime minister who claimed credit for a major constitutional victory at Meech Lake was the same man who had declared in the House of Commons that this very Constitution was not worth the paper it was written on because it contained a derogatory clause![13]

He might have thought of this before signing the Meech Lake Accord! In any event, the extravagance of his hyperbole is amply demonstrated by the fact that Canada's legal landscape has been radically transformed since the Constitution Act of 1982. Members of the Bar and the Judiciary were the first to understand the important new beginning in political and social reality announced by the Charter. And in October 1985, "Chief Justice Dickson declared ... that the Canadian Charter of Rights and Freedoms represent[ed] the greatest challenge in the history of the Supreme Court of Canada."[14] That should give pause to those who say that the Charter is worthless, and that Canadians would be better off without a charter than with one containing a notwithstanding clause.

___ National Identity _____

Finally, I return to the major question I posed for myself early in the previous section of this chapter: how can the Charter strengthen Canadian unity when its pursuit has caused such discord? Or, to expand on the question: when Trudeau entered politics in 1968, he claimed it was to work for Canadian unity; in 1984, after all his federal-provincial conferences on the constitution, did he not leave a country that was more divided than ever?

First, let it be recognized that during my mandates as prime minister I was often criticized for giving too much time to constitutional debates—but I have also been criticized for totally ignoring them from 1971 to 1975. It will probably be said that this chapter, as well, is too absorbed in constitutional questions. Fortunately, this book has other chapters to remind the reader that we also tackled a number of other little problems.

Essentially, I anticipated this criticism long ago. As early as the winter of 1965, having analyzed the groundswells in favour of greater decentralization for the federation, I wrote, "I should be very surprised if real statesmen . . . arrived at the conclusion that our constitution needs drastic revision."[15] After entering politics later that year, I again expressed the opinion that the constitutional debate should not be opened because it was "a hornet's nest."

At the time, I was a constitutional law professor at the University of Montreal and was teaching my students (of whom a number were militant separatists) that, except for exclusive fiscal powers, the province of Quebec already had all the jurisdictional powers it needed to implement the separatist program advocated by Marcel Chaput on pages 98 and 99 of his book, *Pourquoi je suis séparatiste*.[16] As a professor, I was also being paid to know what enormous amounts of bile and wasted time constitutional conferences had produced since 1927 when Mackenzie King had first called the provinces together to look for a way of repatriating the Canadian Constitution from England, only to discover how impossible it was to get all of them to agree on a constitutional amending formula.

Forty years and four prime ministers later, in spite of countless series of federal-provincial meetings at both the political and bureaucratic levels, the problem was still insoluble.

Furthermore, there was no lack of other priorities for governments at all levels: the economy, social questions, regional disparities, taxation, infrastructures, the environment, foreign policy and many other things were demanding the attention of Canadian politicians and civil servants at a time when international interdependence and lightning-fast communications were presenting Canada with challenges as big as the country itself.[17]

But it was too late to ward off the sickness. Quebec was already suffering from acute constitutionitis; as I mentioned earlier, in May 1963 that province's MLAs had voted unanimously in favour of "revision of the Canadian constitutional system," the government of Jean Lesage already having decided to go for "special status" and the Opposition, under Daniel Johnson, for "equality or independence."

Several other provinces, emboldened by postwar prosperity, were also beginning to kick against the traces. I recalled earlier – to change metaphors – how the ball was opened by the provinces that called the constitutional conference of 1967. As minister of justice at the time, I had serious reservations, but Prime Minister Pearson realized that we had no choice. The federal government had to join in.

I was convinced that once the debate began, it had to be carried to a conclusion. Canada was the only country in the world not in control of its constitution. A hundred years after its birth as a country and thirty-six years after the Statute of Westminster formally marked the end of Canada's colonial era and its beginning as a sovereign nation, we still had to ask London to amend our Constitution for us. Prime Ministers King, Bennett, St-Laurent, Diefenbaker and Pearson had all tried to put an end to the anachronism and had called numerous federal-provincial conferences for the purpose, but all of them had failed.

In 1967 the problematics had not changed one iota since 1927. Did Canadian sovereignty emanate from a people with a collective will to live as a nation, seeking a common good throughout the country and governing themselves under a federative form of constitution? Or was it the creature of ten provinces (some would say two nations), dependent on them for its existence and governed by the consensus of its eleven governments – ten provincial and one federal? These two points of view hardened, crystallized and clashed throughout the series of constitutional conferences that began with the interprovincial meeting of 1967 and ended with the federal-provincial conference of November 1981.

Generally speaking, the goal of the provinces was to obtain a greater devolution of constitutional powers, and their strategy consisted of refusing to agree on repatriating the constitution as long as their hunger for power went unsatisfied.

The goal of the government I led was to arrive at a more functional distribution of jurisdictions by giving up certain powers to the provinces in return for powers essential for making Canada an economic entity without internal borders. Our strategy was to win the support of Canadians by offering them measures designed to strengthen the sovereignty of the people: a constitution free of British guardianship, a constitutional amending formula providing for recourse to a referendum, and a charter of rights and freedoms common to the whole country (which would include the right to linguistic and regional equality).

Canada, along with Switzerland, was already one of the two most decentralized countries on earth with respect to jurisdictions and public finances.[18] However, the two countries being very different in size, Canada needed stronger bonds to hold the parts together. Furthermore, although the Swiss comprised four distinct nationalities, they had developed a common sense of belonging over many centuries and would speak without hesitation of "the Swiss nation." Canada, in contrast, had grown territorially as late as 1949, and its writers and politicians were still seeking a national identity. Edward Blake and Henri Bourassa, two of Canada's most brilliant parliamentarians, had both—forty years apart—deplored the absence of a pan-Canadian national feeling.[19] Seventy years later, the provincial premiers would reject a draft preamble to the constitution because they considered the terms "Canadian people" and "Canadian nation" unacceptable!

It was my feeling that the major decentralization being demanded by the provinces would endanger Canada's survival as a country, and I was determined to resist it.

The strategies of both federal and provincial forces were severely tested throughout the 1968-to-1982 period. There were countless skirmishes, some pitched battles, battle fatigue on both sides and reinforcements arriving after elections, and still there was no predicting how and when the conflict would end.

The provincial position reached its zenith on September 12, 1980, when the ten provinces unanimously presented me with the "Château Consensus," proposing a transfer of powers so massive that the Canadian federation would have been left a loose, balkanized confederacy, after which, through other discussions, some day, maybe, the constitution might be repatriated. This position was such that Premier René Lévesque felt he could safely give up his demand for a "special status" and a constitutional right of veto for Quebec—which had been the core of Quebec nationalist demands for twenty years—and accept without quibbling the principle of equality of all the provinces. No doubt he had calculated, with reason, that the Canada envisioned by the Château Consensus would be so anæmic that Quebec's achievement of independence would sooner or later become a mere formality (and rather sooner than later, of course). I really believe that on that September 12 the combattants had decided to fight to the finish.[20]

Faced with such exorbitant provincial demands, I replied that they were out of the question and the federal government would proceed with the repatriation without the consent of the provinces. The premier of Manitoba, Sterling Lyon, lectured me that this "would tear the country apart." I retorted that if, after one hundred and thirteen years of existence and fifty-three of fruitless discussions, the country broke up because our government repatriated the constitution with a charter of rights and freedoms attached, well, it would prove that the country did not deserve to exist. I was convinced that the time had come for Canada to choose to be or not to be.

On October 10, 1980, our government tabled a draft resolution in the Parliament of Canada asking the Parliament of Westminster to Canadianize the Canadian Constitution and to add to it an amending formula and a charter of rights, both defined in the draft resolution.

However, three provinces took court action to have our resolution declared unconstitutional.

On September 28, 1981, the Supreme Court brought down its

decision: the constitutional proclamation would need "sub-stantial" agreement, which in the end meant the consent of more than two but fewer than ten provincial governments.[21] So we returned to the negotiating table.

The decisive engagement took place on November 4, 1981. To break the deadlock, I proposed to the provinces an immediate repatriation of the constitution, followed in two years (if there was still disagreement) by a referendum, through which the Canadian people could say, first, whether they wanted a charter of rights and freedoms, and second, what amending formula they would prefer.

As in the Marienbad game, I knew I could lose, but would not. Several of the most influential provinces (including Quebec) had already adopted their own charters, and it would ill befit them to campaign in a referendum against Canada having one. As for the amending formula, the one the provinces were postulating was that all provinces were equal, whereas in ours all Canadians would be equal. The provinces' formula gave all provincial governments the same weighting of votes, regardless of the number of Canadians represented, while ours counted votes by senatorial divisions (a form of division dating back to Confederation), giving each voter more equal weight; hence, our formula would give an effective right of constitu-tional veto to Quebec and Ontario by virtue of the fact that they had larger numbers of Canadians.

Premier Lévesque accepted my referendum challenge for a brief spell, which took courage, because he had just lost a referendum in Quebec. However, he withdrew his endorsement and beat a hasty retreat when he found himself abandoned by all his provincial allies, who were mightily peeved all of a sudden. Indeed, the nine other provinces had no desire to go into a referendum under these circumstances, particularly in an alliance with a government devoted to independence.

But interprovincial solidarity had collapsed and the war ended with a negotiated peace; an agreement was concluded with the nine other provinces, who accepted repatriation together with a charter of rights, provided that the charter contain a derogatory ("notwithstanding") clause, that the constitutional amending formula be closer to the provincial proposal, and that certain jurisdictions regarding indirect taxation and natural resource marketing be transferred to the provinces.

In subsequent weeks, efforts were made to persuade the Quebec government to define the conditions under which it would resume negotiations[22]— but to no avail.

Our strategy had succeeded on the essential points. The Canadian nation would finally have its very own constitution, which would enshrine a charter of rights and freedoms common to all Canadians. Firm foundations for a national identity had been laid.

___ Canadian Unity and the Future_____

There were a few little shadows in the picture, however . . . The government of Quebec had not signed the constitutional accord but was bound by it nevertheless, and would probably keep on kicking against this, blaming the rest of the country for its own mishandling of its cards. However, a majority of Quebec's elected representatives (federal and provincial) had voted in favour of the accord, and public opinion seemed to ratify their approval.[23]

By this point, the public had grown tired of constitutional confrontations and wanted governments to get on with other things. Somewhere down the line, wiser politicians would no doubt reopen the constitutional debate. Once the French language had gained respect elsewhere in Canada, less defensive Quebec governments would accept the challenge of a pluralist Canada. A more functional division of jurisdictions would be developed and attempts would be made to correct certain anomalies; more open-minded, confident governments would see, for example, that the notwithstanding clause was incompatible with an authentic charter of rights and freedoms, and would get rid of it. And in return, since arbitrary acts would no longer be necessary to counter other arbitrary acts, the federal government would no longer need its power of disallowance and reservation to invalidate provincial laws passed in derogation of the Charter, and would propose that these outdated measures be extirpated from the Constitution.

And then we'd all live happily ever after, wouldn't we? No,

my dreams would have to wait a while ... So back to the
question: when I left politics in 1984, was Canada more united
or more divided than in 1968?

I shall leave the pleasure of arguing this to the historians.
Still, I may perhaps be allowed to put on file a few reflections
that have come to mind on reading the various chapters of this
book, combined with gleanings from my own impressions and
recollections.

Had my years as government leader left me less sensitive to
the injustices dividing Canadians? I hope not. In any event, I
think protest had become less strident than it was in the late
sixties. In the social sphere, the incidence of poverty had
decreased (see Jim Coutts, Chapter 7). Visible minorities and
the disadvantaged had seen their rights affirmed in the Charter,
had formed interest groups and were working toward the
application of these rights. The Métis had been recognized as
aboriginals and, together with the Indians and Inuit, had begun
to negotiate various forms of self-government. The death
penalty had been abolished and for the moment we were not
being pressed to reopen that debate. Legislation on abortion
was holding fast. Unemployment was still too high among
young people, but retraining programs had been put in place
and organizations like Katimavik and Canada World Youth
were attracting the more adventurous (see Jacques Hébert,
Chapter 5).

Economically, Canada had weathered two petroleum crises
and the perils of "stagflation" (inflation with zero growth); its
performance had been one of the best among the seven most
industrialized nations (see Ian Stewart, Chapter 4). Most big
businessmen still claimed to be suffering under the yoke of a
"socialist" government, although this "socialist" government
had never nationalized a single bank or other private
undertaking; in fact, it had come to the rescue of quite a few
ailing capitalist institutions (see Joel Bell, Chapter 3). Regional
disparities still existed but had improved somewhat (see Lloyd
Axworthy, Chapter 10).

On the political scene, a truce had been signed with nine
provinces, ending almost continual constitutional squabbles
since 1927. Canada now had a constitution that was really its
own and it had a charter of rights and freedoms common to all

Canadians. The petroleum crisis dispute between the petro-leum-producing and consuming provinces had been settled through an agreement negotiated by the federal government with the producing provinces (see Marc Lalonde, Chapter 2).

Political structures had also been transformed, reflecting what has become known as "participatory democracy"; the federal Liberal party had opened its doors wide to Canadians from all walks of life and every region of the country, while parliamentary reforms and vastly improved working condi-tions for members of Parliament had made representative democracy in Canada more functional and fairer (see Lorna Marsden, Chapter 11).

Environment policy had brought Canadians together across provincial borders and prompted collaboration among the various levels of government. The Canadian Council of Resource and Environment Ministers had played an important role in this since the early seventies (see John Roberts, Chapter 6).

In international policy, diplomatic recognition of China and of the Vatican had settled two controversial questions that had been dividing Canadians for years. And a stronger, clearer Canadian identity had emerged as a result of our policies toward the United States, Europe and the Pacific, as well as our activities in la Francophonie and North-South and East-West relations (see Tom Axworthy, Chapter 1).

The Official Languages law was no longer being contested, except by a small handful of MPs. Even in the West, where the law had encountered the stiffest resistance, respect for the French language was being demonstrated by the growth in French immersion classes (see Gérard Pelletier, Chapter 8, and statistics given in the introduction to Part IV of this book). Insensitivity as acrimonious as that aroused over the "*Gens de l'air*" dispute looked highly improbable henceforth. And the alienation felt by most French-speaking Quebeckers toward Ottawa had been exorcised by the presence of a contingent of federal members of Parliament and Cabinet ministers from Quebec who were among the most respected and influential. In fact, the government party had the support of almost every riding with a French-speaking majority in the country.

What had happened in Quebec? The separatist movement, which had been dormant since the thirties, had begun to come to life again with St-Laurent's departure from the federal scene in 1957 and Jean Lesage's Quiet Revolution in 1960; René Lévesque put his personal political stamp on the movement when he founded the Parti québécois in 1968. The party had plenty of members and talented candidates. However, in 1970 and 1973, as long as its candidates kept asking to be elected in order to make Quebec independent, they kept getting trounced (only seven and then six MLAs elected). After this, forced to recognize that Quebeckers did not want to vote against being Canadian, the Péquistes adopted a policy of gradualism. The first stage consisted of putting independence on the back burner and presenting themselves to the voters as the "good-government" party. This brought them to power in 1976, replacing the bad government of Robert Bourassa, who had called an early election to ask for a mandate to oppose "Trudeau's constitutional machinations."

Three years later, this Trudeau had lost power and was preparing to leave politics. The Péquistes took advantage of the opportunity to announce their long-awaited referendum; however, sensing that Quebeckers were still not ready to separate from Canada, they drew up a pretty artful referendum question that was not proposing independence outright but asking for authority to negotiate a kind of association with the rest of Canada, with the understanding that, following these negotiations, there would be another referendum. Oh, yes—I almost forgot to add that the question carefully stated that the Canadian dollar would continue to be the currency of this somewhat independent Quebec![24]

All the precautions built into the Péquiste plan were for naught. Quebec voted solidly against it. Meanwhile, the same Trudeau had returned to power in Ottawa and announced the constitutional reform which this chapter has treated at length and about which I shall say no more in this book.

Was Quebec more distant in relation to Canada in 1984 than in 1968? Within Quebec, opposition to membership in the Canadian federation had undoubtedly crystallized and become more articulate and visible with the appearance of a separatist party on the political scene. But each time the Quebec electorate had been called upon, it had rejected independence as such, and year in and year out, the hard-line separatists kept getting the same low score in the polls—about 15 percent. In his latter years in power, Premier Lévesque began to talk about federalism being "a good risk," forgetting, I imagine, that this was exactly the theme I had proposed to Quebeckers in my campaign for the leadership of the Liberal party in 1968. . . .

I can only conclude, therefore, that the fragmentation of Canada began after the election of Brian Mulroney as prime minister in the fall of 1984. He was elected thanks to the support of the provincial premiers, to whom he had promised "national reconciliation," meaning settlement of all federal-provincial disputes to the satisfaction of the provinces: a petroleum policy to please the western provinces, offshore resources for the Atlantic provinces, an end to foreign investment screening for Ontario, and for Quebec an invitation to co-chair international meetings. For Quebec officialdom, appearances are everything!

Since, in Quebec, the Conservative Party of Canada had barely survived forty-nine years of federal Liberal governments (the Liberal tenure was interrupted only twice), Mr Mulroney needed the help of separatists and the Parti québécois's election machine to get himself elected. And since he had to give generously in order to get, he gave positions in his government to these allies and reopened the constitutional debate to satisfy "Quebec's demands," meaning those of the nationalist ilk. Then Robert Bourassa returned to the scene, only too happy to have the opportunity to pad out his five demands. Mr Mulroney gave him satisfaction on seven, and for good measure did as much for the other provinces, too.

It all happened in secret one dark night, beside a pretty little lake in Quebec by the name of Meech. Canada has never been as divided as it has since that night.[25]

So today we have the legal country—that is, a prime minister ready to trade Canada's soul for an electoral victory, and ten provincial premiers all panting to increase their powers by despoiling the Canadian state, with the backing of the small fry sitting on parliamentary Opposition benches who are terrified of incurring the disapproval of officially endorsed Quebec thinking.

And then we have the real country—that is, the unorganized

coalition of Canadian individuals and groups scattered across the nation,[26] for whom Canada is more than a collection of provinces to be governed through wheeling and dealing. To them, Canada is a true nation, whose ideal is compassion and justice and whose desire is to be governed democratically in freedom and equality.

The more they have learned about what Meech Lake really means, the more indignant these people have become that their governments have signed an accord that could break up their country, weaken the Charter of 1982 and undermine shared-cost programs.

The anglophones of Quebec and the francophones of the other provinces began also to realize that the mindset of the Meech Lake signatories was going to be bad news for linguistic minorities. They didn't have long to wait. First, the francophones of Saskatchewan and Alberta were deprived of rights that they had had since before Confederation—by the very people who had signed the Meech Lake Accord. Soon after this, the anglophones of Quebec were deprived of their right to have signs in their language, which they, too, had always had and of which they had been deprived only temporarily under Bill 101.[27] And most disgraceful of all, the government of Quebec took sides with the government of Alberta when the latter province's francophones asked for broader education rights and their request was refused.

This was the climate surrounding the Quebec provincial election of September 25, 1989. The electorate, having to choose between a questionable federalist, Mr Bourassa, and a true separatist, Mr Parizeau, gave the latter 40 percent of the vote, the highest percentage ever received by the Parti québécois when seeking a clear mandate to proceed to independence. (In 1970 and 1973, the only other comparable occasions, the Parti québécois had obtained, respectively, 23 and 30 percent of the vote.)

Calling it national reconciliation, Prime Minister Mulroney has in fact been dismantling Canada for the benefit of the provinces. And under the noble pretext of satisfying Quebec, he has been fostering exactly the kind of dualism that is the stuff of the separatists' fondest dreams: an exclusively

English-speaking Canada alongside an exclusively French-speaking Quebec.

Worse still, the commendable goal of promoting freer trade has led to a monstrous swindle, under which the Canadian government has ceded to the United States of America a large slice of the country's sovereignty over its economy and natural resources in exchange for advantages we already had, or were going to obtain in a few years anyway through the normal operation of the GATT.

Alas, by now it is clear that, barring a sharp and unlikely change of course, our Great Helmsman is indeed steering Canada toward peace and reconciliation — the kind to be found in the graveyards of the deep.

The Poverty of Nationalist Thinking in Quebec

————————— by Pierre Elliott Trudeau —————————

translated by Patricia Claxton

> *"French Canadians have no opinions,*
> *they only have feelings."*
> – Sir Wilfrid Laurier

____ I   Pride and Money_____

Commenting on Quebec nationalist politics in the first issue of *Cité Libre* forty-two years ago, I wrote, "The country can't exist without us, we think to ourselves. So watch out you don't hurt our feelings ... We depend on our power of blackmail in order to face the future ... We are getting to be a sleazy bunch of master blackmailers."[1]

Things have changed a lot since then, but for the worse. Four decades ago, all Duplessis was asking for his province was that it be left in peace to go its own slow pace. His rejection of proposals for constitutional reform was intended mostly to block an updating of Canada's economic and social institutions. And Quebec's "no" was formulated by a relatively small political class. In today's Quebec, however, the official blackmail refrain gets backup from a whole choir of those who like to think they are thinking people: "If English Canada won't accept Quebec's traditional, minimum demands, we'll leave ..."

Leave for where? What for?

Consider that in the last twenty-two years the Province of Quebec has been governed by two premiers. The first was the one who coined the phrase "profitable federalism." We'll stay in Canada if Canada gives us enough money, he argued. However, adds the Allaire report that he commissioned, the rest of Canada must hand over nearly all its constitutional powers, except of course the power to give us lots of money.[2]

And to put a bit more kick in the blackmail, no opportunity is missed to point out that Quebec's (alleged) right of self-determination is written into this premier's party program. This is the premier who prides himself in not practising "federalism on bended knees."

The other premier was the one who invented "sovereignty-association." He demanded all the powers of a sovereign country for Quebec, but was careful to arrange for the sovereign country not to be independent. Indeed, his referendum question postulated that a sovereign Quebec would be associated with the other provinces and would continue to use the Canadian dollar as legal tender. Money, money, money!

So for twenty-two years the Quebec electorate has suffered the ignominy of having to choose between two provincial parties for whom the pride of being a Quebecker is negotiable for cash. And if by some stroke of ill fortune the rest of Canada seems disinclined to go along with the blackmail, as happened over the Meech Lake Accord, it is accused of humiliating Quebec. In Quebec, humiliation is decidedly selective.

Except for a small handful of dyed-in-the-wool separatists, together with the sprinkling of Montrealers who exercised their vote in favour of the Equality Party, just about all the cream of Quebec society approves of this shameful horsetrading, and so without batting an eye has backed one or the other of the above-mentioned premiers for twenty-two years.

Artists in general parade as *indépendantistes* but want the Canadian government to keep giving them money. Big businesspeople and professionals endorsed the independence blackmail over the Meech affair, but with the economic crisis worsening are rediscovering advantages to "profitable federalism." The francophone media line up in great numbers on the side of sovereignty, but remain faithful to their hero and soft-pedal real independence because of the costs it would entail. Political scientists (and their students, of course), instead of analyzing this spineless behaviour with scientific detachment, subscribe to it almost unanimously; some openly advocate knife-to-the-throat negotiations with English Canada, maintaining that with a certain kind of independence, Quebeckers could continue to elect federal members of Parliament (from whence come equalization payments).

Curiouser and curiouser, as Alice said. Want more examples of this ludicrous political thinking?

- In 1964 and 1971, Quebec premiers scuttled two constitutional agreements that they had signed (Fulton-Favreau) or drafted and promised to sign (Victoria). In Quebec they were cheered. But in 1987 when the premiers of two other provinces refused to back the Meech Lake Accord, which they had neither negotiated nor signed, it was claimed that Quebec had been hurt and humiliated by the rest of the country.
- A Canadian prime minister is accused of having broken a promise made to Quebeckers during the referendum of 1980, whereas the words interpreted as a promise were in fact addressed to the other provinces to urge them to resume constitutional negotiations after the referendum.[3]
- Seven provinces that approved the repatriation of the constitution in November 1981 are accused of betrayal (on the night of November 4, the so-called "night of the long knives"), after forming a common front with Quebec in April 1981 to block the repatriation project. The truth is that during the negotiations on the morning of November 4, it was the premier of Quebec who broke ranks with the other provinces of the Group of Eight and left *them* out in the cold. (Max Nemni, professor of political science at l'Université Laval discusses this situation in an excellent contribution to a recent book.)[4]
- In 1992 the premier of Quebec considers a constitutional veto for Quebec a matter of life and death; yet in 1971 he himself rejected this veto when the federal government and the nine other provinces offered it on a silver tray. And his successor, who also considered Quebec's veto sacred, turned it down several times between 1978 and 1981; he even went to the Supreme Court to prevent the federal government, which had the support of Ontario and New Brunswick, from putting a veto for Quebec in the constitution.
- Once the Supreme Court had defined the rules of the game, the repatriation of the constitution was carried out in strict accordance with the rule of law and respect for convention; furthermore, it was backed by a weighted 65 percent of the combined totals of Quebec's members of Parliament in

Ottawa and the Quebec National Assembly. Yet official Quebec history denounces the operation as "strong-arm tactics," and a number of worthy individuals (including a former federal Cabinet minister who had supported the operation) have discovered retroactively that it had humiliated them ...

In short, Quebec governments had blocked all Canadian attempts at repatriation since 1927, and here was a separatist Quebec government trying to do it again in 1980. The premier of Quebec, they say, loved to play the game. Well, he played at referendum and lost. He played at alliances and lost. He played at negotiation and lost. He played the Supreme Court game and lost. Finally he played at getting votes from elected representatives and lost. How have Quebec's nationalist thinkers explained this succession of failures? Since it is out of the question for them to consider that a Quebec government might have played its cards atrociously, they have had to distort history once again in order to blame it all on some imaginary betrayal.

So it goes that, with myths and delusions, the Quebec nationalist élites falsify history to prove that all Quebec's political failures are someone else's fault: the Conquest, the obscurantism of Duplessis's time, slowness to enter the modern age, illiteracy, and all the rest. It is never our leaders' fault; it has to be blamed on some ominous plot against us.

_____II   The Distinct Society_____

The same glaring lack of professionalism is in evidence when nationalist thinkers in Quebec have used terms like "distinct society," which succeeded "sovereignty-association," which followed "equality or independence," which was preceded by "special status." None of these terms stands up to serious scrutiny.

The latest variation, the distinct society, turned up in post-referendum negotiations in 1980, when the premier of Quebec had to invent something to replace sovereignty-association, which had gone down with the referendum. The frivolity of the notion becomes apparent if we recall that its author considered his province so indistinct that he allied it with the other provinces of the Group of Eight in April 1981, when all eight of them formally declared themselves equal to all the others and approved an amending formula by which Quebec gave up its right of veto. Nevertheless, the phrase "distinct society" continues to be a hit.

That Quebec is a distinct society is totally obvious. The inhabitants of the province live in a territory defined by its borders. The majority speak French. They are governed under a particular system of laws. And these realities have been pivotal in the development of a culture which is uniquely theirs.

These are inarguable facts, arising from two centuries of history marked by intense struggles and juridico-political stubbornness. This produced the Canadian Constitution of 1867, whose federative rather than unitary form was imposed by French Canadians, led by Sir George-Étienne Cartier, on other Canadians. It was precisely this federalism which enabled and encouraged the development in Quebec of a province that is a distinct society.

This constitution also gave birth to nine other provinces, all of them distinct from the others by reason of their territorial borders, their ethnic composition, their laws, and hence their cultures. (A society cannot be distinct in relation to another, in fact, without that other being distinct in relation to the first.)

Nonetheless, all these distinct societies share a considerable heritage, despite misconceptions to the contrary. Much is made of the fact, for example, that the civil law is the law in Quebec, whereas common law applies in the other provinces. Yet, however important the Civil Code may be, in reality it occupies a very small place in the total picture of provincial laws by which we in Quebec are governed. Just like the other provinces, Quebec has enacted a vast number of provincial laws; they apply to all aspects of our collective lives and are the product of a juridical culture far more closely related to that of the other provinces than to the laws of New France or the Napoleonic Code.

At any rate, it is a truism if not a platitude to assert that Quebec is a distinct society, since the constitution we adopted in 1867 has permitted it to be a distinct society. Since this is constitutionally recognized already, why are so many Quebec politicians, public law experts and businesspeople clamouring to have it inserted in the constitution all over again? And why do they say they are humiliated when people wonder why this is so necessary?

Because, they say, the constitution of 1982 recognizes the collective rights of other communities: ancestral rights of the native peoples, the multicultural heritage of many newer Canadians, even women's rights. So why such niggardliness when it comes to writing into the same constitution "the promotion of Quebec as a distinct society"?[5]

This is gross sophistry. Unlike Quebeckers, neither the native peoples nor the "multiculturals" nor women are collectivities defined by a specific territory and enjoying executive, legislative and judicial powers. Consequently, the constitution does not give them, as collectivities, any specific jurisdictional power to "promote" their distinct societies. The only effect of these Charter provisions is to give individuals belonging to these collectivities an additional judicial guarantee of protection against any interpretation of the Charter whereby their rights could be overlooked. Somewhat in the same fashion, the Charter has given to members of the French-Canadian collectivity scattered throughout Canada, not the power to make laws to promote the French language, but the power to have the courts insist on the equality of French with English, to the extent guaranteed by the Charter.

On the other hand, when the words "promotion of Quebec as a distinct society" are proposed for insertion either in the body of the constitution or in the Charter, they would apply to a province–that is, a constitutional entity with power to make laws, give effect to them and have the courts impose respect for them. The courts will be called upon to define these words. First they will need to determine what new powers the constitution intends to give to Quebec in order to better enable it to "promote its distinct society." They will also need to consider how the Province of Quebec is different from the other provinces, all of which are distinct societies, and all of which are empowered by the Canadian constitution to promote the interests of their respective populations. Then they will ponder the wording of the proposed insertion whose purpose is to guide their interpretation of the Charter: " 'distinct society'... *includes* a French-speaking majority, a unique culture, and a civil law tradition."[6]

Now the consequences become clear. The Charter, whose

essential purpose was to recognize the fundamental and inalienable rights of all Canadians equally, would recognize thenceforth that in the Province of Quebec these rights could be overridden or modified by provincial laws whose purpose is to promote a distinct society and more specifically to favour "the French-speaking majority" that has "a unique culture" and "a civil law tradition." There is a very good chance, then, that Quebeckers of Irish, Jewish, Haitian or Vietnamese origin—even if they speak perfect French—would have trouble claiming to belong to this "distinct society" in any attempt to protect their fundamental rights against discriminatory laws enacted in a jurisdiction where they are in the minority. And even an "old stock" Quebecker would risk losing his fundamental rights if he were rash enough to pit them against Quebec laws passed for the promotion of "collective rights."

This most recent ideological fad in Quebec, collective rights, has an enthusiastic following. Journalists, academics, students, businesspeople and politicians are all ready to man the barricades to protect the "collective rights" of Quebeckers against any interference from the Canadian constitution or the Charter of Rights and Freedoms. In this they are following the lead of their premier, who at the proclamation of Bill 178 banning signs in languages other than French, bragged that in the name of collective rights his government had trampled individual rights guaranteed by the Charter.

_____ III   Collective Rights _____

The poverty of nationalist thinking in Quebec is abundantly clear from the dispatch with which so many of our Québécois thinkers have embraced the concept of "collective rights."

Under the Charter, all Canadians stand as equals before the state. But Quebec's nationalist élites, who are fearless in the face of competition from the United States and even the whole world, are scared stiff of English Canada. Only in the St. Jean Baptiste parade are we a race of giants; when the next day dawns and we come to measure ourselves against other Canadians as individuals, we are afraid we are not equal but inferior to them, and we run and hide behind our "collective" rights which, if need be, we invoke to override the fundamental rights of "others." But what politician or academic or businessperson will tell us which collectivity is supposed to have those rights?

Is it the French-Canadian collectivity living here and there across Canada? Of course not, since the preponderant ideology in Quebec doesn't give a fig about bilingualism in Canada, and Quebec has gone to bat in court for Alberta and Saskatchewan when they have denied French rights acquired even before these provinces joined Confederation in 1905.

Is it the collectivity of all Quebeckers, then? No, because that collectivity is called a province, and the powers of the province were explicitly recognized long ago by the Constitution Act of 1867.

So it can only be some distinct collectivity within Quebec–but which? Certainly not the anglophone collectivity, since Quebec law denies them any collective rights in relation to signs and certain aspects of education. We can rule out the native peoples too, since they have been clearly given to understand that they cannot be a distinct society with the right to self-determination because the term has been reserved by Quebeckers of another race.

When the nationalists talk about protecting collective rights, then, they are thinking only of French-speaking Quebeckers. But are we sure we know what *that* means? There are plenty of anglophones who speak very good French and plenty of francophones of various cultural backgrounds who speak languages other than French. Will they all get protection of their collective rights at least for the French-speaking part of their being? If so, what will these rights consist of? Can Haitian Quebeckers, for instance, protect certain aspects of their own culture by claiming protection as part of the French-speaking collectivity? Or are they excluded from the "unique culture" which Quebec will have the power to promote through derogations from the Charter? Can neo-Canadian Quebeckers of whatever origin choose to renounce their heritage and origins so as to share with "old stock" Quebeckers the protection sought for the French-speaking collectivity? Or are we dealing with a frankly racist notion that makes second- or third-class citizens of everyone but "old stock" Quebeckers?

There are no certainties here, but what does seem clear is that it will not be for the individual to decide whether or not he or she belongs to the collectivity of "old stock" Quebeckers. This will be decided by a Quebec government through laws adopted by majority vote in the National Assembly. And so from collective rights on down to the distinct society, thirst for power in some, together with apathy and sometimes stupidity in others, will have established that, as a basic element of Quebec society, a legislative majority will have justification for arbitrarily overriding the fundamental rights of any citizen who has the privilege of living in Quebec.

_____ IV   Quebec's "Traditional" Demands _____

Professor Max Nemni has shown, in the work mentioned above, that between 1980 and 1992, Quebec's "traditional" and "minimum" demands have been anything but traditional or minimum.

Looking back further still, it can be seen that there has never been a definitive answer to the question "What does Quebec want?", which is still being asked by the few English-speaking Canadians who are not sick and tired of the evasiveness of Quebec nationalist thinking.

As far back as memory serves, French Canadians were essentially asking for one thing: respect for the French fact in Canada and incorporation of this fact into Canadian civil society, principally in the areas of language and education, and particularly in the federal government and provinces with French-speaking minorities. After two centuries of struggle and a few symbolic victories (bilingual money and stamps, for example), the Official Languages Act was passed in 1969 and minority-language education rights were entrenched in the Charter of 1982. The gates had suddenly opened and institutional bilingualism was recognized in Canada.

Then, equally suddenly, the Quebec nationalists no longer wanted the French language to be made equal with English throughout Canada. They denounced bilingualism as utopic at the very moment it was becoming a reality. With Bills 22 and 101, Quebec declared itself unilingually French and abandoned the cause of French-speaking minorities in other provinces, the better to marginalize the English-speaking minority in Quebec; the Quiet Revolution had suddenly empowered us to become indifferent to the first minority and intolerant of the second. As if we had practised virtue only out of weakness or hypocrisy ...

Yet Premier Jean Lesage, the father of the Quiet Revolution, had spelled out Quebec's traditional demands at the federal-provincial conference held in July 1960, a few weeks after the election that had brought him to power. In substance, they were as follows:

- immediate resumption of talks on the repatriation of the constitution and the constitutional amending formula;
- insertion in the constitution of a charter of rights, to include both language rights and education rights for French-speaking minorities outside Quebec;
- creation of a constitutional court;
- creation of a permanent federal-provincial affairs secretariat;
- annual meetings of provincial premiers;
- an end to conditional grants and shared-cost programs.

But whenever these objectives were about to be reached, Quebec's "traditional" demands would begin to evolve. Then in 1964, Premier Lesage gave in to the nationalists and repudiated the Fulton-Favreau agreement on repatriation, which his government had negotiated and signed, and came up with an entirely new "traditional" demand, which came to be known as "special status." The content of this notion remained deliberately vague, for essentially it had been turned into an instrument of blackmail: Quebec would never allow the Canadian constitution to be brought home unless the country paid a ransom to Quebec. That ransom would vary from year to year, the only constant being that as soon as the ransom was paid, the Quebec government would come up with a new one. Thus, under Lesage, there was a lot of "opting out," by which various federal programs that were applicable throughout the country would be administered in Quebec by the Quebec government, but at the Canadian government's expense. There was also much hoopla over the new *politique de grandeur,* through which it was hoped that Quebec would gain recognition as an international power.

In 1966 Daniel Johnson's government took power, and Quebec's new demand became "equality or independence."

In 1971 the profitable federalism premier scuttled his own agreement on repatriation and as ransom demanded the right to opt out of family allowances. This had barely been paid when he demanded another: cultural sovereignty.

In 1976 the sovereignty-association premier demanded sovereignty-association as ransom, failing which Quebec would become totally independent. After the defeat of the referendum, this premier demanded merely a massive transfer of federal powers to the provinces (the Château Consensus of September 1980) and refused to discuss even the possibility of repatriation until the transfer was assured. Then in April 1981 this premier allied himself with seven English-speaking provinces to demand a "notwithstanding" clause in the Charter and a constitutional amending formula that provided for opting out with compensation.

On November 5, 1981, the same premier spelled out his three conditions for agreeing to the constitutional deal that had just been made: an amending formula with a guarantee of full compensation to a province opting out of a transfer of powers, restrictions on the right to work anywhere in the country and restrictions on minority-language education rights.

The federal government indicated that it was ready to talk, but less than two weeks later, on November 13, 1981, these three conditions had disappeared and been replaced by three others: recognition of Quebec's distinct society, a constitutional veto and limitations to the Charter.

After the federal election of 1984, the self-same premier recommended that Quebec give "the fine risk of federalism" a try.

The profitable federalism premier, when he had returned to power in 1985, demanded that Quebec's "distinct society" be mentioned *in a preamble* to the constitution, failing which he would break off negotiations. A year or two later the "distinct society" was to be incorporated *in the body* of the constitution as an interpretive clause (the Meech Lake Accord), failing which Quebec would "resort to self-determination."

In February 1990, while the Meech Lake Accord was still being negotiated, this premier created the Allaire committee, whose mandate was to define the "traditional demands" to be made *after* the conclusion of the Meech Lake Accord. The Allaire report, published less than a year later, demanded a massive transfer of federal powers just to Quebec. If this ransom were not paid, there would be a referendum on Quebec independence. As we know, this report was set aside by the premier at the policy convention of the Liberal Party of Quebec on August 29, 1992.

Many in Quebec have the cheek to call this incredible grab-bag "traditional demands"! And every time a new demand is announced, the self-appointed élites snap to attention, ready to feel humiliated if the ransom is not paid at once. Most incredible of all, there are still good souls in English Canada who are ready to take these temper tantrums seriously and urge their compatriots to pay each new ransom for fear of losing each "last chance" to save Canada. Poor things, they have not yet realized that the nationalists' thirst will never be satisfied, and that each new ransom paid to stave off the threat of schism will simply encourage the master blackmailers to renew the threat and double the ransom.

It has become clear that all the demands made of Canada by the Quebec nationalists can be summed up in just one: keep giving us new powers and the money to exercise them, or we'll leave.

If Quebeckers are offered the chance to have their cake and eat it too, naturally they will accept. But as Canadians they also know that a country must choose to be or not to be; that dismantling Canada will not save it and the nationalists cannot be allowed to play the game of heads-I-win-tails-you-lose, or to hold referendums on independence every ten years. And anyway, you cannot *really* believe in Canada and at the same time claim the right of self-determination for Canadian provinces.

"French Canadians only have feelings," Laurier said. For unscrupulous politicians, there is no surer way of rousing feelings than to trumpet a call to pride of race. French Canadians will only be rid of this kind of politician if the blackmail ceases, and the blackmail will cease only if Canada refuses to dance to that tune. Impartial history has shown that it was exactly this attitude that pushed separatism to the brink of the grave between 1980 and 1984.

Separatism has regained a lot of ground since 1984, of course, but as the Portuguese proverb goes, "The worst is not always certain." However, to ward it off, our leaders will need a bit of courage ...

Notes

We would like to thank Denis Stevens, Oliver Hobday and Paul Corriveau for their diligent research assistance, and Anne Marriott for her customary professionalism in co-ordinating and preparing the text.

Introduction to the Hardcover Edition

1. Carl Becker, quoted by Peter Gay in *Style in History* (New York: W. W. Norton and Co., 1974), p. 197.
2. Gérard Pelletier, *Years of Impatience*: 1950–1960 (Toronto: Methuen, 1984) and *Years of Choice*: 1960–1968 (Toronto: Methuen, 1987).
3. Arthur M. Schlesinger, Jr., *The Cycles of American History* (Boston: Houghton Mifflin Co., 1986), p. xi.
4. Henry Adams, *The Education of Henry Adams* (New York: The Modern Library, 1918), p. 193.
5. See A. D. Taylor, *Bismarck: The Man and Statesman* (New York: Vintage Books, 1955), p. 70.
6. Jean-Paul Desbiens, quoted by Gérard Pelletier in *Years of Choice* 1960–1968 (Toronto: Methuen, 1987), p. 224.
7. Pierre Elliott Trudeau, *Approaches to Politics* (Toronto: Oxford University Press, 1970), p. 84.
8. Georg Wilhelm Friedrich Hegel, *The Philosophy of History* (New York: Dover Publications, Inc., 1956), p. 8.
9. Lord Acton, *Essays in the Study and Writing of History*, ed. J. Rufus Fears, vol. II (Indianapolis: Liberty Classics, 1985), p. 506.

PART I The Tempest Bursting: Canada in 1992

1. Richard Gwyn, "Canada at Risk" in *Canada at Risk: Canadian Public Policy in the 1990s,* ed. C. Bruce Doern and Bryne B. Purchase (Toronto: C.D. Howe Institute, 1991), p. 117.
2. Quebec, *Report of the Committee on the Political and Constitutional Future of Quebec* (Quebec: Assemblée Nationale, 1991). Better known by the name of its co-chairmen, Michel Bélanger and Jean Campeau.
3. Quebec Liberal Party, *A Quebec Free to Choose: Report of the*

Constitutional Committee of the Quebec Liberal Party ([Montreal]: Quebec Liberal Party, 1991). Usually referred to as the Allaire report after the name of the chairman, Jean Allaire.

4. The pollster Michael Adams summarizes recent public opinion findings in "Populism and Perestroika: Challenges for Canadian Leaders in the 1990s" in *Finding Common Ground: The Proceedings of the Aylmer Conference*, ed. Jean Chrétien (Hull, Quebec: Voyageur Publishing, 1992), pp. 198–207.

5. "Nice Country, Nice Mess," *The Economist*, 29 June 1991, p. 49.

6. Ernest Renan, *Discours et Conférences* (Paris: Calman-Lévy, 1887), pp. 300–301.

7. Ernest Gellner, *Nations and Nationalism* (Ithaca, New York: Cornell University Press, 1983), p.1.

8. Mercredi is quoted by Rhéal Séguin in "Quebec's Right to Self-rule Disputed," the *Globe and Mail* (Toronto), 12 February 1992, p. A4.

9. Vaclav Havel, *Summer Mediations* (New York: Alfred A. Knopf, 1992), p. 92.

10. Lord Acton, *Essays in the Liberal Interpretation of History* (Chicago: The University of Chicago Press, 1967), p. 157.

11. Isaiah Berlin, *Against the Current: Essays in the History of Ideas* (Oxford: Oxford University Press, 1981), p. 346.

12. Barbara W. Tuchman, *The March of Folly* (New York: Alfred A. Knopf, 1984), p. 7.

13. A particularly trenchant critique of the two reports which also places them within the broad tradition of Quebec nationalism is found in William Johnson's *Anglophobie* (Montreal: Stanké, 1991).

14. See, for example, Daniel Bell, "Ethnicity and Social Change" in *The Winding Passage* (New Brunswick, USA: Transaction Publishers, 1991), pp. 184–209.

15. Quebec Liberal Party, *A Quebec Free to Choose* (Allaire report), p. 4.

16. Quebec, *Report of the Committee on the Political and Constitutional Future of Quebec* (the Bélanger-Campeau report), pp. 33–34.

17. Statistics on the current state of the French language and culture in Canada can be found in Jacques Henripin, "The 1986 Census: Some Enduring Trends Abate" in *Language and Society* (Fall 1988): 6–9; the *Twenty-first Annual Report of the Commissioner of Official Languages*, covering the calendar year 1991 (Ottawa: Supply and Services, 1992); and a report for Le conseil du patronat du Québec by André Raynauld, *Les Enjeux Économiques de la Souveraineté* (October 1990), especially pp. 31–40.

18. John McCullum, "Canada's Choice: Crisis of Capital or Renewed Federalism," C.D. Howe Institute Benefactors Lecture, 1992, p. 36.

19. Raynauld, *Les Enjeux Économiques de la Souveraineté*, pp. 31–40.
20. Quoted in Isaiah Berlin, *The Crooked Timber of Humanity* (New York: Alfred A. Knopf, 1991), p. vii.
21. Berlin, *The Crooked Timber of Humanity*, p. 2246.
22. Quebec, *Report of the Committee on the Political and Constitutional Future of Quebec* (the Bélanger-Campeau report), p. 40.
23. Quebec Liberal Party, *A Quebec Free to Choose* (the Allaire report), p. 11.
24. Quebec, *Report of the Committee on the Political and Constitutional Future of Quebec* (the Bélanger-Campeau report), p. 18.
25. Jacques Parizeau, "What Does Sovereignty-Association Mean?" Notes for a speech to be delivered at a special joint meeting of the Empire Club of Canada and the Canadian Club of Canada, 11 December 1990.
26. The secretariat of the Bélanger-Campeau exercise commissioned eight economic studies from some of Quebec's most distinguished economists and then the secretariat drew on the studies "to produce a more political, less analytical and even more sovereignst paper than those of the individual economists" according to Patrick Grady in *The Economic Consequences of Quebec Sovereignty* (Vancouver: The Fraser Institute, 1991), p. 42. Grady provides a useful summary of these eight economic background studies prepared for Bélanger-Campeau.

  The most widely publicized assessment of Quebec's economic viability after independence was contained in the 1991 annual report of the Economic Council of Canada, *A Joint Venture: The Economics of Constitutional Options*. The C.D. Howe Institute commissioned a series of monographs entitled *The Canadian Round,* which examined various aspects of the economy of breakup and renewal. A feature of the C.D. Howe series is that the research was integrated with the earlier work of the Bélanger-Campeau commission. See, for example, John McCullum and Chris Green, *Parting as Friends: The Economic Consequences for Quebec* (Toronto: C.D. Howe Institute, 1991). John McCullum summarized the findings of several of the most prominent studies in the appendix of "Canada's Choice: Crisis of Capital or Renewed Federalism," C.D. Howe Institute Benefactors Lecture, 1992.
27. McCullum and Green, *Parting as Friends,* pp. 17–25.
28. "Independence No longer Easy to Justify: Ex-premier," *Montreal Gazette,* 13 May 1992.
29. Quebec Liberal Party, *A Quebec Free to Choose* (the Allaire report), p. 7.

30. Quebec, *Report of the Committee on the Political and Constitutional Future of Quebec* (the Bélanger-Campeau report), p. 31.
31. Ibid., p. 17.
32. Translation of Premier Bourassa's speeches to the Quebec National Assembly on 18 June 1987 and 23 June 1987 are contained in Appendix B, of *With a Bang, With a Whimper: Pierre Trudeau Speaks Out*, ed. Donald Johnston (Toronto: Stoddart, 1988).
33. Parizeau is quoted by William Johnson, *The Gazette* (Montreal) 14 September 1991.
34. See "Langue malade, école coupable," *L'Actualite*, 15 September 1991 and "School Dropout Rate Hits 36 Percent," *The Gazette* (Montreal) 26 June 1991.
35. See "Frère Untel Sounds Another Warning about French," *The Gazette* (Montreal) 14 March 1992.
36. Statistics Canada, *Public Libraries 1989–90*, cat. 87, 205 annual.
37. See "Rivers of Filth," *Globe and Mail* (Toronto), 27 April 1991.
38. Bell, *Winding Passage*, p. 209.
39. Leon Dion, "The Myths of Quebec," *Daedalus* (Fall 1988): 292–93.
40. Quoted in Brooke Jeffrey, *Breaking Faith* (Toronto: Key Porter Books, 1992), p. 91.
41. Lucien Bouchard, *A Visage Découvert* (Montreal: Boréal, 1992), p. 143.
42. Quoted in Kathleen Hall Jamieson, *Eloquence in an Electronic Age* (Oxford: Oxford University Press, 1988), p. 168.
43. House of Commons Debates, 27 June 1984.
44. Débats de l'Assemblée nationale, 20 décembre 1988, p. 4425.
45. *Dominion Law Reports*, vol. 140 (Aurora, Ontario: Canada Law Book Ltd., 1983), pp. 64–65.
46. Quoted in Tip O'Neill, *Man of the House* (New York: St. Martin's Press, 1987), p. 242.
47. Ralf Dahrendorf, *The Modern Social Conflict* (Berkley: University of California Press, 1988), p. ix. Dahrendorf eloquently pleads for both entitlements and provisions. Other works that have influenced our thinking on these points include David Marquand, *The Unprincipled Society* (London: Jonathan Cape, 1988); Roy Hattersley, *Choose Freedom* (London: Penguin Books Ltd., 1987); and Will Kymlicka, *Liberalism, Community and Culture* (Oxford: Clarendon Press, 1989).
48. Quoted in Hattersley, *Choose Freedom*, p. 30.
49. See R.H. Tawney, *Equality* (London: George Allen and Unwin Ltd., 1931).

50. Quoted in Hattersley, *Choose Freedom*, p. xix.
51. See Robert Cairns, "On a Necessary Tension of a Democratic Society" in *Social Democracy Without Illusions*, ed. John Richard, Robert Cairns and Larry Pratt (Toronto: McClelland and Stewart, 1991).
52. Marquand, *Unprincipled Society*, p. 10.
53. Canada, *A New Direction for Canada: An Agenda for Economic Renewal*, 8 November 1984. p. 1.
54. For a description of this Conservative transformation see Martin Goldfarb and Thomas Axworthy, *Marching to a Different Drummer: An Essay on the Liberals and Conservatives in Convention* (Toronto: Stoddart, 1988).
55. See Charles Murray, *Losing Ground* (New York: Basic Books, Inc., 1984) and George Gilder, *Wealth and Poverty* (New York: Bantam Books, 1981).
56. Quoted in Denis Healey, *The Time of My Life* (London: Penguin Books, 1989), p. 581. Healey's memoir contains both a splendid history of post-war politics 1945-1990 and a sensitive analysis of writers and poets such as Virginia Woolf and W.B. Yeats. Healey approvingly quotes Polish philosopher Lesjeck Kolakowski's definition of political purpose as "an obstinate will to erode by inches the conditions which produce avoidable suffering" (p. 472), a sentiment we repeat in the conclusion to this essay.
57. Canada, *An Agenda for Economic Renewal*, pp. 1-2.
58. Critiques of the Conservative economic record are contained in Jeffrey, *Breaking Faith*, pp. 141-265, and George Radwanski and Julia Luttrell, *The Will of A Nation* (Toronto: Stoddart, 1992), pp. 19-50.
59. "Canadian Economy in Worst Shape Since the War, Bank Economist Says," *The Gazette* (Montreal) 29 July 1992.
60. See Kenneth Courtis, "Globalization: The Economic Impact," *Finding Common Ground*, pp. 15-22.
61. Advisory Council on Adjustment, *Adjusting to Win*, 28 March 1989.
62. Lester Thurow, "The Need for Strategic Approaches" in *Finding Common Ground*, p. 74.
63. Peter Nicholson, "No Where to Hide," *Finding Common Ground*, p. 35
64. Canada, *Agenda for Economic Renewal*, p. 3.
65. Ken Battle, "Limits of Social Policy" in *Finding Common Ground*, pp. 145-68.
66. John Kenneth Galbraith, *The Culture of Contentment* (Boston: Houghton Mifflin Co., 1992), p. 107.
67. The Senate Standing Committee on Social Affairs, Science and

Technology, chaired by Lorna Marsden, produced an outstanding report on this priority. See *Children in Poverty: Towards a Better Future*, January 1991.

68. Economic Council of Canada, *The New Face of Poverty* (Ottawa: Ministry of Supply and Services, 1992), p. 8.
69. Quoted in Alan C. Cairns, *Disruptions: Constitutional Struggles, from the Charter to Meech Lake*, ed. Douglas E. Williams (Toronto: McClelland and Stewart, 1991), p. 57. Cairns' stimulating book emphasizes the impact of the Charter on the values of citizens and includes a description of Canadians as "a united people divided by our governments" (p. 64), which parallels our own view."
70. Pierre Elliott Trudeau, *Federalism and the French Canadians* (Toronto: MacMillan of Canada, 1968), p. 44.
71. Andrew Cohen, *A Deal Undone* (Vancouver: Douglas and McIntyre, 1990), pp. 110–13.
72. C.D. Howe Institute, *Backgrounder* 21 July 1991.
73. "Provinces Defeat Bid to End Trade Barriers," *Toronto Star*, 23 August 1992.
74. "The Rape of the Economic Union," *Globe and Mail* (Toronto), 13 July 1992.
75. Cairns, Disruptions, p. 166.
76. Thomas Paine, "The Rights of Man" in *The Essential Thomas Paine* (New York: New Mentor Library, 1969) p. 246.
77. Quoted in Tuchman, *The March of Folly*, p. 7.
78. Thurow, *Finding Common Ground*, p. 83.
79. Albert Camus, *Resistance, Rebellion and Death*, trans. Justin O'Brien (New York: Alfred A. Knopf, 1972) p. 73.

PART II The Global Transformation

1. Statistics Canada, *Corporations and Labour Unions Returns Act* (Ottawa: Ministry of Supply and Services, 1988), p. 74.
2. From 1966 to 1973, growth in real Gross Domestic Product in Canada averaged 5.5 percent, compared to 3.9 percent in the U.S.; from 1974 to 1979, the comparison was 3.2 percent in Canada and 2.8 percent in the U.S.; from 1980 to 1984, Canada averaged 1.5 percent compared to 2.1 percent in the U.S. See Stephen Brooks, *Public Policy in Canada* (Toronto: McClelland and Stewart, 1989), pp. 182–83.
3. National Council of Welfare, *Progress against Poverty* (Ottawa: April 1988), p. 86.
4 Ian Drummond, "Economic History and Canadian Economic Policy since the Second World War," in *Post-War Macroeconomic*

Developments (Toronto: University of Toronto Press, 1986), vol. 20 in the series of studies commissioned for the Royal Commission on the Economic Union and Development Prospects for Canada, p. 25.

5. Sandra Burt, "Women's Issues and the Women's Movement in Canada since 1970," in *The Politics of Canada, Ethnicity and Change in Canada* (Toronto: University of Toronto Press, 1986), vol. 34 in the series of studies commissioned for the Royal Commission on the Economic Union and Development Prospects for Canada, p. 118.

6. Canada, Royal Commission on the Economic Union and Development Prospects for Canada, Vol. II (Toronto: University of Toronto Press, 1985), p. 16.

7. Drummond, "Economic History," pp. 25–26.

8. Charles de Gaulle, *Memoirs of Hope: Renewal and Endeavour*, trans. Terence Kilmartin (New York: Simon and Schuster, 1971), p. 162.

CHAPTER 1   "To Stand Not So High Perhaps but Always Alone": The Foreign Policy of Pierre Elliott Trudeau

1. See the Melian Debate in Thucydides, *History of the Peloponnesian War*, trans. Rex Warner (Harmondsworth, Middlesex: Penguin Books Ltd., 1966), pp. 358–66. The term "realpolitik" was coined in 1853 by Von Rochau, in connection with the failure of the liberal Frankfurt Assembly of 1848.

2. Ibid., p. 25.

3. Thomas Hobbes, *Leviathan* (Harmondsworth, Middlesex: Penguin Books Ltd., 1981), p. 185.

4. Quoted in Henry A. Kissinger, "The White Revolutionary: Reflections on Bismarck," *Daedalus* (Summer 1968): 907.

5. Immanuel Kant, *Perpetual Peace and Other Essays*, trans. Ted Humphrey (Indianapolis, Indiana: Hackett Publishing Co., 1983), p. 34.

6. Ibid., p. 125.

7. Ibid., p. 46.

8. Quoted in A. J. P. Taylor, *The Troublemakers: Dissent over Foreign Policy* (London: Panther Books, 1969), p. 31.

9. See Michael W. Doyle, "Kant, Liberal Legacies and Foreign Affairs," *Philosophy and Public Affairs* (Summer and Fall, 1983): 205–35.

10. Quoted in Taylor, *The Troublemakers*, p. 49.

11. John Bright, *Selected Speeches* (London: J. M. Dent, 1907), p. 221.

12. Quoted in E. H. Carr, *The Twenty Years Crisis* (London: The Macmillan Press Ltd., 1939), p. 8.
13. Quoted in Michael Howard, *The Causes of War* (Cambridge, MA: Harvard University Press, 1984), p. 229.
14. Pierre Elliott Trudeau, *Federalism and the French Canadians* (Toronto: Macmillan, 1968), p. xix.
15. "Positions sur la présente guerre," *Cité libre* (May 1951): 1 [translation]. Trudeau's article was unsigned because at the time he was working in the Privy Council office.
16. Ibid., p. 11 [translation].
17. See articles in the following issues of *Cité libre*: January 1957, February 1957, May 1958, April 1960, December 1961, and April 1963. From May 1948 to April 1949, Trudeau visited Germany, Austria, Czechoslovakia, Hungary, Poland, Yugoslavia, Bulgaria, Lebanon, Trans Jordan, Syria, Iraq, Turkey, Afghanistan, Pakistan, India, Burma, Thailand, Indo-China, China and Japan. He visited most of Africa in 1951; the Soviet Union in 1952; Pakistan, India, Ceylon, Indonesia, Australia and New Zealand in 1955; Nigeria, Ghana and Togo in 1957; Japan and Viet Nam in 1959; and again China in 1960.
18. Jacques Hébert and Pierre Elliott Trudeau, *Two Innocents in Red China*, trans. M. Owen (Toronto: Oxford University Press, 1968), p. 3.
19. Quoted in John Saywell, ed., *The Canadian Annual Review for 1968* (Toronto: University of Toronto Press, 1969), p. 23.
20. Canada, Office of the Prime Minister, Transcript of Press Conference, 7 April 1968.
21. Canada, Office of the Prime Minister, "Canada and the World," Policy Statement, 29 May 1968.
22. Quoted by Arthur Schlesinger, Jr., *The Cycles of American History* (Boston: Houghton Mifflin, 1986), p. 122.
23. Quoted in Bruce Thordarson, *Trudeau and Foreign Policy: A Study in Decision Making* (Toronto: Oxford University Press, 1972), p. 69.
24. Canada, Office of the Prime Minister, Transcript of interview with Charles Templeton on the CTV Network, 18 December 1968.
25. Quoted in Taylor, *The Troublemakers*, p. 19.
26. Canada, House of Commons, *Debates*, 15 June 1981, p. 1059.
27. In "Economic Summitry Reaches Time of Testing in London," *International Perspectives* (September-October 1977): 33. Alex I. Inglis argues that Prime Minister Trudeau's contributions to the Puerto Rico Summit of 1976 were so useful in focusing the discussion that by 1977 Canada's admission to the club was no longer an issue. When France issued invitations to the first summit in 1975, Canada had been excluded.

28. John W. Holmes, "Most Safely in the Middle," *International Journal* (Spring 1984): 379.
29. Arnold Wolfers, *Discord and Collaboration* (Baltimore: The Johns Hopkins Press, 1962), p. 24.
30. One of the best assessments of the Trudeau foreign policy legacy is John Kirton's article, "Managing Canadian Foreign Policy," in *Canada among Nations, 1984: A Time of Transition*, ed. Brian W. Tomlin and Maureen Molot (Toronto: Lorimer, 1985), pp. 14–29. My summary draws heavily on Kirton's succinct description.
31. Walter Lippman, *U.S. Foreign Policy: Shield of the Republic* (Boston: Little, Brown and Co., 1943), p. 9.
32. Canada, Office of the Prime Minister, "Canada and the World," Policy Statement, 29 May 1968.
33. See Dale C. Thomson, *Vive le Québec libre* (Toronto: Deneau, 1988) and Claude Morin, *L'art de l'impossible: la diplomatique québécoise depuis 1960* (Montreal: Boréal, 1987).
34. Quoted in Thomson, *Vive le Québec libre*, p. 114.
35. René Lévesque, *Memoirs*, trans. Philip Stratford (Toronto: McClelland and Stewart, 1986), p. 206.
36. Quoted in Thomson, *Vive le Québec libre*, p. 276.
37. Max Weber, "Politics as a Vocation," in *Max Weber: Essays in Sociology*, ed. H. H. Gerth and C. W. Mills (New York: Oxford University Press, 1958), pp. 77–128.
38. Morin, *L'art de l'impossible*, p. 389 [translation].
39. This spectacle of duelling delegations was not without humour. In 1969, at the first conference in Niamey, Pauline Julien, a well-known *chanteuse québécoise* interrupted the speech of Gérard Pelletier with de Gaulle's old cry of "*Vive le Québec libre.*" Pelletier laconically replied that he had heard her in better voice.
40. Holmes, "Most Safely in the Middle," pp. 376–77.
41. For a detailed examination of the process leading up to the April 1970 Arctic policy, see John Kirton and Don Munton, "The *Manhattan* Voyages and Their Aftermath," in *Politics of the North West Passage*, ed. Franklyn Griffiths (Montreal: McGill-Queen's University Press, 1987), pp. 95–96.
42. Quoted by D. M. McRae, "Arctic Waters and Canadian Sovereignty," *International Journal* (Summer 1983): 477.
43. Quoted in Dale C. Thomson and Roger F. Swanson, *Canadian Foreign Policy: Options and Perspectives* (Toronto: McGraw-Hill Ryerson, 1971), p. 126.
44. Trudeau, *Federalism and the French Canadians*, p. xxiii.
45. Mitchell Sharp, "Canada-U.S. Relations: Options for the Future," *International Perspectives* (Autumn 1972): 1.
46. Quoted in Michael Tucker, *Canadian Foreign Policy: Contemporary*

Issues and Themes (Toronto: McGraw-Hill Ryerson, 1980), p. 86.

47. Sharp, "Canada-U.S. Relations," p. 4.
48. Statistics Canada, *Corporations and Labour Unions Returns Act* (Ottawa: Ministry of Supply and Services, 1988), p. 74.
49. Canada, Government of Canada, *Energy and Canadians: Into the 21st Century* (Ottawa: Ministry of Supply and Services, 1982), p. 87.
50. Alan M. Rugman, *Outward Bound: Canadian Direct Investment in the United States* (Toronto: C. D. Howe Institute, 1987), p. 5.
51. Pierre Elliott Trudeau, "A propos de domination économique," *Cité libre* (May 1958): 8 [translation].
52. Quoted in Thomson and Swanson, *Canadian Foreign Policy: Options and Perspectives*, p. 8.
53. John Halstead, "Implications for Canada," *International Perspectives* (July/August 1973), p. 12.
54. Michael Tucker, *Canadian Foreign Policy: Contemporary Issues and Themes* (Toronto: McGraw-Hill Ryerson, 1980), p. ix.
55. Kim Richard Nossal, *The Politics of Canadian Foreign Policy* (Scarborough: Prentice-Hall Canada, 1985), p. 97.
56. Pierre Elliott Trudeau, "Positions sur la présente guerre," *Cité libre* (May 1951): 10 [translation].
57. Statement by Pierre Elliott Trudeau to convocation celebrating the Diamond Jubilee of the University of Alberta, 13 May 1968, in *Lifting the Shadow of War*, ed. C. David Crenna (Edmonton: Hurtig, 1987), p. 10.
58. Pierre Elliott Trudeau, "La guerre! La guerre!" *Cité libre* (December 1961): 1 [translation].
59. Harold von Reikhoff and John Sigler, "The Trudeau Peace Initiative: The Politics of Reversing the Arms Race," in *Canada among Nations: 1984*, ed. Tomlin and Molot, p. 50.
60. Quoted by John Kirton in "Concerted Principals and Common Principles: The Peace Initiative of Prime Minister Trudeau," paper delivered to the International Society of Political Psychology, Toronto, Ontario, 25 June 1984, p. 17.
61. Geoffrey Pearson, "Reflections on the Trudeau Peace Mission," *International Perspectives* (March/April 1985): 5.

CHAPTER 2   Riding the Storm: Energy Policy, 1968–1984

1. For a comprehensive overview of Canadian energy politics and policy leading up to and including the National Energy Policy, see G. Bruce Doern and Glenn Toner, *The Politics of Energy: The*

Development and Implementation of the NEP (Agincourt: Methuen, 1985).

2. For an extensive review of the Syncrude deal, see Larry Pratt, *The Tar Sands: Syncrude and the Politics of Oil* (Edmonton: Hurtig, 1976).

3. From "Notes for Remarks by The Right Honourable P.E. Trudeau," Halifax Board of Trade, Halifax, N.S., 25 January 1980. An influential document in the preparation of that policy was a major report made for Energy, Mines and Resources Canada in 1978 by James E. Gander and Fred W. Belaire, entitled *Energy Futures for Canadians* (Ottawa: Minister of Supply and Services, 1978).

4. Press conference held by Premier Peter Lougheed and Mr Mervin Leitch, 1 September 1981.

5. *Daily Oil Bulletin*, 17 July 1988 and *Financial Post*, 18 July 1988.

CHAPTER 4   Global Transformation and Economic Policy

1. I have become particularly conscious of this as a result of an involvement with some oral history work concerning the pre-Trudeau years currently going forward in Ottawa. It used to appear to me that so idiosyncratic were the events, forces and personalities surrounding any policy decision in Ottawa that it would be almost impossible for the external observer or historian to render an adequate account. It now appears to me that time and distance permit some perspective.

2. For a neo-Keynesian's review of these matters, see Alan S. Blinder, "Economic Policy and Economic Science: The Case of Macroeconomics," paper prepared for the Economic Council of Canada's Perspective 2000 Conference, Ottawa, December 1988 (Conference volume forthcoming).

3. Somewhat expanded treatment of some of the views expressed in this account is to be found in "Consensus, Flexibility and Equity," *Canadian Public Policy* 12, no. 2 (1986) or in "Consensus and Economic Performance," paper prepared for the Economic Council of Canada's Perspective 2000 Conference, Ottawa, December 1988 (Conference volume forthcoming).

4. See the Economic Council of Canada, *Fifth and Sixth Annual Reviews* (Ottawa: Queen's Printer, 1968 and 1969) and Canada, *The Report of the Special Senate Committee on Poverty* (Ottawa: Information Canada, 1971).

5. Canada, *Report of the Royal Commission on Taxation* (Ottawa: Queen's Printer, 1966).

6. Canada, Department of Energy, Mines and Resources, *An Energy Policy for Canada* (Ottawa: Information Canada, 1973).

7. Canada, Department of National Health and Welfare, *Working Paper on Social Security Reform in Canada* (Ottawa: Information Canada, 1973).

8. The Carter Commission proposals were followed by: Canada, Department of Finance, *Proposals for Tax Reform* (Ottawa: Department of Finance, 1969) and Canada, Department of Finance, *Summary of 1971 Tax Reform Legislation* (Ottawa: Department of Finance, 1971).

9. For a compendium of the major tax initiatives of the Trudeau years, see Canada, Department of Finance, *The Federal Deficit in Perspective* (Ottawa: Department of Finance, 1983).

10. Canada, Government of Canada, *The Way Ahead* (Ottawa: Ministry of Supply and Services, 1977).

11. For an example of this thesis, see David A. Wolfe, "The Politics of the Deficit," in *Research Volume 40*, co-ordinated by G. Bruce Doern for the Royal Commission on the Economic Union and Development Prospects for Canada (Ottawa: Ministry of Supply and Services, 1985). For a critical and very readable overview of taxing and tax reform during the Trudeau years, see Linda McQuaig, *Behind Closed Doors* (Toronto: Penguin Books Canada Limited, 1987).

12. Canada, Department of Energy, Mines and Resources, *The National Energy Program* (Ottawa: Ministry of Supply and Services, 1980).

13. See Canada, Department of Energy, Mines and Resources, *The National Energy Program: Update 1982* (Ottawa: Ministry of Supply and Services, 1982).

14. See Canada, Department of Finance, *Federal-Provincial Fiscal Arrangements in the Eighties* (Ottawa: Department of Finance, 1981) and Canada, House of Commons, *Fiscal Federalism in Canada*, Report of the Parliamentary Task Force on Federal-Provincial Fiscal Arrangements (Ottawa: Ministry of Supply and Services, 1981).

15. See Canada, Department of Finance, *Analysis of Federal Tax Expenditure for Individuals* (Ottawa: Department of Finance, 1981).

16. Canada, Ministry of State for Economic Development, *Economic Development for Canada in the 1980s* (Ottawa: Ministry of Supply and Services, 1981).

17. Albert Hirschman, *Shifting Involvements*, (Princeton, N.J.: Princeton University Press, 1982).

PART III A Society in Ferment

1. For a description of the last two decades of federal budgets, see Douglas D. Purvis and Constance Smith in "Fiscal Policy in Canada: 1963–84," in *Fiscal and Monetary Policy* (Toronto: University of Toronto Press, 1986), vol. 21 in the series of studies commissioned for the Royal Commission on the Economic Union and Development Prospects for Canada). For a description of the tax policies of the Mulroney government, see Linda McQuaig, *Behind Closed Doors* (Toronto: Penguin Books Canada Limited, 1987).
2. Statistics Canada, *Income Distribution by Size in Canada*, 1969, cat. no. 79, Table 85; 1987, cat. no. 13207, Table 72.
3. National Council of Welfare, *Poverty Profile 1988* (Ottawa: April 1988), p. 115.

CHAPTER 5   Legislating for Freedom

1. Speech delivered at the Liberal Party Policy Conference, Ottawa, 20 November 1970. Cited in *Trudeau en direct* (Montreal: Editions du Jour, 1972), p. 66.
2. Census of 1986.
3. *Hansard*, 8 October 1971.
4. Jean R. Burnet and Howard Palmer, *Coming Canadians* (Toronto: McClelland and Stewart, 1988).
5. *Hansard*, 16 March 1971.
6. Canadian Bar Association, Brief on Bill C-61 (Young Offenders Act), *Minutes of Proceedings and Evidence*, 24 February 1982.
7. Edmonton, 4 June 1968.
8. The Hugessen Report, 1972; the Goldenberg Report, 1974; and the McGuigan Report, 1977.
9. Quoted in *Trudeau* (Ottawa: Deneau Publishers, 1984) [translation].

CHAPTER 6   Meeting the Environmental Challenge

1. Canadian Environmental Advisory Council, *Annual Review 1979-80*, Ottawa, 1981, p. 10.

CHAPTER 7   Expansion, Retrenchment and Protecting the Future: Social Policy in the Trudeau Years

1. The Proceedings of the Liberal Convention of 1919.
2. Prime minister's opening statement to the November 1963 Federal-Provincial Conference, Ottawa.
3. Al Johnson, "Social Policy in Canada: The Past As It Conditions the

Present," Canada-U.K. Colloquium on the Future of Social Welfare Systems, hosted by the Institute for Research on Public Policy, Meech Lake, 16 October 1986.

4. Canada, Department of National Health and Welfare, *Working Paper on Social Security Reform in Canada* (Ottawa: Information Canada, 1973).

5. Ibid.

PART IV   The Challenge of Federalism

1. Quoted in Robert Shepard and Michael Valpy, *The National Deal: The Fight for a Canadian Constitution* (Toronto: Fleet Books, 1982), p. 39.

2. Canada, House of Commons, *Debates*, 10 June 1980, p. 1977.

3. Canada, Department of Finance, *Annual Reference Tables* (June 1989), Tables 49–52.

4. Quoted in Peter Leslie, *Federal State, National Economy* (Toronto: University of Toronto Press, 1987), p. 88.

5. 1971 data calculated from Dominion Bureau of Statistics, *Family Incomes*, cat. no. 13–538, January 1972, Table 2, p. 13; 1984 data from Statistics Canada, *Income Distribution by Size in Canada*, 1984, Table 10, p. 61.

6. Statistics Canada, *Postcensal Annual Estimates of Population by Marital Status, Age, Sex and Components of Growth for Canada, Provinces and Territories, June 1, 1984*, vol. 2, Second Issue, May 1985, cat. no. 91–210, Table 8, p. 51.

7. Donald J. Savoie, *Regional Economic Development: Canada's Search for Solutions* (Toronto: University of Toronto Press, 1986), p. 117.

CHAPTER 8   1968: Language Policy and the Mood in Quebec

1. The Royal Commission on Bilingualism and Biculturalism, whose mandate was to study the situation created in Canada by linguistic duality and the existence of two principal cultures.

2. Privy Council Office of Canada, *A Preliminary Report of the Royal Commission on Bilingualism and Biculturalism*, Ottawa, 1965, p. 135. Reproduced with permission of the Minister of Supply and Services Canada, 1990.

3. On this question, see "Histoire du développement industriel du Québec" by Albert Faucher and Maurice Lamontagne, followed by a commentary by O.J. Firestone in *Essais sur le Québec contemporain* (Québec: Presses de l'Université Laval, 1953).

4. Ibid. p. 219 [retranslation].

5. *A Preliminary Report of the Royal Commission on Bilingualism and Biculturalism*, p. 77.

45454

6. This was also what André Laurendeau had called for in his editorial in *Le Devoir*, which led to the creation of the royal commission that he co-chaired with Davidson Dunton. "After a century of Confederation, or almost," he wrote in this editorial, "no one knows what *a completely bilingual state* might mean in practice [. . .] No one has a clear idea of what *state bilingualism* should or might be." [my italics] *Le Devoir*, 20 January 1962, p. 4.

7. Richard Gwyn, *The Northern Magus* (Toronto: McClelland and Stewart, 1980), pp. 223–24. Used by permission of the Canadian publisher, McClelland & Stewart.

8. Ibid., p. 226.

9. It is interesting to note that the number of these opponents, all Conservatives and most of them from the West, has changed hardly at all. Fifteen years later, in the autumn of 1988, there were still fifteen of them voting against Bill C-72, which amended the Official Languages Act, proposed this time by their own party.

CHAPTER 9   Fiscal Federalism in Evolution

1. This demand came from Premier Maurice Duplessis during the federal-provincial discussions of December 1950.

2. Federal-Provincial Tax Structure Committee, Ottawa, 1961. Statement made by the Honourable M. W. Sharp, Minister of Finance.

CHAPTER 10   Regional Development: Innovations in the West

1. An address by the Right Honourable Pierre Elliott Trudeau, in reply to the Throne Speech, *Hansard*, 16 September 1968, p. 68.

2. In addition to this proposal, $250 million were set aside for a Native Economic Development Fund, designed to promote economic entrepreneurship for aboriginal people.

3. Howard Darling, *The Politics of Freight Rates* (Toronto: McClelland and Stewart, 1980). See especially Chapter 4, "The Twenties: Setting the Pattern of Freight Rate Protest."

PART V   The Institutional Framework

1. Thucydides, *History of the Peloponnesian War*, trans. Rex Warner (Harmondsworth, Middlesex: Penguin Books Limited, 1954), Book 2, p. 119.

2. Quoted in Donald Johnston, ed., *With a Bang, Not a Whimper: Pierre Trudeau Speaks Out* (Toronto: Stoddart Publishing Company Limited, 1988), p. 23.

CHAPTER 11   The Party and Parliament: Participatory
Democracy in the Trudeau Years

1. See John B. Stewart, *The Canadian House of Commons: Procedure
and Reform* (Montreal: McGill-Queen's University Press, 1977).
2. Ibid., pp. 83ff.
3. Members of Parliament spend a great deal of their time helping
constituents with problems related to government services such as
immigration, citizenship, passports, unemployment insurance,
access to a variety of federal programs and innumerable other
matters that have no bearing on legislation before the House. It is for
this work that good staff are essential. The legislative side of an MP's
work in the House and on committees also requires staff who can
undertake accurate, analytical work.
4. For a clear and useful distinction between the "court party" and the
"country party," see John B. Stewart, "Strengthening the Commons," *Journal of Canadian Studies* 14, no. 2 (Summer 1979):
35–47.
5. For this summary of the parliamentary changes during the Trudeau
years, I am grateful to Mr Jack Stilborn of the Research Branch of
the Library of Parliament.
6. Jeffrey Simpson, "The Two Trudeaus: Federal Patronage in
Quebec, 1968–1984," *Journal of Canadian Studies* 22, no. 2 (Summer
1987).
7. Mr Gordon Dryden, a member of the Barbeau Commission, has
kindly provided me with an account of the origins, work and
purposes of the Commission.
8. As has often been pointed out, this gave the greatest benefit to the
New Democratic Party, whose base of corporate donors was rather
small. It also required the parties to develop new and better schemes
of persuading citizens to donate. Contrary to current wisdom,
between 1974 and 1983 the Liberal Party had a net surplus of income
over expenditures, and when the leadership changed in 1984, the
Party was debt-free. According to Liberal Party reports filed with
the Chief Election Officer for 1974–1979, the Party raised $1.8
million more than it spent; for 1980–83, it raised $2.7 million more
than it spent; in the transition year of 1984, there was a deficit of
$400,000 during the year, and a deficit of $4.9 million for the
election. Thus the Election Expenses Act continued to serve in the
reformed context (Thomas S. Axworthy, "The Government in
Opposition: Is the Liberal Century Over?" in *Party Politics in
Canada*, 6th ed., ed. Hugh G. Thorburn (forthcoming).
9. The changes in structure and organization of the Liberal Party have

been complex. In November 1970, the name was changed from the National Liberal Federation to the Liberal Party of Canada. In each province there exists either one Liberal Party organization with a federal and a provincial leader, or two separate parties, one federal and one provincial. In the first type, members buy one card to belong to the federal and provincial wings. In the second type, now more common, members join each branch separately. Funding structures have become separate, partly because of federal and provincial election expenses legislation. In several provinces, the federal wing is called "The Liberal Party of Canada of [name of province]." The provincial wing is then called "the [provincial name] Liberal Party." It is impossible here to detail all the many changes that occurred between 1968 and 1984 inside the federal party, although the most important of these are described in the text.

10. Richard Stanbury, president of the Liberal Federation from 1968 to 1973, identifies these estates—the federation, the caucus and Cabinet. Our formulation of the estates is rather different, based on their relationship to the leader and their power vis-à-vis one another and the leader. For the Stanbury formulation, see Joseph Wearing, *The L Shaped Party: The Liberal Party of Canada, 1958-1980* (Toronto: McGraw-Hill Ryerson, 1981), p. 148.

11. In a conversation I had with Mr Trudeau in the mid-1970s, he expressed a desire to have a "mass party," as open as possible, which all those who shared Liberal beliefs would join. This leads me to believe that Pierre Trudeau would share my judgment that this is the most important estate in the Party.

12. It should be noted that, with the exception of Norm MacLeod, each of these presidents was experienced in the parliamentary caucus. Iona Campagnolo had been in Cabinet and the others were senators.

13. For accounts of these events, see Joseph Wearing, *The L Shaped Party*; Christina McCall-Newman, *Grits: An Intimate Portrait of the Liberal Party* (Toronto: Macmillan, 1982); and Keith Davey, *The Rainmaker: A Passion for Politics* (Toronto: Stoddart, 1986).

14. See chapter 5 of Joseph Wearing, *The L Shaped Party*, for a description of these memoranda.

15. This accountability provision and the provision that each Cabinet minister should hold an accountability session at each national convention was removed by the "reforms" of 1986. The accountability provisions, which required the Party president and other executive officers to explain their actions to the convention, had been added to the constitution before the 1980 and 1982 conventions.

16. The Party had used this name for a magazine when under the leadership of Mackenzie King. It would be used again when a magazine format was revived in 1975. But in this case the name was applied to a newspaper.

17. These regional desks were disbanded by Tom Axworthy after the 1980 election when a major reorganization of the PMO responded to Party dissatisfactions and to new requirements of the caucus and government.

18. The policy papers were prepared under the chairmanship of the late Senator Maurice Lamontagne, who represented the caucus, and Lorna Marsden, who represented the Party.

19. Led by Blair Williams and composed of a group of friends who had worked largely on the policy side of liberalism, the group met annually on Grindstone Island for a weekend of debate and friendship. Never part of the party apparatus and openly resented by some who saw them as a group of dissidents, the Grindstone Group is now seen as *the* place to debate many issues.

20. These proposals are found in a document entitled "The Liberal Party and the Critical Choices of the 1980s" dated November 16, 1979, addressed to members of the national executive by Pierre Trudeau and released at the Annual Meeting of the Liberal Party of Canada (Ontario).

21. It should be noted that what the national executive saw as their own demands for changes in return for their support were ideas that had been proposed by Mr Trudeau in 1979. It is in the context of anger with the caucus and with what some felt was the influence of the PMO that this meeting can be seen as a bargaining process.

22. The person who worked out these innovations in practice was Tom Axworthy, assistant principal secretary (1978-81), who was later principal secretary—from 1981 to 1984.

23. The commissions on women and youth replaced the earlier Women's Liberal Federation of Canada, the Young Liberal Federation and the Canadian University Liberal Federation. In 1971 funds to the Women's Federation were cut off and a task force was established, chaired by Esther Greenglass, a psychology professor. At the 1973 National Convention, the new National Women's Liberal Commission and the National Youth Commission were established. The latter has since been replaced by the Young Liberals of Canada.

24. When the leadership changed in 1984 and an election was imminent, the platform committee was summoned but there were new players who did not understand the organization, purpose or structure of policy making that it implied. The committee met and made

proposals but they had nowhere to go, either in the leader's office or into the campaign committee, which, consisting of an entirely new membership, did not understand its purpose. Because of this, the platform committee idea became somewhat discredited and the earlier "inside track" method was restored for the 1988 election through the Canada Conferences and the work of a more deliberative committee under the able chairmanship of Patrick Johnston and Manon Vennat. The work they produced was very well designed but the process lacked the immediacy of calling a platform committee after an election announcement. So, for example, the caucus was only able to see the 1988 platform after the Party activists instead of at the same time and the election campaign committee did not feel the same constraints on policy as it had in 1979 and 1980.

CHAPTER 12   Bringing the Constitution Home

1. *Hansard*, 15 April 1980.
2. Claude Morin, *Lendemains piégés: du référendum à la nuit des longs couteaux* (Montréal: Boréal, 1988).
3. Ibid., pp. 282–83.
4. Statement made to the press, November 1981. Cited in speech made by the Honourable Jean Chrétien to the House of Commons, in Canada, House of Commons, *Debates*, 20 November 1981, p. 13,042.

CHAPTER 13   The Quiet Revolution: A Turning Point

1. Linteau-Durocher-Robert-Ricard, *Histoire du Québec contemporain. Le Québec depuis 1930* (Montreal: Boréal, 1986), vol. II, pp. 725ff.
2. Marcel Rioux and Yves Martin, eds., *The French-Canadian Society* (Toronto: McClelland and Stewart, 1964), 450 pp.
3. Fernand Ouellet, "La Question sociale au Québec, 1880-1930. Perspectives historiographiques et critiques," in Ginette Kurgen-Van Henteryk, ed., *La Question sociale en belgique et au Canada, XIXe-XXe siècle* (Brussels: Université libre de Bruxelles, 1988), p. 54.
4. Jean-Charles Falardeau, ed., *Les Essais sur le Québec contemporain* (Quebec: Presses de l'Université Laval, 1953), 257 pp.; Pierre Elliott Trudeau, *La Grève de l'amiante* (Montreal: Editions Cité libre, 1956), pp. 2–91; see also the journal *Cité libre*.
5. Falardeau, Ibid., p. 32.
6. André Raynauld, *Croissances et structures économiques de la*

Province de Québec (Quebec: Ministère de l'industrie et du commerce, 1961), 657 pp.

7. Canada Census, 1851–52.

8. Ouellet, "Ruralization, Regional Development and Industrial Growth before 1850," forthcoming.

9. Ouellet, *Lower Canada: Social Change and Nationalism*, trans. and adap. Patricia Claxton (Toronto: McClelland and Stewart, 1980), pp. 158–82.

10. *Mandement* of 12 March 1839, *Mandements, lettres pastorales et autres documents publiés dans le diocèse de Montréal* (Quebec: Imprimerie générale A. Côté, 1888), pp. 48ff.

11. Lartigue to the Bishop of Quebec, 28 March 1836, *Rapport de l'Archiviste de la Province de Québec, 1944–1945*, pp. 185ff.

12. Louis-Edmond Hamelin, "Evolution numérique séculaire du clergé catholique dans le Québec," *Recherches sociographiques* 2 (1961): 189–241.

13. Paul Lemieux, "L'Evolution numérique du clergé québécois, 1756–1945," M.A. thesis, University of Ottawa, 1986.

14. Gérald Bernier and Robert Boily, eds., *Le Québec en chiffres de 1850 à nos jours* (Montreal: ACFAS, 1986), p. 219.

15. Jean Hamelin, *Histoire du catholicisme québécois. Le XXᵉ siècle à nos jours* (Montreal: Boréal, 1984), vol. 2, pp. 245–47.

16. Hamelin-Gagnon, *Histoire du catholicisme québécois. Le XXᵉ siècle, 1898–1940* (Montreal: Boréal, 1984), vol. 1, pp. 123–25.

17. Ouellet, "La Question sociale au Québec, 1880–1930," p. 72.

18. Ouellet, "La Condition féminine et le mouvement des femmes dans l'historiographie," *Histoire sociale-Social History* 21 (1988): 337–42.

19. Ibid.: 329.

20. *Parent Commission Report*, vol. 5, p. 216.

21. André Labarrère-Paulé, *Les instituteurs laïcs au Canada français. 1836–1900* (Quebec: Presses de l'Université Laval, 1965), pp. 149–93; *Province of Quebec Statistical Annual*, 1914; *Parent Commission Report*, vol. 5, p. 53.

22. Micheline Dumont and Nadia Fahmy-Eid, *Les Couventines. L'éducation des filles au Québec dans les congrégations religieuses enseignantes* (Montreal: Boréal, 1986), p. 264.

23. On this subject, see several works published by the rector of Laval University between 1962 and 1964, all published in Quebec by Les Presses de l'Université Laval: *Communauté universitaire*, 1963, 121 pp.; *Apostolat de l'université catholique*, 1963, 85 pp.; *Vérité et liberté*, 1962, 71 pp.; *Responsabilité collective des universitaires*, 1963, 85 pp.; *Progrès de l'université et consentement populaire*, 1964, 190 pp.

24. Data based on figures from Bernard Denaut and Benoit Lévesque, *Eléments pour une sociologie des communautés religieuses aux Québec* (Montreal/Sherbrooke: Presses de l'Université de Montréal, 1975), p. 43.
25. Marie Lavigne and Yvonne Pinard, eds., *Travailleuses et féministes. Les femmes dans la société québécoise* (Montreal: Boréal, 1983), p. 286.
26. Trudeau, *La Grève de l'amiante*, 420 pp.
27. André Raynauld, *La Propriété des entreprises au Québec. Les années 1960* (Montréal: Presses de l'Université de Montréal, 1974); *Bâtir le Québec. Enoncé de politique économique* (Quebec: Editeur officiel, 1979); André Raynauld and François Vaillancourt, *L'Appartenance des entreprises. Le cas du Québec en 1978* (Quebec: Editeur officiel, 1985).
28. Gagnon-Montcalm, *Quebec beyond the Quiet Revolution* (Scarborough: Nelson, Canada, 1989), pp. 106–26.

CHAPTER 14 "I never thought I could be as proud . . .": The Trudeau–Lévesque Debate

1. *Le Devoir* (Montreal), 17 July 1980 [translation].
2. René Lévesque, "Quebec's Economic Future," in *The Montreal Star, Seminar on Quebec* (Montreal 1963), p. 78.
3. Albert Breton, "The Economics of Nationalism," *Journal of Political Economy* 72 (August 1964): 376–86.
4. Jacques Lazure, *La Jeunesse de Québec en révolution* (Montreal: Presses de l'Université de Québec, 1970), pp. 23–62.
5. Quoted in Gérard Bergeron, *Notre miroir à deux faces* (Montreal: Québec/Amérique, 1985), p. 42.
6. Quoted in Gérard Pelletier, *Les Années d'impatience 1950–1960* (Montreal: Stanké, 1983), p. 49 [translation].
7. Ibid., pp. 50–51 [translation].
8. Gérard Pelletier, *Le Temps de choix 1960–68* (Montreal: Stanké, 1986), p. 214.
9. Pierre Elliott Trudeau, *Federalism and the French Canadians*, (Toronto: Oxford University Press, 1968), p. 179. For detailed accounts of Trudeau's ideas, see Reg Whitaker, "Reason, Passion and Interest: Pierre Trudeau's Eternal Liberal Triangle," *Canadian Journal of Political and Social Theory* 4 (Winter 1980): 5–32; and Ramsay Cook, *The Maple Leaf Forever* (Toronto: Macmillan, 1977), pp. 22–44.
10. René Lévesque, *Option Québec* (Montreal: Les Editions de l'Homme, 1968), p. 14.
11. Jacques Guay, "Comment René Lévesque est devenu indépendan-

tiste," *Le Magazine Maclean* (février 1969): 27 [translation].

12. Jean Provencher, *René Lévesque: portrait d'un Québécois* (Montréal: La Presse, 1973), p. 33 [translation].

13. René Lévesque, *Memoirs* (Toronto: McClelland and Stewart, 1986), 74. Lévesque doesn't help much by writing that "the nation-state has had its day" and that "one cannot be anything but federalist . . . at least in world terms" (p. 117).

14. Quoted in Jean-Louis Rioux, "Radio-Canada, 1959," in *En Grève* (Montreal: Les Editions du Jour, 1963), p. 265. It is interesting that the editor of the nationalist daily, *Le Devoir*, Gérard Filion, rejected Lévesque's claim, writing sarcastically, " . . . when honour is lost, nothing is left but shame," Ibid., p. 265 [translation].

15. *La Presse*, 2 November 1967 [translation].

16. René Lévesque, "For an Independent Quebec," *Foreign Affairs* 54 (1976): 737, 742.

17. Pierre Elliott Trudeau, "L'Ascéticisme en canot," *JEC* 6 (June 1944):5 [translation]. The official English version (not this translation) appears in Borden Spears, ed., *Wilderness Canada* (Toronto and Vancouver: Clarke, Irwin, 1970), p. 5.

18. Borden Spears, ed., *Wilderness Canada* (Toronto and Vancouver: Clarke, Irwin, 1970), p. 5.

19. Pierre Elliott Trudeau, ed., *La Grève de l'amiante* (Montreal: Les Editions Cité libre, 1956), p. 41 [translation].

20. Ibid., p. 404 [translation].

21. "Manifeste pour une politique fonctionelle," *Cité libre* (May 1964) [translation].

22. Quoted in Pelletier, *Le Temps*, p. 222; Dorval Brunelle, *Les Trois Colombes: essai* (Montréal: blb Editeurs, 1985), p. 18 [translation].

23. Trudeau, *Federalism*, p. 211.

24. Ibid., 31–32.

25. Bergeron, *Notre miroir*, p. 124 [translation].

26. Pierre Elliott Trudeau, "La Consolidation du Canada passe par le renforcement organique de la fédération," *Le Devoir*, 2 April 1984, p. 8 [translation].

27. Hubert Aquin, "L'Existence politique," *Liberté* 21 (March 1962): 69 [translation]. See also Eli Kedourie, *Nationalism* (London: Hutchinson University Library, 1960), p. 101: "These movements are ostensibly directed against the foreigner, the outsider, but they are also the manifestation of a species of civil strife between the generations; nationalist movements are children's crusades. . . ." Brunelle, in *Les trois colombes*, also touches upon this theme of generational conflict. No one has applied it, in detail, to Quebec and it could not be done mechanically, since Trudeau and Lévesque were of the same generation.

28. Bergeron, *Notre Miroir* [translation].
29. *Le Devoir*, 16 November 1976; *Le Devoir*, 22 May 1980 [translation].

PART VII   The Values of a Just Society

1. Gérard Pelletier, *Years of Impatience*, trans. Alan Brown (Toronto: Methuen, 1984).
2. At a seminar in London. The theme reappears in "Les séparatistes: des contre-révolutionnaires," *Cité libre*, no. 67 (May 1964): 4.
3. In *Les droits de l'homme et la Loi Naturelle*, p. 53, Maritain quotes Saint Thomas Aquinas commenting Aristotle: "Equality comes after justice, and underlies the principle and origin of friendship."
4. "Pelletier et Trudeau s'expliquent," *Cité libre*, no. 80 (October 1965): 4.
5. Pierre Elliott Trudeau, *Federalism and the French Canadians* (Toronto: Macmillan, 1968), p. xxiii.
6. Ibid., pp. 38-39. "Final" expenditures include those made with funds received from another level of government.
7. These rights may, however, be limited in their exercise by the necessity of also guaranteeing their exercise to other members of the society; this is the role of Section 1 of the Charter, which I discuss later.
8. The family itself, a natural and basic community, has only that authority which works to the benefit of its members.
9. Trudeau, *Federalism*, p. 4. These lines were written in 1965, but as the proportion of French-Canadian Quebeckers of "old stock" in the population declines, nationalist thinking tends all the more readily to define Quebec in terms of language rather than ethnicity. However, there is no certainty that intolerance is any the less healthy, judging by the Bill 178 episode which I discuss further on.
10. Charles Baudelaire: "*hyprocrite lecteur, mon semblable, mon frère.*"
11. That which has been held "always, everywhere, by everyone."
12. As I mentioned earlier, the derogatory clause applies only to Sections 2 and 7 to 15. Bill 178 limiting signs in English in Quebec was in derogation of Section 2 (freedom of expression).
13. *House of Commons Debates*, 6 April 1989, p. 153: ". . . is not worth the paper it is written on."
14. Quoted in September 1988 by Beaudoin and Ratushny, *Charte canadienne des Droits et Libertés*, 2nd ed. (Montreal: Wilson Lafleur, 1989), p. iii. In this book of over a thousand pages, "twenty-one authors from all parts of the country . . . have analyzed the fifty judgments pronounced by the Supreme Court on the *Canadian*

Charter of Rights and Freedoms, and also a great many judgments pronounced by other courts in the country." (Ibid.) See also Neil Finkelstein, *Laskin's Constitutional Law*, 5th ed. (Toronto: Carswell, 1986). About 30 percent of the 1500 pages of this book are devoted to the Charter. It will be noted further that the Charter occupies an increasing place in the teaching at all the law faculties in the country.

15. Trudeau, *Federalism*, p. 36.

16. See Ibid., pp. 152 and 180, for references to this book by Marcel Chaput, which was published in Montreal in 1961.

17. On the Constitution, I used to say rather the same thing I would reply to those who thought I should attack the monarchy: that the system worked alright and that opening the debate then would create enormous bitterness and divisions among Canadians without solving the problem.

18. In 1985, Swiss Confederation revenues accounted for 43 percent of the total, compared to 57 percent for the cantons. Confederation expenditures were 44 percent, while those of the cantons were 56 percent.

19. Cited in Pierre Elliott Trudeau, *A Time for Action* (Ottawa: Government of Canada, 1978).

20. I discuss the Château Consensus in Don Johnston, ed., *With a Bang, Not a Whimper* (Toronto: Stoddart, 1988), Chapter 4.

21. Supreme Court judgment of 6 December 1982.

22. I wrote to Premier Lévesque to this effect on 1 December 1981.

23. See Appendix A in Don Johnston, ed., *Lac Meech — Trudeau Parle* (Montreal: HMH, 1989), p. 141.

24. For an interesting discussion of the referendum question, see Maurice Lamontagne, *The Double Deal* (Montreal: Optimum, 1980), pp. 87ff.

25. On November 27, 1989, the Montreal daily, *La Presse*, published the results of a Gallup poll headlined, "Most Canadians know nothing about Meech Lake." The poll revealed that only 25 percent of Canadians support the Accord, against 31 percent who "consider that the Accord would not be a good thing for Canada." And on December 27, 1989, a Canadian Press story read: "More than half of Canadians think their country has become more divided in recent years, a year-end poll conducted by Decima Research suggests."

26. A sampling of these individuals and groups will be found in Johnston, ed., *With a Bang, Not a Whimper*, Appendix A, pp. 111-35.

27. Supreme Court judgment of 15 December 1988.

POSTSCRIPT   The Poverty of Nationalist Thinking in Quebec

1. "Pour un politique fonctionnelle," *Cité Libre*, vol. 1, no. 1 (June 1950): p. 24.
2. At the moment of going to press, we have learned that the recommendations of the Allaire report, although favourably received by the premier when they were presented, were rejected by the Liberal Party of Quebec at its policy convention on August 29, 1992. These latest "traditional demands" thus lasted less than two years. Don't miss the next instalment . . .
3. Max Nemni, in Balthazar, Laforest and Lemieux, eds., *Le Quebec et la restructuration du Canada, 1980–1992*, (Quebec: Septentrion, 1991); see especially pages 175–76. See also Don Johnson, ed., *Trudeau Speaks Out on Meech Lake* (Toronto: General, 1990), p. 114–15.
4. Nemni, Ibid., 177–78.
5. I was shocked to see this argument taken up by one of no less stature than the federal minister of justice, in a document dated October 25, 1991: "Article 25.1 [proposing the recognition of Quebec's distinct society] is similar to the provisions already set forth in the Charter [of 1982] in respect to the native peoples, multicultural heritage, and equality of the sexes."
6. We do not know whether or not this clarification of "distinct society" will be retained in the final text of the constitutional amendment. If not, the judges will have to decide for themselves what "distinct society" means, and they will undoubtedly take language and culture into account (and perhaps a lot of other things).